VOICES OF THE MARKETPLACE

TWAYNE'S
AMERICAN THOUGHT
AND CULTURE SERIES

Lewis Perry, General Editor

VOICES OF THE MARKETPLACE

American Thought and Culture, 1830–1860

ANNE C. ROSE

Twayne Publishers • New York
Maxwell Macmillan Canada • Toronto
Maxwell Macmillan International • New York   Oxford   Singapore   Sydney

Voices of the Marketplace: American Thought and Culture, 1830–1860
Anne C. Rose

Copyright © 1995 by Anne C. Rose

Twayne Publishers
Macmillan Publishing Company
866 Third Avenue
New York, New York 10022

Maxwell Macmillan Canada, Inc.
1200 Eglinton Avenue East
Suite 200
Don Mills, Ontario M3C 3N1

Library of Congress Cataloging-in-Publication Data

Rose, Anne C., 1950–
    Voices of the marketplace : American thought and culture, 1830–1860 / Anne C. Rose.
        p.   cm.—(Twayne's American thought and culture series)
    Includes bibliographical references and index.
    ISBN 0-8057-9065-9—ISBN 0-8057-9075-6 (pbk.)
    1. United States—Civilization—1783–1865. I. Title. II. Series.
E165.R7 1994
973.081—dc20   94-19732
                                                                                    CIP

The paper used in this publication meets the minimum requirements of American National Standard for Information Sciences—Permanence of Paper for Printed Library Materials. ANSI Z3948-1984. ∞™

10 9 8 7 6 5 4 3 2 1 (hc)
10 9 8 7 6 5 4 3 2 1 (pb)

Printed in the United States of America

For my wonderful children,
Eleanor and Jonathan

Contents

ILLUSTRATIONS   ix

FOREWORD   xi

ACKNOWLEDGMENTS   xiii

INTRODUCTION   xv

ONE

The Transformations of Faith   1

TWO

The Struggles of Political Loyalties   30

THREE

The Languages of Capitalism   60

FOUR

American Renaissance   90

FIVE

The Flowering of Minority Cultures   130

SIX

America at a Crossroads: The 1850s   162

CHRONOLOGY   185

NOTES AND REFERENCES   189

BIBLIOGRAPHIC ESSAY   227

INDEX   239

Illustrations

Daguerreotype of an outdoor antislavery meeting (ca. 1850)   16

Lithograph of Andrew Jackson (ca. 1833)   34

Painting of Daniel Webster (1830)   35

Osceola, the Black Drink, a Warrior of Great Distinction (1838),
painting by George Catlin   66

American Country Life: October Afternoon (1855),
lithograph by Nathaniel Currier   68

View of New York from Brooklyn Heights (1849),
lithograph by Nathaniel Currier   69

The Greek Slave (1846), sculpture by Hiram Powers   105

The Bone Player (1856), painting by William Sidney Mount   106

Daguerreotype of Edgar Allan Poe (1849)   110

*An Imaginary Gathering: Washington Irving and
His Friends at Sunnyside, 1864*   120

Authors of the United States (1866), engraving
by Alexander Hay Ritchie   121

Isaac Mayer Wise in 1854   134

Mary Anne Sadlier (1897)   144

Frederick Douglass (ca. 1850)   150

A Beautiful Representation of the New York Crystal Place (1853),
wood engraving by J. W. Orr   163

Illustrations from *Harper's New Monthly Magazine* accompanying
William Allen Butler's 1857 poem "Nothing to Wear"   172 and 173

Foreword

Twayne's American Thought and Culture Series surveys intellectual and cultural life in America from the sixteenth century to the present. The time is auspicious for such a broad survey because scholars have carried out so much path-breaking work in this field in recent years. The volumes reflect that scholarship as well as valuable earlier studies. The authors also present the results of their own research and offer original interpretations. The goal is to bring together books that are readable and well informed and that stand on their own as introductions to significant periods in American thought and culture. There is no attempt to establish a single interpretation of all of America's past; the diversity, conflict, and change that are features of the American experience would frustrate any such attempt. What the authors can do, however, is to explore issues that are of critical importance to both a particular period and the whole of American history.

Today the culture and intellectual life of the United States are subjects of heated debate. While prominent figures summon citizens back to an endangered "common culture," some critics dismiss the very idea of culture—let alone American culture—as elitist and arbitrary. The questions asked in these volumes are directly relevant to that debate, which concerns history but too often proceeds in ignorance of it. How did leading intellectuals view their relations to America, and how did their compatriots regard them? Did Americans believe that theirs was a distinctive culture? Did they participate in international movements? What were the links and tensions between high culture and popular culture? While discussing influential works, creative individuals, and major institutions, the books in this series place intellectual and cultural history in the larger context of American society.

The period examined in this book has long been recognized as a time of crucial change in American society. Interpretations of American culture in this period have emphasized a single theme, such as revivalism, slavery, reform, Jacksonian democracy, or New England's transcendentalist authors. Some interpretations have been preoccupied with the Civil War that followed in the 1860s and therefore have overlooked links between antebellum culture and the late nineteenth- and twentieth-century eras. Anne C. Rose's searching and comprehensive reinterpretation considers sharply divergent tendencies in religion and politics and a wide range of reformers, authors, and other public figures. It illuminates major changes in intellectual life that occurred between 1830 and 1860; at the same time it clarifies enduring questions about the roles of ethnicity, gender, and class in the formation of American national identity.

Voices of the Marketplace examines *Walden, Uncle Tom's Cabin, Moby-Dick, The Scarlet Letter*, and other celebrated works associated with the American Renaissance, but it also discusses works by African Americans, Irish immigrants, Native Americans, and Jewish Americans that have seldom been seen in relation to the more famous masterpieces of the same era. Rose explains how the "market revolution"—to use a term prominent in economic and political histories of the antebellum period—made it possible for individuals to pursue fame and fortune through personal expression as never before and encouraged groups to reshape their identities in quest of public influence or protection from public criticism. In doing so Rose is able to explain how the same era could foster works of individual genius, inspire visions of collective moral improvement, and give rise to widespread suspicion and violence.

While offering a compelling portrait of the antebellum decades, *Voices of the Marketplace* points to the emergence of a middle-class Victorian culture that would prevail later in the century. In discussing how the marketplace stimulated groups to assert their separate identities within American culture, Rose uncovers some origins of issues of great moment in our own time.

LEWIS PERRY
Series Editor

Acknowledgments

I am grateful for the assistance of many individuals and institutions. I am most indebted to Lewis Perry, not only for the opportunity to write this book but for his excellent advice about successive versions of the manuscript. His dedicated work on Twayne's American Thought and Culture Series makes a valuable and lasting contribution to the field of American intellectual history. I also thank Carol Chin, Lesley Poliner and Barbara Sutton of Twayne Publishers for their expert help and hard work, as well as Karen Day for her support at a crucial point in the production process. My good friend and colleague Susan Harris generously read and commented on the manuscript. The observations of an anonymous reader for Twayne also enabled me to see key issues more clearly. I have been lucky to benefit from the proofreading skills of Laura Gordon-Murnane. Barbara Cohen has prepared an excellent index.

The Department of History and the Religious Studies Program at Penn State University have provided me with an exceptionally congenial atmosphere for pursuing scholarly work. I thank all the faculty and staff, especially Gary Gallagher, Philip Jenkins, Gary Cross, and Mona Perchonok. A National Endowment for the Humanities Fellowship for College Teachers and Independent Scholars gave valuable assistance to this project. The staffs at Penn State University's Pattee Library and at the American Jewish Archives, Cincinnati, helped to locate research materials. I have acquired illustrations through the generous and efficient cooperation of the following institutions: the American Jewish Archives; the Archives of the University of Notre Dame; the Corcoran Gallery of Art; the Free Public Library of Philadelphia; the J. Paul Getty Museum; the Museum of the City of New York; the Museum of Fine Arts, Boston; the National Academy of Design, New York; the National Museum of American Art and the National Portrait

Gallery, Smithsonian Institution; the New-York Historical Society; and the New York Public Library.

My family, as always, brings me the happiness that enables me to work. My children, Eleanor and Jonathan, so different from each other, are both wonderfully inquiring and creative people. It is a great joy to dedicate this book to them. My husband, Adam, shares with me the strains and rewards of belonging to an academic family. I could not do this without his love. Our lively Pembroke Welsh corgis, Lucy and Wally, know how to have fun and make us all laugh. Often that is what we, as a family, need the most.

Introduction

The Languages and Social Conditions of Antebellum Thinking

The decades between 1830 and 1860 were a period of extraordinary intellectual fertility. These were the years of the Second Great Awakening, religious revivals that began at the turn of the century and, particularly after 1830, inspired a wide range of spiritual movements and social reforms. It was the Age of Jackson, an era characterized by a democratic political culture descended from the founders' original republicanism and now based on strenuous partisanship and aspirations for popular participation. It was a time of such literary "flowering" that the decades before the Civil War are remembered as the American Renaissance. This exuberant creativity was based, paradoxically, on a consolidating process of institutional formation and intellectual definition. A mainstream Victorian culture took shape after 1830 based on loyalties to Protestant denominationalism, party competition, and middle-class values. At the same time, a wide range of dissenting speakers adopted the available means of organization and communication to articulate their distinctive points of view. Free expression—whether practiced by white, native-born Protestants, escaped slaves, or Irish-Catholic immigrants—thrived because the tools of intellectual exchange were widely shared and because the terms of debate were increasingly clear.[1]

This book seeks to record the diverse voices of the antebellum cultural marketplace. The dialogues that evolved in the decades before the Civil War were sometimes spoken in tones of acrimony and often stirred conflict. Nonetheless, three sets of concepts provided common languages of discourse: Christianity, democracy, and capitalism. Americans at least recognized, even if they disagreed with, the meaning of one another's words.

In 1830 Christian beliefs and democratic ideas were established means that Americans used to judge their lives and to try to direct social development. Evangelical Protestantism, with its goals of personal salvation and social regeneration, was a dominant force in American culture from the earliest days of colonial settlement. In civic life the American Revolution had nurtured a commitment to representative government chosen by a self-determining people.

These religious and political values continued to inform the way Americans perceived society in the years before the Civil War, but they also changed dramatically as new situations arose. Opposing intellectual responses to the issue of slavery exemplify this process of transformation. Christian conscience pushed many northerners to question the morality of slavery, yet it equally induced pious southerners to believe that they should treat their slaves with benevolence. Established views of sin and virtue took on revised connotations in the process: abolitionists identified slaveholding as a sin, in striking contrast to proslavery advocates who offered biblical justifications of bondage. The slavery debate thus opened new rifts in Christian thinking.

In political ideology, the eighteenth-century republican focus on free and virtuous citizens gave way during the sectional controversy to a new vocabulary involving concepts of the Union and minority rights. Under what conditions should the Union endure? How could the white South, a political minority, protect itself from the growing antislavery majority? Could electoral democracy survive political conspiracies, plots suspected of abolitionists and slaveholders alike? Theories of the Union, nullification, concurrent majorities, popular sovereignty, and secession competed in the political arena as answers to these questions. As antebellum Americans reinterpreted Christian and democratic doctrines in light of the concerns of their time, both intellectual systems proved vital and adaptable tools for reflection and debate. They were joined by a much newer influence in national discussion: capitalism.

The culture of capitalism began less as an original set of ideas than as a series of answers to questions about the nation's identity raised by new economic strategies. The desire to seek profits in markets dates far back in human history. Yet in America's post-Revolutionary democracy unprecedented opportunities for profit for large numbers of citizens impelled profound social changes that began around 1800 and accelerated throughout the century. Communities became connected with one another through regional and national markets. People migrated to the frontier or perhaps to growing cities. Entrepreneurs encouraged new technologies. Along with Americans' excitement at the promise of wealth, they faced troubling prospects. How could an individual's moral character be secured in a mobile society? Could government by free men be maintained if prosperity was unequally shared to the point that there were wide differences in wealth? Should marginal social groups such as women, blacks, Indians, and Catholics have unrestricted access to society's rewards? Should slavery have a role in a progressive nation?

Responses to these and other ethical questions were phrased in terms that blended old and new ideas. The work ethic for men and a domestic ideal for women—twin solutions to the problem of character formation—recast Protestant morality in language appropriate to increasingly separate social settings: the workplace and the home. In a similar intellectual patchwork, advocates of both proslavery and antislavery combined arguments about slave labor's compatibility or incompatibility with Christianity and free government with judgments on the system's utility as a form of production. During the pre–Civil War era, capitalism moved toward coherence as an ideology and endorsed such key concepts as self-control, gender distinctions, reward for merit, and practical thinking. Largely a product of popular, mass-marketed writing and art, the culture of capitalism was an eclectic intellectual solution to Americans' contradictory social desires.

The capitalist mind-set was thus the newest of the three antebellum systems of values and spoke eloquently of this generation's powerful ambitions and anxieties. It was based on a faith that words and images, if carefully chosen and ordered as ideology, could bring tranquility of mind and peace in social relations. Even so, capitalist values did not eclipse the cultural power of Christianity or democracy. This study's title, *Voices of the Marketplace*, spotlights the exchange of goods and ideas as the most distinctive development of the antebellum period. But the "voices" expressed themselves in established languages as well as new ones, and the "marketplace" invited meetings between ideas that had dominated the past and those that would sway the future. Equally important, all three sets of ideas provided motives as well as explanations. The majority of Americans wished to be Christians, democrats, and capitalists, and their desires gave each area of culture its own internal dynamic of change. What antebellum Americans thought and felt directly affected their choices.

The literary and artistic achievements of the American Renaissance were equally influential in the everyday lives of antebellum Americans. The growing number of magazines, novels, photographs, plays, and musical compositions did not provide a systematic intellectual viewpoint. Yet these works of culture served, perhaps more decisively, as a new lens on experience. They encouraged the use of imagination, an involvement with language, and a fascination with visual images. In this exceedingly literate and generally prosperous society, reading books, displaying pictures, and attending performances intimately colored an individual's responses and decisions. Particularly for social minorities—Irish, Jewish, African, and Native American—prose was an essential instrument for forging a collective consciousness in lieu of an established network of reliable institutions. In sum, words and images expressed what Americans were thinking as Christians, democrats, and capitalists. Even more, literature and the fine arts conveyed their own message about the desirability of reflection, communication, and pleasure.

What were the social circumstances in which thinking took place in ante-bellum America? The three following sketches show how the American religious community, political system, and cultural marketplace were organized in the decades before the Civil War. In all three areas of culture similar trends distinguished this period: growing national unity, the increasing influence of professionals, and the availability of a wider range of choices to ordinary people.

When the Constitution was drafted in 1787, Congregationalists were the largest American religious group. In 1850 the Methodists were the Protestant denomination that claimed most members. The change reflects the transition in American religion from a local to a national orientation. Eighteenth-century Congregationalists were committed to the autonomy of churches in established communities. Methodists, in contrast, thrived on connections and mobility. In the early decades of the nineteenth century circuit-riding Methodist preachers spoke in towns to sometimes hastily gathered listeners, and camp meetings drew people away from their homes for protracted open-air worship. Methodists learned to look beyond their local towns and to identify with a religious community of regional and national scope. After 1830 the Methodists' expertise at building a large-scale religious organization became the main source of denominational unity, displacing frontier-style traveling preachers and transient audiences. As far back as Methodism's eighteenth-century beginnings in America, the denomination had a hierarchy of ministers and a system of conferences that ruled in a way one scholar has called "basically autocratic."[2] From about 1830 on, Methodists increasingly used these bureaucratic skills to develop new tools of persuasion. They established denominational colleges (Wesleyan University in Connecticut was founded in 1831, for example) and periodicals (Methodists in Cincinnati began publishing the *Ladies' Repository* in 1841). Developments in Methodism exemplified changes occurring in other denominations as well: emphasis of translocal ties, reliance on more sophisticated organization, and interest in new means of communication to ground religion more firmly in culture.[3]

This expansive religious setting produced a new kind of leadership. Antebellum religious spokesmen were "professionals" in this sense: they conceived their role, measured their success, and selected their peers according to an abstract notion of their work rather than in relation to the specific social situation of the parish ministry.[4] The revivalist Charles Grandison Finney did not think of himself as a minister because he settled with a single congregation, but because he spread God's saving message as a much sought-after preacher, writer, and professor. This disengagement of religious labor from the traditional sphere of the church encouraged leaders to experiment with new roles that helped to transform religion. Some seminary students, for example, who were educated to see their purpose as bringing holiness and morality to American society, moved easily from their original aim to enter the ministry to a more radical determination to become advocates of the immediate abolition of slavery.[5] The broad ways in which religious spokesmen exerted their influence, moreover, had the unintended effect of offering a voice to new social groups. In the 1840s Catharine Beecher highlighted women's religious capabilities when she recruited a corps of female teachers to help establish Christian culture in the West. With religious leaders now identified more by the task of evangelism than by traditional parochial duties, women could legitimately claim a public, though still subordinate, spiritual role.[6]

Ordinary Americans similarly enjoyed a widening range of religious choices in the antebellum decades. When Massachusetts became the last state to disestablish its tax-supported church (the Congregational) in 1833, there were no more legal disincentives to keep Americans from freely selecting their religion among a growing number of denominations—not simply popular mainstream Protestant churches such as the Methodists and Baptists but groups with more controversial views such as the Mormons, Millerites, and Catholics.[7] Whether or not a person joined a congregation in a specific denomination, he or she might elect to participate in a nearly daunting number of voluntary associations intended to promote reform, some of them church-affiliated, but others ecumenical and autonomous. The New York Female Moral Reform Society, for instance, was established in 1834 by a group of women with Charles Finney's wife, Lydia, as its first director. The organization aimed to encourage conversion experiences among the city's prostitutes and more generally to champion moral purity.[8] Rising literacy, finally, was a key factor in giving Americans the option of pursuing religion in private and developing personalized views. More than 90 percent of adult American whites could read and write in 1850. Growing religious organizations produced a tremendous amount of printed matter including tracts, advice literature, and religious novels.[9] Many Americans read on spiritual subjects in addition to their participation in public worship and reform. For others, private reflection was an alternative to organized religion. Either way, antebellum Americans had increasing liberty to define their own beliefs. The principal setting of religious experience in 1800 had been the local church. After 1830, however, there were many centers of religious culture, public and private, among which individuals could choose.

The same trends toward national connections, professional leadership, and popular choice appeared in antebellum politics. To some extent, Americans gravitated toward either the arena of religion or politics as a place for self-expression and social influence. The urban working class was one social group that favored political parties rather than religious organizations as vehicles for their points of view. Still, most Americans thought and acted in both religious and political capacities at different times in their lives.

Between the election of Andrew Jackson to the presidency in 1828 and the victory of Abraham Lincoln in 1860, Americans' long-standing fear of party contention gave way to an appreciation of the uses and drama of partisan competition on a national scale. Profound ideological and organizational realignments took place during these decades. The Second Party system, based on opposition between the Democrats and the Whigs, emerged in the 1830s. It was superseded in the midst of turmoil in the 1850s by the Third Party system, centering on electoral contention between the Democrats and the Republicans. The effect of active political parties was to fix Americans' attention on regional and national issues rather than local ones. One symbol of these broader horizons was a Whig procession in 1840—one of many parades in an election year—that trekked 20 miles from the small town of New Haven, Vermont, to Burlington behind the party's emblem, a log cabin drawn by oxen.[10]

An ironic and critical consequence of growing political interdependence was the heightening of self-conscious sectionalism. Northerners and southerners, now in closer contact, became more aware of their differences and felt more vulnerable by proximity to the other side. Indeed, one apparent motive for southern secession was the determination to limit the spread of the new style of party contention, judged by southerners to be northern in origin, and to protect the South's custom of political deference.[11] Whatever southerners' perception of their superior civic purity, however, all antebellum parties except the Republicans were national organizations. Members of the political community, North and South, helped to bring about the shift to competitive tactics that was part of the new nationwide political culture.

Political leaders became more professionalized during these decades, as they grew more attached to party ideologies and organizations and less concerned with local affairs. When Martin Van Buren of New York became president in 1836 with the help of a Democratic faction called the Albany Regency, he was the first chief executive to appreciate the utility of building coalitions of fellow politicians in order to win elections.[12] This kind of professional reliance on peers might seem at first glance the foundation for a new kind of elitism, but during this era, strong party loyalty among office seekers was consistent with the extension of mass democracy. The disengagement of politicians from small-town issues meant freedom from social elites that dominated communities. At the same time, aspiring leaders adopted more accessible styles of communication to secure a popular political base. Although this was an age when people had a great appetite for political oratory, politicians nonetheless moved toward terse forms of public speaking. Lincoln's carefully selected and poignant images, for example, epitomized by his Gettysburg and second inaugural addresses during the Civil War, superseded the expansive legalistic expositions of his political predecessor, Daniel Webster. In sum, antebellum political parties both heightened professional self-consciousness among politicians and encouraged experimentation with popular leadership.[13]

As these political spokesmen realized, ordinary men could now register their opinions in increasing numbers of ways. With the important exceptions of efforts in the 1850s to limit the voting rights of immigrants and free blacks, there was a general movement in antebellum America toward universal suffrage for white men, as revisions of state constitutions from the 1820s on eliminated property requirements for voting. Men enthusiastically took advantage of their right. Sixty-nine percent of eligible voters turned out for presidential elections between 1840 and 1872, a proportion that rose to 77 percent between 1876 and 1900, in contrast to about 50 percent today.[14] It was the combination of democratic reforms and party activity that drew people toward politics. Not only did the simple fact of competition over ideas and programs stimulate interest in government, but parties offered men new roles beyond casting votes. Parties understood the power of pageantry to arouse excitement. In 1856, the first year that Republicans ran a candidate for president, they formed marching companies in towns across the nation called Wide Awakes, composed of men who dressed in uniforms, paraded by torchlight, and listened to speeches.[15] Although most of these marchers had little real voice in party affairs, ordinary people in the antebellum political community were nonetheless better informed, more visible, and more influential through demonstrations of their collective presence than were the majority of men in the past.

The marketplace was the third major social setting where Americans articulated their values, and it was by no means the least important. Antebellum markets grew because of the expansion of international trade (centering on the export of cotton), the accumulation of investment capital, the rise of manufacturing, the construction of railroads, and the aggressive promotion of goods. People in both the cities and countryside were exposed to the social rhythms of capitalism and its pressures toward productivity, competitiveness, and success.[16] Commodities, however, were not the only things briskly traded: there was also an explosive exchange of ideas, as literature and the arts were established on a cash basis. The three social developments visible in religion and politics—growing national coherence, professional leadership, and popular self-expression—also appeared in the context of cultural production.

By almost any measure of literary or artistic culture, the years between 1830 and 1860 were a time of revolution in communications. As late as 1820, intellectual exchange in America remained largely a local affair. Authors tended to write anonymously, pay printers to issue their work, and rely for distribution on subscribers, people who knew of the publication without the intervention of advertising. Other books were imported from Europe, but public discussion of their contents occurred mainly within literary societies composed of a town's gentry. In the following decades the circulation of ideas achieved far greater breadth. Entrepreneurs, both writers and publishers, carved out new markets of customers. Magazines rose in number from 125 in 1825 to 600 in 1850 and served not only as a cheap medium for serialized fiction but also as a key form of advertising through the device of book reviews.[17] The result was an increasingly national audience. Writing in her diary in South Carolina in 1861, Mary Chesnut castigated Harriet Beecher Stowe as one of "these holy New Englanders," self-righteous reformers who prescribed for a slave society about which they knew little firsthand.[18] The underlying message of Chesnut's defensive sectional outburst was that she had read *Uncle Tom's Cabin*, first published serially in 1851 in the antislavery journal, the *National Era*, and that she understood the social power of mass-circulated ideas.

Not only did books cover geographic and social distances, but speakers traveled the lecture circuit bringing culture to cities and towns. Until the 1840s, audiences at local lyceums listened mainly to presentations by their members. Thereafter, people of prominence such as Ralph Waldo Emerson were more often booked for paid performances by agreement between the lyceum's managers and professional agents. Whether the medium of intellectual exchange was written or verbal, the cultural marketplace ensured broad exposure to a common stock of ideas.[19]

The professional aspirations of writers, artists, and entrepreneurs of culture were encouraged by market expansion. Prior to the 1820s, men of intellectual inclinations commonly made their living in established professions, most often the ministry or law, and wrote without expectation of profit. In contrast, men and women in the antebellum years sought to become novelists, painters, and actors, supported financially by their crafts. Their ambition arose both from the simple possibility of making money from the arts in a mass market and from the desire to seize the freedom involved in fashioning entirely new kinds of careers. One of the motives for the commonplace use of pseudonyms and distinctive clothing by literary figures was the impulse to assert the possibility of self-creation in artistic vocations. The writer Sarah Hale wore widow's clothes for half a century after her husband's death as proof for readers of her loyalty to conventional standards of gender behavior—a guarantee essential for her acceptability and success as a professional woman. Walt Whitman, in a different frame of mind, dressed as a workingman to advertise his enthusiasm for democracy. In both cases, imagination applied to the writer's appearance helped to establish broad boundaries for literary professionalism.[20]

Behind writers and artists was a new kind of businessman who worked to carve out markets for highbrow and lowbrow entertainment. James T. Fields, a Boston publisher, not only created practical opportunities for such poets as Henry Wadsworth Longfellow and James Russell Lowell but, along with his wife, Annie, made his home a salon for writers. Robert Bonner, a Scotch-Irish immigrant and New York publisher, gave professional support and counsel to best-selling women authors. With great flourish and daring, P. T. Barnum brought the American public varied diversions: the midget Tom Thumb and other curiosities in the 1840s, the Swedish singer Jenny Lind in the 1850s, and his spectacular traveling circus ("The Greatest Show on Earth") after the Civil War.[21] All of these producers of culture—the artists themselves and their backers—pursued careers that would not have been possible without the growing wealth, literacy, and enthusiasm for imaginative efforts of antebellum Americans.

Just as much as professionalism in the arts depended on the emergence of receptive audiences, market-oriented writers and artists extended the horizons of the public in turn. The range of intellectual options available to Americans after 1830 can be conveyed by surveying the locales connected with the cultural marketplace where people encountered ideas. Homes, now less essential as places of production of everyday goods, increasingly became centers of consumption. Family members read and passed on books to one another, perhaps gathered around a piano to listen and sing, and enjoyed the architecture, furnishings, paintings, and photographs that made households, particularly prosperous ones, aesthetic displays in themselves.[22] Outside the family Americans attended art exhibitions, concerts, and plays that were available not simply in cities but, because most performers toured, in towns as well. Many of these forms of entertainment were within the economic reach of the mass of Americans, including such struggling groups as young migrants to cities and the urban working class. This social inclusiveness helps explain why book reviewers took care to determine the moral tenor of literature—lest novels corrupt the young—and why critics of the theater decried the presence of prostitutes soliciting clients during performances.[23] Anxieties about the content of imaginative works and the social conditions of consumption were not without some foundation. Never before were Americans introduced to so great a quantity of new ideas, nor had they ever mixed so freely with strangers in public settings. But second thoughts about artistic developments were more than balanced by the exhilaration of nurturing a more lighthearted side of human nature than that acknowledged by religion or politics. Not surprisingly, opportunities for cultivation and entertainment continued to expand.

The key characteristic of the society in which antebellum Americans explored their ideas—in religion, politics, or the cultural marketplace—was openness. Yet the freedom and creativity of antebellum thought depended on conditions of cultural security. The chapters that follow emphasize the construction of cultural institutions and intellectual patterns that supported both maintream American Victorian culture and the dissenting points of view that contested conventional assumptions. The commitment of many white, Protestant Americans to such ideas as gradual moral improvement, controlled partisan competition, and upward social mobility grew simultaneously with numerous alternative sets of values articulated by marginal groups—"minorities" from the point of view of rights—defined by their gender, class, ethnicity, or race.[24] Whether the language of public discussion was Christianity, democracy, or capitalism, antebellum thought developed through the fervent and often tense interaction among advocates of diverse ideals.

one

The Transformations of Faith

When Americans surveyed their religious situation in 1830, they saw a diverse but familiar landscape. In keeping with trends dating back to the turn of the century, Methodists and Baptists were gaining members at the expense of older evangelical denominations. Groups that questioned the value of sudden conversion, most notably the Unitarians, dissented from their culture's predominant commitment to revivalism. There were small minorities of Catholics (about 300,000) and Jews (fewer than 15,000) and a few vocal atheists, such as the social reformers Robert Dale Owen and Fanny Wright. When contemporaries looked again in 1860, religious patterns had radically changed. The Catholic church had grown tremendously as a result of Irish immigration. With over three million members, Catholicism was the largest American denomination. There were now 150,000 Jews. Although many Protestants had moved in the intervening decades toward a consensual position, the era was nonetheless marked by heterodoxy and conflict. Mormonism, transcendentalism, adventism, abolitionism, communitarianism, and High Church Episcopalianism had all been sources of controversy. Mob violence and legal initiatives were aimed at Catholics. The Presbyterian, Methodist, and Baptist churches had split into northern and southern branches in large measure over slavery. As the Civil War approached, most Americans still thought of their country as a Christian nation. Still, they must have wondered about the process of change that produced such sharp religious differences.[1]

Among the many reasons for the proliferation and clash of religious ideas, perhaps two are most basic: the impulse rooted in spiritual enthusiasm to explore the possibilities of the Judeo-Christian tradition and the openness of antebellum society, which offered new opportunities for religious expression. Most Americans in the pre–Civil War decades approached religion with con-

1

viction and passion. At a time of social and institutional transformation, this frame of mind impelled people in varied religious directions. Within Protestantism there were three principal trends: the entrenchment of mainstream denominations in new institutions, the rise of radical reform movements inspired by religion, and the search for ways to tie Christianity more closely to social and religious traditions. Despite internal divisions, Protestant Christianity retained its long-standing cultural dominance. But the new strength of the Catholic and Jewish communities began to tip the balance of religious power away from Protestantism. At the root of all these changes was an impulse to create a more human-centered religion. Antebellum Americans did not subordinate themselves to inherited beliefs but sought ways to make tradition serve their needs. Although they did not lose sight of God in heaven, they were far more interested than previous generations in religion's possibilities on earth.[2]

From Revivalism to Victorianism

The pioneering intellectual historian Perry Miller judged revivals to be the characteristic religious expression of American Protestants from the turn of the nineteenth century until the Civil War. The Second Great Awakening, in Miller's view, began with the protracted outdoor meeting in Cane Ridge, Kentucky, in 1801, where Baptist, Methodist, and Presbyterian ministers all preached to inspire conversions, and closed with the largely urban and lay-led revivals of 1857 and 1858. The numerous seasons of awakening in the intervening years together constituted "a religious revolution."[3] Even though Miller stressed the importance of these periods of public fervor, however, when born-again individuals left behind a life of sin for the hope of salvation, he saw that revivals occurred less frequently after the late 1830s. He sensed that their decline was connected with increasing formality in the churches, as ministers wrote books about how to conduct revivals, for example, at the same time that they had less practical success.[4] There is more than Miller grasped to this shift away from revivalism between 1830 and 1860. As Protestants threw their energies into a host of reform organizations that were in theory subsidiary to the revivals themselves, doctrine, too, moved from an evangelical insistence on sudden conversion to a new focus on the gradual nurture of faith, an end to be achieved through a peculiar combination of sentimentalism and bureaucratic efficiency. By the late 1850s revivals were more an anomaly than the characteristic feature of antebellum Protestant practice.

The most immediate catalyst in the new emphasis on religious gradualism was the creation of a series of agencies that functioned in a predictable and ongoing way. These benevolent organizations were the product of the revivals themselves. Whether the social setting was rural or urban, northern or southern, the pattern of institutional formation was essentially the same. Revivals generated a commitment among believers to spread the message of the Gospel, and voluntary associations were the chosen vehicle of reform. Before 1830 the goal of these societies was usually spiritual awakening. Following an 1827 revival in Baltimore, for example, Presbyterians established Sunday schools and made efforts to provide the poor residents of the city with tracts, preaching, and lay visitors to stimulate religious reflection. Such evangelical activities continued after 1830, but Protestants increasingly envisioned the work of religion in broader social terms. In Oneida County, New York, for example, a temperance organization begun in 1824 was the first evangelically inspired association in the region to challenge secular habits directly. Local campaigns in Oneida County to promote the abolition of slavery and to stamp out prostitution joined temperance in the 1830s as reforms with definite social ends.[5]

The same trend toward an interest in Christianity's social applications appeared after 1830 in the South. White citizens in this slave society were anxious about tinkering with the status quo, and they tended to restrict voluntary associations to the pursuit of spiritual goals, using such means as tract distribution and religious education. Nonetheless, white ministers in the 1830s and 1840s did advocate special missions to slaves, both to fulfill a Christian duty to dependents and, as the clergy assured masters, to secure willing obedience through an emphasis on Christ's meekness and subordination. To advance all of these causes, in the North as well as the South, organizations grew up outside established congregations that were essentially bureaucratic in structure. Leaders exercised authority through functional hierarchies, workers performed specialized tasks, and the exchange of information helped to coordinate wide-ranging efforts. Even proselytizing slaves, as the historian Albert Raboteau points out, gave rise to an institutional infrastructure similar to that of other reforms: "Addresses before planter associations, printed sermons and essays, committee reports and resolutions of clerical bodies, meetings of concerned clergy and laymen, annual reports of associations, interdenominational cooperation, and networks of correspondence were all devoted to spreading the message."[6]

What were the intellectual assumptions that encouraged the pursuit of spiritual renewal and social improvement by means of an unprecedented range of organizational tools? Did Protestant evangelicals, who tended to be more self-righteous and prosperous than their neighbors, seek to control such potentially disruptive groups as working people and slaves through the ideological bonds of religion, as some scholars have contended?[7] At least at some times and places, middle-class Protestants almost certainly encouraged churchgoing and temperance to reinforce social order. Still, this line of argument in a way misses the point. The Second Great Awakening was in its inception and inspiration a religious movement, and it took its basic direction from religious ideas whose tenor was optimistic, activist, and millennial.

Antebellum Protestants were more confident of people's ability to act morally and to transform society in accord with religious precepts than was any previous generation of Americans. In classic seventeenth-century Puritanism, there was an exhilaration for the select minority who, the Puritans believed, would be converted. But hopefulness for these few still grew from the privilege of participating in the drama of salvation made possible solely by God's power, not by human will. Nineteenth-century Protestants, in contrast, generally conceded that men and women could distinguish good from evil and that, with some help from God, they could make virtuous choices. Both the orthodox (evangelical) majority and the liberal (primarily Unitarian) minority based their theology on Scottish common sense philosophy, a set of eighteenth-century ideas proposing that human beings had an innate understanding of moral laws that was largely undamaged by original sin. Neither religious party believed that people could actually do good without divine assistance. Even so, each one located a foundation for moral growth in human nature itself.

Among many specific doctrinal statements that captured this basic optimism, none was more popular than the Methodist notion of conversion. Although the power of offering salvation was still God's alone, according to the Methodists, God made grace so pervasive—"prevenient"—that it seemed that people needed only to reach out and choose a gift close at hand. After conversion, human nature was so changed by grace that perfection was possible. People could not expect unerring behavior, but they could strive for a total commitment to good. Perfectionism was not an undisputed position either among Methodists or in other denominations where the idea appeared. Conservative ministers and laypeople balked at such radical claims for human ability. Still, perfectionism had wide appeal. Phoebe Palmer of New York, a leading Methodist perfectionist, sold out 20 editions of *Entire Devotion to God* (1845) and 24 editions of her *Faith and Its Effects* (1854) by 1859. Many Americans were ready to dedicate themselves to moral and social improvement and were convinced of their power to do so.[8]

The Protestantism of the antebellum decades was also strenuously activist, and the goal toward which many looked was indeed an inspiring one—the millennial reign of peace on earth that was promised in the New Testament Book of Revelation. New thoughts about people's moral capacity justified taking an initiative in religious affairs that was once thought to be God's alone. *"Religion is the work of man,"* declared Charles Finney in his *Lectures on Revivals of Religion* (1835): "It is something for man to do."[9] After backing off from so bold a proposal by continuing with the thought that religion "consists of obeying God," Finney returned to his brash line of reasoning by concluding that a revival is not a "miracle" but "the *right exercise* of the powers of nature," of "the appropriate means."[10] From a psychological standpoint, the leap from Finney's proposition that men and women may act to promote religion to making them actually want to do so was achieved through the will to seek personal moral perfection. People who experienced "justification"—saving faith—in the revivals longed to make the sustained dedication to Christian work associated with "sanctification." The reform agencies of the Second Great Awakening were an ideal channel for commitment.

These private motivations were reinforced by the conviction, widely shared among Americans, that they lived at a portentous historical moment. When the minister Lyman Beecher first learned of Jonathan Edwards's eighteenth-century belief that the millennial reign of Christ would begin in America, he thought the idea "chimerical." But by 1835 he saw that "mighty causes, like floods from distant mountains, are rushing with accumulating power, to their consummation of good or evil," and "if this nation is, in the providence of God, destined to lead the way in the moral and political emancipation of the world, it is time she understood her high calling, and were harnessed for the work."[11] Like most contemporary invocations of this awe-inspiring prospect, Beecher concluded his "Plea for the West" with specific proposals. He called for ministers, churches, and schools—some of the key agents and agencies of the awakening—to bring "universal education and moral culture" to the frontier.[12]

Perhaps the very exuberance of this religious outlook fostered diversity among the intellectual and social movements to which it gave rise. Campaigns for radical social change and conservative efforts to recover links with the past—a series of religious expressions on the left and right—owed a debt to the evangelical perspective. But even in mainstream Protestant churches, such as the Methodist, Baptist, Presbyterian, and Congregational, there were unanticipated consequences of institutionalizing revivalism. In the context of the network of voluntary associations, a new perspective on regeneration emerged that centered on gradual nurture, sentimentalism, and orderliness. This outlook did not directly challenge the optimism, activism, and millennialism of the awakening but tended nonetheless to subvert the revivals' enthusiasm.

The simple existence of ongoing religious institutions opened the possibility of steady growth in faith rather than sudden conversion. It is significant that Sunday schools on a more or less modern model appeared in the1820s and 1830s. No longer charity schools held on Sundays for the convenience of the working poor, Sunday schools now instructed the middle-class children of a congregation, focused on religious education in lieu of basic literacy, and sought conversions in an institutionalized setting.[13] Horace Bushnell, the Hartford Congregational minister and theologian, drew the inevitable lesson from this delicate balance of patient instruction and expectations of a sudden change of heart. Would it not be better, he proposed in *Christian Nurture* (1847), to form Christian character step by step rather than to take a chance with uncertain seasons of awakening?[14] The appealing simplicity of Bushnell's logic belies how radically he questioned the central tenet of the evangelical tradition in America: the need for a single conversion experience. Critics strongly contested his argument. Yet precisely because this proposition was voiced within the evangelical mainstream, and not, like the Unitarians' similar case for gradualism, in deliberate opposition to the majority, Christian nurture gained widespread acceptance in the decades that followed.

Bushnell's use of the concept of "nurture" and his interest in regular methods highlight the growing importance of both sentimentalism and system in mainstream Protestantism. In the early decades of the century Unitarians criticized evangelicals for their reliance on transient passions that could not sustain faith much beyond the end of a revival without, the liberals concluded, the support of reason. The kind of sentiments that Bushnell associated with moral nurture were not excited feelings but the devoted, thoughtful care identified by contemporaries with motherhood. Women were so prominent in evangelical voluntary associations that a convergence of ideas about religious growth and women's role is not surprising. In the 1830s and 1840s women were probably the majority of Sunday school teachers, visitors to the poor, and moral reformers of prostitutes and their clients. Moreover, the family was increasingly seen as the primary religious institution. It was mothers at home who began the work of forming their children's characters.

Part of the appeal of enlisting women and maternal feeling in the cause of moral regeneration was their reliable constancy. In her influential *Treatise on Domestic Economy* (1841), Catharine Beecher reminded American women that they were descendants of the English, "who, as a nation, are distinguished by systematic housekeeping, and for a great love of order, cleanliness, and comfort."[15] Women's sentiments, naturally inclined to orderliness in Beecher's opinion, had to be harnessed to efficiency to be morally effective. Independently of this high esteem of domestic regularity, evangelicals who were active in social reform came to see the value of systematic effort through their day-to-day work. In the decades following the founding of the New York Female Moral Reform Society in 1834, the women reformers involved in the society realized that persuasion alone would not end prostitution without concurrent improvement in opportunities for women. By the 1860s the renamed American Female Guardian Society ran a women's shelter, employment agency, and industrial schools. This change in program reflected the women's growing determination to support their benevolent intentions with organization in order to accomplish spiritual and social renewal.[16]

To an extent, the new Protestant emphases on sentimentalism and orderliness worked at cross purposes in practice. As time went on, reform agencies involved in causes ranging from tract distribution to urban reform increasingly employed paid professionals (almost always men) rather than volunteers (often women) in order to achieve maximum efficiency. Religious feeling and scientific method could each assume a role in a new religious synthesis as the dominant outlook of a distinctive social sphere—the home and the charitable organization, respectively. But an increasingly rigid identification of sentimentalism with women and systematic behavior with men tended to exclude women from work in public benevolence.[17]

6

The affirmation of nurture, feeling, and system that emerged by about 1850 is generally associated by historians with the appearance of American Victorian culture. Although Victorianism did not contest evangelicalism's self-confident activism, there was a shift in religious temper as revivalism yielded to voluntary association. The earlier thirst for the renewal of individual awakening, experienced in the revivals' ritualized setting away from daily routine and as if on the edge of time, gave way to an appreciation of collective, long-term efforts where participants played specialized roles. Firmly rooted in a network of institutions including churches, Sunday schools, and benevolent societies, American Victorian religion provided a definite center to Protestantism. Here old religious differences were surprisingly reconciled, and, outside of this sphere of consensus, new marginal groups found themselves in dissent.[18]

The views of New England evangelicals and Unitarians, for example, bitter antagonists in church schisms and pamphlet wars between about 1800 and 1830, nearly converged by the Civil War. Unitarians, the liberal descendants of colonial Congregationalists, never commanded large numbers of followers. The fact that they were generally prosperous and educated city dwellers, however, guaranteed an audience for their message: human beings could be improved and indeed perfected through gradual moral growth under the guidance of reason. When William Ellery Channing, the most eloquent spokesman of the liberal viewpoint between the turn of the century and his death in 1842, praised "Unitarian Christianity" in 1819 as a "purifying truth," he highlighted Unitarians' twin commitments to religious enlightenment and moral effort.[19]

Part of the reason that evangelicals and Unitarians grew closer after 1830 was that orthodoxy changed. Evangelicals such as Bushnell increasingly favored steady nurture of moral character instead of conversion. But the Unitarians changed as well. Their experience of administering voluntary associations almost identical to those of the evangelicals heightened liberals' awareness of the value of sentimentalism and efficiency, at the expense of their original, more contemplative rationalism. In the 1830s and 1840s Unitarians in and around Boston organized a ministry to the poor, sent missionaries to the West, and advocated such social reforms as temperance and antislavery. In so doing they reached many of the same conclusions as did evangelicals. They recognized the power of warm sentiment in persuasion and welcomed the quickening of their own religious feelings that came with moral activity, to the point that the historian Timothy Smith has identified in the 1850s an "evangelical Unitarianism," centering on the desire for intimacy with a mediating Christ.[20] At the same time, Unitarians increasingly argued that sentiment must yield to planning and method in public benevolence.

Broad as the Victorian synthesis was, particularly in contrast to the denominational infighting of earlier decades, it did not include all Americans. Class and ethnic identity were two social factors that complicated religious participation and set many people at odds with mainstream Protestants. The experiences of white, working-class Protestants and Catholics of all social ranks are exemplary.

The relationship of urban Protestant workers to middle-class evangelicals and liberals active in benevolence was uneasy throughout the antebellum decades. Many laborers came from rural or small-town backgrounds and were sincerely pious. Lucy Larcom recalled in her memoir, *A New England Girlhood* (1889), that most of the female texile workers in Lowell, Massachusetts, in the 1830s and 1840s avoided the Episcopal church provided by the mill owners, but sought out other congregations, such as the Congregationalist and Universalist, without wealthy patrons.[21] As the expanding network of voluntary associations increasingly determined working people's religious choices, however, many sensed that belief could no longer be considered simple assent to doctrine but involved a response to implicit social assumptions as well. The pattern of outreach to workers that followed revivals in Rochester, New York, around 1830 was typical. Well-to-do converts formed a free Presbyterian church for laborers who worked on the Erie Canal and assisted struggling Methodist and Free Will Baptist congregations.[22] Workers who accepted the evangelical call must have understood that the offer of saving grace was also an invitation to upward social mobility, if they conformed to the behavioral standards expected of converts for sobriety, industry, and self-discipline.

The condescension of patrons must have been difficult to endure, however, and other workers expressed their desire for autonomy from their social superiors through vocal irreligion. In a tradition linking social radicalism and skeptical rationalism that dated back at least to Tom Paine's *The Age of Reason* (1793–95), antebellum working-class spokesmen championed free inquiry to expose Christianity's supposed irrationalities and thus to question religion's authority. Tensions climaxed when Abner Kneeland, editor of a Boston newspaper called the *Investigator*, was imprisoned for blasphemy in 1838 on the grounds, according to one judge who tried him, that the workers who listened to Kneeland would not obey human law if they disdained God's commandments. A few religious leaders attempted to offer working people an alternative to both an assimilationist Protestant ethic and alienated infidelity. Orestes Brownson, a Unitarian minister in the 1830s, told Boston workers that Christ's true message was not competition and individual success but a "Gospel of human brotherhood."[23] Nonetheless, most native-born working people, torn between Protestant upbringings and emerging class consciousness, probably remained on uncertain ground between wholehearted acceptance of evangelicalism and hostile dissent.

The religious situation of working-class Protestants was less problematic, though, than the dilemma of Catholics. Whereas the distance of Protestant workers from the evangelical establishment was to a large extent voluntary, Catholics were forcibly denied legitimacy by the prejudice of Protestants. Rather than organize to persuade Catholics, like workers, to accept the awakening's Gospel, Protestants used voluntary associations to preach the evils of Catholicism. With a benign sounding name, the American Society to Promote the Principles of the Protestant Reformation was one anti-Catholic agency formed in New York in 1836 according to the same blueprint as other evangelical causes: interdenominational cooperation, bureaucratic structure, and an emphasis on spreading its message through printed literature. Such efforts were not the work of a fanatical minority. An integral part of the millennial vision of Lyman Beecher's "Plea for the West" was that the contest for Protestant dominance must be fought against Catholics, the "locusts of Egypt." At stake was the triumph of "superstition, or evangelical light; . . . despotism, or liberty."[24] The intolerance of Protestant leaders created an atmosphere where verbal and physical violence seemed acceptable. Provocative exposés, such as Maria Monk's *Awful Disclosures of the Hotel Dieu Nunnery of Montreal* (1836), titillated readers with intimations of illicit sexual relations and infanticide in monastic communities. In 1834 a mob burned the Ursuline Convent in Charlestown, Massachusetts. In 1844 riots outside Philadelphia between anti-Catholic nativists and Irish residents left two Catholic churches destroyed and 13 people dead.[25]

The source of this virulent anti-Catholicism was in part strictly doctrinal. Protestant denunciations of Catholic errors began with the Reformation, and Americans influenced by eighteenth-century Enlightenment rationalism identified the Catholic church with superstition and repression. As in the case of Protestant workers, however, social conflict fanned religious discord. The tremendous influx of Irish immigrants to the American Northeast in the antebellum decades made anti-Catholic bias one aspect of a broader nativism— that is, hostility to foreigners. The fact that most of the Irish were laborers exacerbated the tension. When Emily Dickinson, living in the comparatively rural Connecticut Valley of Massachusetts, pictured "Shanties—by the sides of Roads" in a poem around 1860, she seemed to allude to the widespread (and often accurate) view of Irish men as poor workers who helped to build railroads.[26] Thus it is not surprising that the perceived threat of Catholics was often described in social, not theological, terms. Nativists imagined a Catholic plot to subvert American freedom that was directed from Rome and executed by the obedient members (frequently identified as Jesuits) of a tight-knit ecclesiastical organization. Samuel F. B. Morse, remembered for inventing the telegraph but also an aggressive nativist, spoke quite accurately in 1835 when he claimed that he was not concerned with "the *religious tenets* properly so called, of the Roman Catholic" but with "the foreign political conspiracy . . . identified with that creed."[27] Whether Protestants' quarrel with Catholicism was intellectual or social, the consequences were pernicious either way. Nativism made religion a badge of personal identity that determined if an individual would be granted full social equality.

Despite such prejudice, the American Catholic church worked strenuously during the antebellum decades to establish institutions to serve the growing

Catholic population. Catholic parishes were much less like the conspiratorial model projected by Protestants' fears than they were similar to contemporary Protestant congregations. Individual churches served as spiritual centers within neighborhoods. Parish missions, periods of intense preaching designed to stir conviction, were the popular counterpart of Protestant revivals. A taste for devotions, rituals performed by individuals, corresponded to the attachment of Victorian Protestants to religious nurture and feelings. Literate Catholics studied manuals of instruction in devotions in an effort to enhance their personal piety through a routine of observances and prayers. These common practices linking American Catholics and Protestants did not erase important differences between them. The Catholic church experienced internal conflicts, for example, over the meaning of its commitment to ecclesiastical authority. Disputes concerning the balance of power between the lay trustees of a church and its priest arose within parishes. In a far broader perspective, the relation of the distant, scattered, and relatively free American congregations to the Roman hierarchy loomed as a contested issue. Whatever the distinctiveness of Catholicism, however, the Catholic church was hardly the insidious anomaly on the American religious landscape portrayed by Protestant bias.[28]

The historian David Brion Davis has proposed that anti-Catholicism betrayed Protestants' divided mind about their own changing identity. Protestants attacked not only Catholics but also Freemasons and Mormons for being members of centralized organizations united behind rigid ideologies, a pattern of behavior at odds with the perceived freedom of American society. The irony was that the Protestant majority acted much like their enemies in their campaigns to suppress dissent. They, too, organized behind well-defined positions on the limits of acceptable belief, and the root of their anxiety about conspiracy was their increasing similarity to the supposed conspirators.[29] Mainstream Protestants were involved in a process of consolidation that entailed an organizational transition from revivalism to voluntary association and an intellectual transformation from evangelical millennialism into Victorianism. By 1860 American Protestantism had developed a settled core of institutions and values. In a culture that began in 1830 with great openness and energy, forming predictable routines was one way to control potentially frightening historical change. Not all Protestants chose this cautious route, however. Bolder individuals, fired with spiritual enthusiasm, explored Christianity's radical possibilities.

Radicalism

The history of antebellum American religion is filled with odysseys of simultaneous spiritual transformation and geographic movement. They reveal the potential of the Second Great Awakening to open questions and instill convictions that could not be contained in the middle-of-the-road vision of conventional Protestantism. Joseph Smith, for one, published his alleged transcription of a new revelation that he called *The Book of Mormon* in 1830. He led his followers to accept doctrines of communal ownership and polygamy while they moved to flee persecution from New York through Ohio, Missouri, and Illinois. Sarah and Angelina Grimké of South Carolina and Henry Wright of upstate New York, converts to Quakerism and evangelical Christianity, respectively, crossed paths in New York and New England in the 1830s as agents of the American Anti-Slavery Society. Henry David Thoreau, a transcendentalist, sojourned at Walden Pond in the 1840s in a spirit that mirrored the efforts of many communitarians to begin society anew on a moral basis. He captured the mythic quality of their treks to inward and outward frontiers when he wrote in *Walden*, "I long ago lost a hound, a bay horse, and a turtle dove, and am still on their trail."[30]

The rise of heterodox challenges to mainstream doctrines characterizes most periods of spiritual excitement, and the decades between 1830 and 1860 were no exception. The same culture that encouraged the formation of evangelical institutions and the consolidation of Victorian values gave rise to claims of special revelations, prophecies of doom, communications with spirits, and a variety of new religiously inspired behaviors pertaining to diet, sexuality, property, and government. The core assumptions behind conventional and radical religion were much the same: optimism about human nature, an activist orientation, and millennial expectancy. But the social marginality of many dissenters, whose leaders were often ne'er-do-wells, young people, and women, combined with their intense enthusiasm to produce unusual intellectual discontent and new interpretations of shared ideas.

Some radical religious initiatives were intellectually disruptive to the extent that they challenged established notions of time and space. Mormonism, Millerism, transcendentalism, and spiritualism may be analyzed together as religious philosophies that offered new modes of perception. Radical abolitionism and communitarianism, on the other hand, were movements with social programs as well as spiritual objectives. All of these religious expressions were seen by contemporaries as "radical" in the sense that they threatened to upset widely accepted beliefs and mores. Their adherents did value moral absolutes above established practices, yet they did not disdain order altogether. They aimed to direct spiritual life and social change through the application of self-conscious principles, however unorthodox those ideas might be.

The radical perspectives that pictured the world in terms that contradicted the usual conceptions of time and space underscore how much religious dissent touched issues of elemental human importance. Most antebellum Americans saw time as linear and space as dualistic. Their hopes for achieving perfection in history were what historians call "postmillennial." Jesus's return to earth to rule the millennial kingdom would follow gradual moral improvement initiated by human beings. His reign of peace would not begin, as imagined in a "premillennial" vision, with the sudden, apocalyptic destruction of the sinful majority. Just as most Protestants saw present divided from future by steadily unfolding time, they perceived the visible and invisible worlds as related but still distinct. Matter and spirit were essentially different in nature rather than varying manifestations of a single principle. The universe was "dualistic," not "monistic."[31]

The excitement of the revivals invited departures from this intellectual status quo. Vocal premillennialism was a phase in both the Mormon and Millerite movements in the 1830s and 1840s. The minorities' condemnations of social depravity and predictions of doom for the unrepentant fueled adversarial relations with the Protestant majority. But on a deeper level, conflict grew from their diverging conceptions of time. In a rapidly changing society where time and its transformations could be a source of fear as well as hope, disagreements about how history would unfold touched people's deepest concerns.

Joseph Smith's personal history reveals the way the awakening's fervor nurtured radical dissent. Born into a family that could find neither economic prosperity nor religious stability as they migrated from Vermont to western New York, Smith (1805–44) came of age in an area along the Erie Canal known as the "burned-over district," so intense were its revivals' spiritual fires. Smith did not find religion in controlled settings such as churches or open-air meetings where the Bible dictated doctrine; instead he experienced a series of private visions and revelations beginning in 1820. In 1823 he alleged that an angel told him where to dig to find a new gospel engraved on golden plates, the document that became, in Smith's purported translation, *The Book of Mormon*. Like the Bible, *The Book of Mormon* is a historical text in the sense that it tells a story about the past. Smith recounted the prolonged conflict in ancient America between the virtuous though corrupt Nephites and the irreligious Lamanites. Their war of mutual extermination was primarily important, however, for its lesson about the future. Armageddon was drawing near for nineteenth-century Americans, Smith implied, much as the final judgment had for the extinct peoples of the New World. One motive for the Mormons' migrations from state to state was to find a refuge where they could call sinners out of the world during its last, violent days. When Smith was killed by a mob in Carthage, Illinois, in 1844, Mormons concluded that American society was irredeemably corrupt and withdrew farther to the West to await Christ's judgment. Once the Mormons' premillennialism assumed this alienated form, their apocalyptic view of time temporarily ceased to provoke confrontation with mainstream Protestants.[32]

The fascination with time of antebellum Americans can also be seen in the controversy surrounding the millennial prophecies of William Miller (1782–49). As a young man in Vermont, Miller was a skeptical deist; during the War of 1812, however, he returned to evangelical Christianity and became a Baptist preacher, whose study of the Bible led him to believe by the 1830s that the apocalypse was near. As Miller attracted followers, the doctrinal center of the movement was the assurance that Jesus would soon intervene in history, not agreement on a specific date. Yet it is no less true that neither the Millerites nor their critics could resist forecasting precisely when the end would come. At successive Millerite conferences in the early 1840s, leaders had to work out compromises among those with differing views on particular dates and on the wisdom of date-setting itself. Their opponents attacked the whole enterprise of prophecy, but many still became immersed in disputes about why the Millerites' time tables were wrong.[33] On an important level, both partisans and foes of Millerism sought to reassert their control of time by predicting its outcome with a traditional tool of interpretation, the Bible. The danger of disappointment inherent in prophecy was realized when expectant Millerites watched the last date chosen, 22 October 1844, come and go without incident. For the most part, the Millerites' Christian frame of reference reinforced their suspicion that the details of God's designs should not be probed. They did not succumb to the more cynical view that secular history developed without relation to the timetables of religion. Millerism survived as a religious movement by transforming itself in the 1850s into a broader adventism, a perspective that surrendered some of its preoccupation with time and regrouped around such doctrines as biblical literalism, seventh-day sabbath observance, and vegetarianism.

Just as Mormons and Millerites had a radical sense of the nearness of time and eternity, transcendentalists and spiritualists were convinced that the veil dividing the visible and invisible worlds could easily be drawn aside. Transcendentalism and spiritualism were less coherent from an institutional standpoint than were Mormonism and Millerism. They produced no authoritative leaders or system of operating procedures. But both were distinctive viewpoints that provoked reactions from contemporaries of disapproval mixed with fascination.

Most antebellum Protestants believed that the distance between divine and human spheres was closed partly by the insights of common sense but bridged finally only by revelation, Jesus's message of salvation recorded in the Bible. The transcendentalists were a group of intellectuals who lived in and around Boston and who took one version of this common perspective—the liberal Christian doctrines of the Unitarians—in unorthodox directions in the 1830s. By asserting that human nature made a full revelation available to all people, they invited the proliferation of equally authoritative readings of divine truth and encouraged the sense that the spiritual and material worlds were intimately bound. It might seem innocent to say, as the transcendentalists did, that people grasped God's message by intuition rather than by a combination of common sense and revelation. Still, the self-sufficiency of private insight, the conclusion implicit in their position, reduced Christianity—and all the institutions that defended it—to the same level as anyone's sincere understanding of enduring truths. To a conventional Christian, whether liberal or evangelical, Ralph Waldo Emerson's definition of "true Christianity" as "a faith like Christ's in the infinitude of man" did violence to reasonable language and threatened corresponding social confusion.[34]

Although not all transcendentalists went on to link their assertion that human beings could traverse the boundaries of the visible world to philosophical monism, Emerson was one who traced human potential to the fact that nature and spirit were simply different manifestations of the same substance. He wrote in *Nature* in 1836 that "the Supreme Being, does not build up nature around us, but puts it forth through us, as the life of the tree puts forth new branches and leaves through the pores of the old."[35] Transcendentalism did not provoke mob violence, but it elicited much criticism in the press in the late 1830s, primarily from more conservative Unitarians. The reasons were clear. Transcendentalism challenged traditional landmarks and ingrained habits that ordered perceptions of space: the preeminence of Christian institutions and the commonsense view of the physical world as a solid entity in itself.

Spiritualism, the practice of seeking to communicate with disembodied souls, lacked much of the intellectual sophistication of transcendentalism, but it rested on the same view that the bounds of visible nature were more permeable than commonly supposed. Spiritualism gained widespread attention in the late 1840s after Katherine and Margaret Fox, ages 12 and 13, respectively, used code to converse with a spirit they heard rapping in their house in upstate New York's burned-over district. The girls soon publicly displayed their talent as mediums under the aegis of the impresario P. T. Barnum. Far more than a passing curiosity, however, spiritualism drew on keen interest throughout the 1830s and 1840s in efforts to probe and manipulate invisible forces. These movements included Swedenborgianism, a philosophy based on the mystical idealism of the eighteenth-century Swedish philosopher Emanuel Swedenborg, and mesmerism, the experimentation with forms of animal magnetism such as hypnotism. In the wake of the Fox sisters' fame in the 1850s, mediums appeared across the country, holding séances primarily intended to help grieving individuals make contact with deceased kin and friends.[36]

Although spiritualists' claims for the power of human insight were heterodox and the appeal of mediums threatened the clergy's authority, spiritualism provoked fewer of the fears of doctrinal and social disorder that surrounded earlier radical religious movements. George Templeton Strong, a New York lawyer and High Church Episcopalian, wrote in his diary in 1855 that spiritualism was "a new Revelation, hostile to that of the Church and the Bible." Still, he had attended at least one séance himself and knew respectable people who were attracted by spiritualist ideas.[37] Perhaps conventional Protestants could flirt with spiritualism because it was not a coherent religious system whose adoption required rejection of prior beliefs. But the growing toleration of dissenting perspectives on time and space was also a function of a basic intellectual change. By the 1850s mainstream Protestants could approach unorthodox ideas about futurity and transcendence from the safe haven of Victorian religion, with its comforting conviction that slow, systematic growth was God's preferred way. To be sure, the evangelicalism of the revivals had never let go altogether of dualistic concepts of present and future and of nature and spirit. Strong millennial and perfectionist tendencies in earlier decades had made the Protestant majority enough akin to the radical fringe, however, to make them worry about their own proximity to heterodoxy when they confronted Mormons, Millerites, and transcendentalists. The comparative emotional equilibrium with which Protestants handled spiritualism was to an important extent the result of the religious resolution they achieved.

None of the foregoing expressions of religious dissent linked systematic social reform objectives to heterodox ideas. Radical abolitionism, in contrast, interpreted ordinary evangelical assumptions in a way that mandated an immediate end to the institution of slavery—an unnerving prospect to white southerners and most northerners alike. For the abolitionists themselves, participation in reform agitation raised further questions about social justice and led to the development of anarchist and feminist ideas. Most antebellum white Protestants concurred that abolitionism posed social and philosophical dangers. Far fewer were willing to acknowledge the intellectual roots of abolitionism in ordinary religious assumptions.[38]

Around 1830 a number of conscientious people scattered across the nation grew impatient with the moral compromises and implicit racism of colonization, the prevailing approach to the termination of slavery that aimed to return blacks to Africa after voluntary manumissions by their masters. The publication of the first issue of the *Liberator* in 1831 by William Lloyd Garrison (1805–79) in Boston is often seen as the beginning of abolitionism. It is more accurate to say, however, that Garrison's moral absolutism and commanding rhetoric drew individuals already concerned about slavery into the American Anti-Slavery Society in the 1830s. Many of Garrison's earliest allies were free African Americans. A number of leaders of black churches in northern cities had preceded Garrison in their opposition to colonization. *Freedom's Journal* (1827–29), a periodical devoted to immediate emancipation and the promotion of black pride, was published in New York City through the initiative of a group of men composed mainly of ministers. These included Nathaniel Paul of Albany's First African Baptist Church, Peter Williams, Jr., of New York's Saint Philip's African Episcopal Church, and Samuel Cornish of New York's First Colored Presbyterian Church, who served as the magazine's editor.

After 1831 black and white abolitionists generally worked cooperatively. An estimated three-quarters of the subscribers to the *Liberator* were black, for example, and the founding meeting of Garrison's New England Anti-Slavery Society in 1832 was held in Boston's African-American Joy Street Baptist Church. Many of Garrison's white supporters came slightly later to the movement than his black co-workers. Among those who became prominent abolitionists in the1830s were former slaveholders James G. Birney, Sarah Grimké,

This daguerreotype of an outdoor antislavery meeting around 1850 shows that black and white abolitionists worked together to achieve the abolition of slavery. Frederick Douglass appears to the left of the woman seated at the table. The daguerreotype is the work of an unknown American maker. *Collection of the J. Paul Getty Museum, Malibu, California.*

and her sister Angelina Grimké; Philadelphia Quakers James and Lucretia Mott; converts of Charles Finney, such as Arthur Tappan, his brother Lewis Tappan, and Theodore Weld; evangelical minister and reformer Henry Clarke Wright; and Unitarians such as Samuel J. May. One reason for this alliance of black and white abolitionists was the participation of reformers of both races in evangelical churches and their consequent agreement on the basic religious orientation that informed radical abolitionism.[39]

The intellectual ground on which all converged was that slavery must be judged as an ethical problem, a provocative approach in a nation caught up in a religious awakening. "Wo to that policy or system which has no other foundation than injustice, tyranny, and wrong," Garrison wrote in the *Liberator* in 1832, "which consults expediency and not right!"[40] Abolitionists identified moral accountability as the solution to the problem of slavery and thus drew on evangelicals' sense of the power of the converted will to triumph over circumstance.[41] Slaveholding was a sin, the abolitionists argued, and it must be renounced immediately in spirit and fact, no matter how adverse the practical consequences or how opposed manumission was to social mores or human law. In her "Appeal to the Christian Women of the South," Angelina Grimké wrote in 1836, "The doctrine of blind obedience and unqualified submission to *any human* power, whether civil or ecclesiastical, is the doctrine of despotism, and ought to have no place among Republicans or Christians."[42] Nor did abolitionists view slaveholders alone as in need of purification. The movement drew its internal force from the impulse of the abolitionists themselves, as converted Christians, to seek personal sanctification through dedication to a moral cause. "We are guilty—all guilty—horribly guilty," Garrison wrote, if we obey the federal government without protest, because it endorses slavery by its equivocation and implicit readiness to protect slaveholders in a crisis.[43] Opposition to slavery was an opportunity to redeem both society and one's own soul.

The religious roots of abolitionism were thus visible in its moral vision, inward focus, and fervent activity. During the 1830s the American Anti-Slavery Society achieved its goal of agitation in almost precisely the terms outlined by Garrison in the *Liberator* in 1831: members issued tracts, employed traveling agents, formed local auxiliaries, and petitioned Congress to abolish slavery where the federal government had the authority.[44] But abolitionists met more resistance than support even in the free states. They did help to stimulate debate about slavery that contributed to complex schisms, more or less along sectional lines, in major Protestant denominations. The Presbyterians divided in 1837, the Methodists separated in 1844, and the Baptists formed sectional branches in 1845 in part because of disagreements over slaveholding. Yet moral uneasiness about slavery among northern white church members remained a far cry from endorsement of immediate abolition. The majority of Protestants in the 1830s and 1840s saw abolitionism as a threat to national harmony and an unwelcome conclusion to be drawn from common religious beliefs. Mobs composed of "gentlemen of property and standing" disrupted abolitionist meetings and killed at least one reformer, the editor Elijah Lovejoy in Alton, Illinois.[45] For the abolitionists, the experience of encountering opposition pushed some toward more unconventional social views.

Nonresistant anarchism was one offshoot of abolitionism. In the writings of both proslavery and antislavery advocates, slavery and anarchy appeared as opposites, although each side evaluated the antinomy in different terms. Slavery's defenders warned that disorder was inevitable without subordination. Slavery's opponents looked forward to perfect freedom from human law under the moral government of God. One reason that a number of abolitionists moved toward anarchism in the late 1830s was the power of their own logic. But their sense that the arena of sin was wider than the institution of slavery and, indeed, included all human agencies, such as governments and churches that exerted authority over individuals, grew, too, from their frustrated efforts to change national policy. The New England Non-Resistance Society, established in 1838, applied the doctrines of immediatism and self-purification in a new context: individuals must separate at once from all social authority based on force and must act in a spirit of nonviolence. This did not preclude strenuous protest among those who took the principles of passive resistance in more specific directions. "Come-outers" not only withdrew from conventional churches but disrupted worship. The best known agitator was Stephen S. Foster, who made a practice of rising in the midst of services and speaking out against slavery. Similarly, Garrison preached "disunionism," the idea that the Constitution was a compact with sin and that the free states should peacefully withdraw from the Union. Nor did anarchism exclude the possibility of new social compacts based on consent among purified members. Adin Ballou, a former Universalist minister and a committed nonresistant, set up the Hopedale Community (1841–58) in Milford, Massachusetts, where order depended primarily on the Christian law of love.[46] Nonresistant anarchism, despite its insistence on uncompromised personal liberty, clearly inspired multiple forms of social activism.

More profoundly, anarchism raised essential questions about the often competing claims of social stability and justice. In the 1880s Leo Tolstoy, the Russian novelist and Christian pacifist, discovered New England nonresistance and valued the movement as an earlier attempt to measure human society by ethical standards. Yet in the late 1830s conservative members of the American Anti-Slavery Society argued that to link antislavery to other radical doctrines alienated potential followers, and they withdrew to form the single-issue American and Foreign Anti-Slavery Society in 1840.[47] These prudent abolitionists were upset not only by their colleagues' support of nonresistance but of women's rights.

The Seneca Falls Convention of 1848, rightly remembered as the beginning of organized advocacy of women's rights in America, was still a decade away when a number of abolitionists spoke out for the rights of women. As was true in the case of the nonresistant anarchists, these early feminists were impelled to explore the implications of their principles for gender relations because of the opposition they met in antislavery reform. When Sarah Grimké (1792–1873) and Angelina Grimké (1805–79) spoke publicly against slavery, the Congregational clergy of Massachusetts issued a "Pastoral Letter" in 1837. The document denounced the Grimkés' decision to assume "the place and tone of man as a public reformer" as "unnatural" for women; it predicted social "degeneracy and ruin."[48] The Grimkés were not caught off-guard by the ministers' protest. They had given thought to the way women should participate in reform. Angelina's "Appeal to the Christian Women of the South," written the previous year, posed the rhetorical question she knew she must answer to gain her reader's support: "But perhaps you will be ready to query, why appeal to *women* on this subject?"[49] Angelina answered that women had more power than they were aware. They could read, pray, speak, and act against slavery. Women might have less public influence than men, she implied, but they were certainly not helpless.

In 1838 Sarah strengthened Angelina's argument when she replied to the ministers in *Letters on the Equality of the Sexes and the Condition of Women*. She wrote that it was women's duty to behave as equal moral agents: "Men and women were CREATED EQUAL; they were both moral and accountable beings, and whatever is *right* for man to do, is *right* for woman."[50] Grimké's language of equality harked back to the Declaration of Independence, but her principal standard of judgment was the Sermon on the Mount. Jesus "lays down grand principles by which [his followers] should be governed, without reference to sex or condition."[51] By the time of the Seneca Falls meeting, the model for its "Declaration of Sentiments" was more clearly republican theory than biblical doctrine. Sarah and Angelina Grimké, retired from active reform after Angelina's marriage to Theodore Weld in 1838, did not attend. Nonetheless, many at Seneca Falls remembered that abolitionists had drawn a belief in the equality of the sexes from their interpretation of evangelical Christianity and recognized that the rhetoric of earlier advocates helped indirectly to launch women's rights as a reform movement.

Within the course of a decade, radical abolitionism thus challenged the institution of slavery, the legitimacy of human authority, and the justice of gender conventions. All of these critiques grew from the insistence that society must be judged by a religious standard of value and the conviction that a recognition of the power of the spirit was the key to reform. For many of the abolitionists' contemporaries, antislavery immediatism and its derivative social theories were disturbing because they directly attacked the legitimacy of conventional social arrangements. But radical Protestantism also inspired a more indirect kind of social protest: the formation of utopian communities.

The impulse to begin society anew by setting up purified communities outside the bounds of civilization was not unique to antebellum America. From seventeenth-century Puritan towns to the commune movement of the 1960s, community builders have sought to liberate themselves and instruct society by creating exemplary social alternatives. Even so, communitarian fervor between 1830 and 1860 was particularly intense. A. J. Macdonald, a Scottish printer and admirer of the reform ideas of Robert Owen, spent a decade in

America before his death in 1854 traveling among communities to collect information. By his count, only 19 societies were formed between 1724 and 1829, but 53 appeared between 1830 and 1854.[52] Many antebellum experiments were the result of a desire originating in the Second Great Awakening to construct a social milieu in which spiritual perfection could be achieved. But many also looked beyond religion to the theories of science and social science for means of implementing their goals. Social concerns initiated by religion brought reformers in contact with secular points of view. The cases of the Oneida community and Brook Farm suggest the ways in which these intellectual odysseys came about.

The Oneida community in upstate New York (1848–79) was based on a combination of Christian perfectionism and millennialism, on the one hand, and theories of male sexuality and eugenics on the other. John Humphrey Noyes (1811–86), the community's founder, experienced conversion during a revival in 1831 and studied for the ministry at Yale. When he announced that he was perfect in the sense of being incapable of committing sin (a position that came to be called New Haven Perfectionism), his license to act as a Congregational preacher was revoked and his social marginality virtually assured. During the early 1840s Noyes and his followers at a community in Putney, Vermont, added unconventional sexual practices to radical religion. They instituted "complex marriage," a sexual arrangement that permitted multiple partners yet proscribed male orgasm. The rationale was not simply that the spiritually perfect could not sin but that intercourse was a form of religious communion and hence worship. Their neighbors' outrage drove them out of Vermont in 1847 and pushed them in even more radical intellectual directions. Noyes declared that the millennial kingdom had already begun. In order for the children of the saints in the "resurrection state" to grow even more perfect, the Oneida community introduced "stirpiculture" in 1867, a system of selective breeding controlled by Noyes and the group's elder members. Significantly, the Oneidans also called their practice of eugenics "scientific propagation." The term underlines the way their attention to theories of health paralleled their religious enthusiasm. Thus "male continence" incorporated the common medical belief that men sacrificed some of their strength with each ejaculation. Unconsummated intercourse also freed women from the physical difficulties that many contemporaries observed came with frequent pregnancies. Overall, Oneida kept its religious goal preeminent but bowed, too, to the authority of science, a combination of allegiances characteristic of antebellum communities.[53]

At Brook Farm in West Roxbury, Massachusetts (1841–47), reformers looked to social science to help realize religious expectations. The community was begun by George Ripley (1802–80), a Unitarian minister who had become a transcendentalist, and his wife, Sophia. The experiment aimed at the outset to create social conditions hospitable to the growth of the individual soul. If all shared labor and had access to education, the Brook Farmers reasoned, then both the social and consequent spiritual inequalities of capitalism would be resolved. Brook Farm was rooted in a developmental perfectionism derived from liberal Christianity, a view akin to the immediatist view of possible sinlessness drawn from evangelicalism by John Humphrey Noyes. Ripley also entertained an expectant millennialism that linked him to Noyes's sense of the imminence of the end of human time. He wrote in 1843, "I long for action, which shall realize the prophecies, fulfil the Apocalypse, bring the new Jerusalem down from heaven to earth, and collect the faithful into true and holy brotherhood."[54]

Unlike the Oneida reformers, however, the Brook Farmers did not adopt medical science but rather the social science of Charles Fourier, a French thinker, to achieve millennial perfection. Whereas social arrangements in the early years of Brook Farm grew from Christianity directly, Fourierism provided both theory and methods after 1844, including guidelines for the redistribution of wealth, the introduction of economies of scale, and the organization of specialized labor. The Brook Farmers were not alone in their attraction to Fourier's ideas. During the height of enthusiasm for Fourierism in America between 1843 and 1845, 25 other communities were established across the nation. By far the highest proportion (10) appeared in New York's burned-over district, a sign that religious fervor impelled other Fourierists as well to adopt social-scientific means to attain spiritual ends.[55]

To penetrate the sources of antebellum religious radicalism, it is helpful to observe that only three Fourier communities began in the 1850s. Similarly, most of the other unsettling interpretations of Christian principles— Mormonism, Millerism, transcendentalism, and abolitionism—ceased to preach an aggressive, coherent message even before mid-century. Part of the reason for their decline as clear alternative voices was the difficulty of maintaining intellectual coherence among exceptionally volatile people. Abolitionism, for example, split in a variety of directions in the 1840s, as those who once concurred on immediatism became nonresistants, feminists, disunionists, communitarians, or advocates of political antislavery. Awareness that original formulas might not work, including doubts about the possibility of persuading slaveholders to renounce bondage or the certainty that the millennium had not come at the predicted time, also contributed to intellectual disarray. Simple exhaustion of high-pitched fervor was a final internal cause of the radical movements' waning force. Most people cannot live indefinitely as if on the verge of momentous events.

From a broader perspective, the diffusion of radical Protestantism roughly coincided with the transformation of evangelical revivalism into Victorian religion. The concurrence of these trends was not accidental. The excited instability of revivalism, reaching a climax around 1840, was the seedbed of heterodox perspectives. Even in its mainstream forms, evangelicalism permitted a fair measure of infatuation with the power of the spirit, both in the drama of conversion and the prospect of millennial perfection. Most Protestants accepted implicit limits to spiritual exuberance set by the Bible, the church, community norms, and the physical world. Religious radicals, in contrast, broke with their contemporaries by disdaining such temporal bounds to spiritual expression. But heterodoxy nonetheless thrived in the charged atmosphere of revivalism. Victorian gradualism was less likely to produce rebellious religious enthusiasms. Indeed, it is possible to argue that middle-of-the-road Victorian religion took shape at the expense of unconventional viewpoints. Through contention with dissenters whose ideas were identified as unacceptable, mainstream Protestants defined a safe intellectual position for themselves.[56] Religious heterodoxy declined, in part, because influential spokesmen worked actively to discredit it. Other characteristics of antebellum religious life still remain unexplained, however. Why, for example, did religious conservatism arise alongside spiritual radicalism?

Conservatism

It may seem strange to trace an intensified commitment to traditional institutions to personal odysseys like those that gave rise to Protestant radicalism. But for some Americans, conscientious self-examination inspired by the Second Great Awakening produced a new appreciation of agencies that assured the transmission of inherited values, such as the church, the family, and slavery. George Templeton Strong, the New York lawyer who dabbled in spiritualism, moved in the early 1840s from Presbyterianism to High Church Episcopalianism. About 50 Episcopal priests and seminary graduates went further when they entered the Roman Catholic church during the pre–Civil War decades.[57] Far more Americans were affected by the new emphasis on the Christian mission of established institutions through proslavery thought. Both ordinary slaveholders who were awakened by revivalism and intellectuals who became proslavery apologists identified slavery, as administered through the patriarchial family, as the necessary center of Christian society.

Overall, antebellum religious conservatism grew from desires strikingly similar to those that fired spiritual radicalism: the inclination to achieve a rich and, indeed, enveloping religious experience and the impulse to use religious patterns of thought and behavior to attain a sense of personal order. Certainly mainstream revivalism stimulated spiritual interests in many contemporary Protestants, but both radicals and conservatives wished to infuse their lives with religious feelings and to direct them according to religious principles to an unusual degree. Whereas radicals defended spiritual expression even at the expense of social order, however, conservatives insisted that God's will acts through historical institutions. Radicals aspired, too, toward future perfection, while conservatives located ideals in the past. Among conservative Christians, several groups focused attention, to a degree nearly unprecedented in America, on the historical church. These included the Mercersburg theologians, High Church Anglicans, and Protestant converts to Roman Catholicism. More unconventionally, proslavery apologists insisted on the religious value of slavery as a familial institution. Judaism, a traditional faith in light of its loyalties to the Torah and to inherited Talmudic learning, gained strength as a result of the arrival of many German-Jewish immigrants. The Jewish community received little attention from American Christians, however, and stood on the margin of these expressions of Christian conservativism.

Conservative advocates of the preeminence of the church as an avenue of faith commonly criticized the individualistic, ad hoc tenor of revivalism. But their ardent longing for a religious experience of greater depth and structure was often aroused, though not satisfied, by mainstream Protestantism. Events that involved the German Reformed seminary at Mercersburg, Pennsylvania, and in particular John Williamson Nevin (1803–86), suggest the evangelical roots of conservative dissent. Nevin experienced conversion in the Presbyterian church while he was a student at Union College in Schenectady, New York. After his graduation from Princeton Seminary, he became a professor at a Presbyterian theological school outside Pittsburgh and participated in a wide range of voluntary associations. In 1840, however, Nevin left the Protestant mainstream for the German Reformed church, a small denomination with close ties to German immigrants and scholarship. From his new position as a professor at Mercersburg seminary, he articulated his dissatisfaction with revivalism and developed his views on the historical church.

Any contemporary familiar with the potential emotional roller coaster of revivalism and the impetuous tenor of voluntary reform efforts must have recognized the basis for Nevin's attack, in *The Mystical Presence* (1846), on the "spirit of sect," a religious temper so narrowly focused on the "personal and experimental" that it encouraged attitudes that were "fanatical and wild; especially in the way of opposition to outward forms and the existing order of the Church generally."[58] As an alternative to personal isolation and institutional transience, Nevin offered the historical church and particularly the sacrament of the Lord's Supper as envisioned by John Calvin. Communion effected a mystical union with Christ, Nevin argued, a bond "not figurative merely and moral, but *real, substantial* and *essential*," an "*objective* force" transmitted from Christ to believers through the church.[59] Thus Nevin used the freedom of self-discovery permitted by mainstream evangelicalism to move toward the more definite, inherited rituals of the Christian tradition. It is not surprising that, even in a nation inclined to aggressive anti-Catholicism, Nevin's longing for connections with the past at one point brought him close to conversion to the Roman Catholic church.[60] Although his ideas had little impact outside the German Reformed denomination, the pattern of his experience—spiritual awakening leading to a search for historical forms of observance to satisfy heightened feelings—was widely shared.

Most Americans who followed this path did so in the context of the "Catholic" movement in the Episcopal church, an expression of religious commitments akin to the Oxford movement in contemporary British Anglicanism. American Protestants of conservative leanings watched closely as a group of scholars at Oxford University published 90 *Tracts for the Times* between 1833 and 1841. John Henry (later Cardinal) Newman, the most prominent Oxford figure, summed up his position of the 1830s when he looked back in his auto-biographical *Apologia Pro Vita Sua* in 1864: advocacy of definite dogma rather than liberal ecumenicalism, defense of the visible church with its sacraments and episcopal hierarchy, and adherence to the Anglican "via media" as opposed to Roman Catholicism.[61]

Historical Christian doctrines and institutions were central to Oxford thinking, and the *Tracts* were read eagerly by Americans dissatisfied with the experimental tenor of evangelicalism. The result of discussion and reflection on Oxford doctrines was the strengthening of a controversial High Church party in the American Episcopal church. For laypeople from mainstream denominations attracted to this form of Episcopalianism, the choice of a church-centered religion seemed to channel a more general impulse to achieve an orderly life through connections with the past. As a young man, George Templeton Strong left the Presbyterian church, a faith he judged "without form and comeliness, and greatly wanting in decency and order," for an Episcopalianism that embodied "submission, humility, and reverence."[62] Alongside comments in his journal on church issues per se, Strong praised diverse aspects of a resurgent, religiously oriented traditionalism, including the use of liturgical music, the celebration of Christmas, and an interest in medieval life.[63] Despite these affinities of High Church Episcopalianism with a broader cultural conservatism, however, Anglican Catholicism was at base a religious movement that aimed to restore the strength of the traditional church. Had adherents been less seriously devoted to principles, fewer would have chosen the socially risky course of conversion to Roman Catholicism.

The longing for an all-encompassing religious experience within a church whose authority was continuous in time and universal in space almost inevitably led to consideration of the claims of Roman Catholicism. Most American Protestants, reared on the Reformation's image of the Roman church as a "scarlet whore" and sensitive to contemporary nativism, drew back from Catholicism in the end. "In the abstract, I prefer the positive errors of Romanism . . . to the miserable negative syncretism of the other side," George Templeton Strong wrote during controversy over New York's common school curriculum in 1843. "But as a practical matter . . . I think it's safer, better, and altogether more discreet to vote the Protestant ticket."[64] Not everyone, however, made the prudent choice. In the course of the nineteenth century as many as 700,000 Protestants became Catholics.[65] Although mixed marriages account for many conversions, there were also tormented decisions among prominent Anglicans in the Oxford and Catholic movements in Britain and America, respectively, the most dramatic of which resulted in the conversion to Roman Catholicism of John Henry Newman in 1845. To appreciate the broad appeal of Catholicism in America, it is important to see that not all converts arrived by a small step from High Church Episcopalianism. Even among the transcendentalists there were a significant number of conversions. The history of Orestes Brownson is exemplary.

It would be easy to picture Brownson (1803–76) as a man who reached an intellectual precipice armed only with the transcendentalist's faith in intuition and, realizing his vulnerability, fell back on the historical church. But the half-truth of this view must be balanced by an understanding of how Brownson's conversion in 1844 grew logically from his transcendentalism as well. By the time he arrived in Boston in 1836 as the Unitarian minister of the Society for Christian Union and Progress, he had already been a Presbyterian and a religious skeptic. From at least 1836 on, however, his underlying goals remained the same: to reunite humanity by improving conditions for the working class, to guide reform by religious principles, and, indeed, to create a new religion by drawing what was best from all versions of Christianity.[66] Like many radical religious reformers, Brownson sought universal social harmony and pervasive spiritual power. More than most, however, he located the roots of future perfection in the past. He argued in *New Views of Christianity, Society, and the Church* (1836) that a progressive religion must unite the spiritual focus of Catholicism and the material interests of Protestantism in order to achieve millennial peace.[67] Perhaps Brownson's appreciation of history made him turn back from utopian visions to the Catholic church. By its own profession, the church was a corporate body essentially spiritual in nature. It was the only religious institution, as Brownson wrote in 1844 on the eve of his conversion, that embodied "the profound REALISM of the Gospel" because of the vital presence of Christ.[68] Through all his intellectual gyrations, Brownson searched with a radical's fervor for a religious state of perfect coherence, changing his mind only about whether it must be made or found close at hand.

All of these movements of ecclesiastical renewal drew on the frustrations of awakened enthusiasm in an evangelical setting. Conservatives sought spiritual satisfaction by appropriating the institutions of the past. There were self-imposed limits to Protestants' choices, however. So decisively did the majority conceive of themselves as a Christian nation that they gave no thought to Judaism as an alternative faith. In contrast to Protestants' highly charged relationships to Roman Catholicism, either of attraction or disdain, their perspective on Judaism was generally distinguished by lack of concern. There was some curiosity about Jewish rituals in East Coast cities where most Jewish Americans settled and, in a more negative mood, some anti-Semitism. Rebecca Gratz (1781–1869), a leading Jewish citizen of Philadelphia, intimated in a letter to her niece in 1840 that it was still common for Gentiles to "stigmatize [a Jewish man] with opprobrious names."[69] In public Christian writings, however, Judaism was slighted more often than not, perhaps because the number of Jewish Americans remained small and the Old Testament focus of their faith seemed far removed from Christian concerns.

Against this Christian background, the American Jewish community changed during the pre–Civil War decades in ways that were liberalizing in theory but in practice strengthened tradition. Eighteenth-century immigrants had been predominantly Sephardic Jews of Iberian descent who were orthodox in belief and ritual. After 1830 the growing numbers who arrived in America were mainly Ashkenazic Jews of northern European and particularly German origin. Many had been influenced by the Enlightenment in Europe and were hospitable to reforms of traditional practices. The influence of respected rabbis, most notably Isaac Mayer Wise of Congregation B'nai Jeshurun in Cincinnati, brought a new sense of direction to congregations that in earlier years were commonly lay-led and contentious. Wise in particular was a consistent advocate of reforms, including so-called "family seating" in services to replace the separation of men and women and the production of English-language literature devoted to Jewish subjects.[70]

Yet despite this liberalizing temper, antebellum American Jews had a deeper sense of their Jewishness than did earlier generations. Part of the reason was circumstantial: only now were there sufficient numbers of Jews in America to form communities able to deflect the temptations of assimilation or laxity. Before 1840 the rate of interfaith marriage may have been as high as 50 percent in a cosmopolitan city such as New Orleans. Even Jews who married within their faith found it difficult in a Christian society to adhere consistently to Jewish law. Many worked on Saturdays, ate nonkosher foods, and failed to circumcise sons. From the 1830s on, in contrast, expanding congregations, vocal rabbis, and the availability of Jewish writings all stimulated a renewed commitment to Judaism. Although Rebecca Gratz remained loyal to Judaism throughout her long life, her letters after 1830 to her Jewish correspondents registered her excitement about increasing Jewish observance, education, and benevolence and her pride in being a Jew. "An enlightened Jew occupies as high a station as any other man," she wrote in 1840.[71] Jews may have stood on the margin of contemporary religious dialogue, but their distance from Christian activity seemed to help them to establish an autonomous religious life.

Far more Americans were affected by the emerging interpretation of slavery as a Christian institution. Next to the efforts of other Christians to revive church traditions, religious defenses of slavery may seem, despite similarly conservative intent, shallow self-justifications rather than sincere expressions of piety. The escaped slave and abolitionist Frederick Douglass was certainly convinced, as he wrote in his autobiography, that one particularly cruel master "seemed to think himself equal to deceiving the Almighty" when he gathered his slaves for daily prayers and hymns to cloak his evil ways.[72] Yet it is important to read Douglass's statement with caution because his *Narrative of the Life of Frederick Douglass* (1845) was an antislavery polemic. Although some slaveholders were simple hypocrites, others were well-intentioned Christians who felt compelled to explain, as much for their own peace of mind as to win public approval, why slavery was an ethical system. Like other forms of religious conservatism, the rhetorical transformation of slavery into a Christian institution put slaveholders in touch with tradition in a way that allowed them to discharge the demands of awakened consciences.

Neither apologies for slavery nor arguments focusing on the institution's religious value began in the 1830s, but proslavery thought grew more insistent than ever before in the decades before the Civil War. Part of the reason was the need to defend slavery as an anomolous institution in an increasingly free-labor world and particularly to respond to the abolitionists' attacks. At least as important to individual slaveholders, religious conversion impelled white southerners to look for a way to see slaveholding in Christian terms. The historian Eugene Genovese has explained that the slaveholders' answer to this intellectual dilemma blended images of slavery as a missionary and family institution. In both private and public writings, masters pictured their relation to their slaves as involving "a duty and a burden." In theory they cared for their dependents like authoritarian fathers overseeing an extended family, black and white.[73] Among the "duties of our guardianships" ennumerated in a proslavery polemic in 1850, the novelist William Gilmore Simms listed obligations to provide a slave with moderate labor, an adequate return in food and care, education "in correspondence with his condition," lessons in "moral duties," and punishment "in obedience to a scrutinizing conscience" and "in compliance with his desserts."[74] Public defenses nearly always appealed as well to Old Testament precedents to establish slavery's legitimacy. These images stood in conflict with the essential violence of slavery. Slavery denied the slaves' humanity by definiting them as chattel, and this legal arrangement in turn permitted the unrestrained authority of masters, the breakup of slave families through sale, and the restriction of slaves' opportunities for individual material, intellectual, and moral advancement.[75] Most scholars also agree, however, that the Christian social vision enouraged actual reforms that made antebellum American slavery more humane on a day-to-day basis.

For the slaves, the movement to Christianize slavery provided weapons of moral self-defense. Although the literal, intended message of white missionaries was the duty of obedience to masters as an expression of willing subservience to Christ, slaves drew other lessons from their religious experience that gave them, as the historian Albert Raboteau has said, "a sense of personal value."[76] The very act of proselytizing slaves contained the implicit acknowledgment that slaves were men and women rather than property. As slaves experienced conversion, joined evangelical congregations sometimes interracial in composition, or met clandestinely for religious celebrations, they grasped the egalitarian potential of Christianity and entered into relations of "religious mutuality" with their masters.[77] That is not to say that masters treated slaves as equals even in religious affairs. Having expected to create a benevolent institution based on subordination, however, slaveholders had to live with the unanticipated and uncomfortable awareness that their slaves were Christians like themselves. Slaves understood the psychological power they exerted over their masters when they saw the slaveholders' guilt and remorse, particularly evident at the time of death. One slave recalled, "It is a common belief amongst us that all the masters die in an awful fright, for it is usual for the slaves to be called up on such occasions to say they [the slaves] forgive them [the masters] for what they have done."[78] Like the culture of slavery in general, southern Christianity was a joint product of white and black perspectives. Precisely because slaveholders so successfully infused slavery with religious goals, slaves gained leverage in a society that strove in theory to reaffirm Christian traditionalism.

Overall, movements of antebellum religious conservatism mirrored expressions of radicalism to an intriguing extent. On the right as well as the left, people aimed with unusual insistence to make their lives altogether conform to religious principles. Radicals and conservatives differed mainly, though importantly, about whether the spirit ruled without mediation or through inherited institutions. Dissent on both sides reached a height in the 1840s. The most intense phases of the Mercersburg movement, High Church Anglicanism, and conversions to Roman Catholicism coincided with the peak of Millerite adventism and Fourierist communitarianism in the middle of the decade. Perhaps the numerous controversies between mainstream Protestants and Christian conservatives deflated the intellectual authority of minority positions. No less than the contests with radicalism, quarrels with Christian conservatism helped to define the contours of Victorian Protestantism: commitment to gradual change rather than backward-looking traditionalism, affirmation of the value of institutions as means of growth rather than ends in themselves, and attachment to sentiment as a spur to action rather than a goal of ritual observance.[79] As middle-of-the-road Protestantism gained a self-assured stability, conservative dissent did not disappear but moved to the margin of religious life. With this process of evolution in mind, how, in the broadest terms, should the role of religion in antebellum culture be understood?

Toward a Christian Humanism

Revisionist interpretations of American colonial history rightly stress that the early settlers' aim to set up Christian commonwealths coexisted socially with ambitions for private advancement and intellectually with persistent folk beliefs. Yet it remains true that Protestant Christianity was the original language through which most Americans understood their purposes as individuals and as a people. By the 1830s democratic and capitalist ideas offered Americans alternative ways to view their world. Religious motives and values were still powerful forces, however, in antebellum culture. People awakened by the promises of the Christian gospel for individual and social salvation rushed to transform their lives to satisfy heightened feelings and to match visions of Christian perfection. So open a culture permitted the expression of many diverging and often conflicting perspectives. The kind of closure represented by the rise of a centrist Victorian religion was a nearly inevitable response, a means to limit debate in the interest of social peace.

In light of this undeniable religious vitality, it is puzzling that a number of scholars consider the antebellum era to be a time of spiritual decline. The core of their arguments is that pious individuals became so involved in transforming society to embody religious ideals—in activities ranging from mothering to abolitionism to ecclesiastical renewal—that they lost sight of the transcendent point of reference that anchored American religion in the past. Sentimentalism displaced theology, moralism overshadowed biblical precepts, and human beings mistook their well-intentioned programs for God's designs.[80]

If this view is appreciated as a description of religious change and not, as is often true, a reason for disapproval or regret, it offers an incisive perspective on antebellum American piety. Between 1830 and 1860 religion did become more human-centered. Antebellum Americans in effect asked the Judeo-Christian tradition to provide concepts to explain and direct numerous aspects of cultural life in an expanding society. Religious values shaped the way people thought about changes in individuality, family, community, and institutions such as the church and state. To be sure, Protestantism had long influenced social development in America. But in the pre–Civil War era there were so many new issues pursued by men and women who assumed that they had the moral ability to act vigorously in religion's interest that the balance shifted away from questions that concerned eternity and that required reliance on God.

This increasingly worldly focus of antebellum religion may be judged a form of secularization. If so, however, the departure of this generation from the rigorous spirituality of the past was neither deliberate nor complete. Americans backed toward human self-reliance because they were fired with religious enthusiasm. In seeking so aggressively to build the kingdom of heaven on earth, they moved toward an unanticipated distance from God. Even then, they did not end the antebellum decades situated altogether in a secular world. Although the spiritual exuberance that ignited revivalism waned in the 1850s, the vast majority of Americans continued to think of their nation as a Christian one. Their self-confident attention to social improvement made them religious humanists, yet they also remained Christians in the sense that they drew their basic values from the Christian past.

It was another index of antebellum Americans' more secular orientation that, in seeking to comprehend their world, they could use languages that did not involve religion. In particular, they explored the possibilities of democratic ideas to debate their future as a people.

two

The Struggles of Political Loyalties

When the French intellectual and statesman Alexis de Tocqueville visited the United States in 1831 and 1832, he judged contemporary religious ferment less crucial in setting the tone of American culture than what he would call the nation's "democracy." In his classic text *Democracy in America* (1835–40), Tocqueville no doubt focused on America's civil affairs because of his own involvement in France's tormented movement toward republicanism in the early nineteenth century. He drew the outlines of democracy in bold yet ambivalent terms. Whereas traditional society, in Tocqueville's view, was characterized by connections in space among mutually dependent social classes and in time among generations, democracy's fundamental "equality of conditions" severed these relations. Instead, democracy gave rise to an individualism that ominously mixed freedom with both personal isolation and the tyranny of the crowd. At best, moreover, the culture of democracy was distinguished by salutary mediocrity. One "might find less glory," but also "less wretchedness." Despite his misgivings about the customs of the common man, Tocqueville was convinced that this "great democratic revolution" was "irresistible."[1] He believed that the democracy he saw in America represented all humanity's future.

In some important ways, social and political conditions in antebellum America did not match Tocqueville's description. Most historians concede that American society between 1830 and 1860 was not characterized by political or social equality, and some contend that inequities increased with market growth. Individualism was not the prerogative of all. Traditional customs, social disadvantages, and political restrictions combined to limit the choices of blacks, women, working people, and other minorities. In addition, various social groups interpreted political values so differently from one another that it is questionable if there was any common allegiance to unambiguous democratic ideals.[2]

Despite these qualifications, Tocqueville's argument retains enough of its considerable authority to serve as a touchstone for discussion of American democracy in the decades before the Civil War. Tocqueville shrewdly discerned three main traits of political life. First, he saw that by the 1830s America possessed not simply a political ideology—an abstract set of commitments such as guided the founding of the republic—but a political culture rich in symbols and rituals that evoked feelings and molded behavior as well as engaged reason. Second, his use of the term "democracy" highlights the change in temper of the nation's original republicanism. By the antebellum decades Americans modified their commitment to a virtuous polity by admitting greater tolerance of partisanship and individualism and by succumbing to growing worry about slavery and the Union. Third, Tocqueville's sensitivity to democracy's potential for both anarchy and tyranny mirrored Americans' own anxieties about their future. Whereas the founding generation perceived their task as protecting liberty from the encroachments of power, antebellum Americans saw that freedom itself might nurture disorder that was capable of curtailing civil rights as problematically as did institutional restraints. The expanding freedom of democratic culture propelled more than one search for new sources of order.

This chapter examines American political culture between 1830 and 1860 from three perspectives: the rhetoric and rituals of party as sources of political unity, debates within the political mainstream about the balance between liberty and order, and ideological discord produced by class, gender, and, most critically, sectional differences. In all aspects of civic life, political ideas, transmitted through families, schools, and public discussion, provided Americans with motives as well as framed their perceptions. Indeed, the key political problem of the antebellum generation was how to adapt the republican commitments of earlier generations to a more open, competitive, and, finally, divided society. The term "democracy" will be used to refer to the new version of republicanism that stressed individualism, competition, and party loyalty. This outlook did not subvert such basic tenets of classical "republicanism" as the sovereignty of the people and the authority of the Constitution. But democracy did deemphasize the older ethic's insistence on citizens' virtue in a harmonious polity. Americans would have worried less about modifying their political culture to accommodate social changes had they not been so committed to behaving as republicans, in the deepest sense, themselves.[3]

Parties

Perhaps the most eloquent statement of the founders' aversion to political discord was made by James Madison in No. 10 of *The Federalist Papers* (1787–88).

A "well-constructed Union," Madison wrote, must "break and control the violence of faction," with a "faction" defined as a group of citizens "actuated by some common impulse of passion, or of interest, adverse to the rights of other citizens, or to the permanent and aggregate interests of the community."[4] Americans continued to worry in the decades after 1830 about internal tensions provoked, for example, by mobs and sectional conflict. But unlike the founding generation, they were increasingly comfortable with the structured competition of national parties. Following bitter contests between the Federalists and Jeffersonian Republicans in the early republic and a decade without organized partisanship in the 1820s, Americans embraced parties as "sentinels on guard" against threats to the liberty of the people.[5] Democrats opposed the National Republicans in 1828 and 1832, then faced the Whigs from 1836 to 1852, and finally set themselves against the Republicans after 1856. Minority parties articulating the views of workingmen, antislavery advocates, and nativists appeared in the political arena as well. Because partisanship allowed individual choice, loyalty to a specific group, and amicable debate, it was a device well suited to provide a kind of dynamic order in an expanding, differentiated society. To the extent that antebellum political culture resembled Tocqueville's image of "democracy" as a system based on personal independence and voluntary association, these characteristics were grounded in the mechanism of parties.

The foundations of antebellum partisan culture were laid, strangely enough, in the anti-competitive early republic. So concerned were Americans at the turn of the century about the republic's potential instability that they multiplied agencies to teach civic virtue. As Revolutionary ideology thus gained depth and became a republican culture, citizens more assured of possessing a shared national identity also felt more at liberty to risk taking partisan stands.[6] A look at these efforts to nurture patriotism may helpfully precede an analysis of party debate.

Before 1830 Americans seemed to waste no opportunity to erect symbols of national unity intended to have a didactic effect. Mason Weems's *Life of Washington* (1800) appeared in at least 29 editions by 1825, for example, and not only helped to create a public image of a common hero but, as the historian George Forgie has said, transformed "historical experience into moral possibility" for young people taught to imitate Washington's character.[7] Similarly, Greek and Roman architectural styles were favored for their associations with historical republics and for the presumed influence of their pure visual lines on citizens' characters. The fact that both public buildings and the private homes of those who could afford to choose distinctive designs resembled ancient temples indicates how thoroughly Americans assimilated civic ideals.[8] Americans encountered much the same lesson on the connection between liberty and virtue in the Fourth of July orations that every year in nearly every community invoked the spirit of the signers of the Declaration of Independence. Even more dramatically, as the fiftieth anniversary of the

American Revolution approached, President James Monroe and the U.S. Congress invited the Marquis de Lafayette to return to the thriving nation he had fought to free. Lafayette's 13-month tour of the states in 1824 and 1825 became "a communal pagent, enacted over and over," according to the scholar Fred Somkin, as the towns he visited reaffirmed their loyalty to republicanism by welcoming the aged hero.[9] All of these demonstrations of civic fervor, in private and public life, indicate how political ideals took root in the early republic. By 1830 the liberty of the people was a concept enmeshed in rhetorical and social conventions.

This nonpartisan political culture continued to thrive after 1830. George Washington remained such a powerful national symbol, for example, that a group of southerners and northerners united in the 1850s to save his home, Mount Vernon, from public sale. When the 62-year-old statesman Edward Everett spoke on behalf of the project in New York, a crowd of more than 7,000 filled even the aisles and stage of the Academy of Music.[10] Towns, too, developed a proud awareness of their history. Concord, Massachusetts, claimed distinction as the site where the Revolution began when the community erected a monument to the men who had defended Concord bridge in 1775. At the marker's dedication on 4 July 1837, the "Concord Hymn," composed by local resident Ralph Waldo Emerson, was sung to honor the "embattled farmers" who "fired the shot heard round the world."[11] No special civic achievement was really needed, however, to make localities wish to transform memories of their founders' early struggles into objects of mutual reverence. During a growing wave of nostalgia in the 1850s, Sangamon County, Illinois—Lincoln's home—was one of many places to organize commemoration of the past when a group of citizens began a county historical society in 1859.[12] Whether patriotic celebration focused on national or local heritage, a political culture that skirted divisive issues persisted alongside rising parties.

Precisely how party activity related to political ideals is not altogether clear. Some scholars argue that Americans were so caught up in the race for material advancement that party debates about tariffs, internal improvements, and even slavery were mere policy discussions—extensions of self-interest—that did not touch deeper issues of political theory. Others read party rhetoric as a clear index of philosophical position. The Democrats' loyalty to the "common man," according to at least one historian, signified the party's commitment to social egalitarianism. Still others contend that public language bore a more complex relation to cultural orientation. One interpretation proposes that Democrats implicitly defended a traditional communal social ethic at the same time that Whigs envisioned a society of self-directed, progressive individuals.[13] At least one conclusion from so much scholarly discussion seems apparent: parties were vehicles for overlapping social and intellectual commitments, and as such they need to be taken seriously not simply as tools of practical interest but as expressions of political identity.

Andrew Jackson was pictured as a military hero in this lithograph made by the Charles Risso and William R. Browne lithography company during Jackson's presidency (ca. 1833). *National Portrait Gallery, Smithsonian Institution.*

Daniel Webster appears as a man of seriousness and dignity in this sepia watercolor by James Barton Longacre painted in 1830. *National Portrait Gallery, Smithsonian Institution.*

Partisanship became a key trait of American political culture during the so-called Second Party system, when Democrats and Whigs opposed one another for elected office. Because both parties encompassed diverse constituencies (northerners as well as southerners, urban residents as well as rural, and well-to-do people as well as men of ordinary means), there was more than one interpretation of what each party stood for. Still, voters assumed that the party system was based on competition between distinctive viewpoints and on their freedom to choose one set of symbols over another. Consider, for example, the different understandings of democracy's meaning implicit in making one's hero the Democrat, Andrew Jackson (1767–1845), or the Whig, Daniel Webster (1782–1852). Public statements about Andrew Jackson consistently attributed three traits to the Democratic leader: untutored natural intelligence, a sense of acting as an agent of God's providence, and iron will. Throughout Jackson's years as president (1828–36) the image of the victorious commander at the Battle of New Orleans in 1814—rough, unpretentious, and determined—not only informed public perception of the man but lent the Democratic party's agenda a genuinely popular aura. The Democrats' laissez-faire economic policies of opposition to tariffs, centralized banking, and federal funding for internal improvements may or may not have actually aided the common man. But the myth of Jackson as a leader of natural force interacted with campaign promises and administration policies to make the Democrats seem the party of independent yeomen and artisans.[14]

The Whig view of democracy's potential stood in contrast to the ideals associated with Jackson. Whereas Jackson commanded respect as a spontaneous man of the people, Daniel Webster, the Whig lawyer from New Hampshire, represented "civilization and law," "progress through history," and "the gentler sentiments of a peaceful negotiator," in the words of the historian Daniel Howe.[15] The impression of Webster as a man of cultivation validated the Whig program of economic and social initiatives sponsored by the federal government (including internal improvements, temperance, and, to an extent, antislavery), much as Jackson's image reinforced the Democratic position. Whigs must have reasoned that if Webster profitably used education, the legal profession, and political power to succeed in his own life, then public institutions might similarly aid the nation's progress.

In sum, party symbols invited Americans to champion values that were different from yet not fundamentally hostile to one another. The images of Jackson and Webster clustered, respectively, around traits of natural and civilized virtue. But both men were revered for their individual success and their ability to promote social progress in a partisan setting. The underlying message of party competition was the republic's ability to accommodate more than one version of democratic ideology.

Party dialogue also facilitated change in political ideas over time. Without altering the fundamental republican principles articulated in the Constitution, new patterns of party opposition gave expression to emerging points of view.

When the Third Party system arrayed Democrats against Republicans after 1856, following a period of voter realignment, the terms of discourse resembled the concerns of the Second Party system but were enough revised to register Americans' new preoccupations as well. The crux of the debate between Democrats and Whigs in the 1830s and 1840s may be seen as the value of institutional initiatives to improve human nature. The same basic issue informed the exchanges of Democrats and Republicans in the 1850s. The Democrats' idea of "popular sovereignty," formulated by the Illinois politician Stephen Douglas, assumed that communities (now conceived as territories in the process of becoming states) were best qualified, as if by natural virtue, to determine the status of slavery in the West. The Republicans' insistence on "free soil, free labor, free men" aimed at self-advancement made possible by the exclusion of slavery from the territories by federal government policy, a position that betrayed the Whig background of many Republicans.[16] Here once again was the dispute between popular control and centralized decision-making.

Yet beyond these continuities in ideology there was a new temper to each party's position. Whereas the Republicans' rhetoric of "free labor" highlighted their interest in economic achievement for individuals in expanding markets, the Democrats' old-fashioned emphasis on community, even to the point of accepting slavery if that was the popular will, had a defensive tone characteristic of people uncertain about the stresses and inequities of economic progress. Party dialogue in the 1830s had centered on how economic development should occur. By the 1850s more polarized sides posed enthusiasm for entrepreneurship against serious reservations about the consequences of the competitive ethic. All this is not to say that debate between Democrats and Republicans was limited to differences about capitalism. Other issues, most critically slavery, also shaped contention and in potentially explosive ways. The point is that as economic conditions changed, the party system allowed Democratic-Whig exchanges about the means of progress to grow into Democratic-Republican dialogue. For the first generation of Americans willing to experiment with partisanship, party competition on the whole fulfilled expectations of keeping ideological differences under control.

Indeed, although political parties brought a kind of dynamic order to an intellectually diversified nation, it is ironic that competition for votes made each party seek a centrist position. Antebellum Americans depended on conflict to make partisanship meaningful and exciting, but politicians' inevitable impulse to copy winning strategies enhanced at least the impression of ideological consensus. The best known instance of this frame of mind involved the Whigs' decision to present themselves in the rustic, hard-fighting image of Andrew Jackson. Whig leaders chose William Henry Harrison, a military hero of battles against the Indians on the Indiana frontier, as their presidential candidate in 1840. Log cabins built to imitate the house where Harrison was born were the centerpiece of Whig rallies across the nation. Not untypically, 150 people inside a cabin set on wheels were pulled from Lowell, Massachusetts, to Concord by 23 horses. Almost comically, sophisticated Whigs dressed up as plain folk when they spoke in rural districts. Boston lawyers put on boots and homespun to woo voters outside the city, and the South Carolina aristocrat Hugh Legaré wore a coonskin cap when he left Charleston to deliver stump speeches in the country.[17]

Over time, images of military prowess gained currency at the expense of demonstrations of humble roots, perhaps because fewer candidates could honestly be portrayed as common men. Thus the Whigs ran the Mexican War hero Zachary Taylor for president in 1848, "Old Rough and Ready" to his troops, though he was sufficiently wealthy to own a Louisiana plantation.[18] Whether symbols surrounding Whig politicians focused on their yeoman origins or military prowess, the message was much the same as the ideas associated with the prototypical partisan hero Andrew Jackson: plain life predominated over genteel tastes, action won over intellect, and willingness to fight for the nation's glory prevailed over loyalty to special interests. This convergence of popular images did not erase the differences in the Whigs' and Democrats' programs that made competition meaningful. Yet in delicate balance with their disagreements about democracy, the parties in effect produced a shared commentary on what an American leader of their era should be.

As if to come back full circle to the nation's common political culture, parties also angled for electoral majorities by borrowing patriotic images for partisan causes. Each side tried to be more persuasively American than the other. Fourth of July orations had for decades preached the evils of faction. But it was a sign of changing times that in 1840 Massachusetts Whigs chose 4 July as the day to wheel their log cabin into Concord. A red-white-and-blue ball at least twelve feet across was pushed at the head of the parade.[19] The message to observers was that to be a Whig was to be an American.

As might be expected, there were plenty of counterclaims from the Whigs' political opponents. Virtually all parties chose names with allusions that made their organization seem the true bearer of the republican tradition. The Democrats and Republicans split the words that once designated Jefferson's "Democratic-Republican" party. The word "Whig" referred to the British opposition political philosophy—the "Whig" or "Country" party—that inspired the American Revolution.[20] Minority parties tried to enter the political mainstream by selecting names that summoned images of national consensus. A group of antislavery advocates became the "Liberty" party in the early 1840s. The anti-immigrant secret society, the Order of the Star-Spangled Banner, launched the "American" party (better known as the Know-Nothings) in the mid-1850s. Beyond the self-interested intentions of party organizers, the encroachment of partisanship on the carefully cultivated ground of unifying patriotism contained two principal lessons. Optimistically, the blending of party rhetoric and shared symbols reflected growing confidence that democracy could thrive despite political rivalries. More soberly, this political style reflected the realization that citizenship in a pluralistic society would be conditioned by loyalties to particular, and limited, points of view.

What effect did the rise of partisan culture have on the common men who figured so prominently in antebellum political thought? For the white adult men who composed the body politic, the availability of alternative political philosophies on the whole enhanced opportunities to create individual public identities. Political leaders made their style of address more colloquial in order to induce potential voters to take political stands. Jackson's speeches epitomized the kind of plain, serviceable language that all could comprehend. He addressed his "fellow citizens" in his farewell address in 1837:

> The planter, the farmer, the mechanic, and the laborer all know that their success depends upon their own industry and economy, and that they must not expect to become suddenly rich by the fruits of their toil. Yet these classes of society form the great body of the people of the United States; they are the bone and sinew of the country—men who love liberty and desire nothing but equal rights and equal laws, and who, moreover, hold the great mass of our national wealth, although it is distributed in moderate amounts among the millions of freemen who possess it.[21]

The efforts of politicians to communicate with ordinary people generated enthusiasm for partisan speeches. When Lincoln debated the Kansas-Nebraska Act with Stephen Douglas in Peoria, Illinois, in 1854, he asked the crowd to recess for dinner before he spoke, because Douglas had talked for three hours and he intended to do the same. People faithfully returned to hear Lincoln after their meal.[22]

During Jackson's administration, humor also emerged as a form of down-to-earth commentary on political events. Perhaps the best known humorist was "Major Jack Downing," a persona created by a journalist, Seba Smith, from Portland, Maine. Posing in one series of fictional letters as Jackson's confidant on the president's trip to New England in 1833, during which Harvard College presented Jackson with a doctor of laws degree, Downing humanized the president and brought politics within the intellectual reach of a mass audience:

> Major [Jackson supposedly began], I feel a little kind of streaked about it [getting the degree] after all, for they say they will go to talking to me in Latin, and although I studied it a little once, I dont know any more about it now than the man in the moon. And how I can get along in that case, I dont know. I told him my way, when anybody talked to me in a lingo that I didn't understand, was jest to say nothing, but look as knowing as any of 'em, and then they generally thought I knew a pesky sight more than any of 'em. At that the Gineral fetched me a slap on my shoulder, and haw-hawed right out. Says he, Major Downing, you are the boy for me; I don't know how I should get along in this world if it wasn't for you.[23]

So effective was political humor as a means of communication that writers other than Smith adopted the name and style of "Jack Downing." Outside New England, similar fictional personae offered droll, down-home views of public life, including "Davy Crockett" from Tennessee, the creation of at least six different writers, and "Captain Simon Suggs," the voice of the Alabama newspaper editor Johnson Hooper.[24] Thus new strategies of language and style introduced by political leaders in effect invited men to participate in the political process.

Overall, antebellum political culture strongly resembled Alexis de Tocqueville's "democracy": popular, individualistic, and ordered by freely formed voluntary associations. Whereas Tocqueville saw democracy as socially rooted in "equality of conditions," it is more accurate to say that equality was a political fiction (though with real significance and consequences) cultivated by parties vying for votes. Antebellum men were not even roughly equal in wealth, but party organizations opened new avenues for civic participation that gave each one who decided to get involved a measure of public power. In addition, party contests helped to order the ideological differences that inevitably appeared in a growing society and motivated leaders to look for compromise positions. These benefits of partisanship suggest why contemporaries praised parties as "sentinels" protecting liberty.

Serviceable though party politics was, however, it is hard to imagine people concerned with their spiritual well-being involved in political exchanges that were often self-interested, belligerent, and crude. Antebellum America remained a seriously Christian nation, and how partisanship coexisted with piety is not self-evident. This puzzle may be resolved to an extent by the observation that the same social groups did not always participate in both religious and political life. Because most antebellum Americans viewed women as more spiritual by nature than men and men as more enterprising, social conventions and legal restrictions kept women from politics. The different tone of the two areas of culture was in part a self-fulfilling prophecy of contemporary ideas about the characteristics of the sexes.[25] Similarly, the opposition of many religious leaders to politics as low-minded, divisive, and hence unchristian steered their more conscientious followers away from partisanship. Political interest, conversely, was the result of the comparatively secular orientation of an increasing number of men.

Nonetheless, probably the majority of antebellum men were active in both churches and parties. Like Lyman Beecher, the minister who vowed to "banish party spirit" yet campaigned for Whig candidates, they were able to tolerate inconsistencies in their own attitudes and to observe discrete standards of behavior in different settings.[26] Yet there was also a subtle continuity in ideas about institutions that helped bridge the distance between religion and politics. Much like the assumption of mainstream Victorian Protestantism that an individual's piety should be nurtured within steadily evolving organizations, antebellum parties assumed that private interest could best be pursued through mass voluntary associations. Neither the revivalist model of sudden conversion nor the classic republican ideal of consensus took sufficient account of change over time to make them workable in a complex, dynamic society. Once Americans came to appreciate the value of ongoing institutions, they could function within a gradualist framework in more than one social sphere. Indeed, men committed to advancing religious and moral issues looked to political parties, particularly the Whig, Republican, and minority parties, as new organizational vehicles for such causes as temperance, anti-slavery, and anti-Catholicism.[27] A uniform style of public behavior that involved competition, choice, institutional loyalty, and compromise brought religious and political initiatives closer together.

Although parties were the distinctive contribution of antebellum Americans to the nation's political culture, these organizations did not occupy the civic landscape alone. Citizens also formed majorities, joined to mobs, and inhabited rival geographic sections. Much as Tocqueville viewed the appearance of democracy with foreboding as well as with awe, Americans who looked beyond the neat boundaries of party worried about their country's potential for oppression and disorder as well as for progress.

Images of Tyranny and Anarchy

Americans in the decades between 1830 and 1860 were not the first generation to reflect on sources of political instability and decline. The ideology of the American Revolution, based on the political thought of British dissenters called the "Country" party, was centered in an image of degeneration: power inevitably encroached on liberty, the founders believed, unless the guardians of freedom resisted. After the Revolution Americans' apprehension that liberty itself would grow corrupt without the careful nurture of virtue stood behind efforts to build an inspiring civic culture. To these persistent anxieties observers after 1830 added vivid impressions of the dangers inherent in a popular government becoming ever more democratic. Tyranny, on the one hand, no longer loomed as the threat posed by corrupt rulers but as the risk incurred by the free exercise of will by the people themselves. Anarchy, on the other hand, was equally portended by the essentially democratic assumption that combinations of citizens might act on what they defined as the people's interest, unconstrained by law. Public discourse on these perils of democracy added new words to the nation's fund of political terms. Commentators spoke of majorities and minorities, the individual and the state, and the "slave states" (even the "slave power") and the "free states." Although antebellum Americans shared anxieties with their forebears about republican government, they expressed their misgivings through concepts that focused unprecedented attention on the problems—most essentially, tyranny and anarchy—of popular democracy.[28]

Tocqueville's *Democracy in America* was perhaps no more widely read than the many other reports by European visitors, but it was unmatched in its ability to crystalize the danger of "tyranny of the majority." Tocqueville was accustomed to a European social landscape where, at least in the recent past, castes with distinctive rights and duties—the monarchy, nobility, clergy, and people—had divided sovereignty and in theory averted oppression by any one of these estates. It is no wonder that Tocqueville viewed democracy, a system that declined to incorporate social differences formally into political life, as a vast empty expanse inviting usurpation by a new kind of political combination: the majority. Even though many Europeans complained of the "weakness" of democratic government, Tocqueville wrote, he found fault with its "irresistible strength":

> When a man or a party suffers an injustice in the United States, to whom can he turn? To public opinion? That is what forms the majority. To the legislative body? It represents the majority and obeys it blindly. To the executive power? It is appointed by the majority and serves as its passive instrument. To the police? They are nothing but the majority under arms. A jury? The jury is the majority vested with the right to pronounce judgment; even the judges in certain states are elected by the majority. So, however iniquitous or unreasonable the measure which hurts you, you must submit.[29]

Two circumstances tempered oppression by the majority: the decentralized administration of the American government and the prestige of lawyers, a profession with "the tastes and habits of an aristocracy," including a "preference for order," a "love of formalities," and a secret "scorn [of] government of the people."[30] As a man of noble ancestry who was trained as a lawyer himself, Tocqueville's remedy for democracy's excesses reflected his own inclinations. Even so, his myopic thoughts on reform did not diminish the brilliance of his definition of the problem of majority tyranny.

Part of Tocqueville's genius was his ability to listen to what Americans said about themselves and to transform their self-revelations into political analysis. His sophisticated dissection of mass tyranny might well have been inspired by Americans' own misgivings about rampant democracy. Contemporary cartoons, for example, depicted "King Andrew" Jackson and boisterous crowds of Democrats who stampeded through the White House after Jackson's 1829 inauguration as invited, though unruly, guests.[31] More important, Tocqueville toured the United States in 1831 and 1832 at the height of the Nullification Crisis, a fiery controversy centered, intellectually, in the options for self-protection of minorities. Tocqueville almost certainly read, and was influenced by, the literature generated by these bitter political events—a conflict that brought prominence to John C. Calhoun of South Carolina as perhaps the preeminent American polemicist for minority political rights.

Whereas Tocqueville, as an observer of American mores, had the luxury of diagnosing democracy's ills without identifying immediate solutions, Calhoun (1782–1850) was a politician who had to protect his constituents' interests and to justify his strategy in acceptably republican terms. The Nullification Crisis was precipitated by the enactment of federal tariffs that many southerners judged injurious to the prosperity of their agricultural and, on this issue, minority section. In his *Exposition and Protest* (1828), Calhoun still spoke in the traditional language of the Constitution when he posed states' against federal rights. Yet the sense of his argument took account of "tyranny of the majority": when a powerful combination imposed its will on one of the polity's lesser members, the aggrieved party, now conceived as a state, might legitimately declare the law void within its borders.[32] Although South Carolina eventually seceded from the Union by the act of a special convention, lower federal tariffs enacted in 1833 ended the crisis. But Calhoun continued to ponder the dilemma of how a minority might be represented justly in a democracy and offered a solution in his *A Disquisition on Government*.

Composed in the years just before Calhoun's death in 1850 and published posthumously, the *Disquisition* (1851) represented an impressively modern understanding of a complex state that Calhoun developed, ironically, to protect the traditional institution of slavery. Calhoun traded his earlier formalistic dichotomy between federal and state governments for a functional view of political life. He envisioned the nation organized around "numbers," electoral majorities and minorities, and "interests," the diverging economic pursuits and social conditions within a community.[33] Like many prominent white South Carolinians, Calhoun might have preferred politics based on deference and compromise among gentlemen to the hurly-burly of democratic parties. Not only did he condemn democracy's inevitable tendency toward majority tyranny, but he predicted that competition for votes would bring "deception, slander, fraud, and gross appeals to the appetites of the lowest and most worthless portions of the community." Such "disorder" would end in an appeal to force and finally to monarchy.[34] Yet Calhoun was enough of a republican by conviction, as well as a practical politician, to know that he could not banish majoritarian politics. So he devised a way to reconcile popular government with both the protection of minority interests and the choice of responsible leadership. Government would not follow the will of a simple majority but the combined or "concurrent" decisions of the several majorities representing each of the principal interests in the state. Since the veto of any one interest would block legislation, minorities had an instrument of self-defense. In addition, the wealthy and poor who identified with each interest would see their cause as a united one. Averting the class conflict Calhoun perceived as more prevalent in advanced societies, the ordinary men who composed the majorities would trust their superiors to lead them.[35]

Looming behind Calhoun's work on the theory of "concurrent majorities" was his hope to guarantee the survival of slavery without having to resort to secession. But despite the intellectual intricacy of *A Disquisition on Government*, Calhoun's ideas were bound to have limited practical impact. How, for example, would an "interest" be defined? Although Calhoun assumed that interests would be the nation's sections, with their distinctive economies, there was no precedent in the Constitution for any such political entity and hence no guidelines for predictably heated debate about how to implement so major a restructuring of the political system. By 1850, moreover, northerners could clearly see that Calhoun's rhetoric of minority rights veiled a defense of slavery. Growing numbers of citizens of the free states viewed slavery as a moral issue that could be compromised only to an extent in the ordinary give-and-take of democratic politics, whether based on simple or concurrent majorities. Many Americans might have sympathized with Calhoun's concern for minority freedom if the minority he represented had not been slaveholders. Indeed, northerners in the 1850s were less likely to see slaveholding southerners as victims of democracy's excesses than as devious tyrants.

As rapid westward expansion after the Mexican War (1846–48) gave poignancy to the question of whether slavery should grow with the nation, many northerners and southerners were convinced that politicians from the opposing section had designs to monopolize the power of the federal government for their own ends. Unlike the analyses of majority tyranny, these conspiracy theories did not assume that the aggressors commanded numerical strength. Still, they built similarly on anxiety about the openness of democracy, latitude that allowed a party legitimately represented in government to extend its influence through persuasion and coalition.

Accusations of schemes to hoard federal power were made by polemicists of both sections. George Julian, a Free-Soil and eventually Republican politician from Indiana, called slaveholders the "real sovereigns of this Republic" in a speech in Cincinnati in 1852. He painted a lurid picture of how they manipulated their "Northern slaves," implicitly the Democrats, to make the extension of slavery national policy.[36] On the other side, Robert Hunter, a senator from Virginia, intimated in a speech on the Senate floor in 1850 that abolitionism represented the general will of the free states and said that the agitators' goal was "to commit the Government of the United States, through a series of measures, to the proposition that there can be no *property* in *man*."[37] This rhetoric of political usurpation was polemically effective because it shifted attention from slavery's denial of liberty to blacks to intrusions on the freedom of whites. The suppressed ambivalence of southerners about the morality of slavery and the worry among northerners that abolition might lead to racial equality made it expedient, strangely enough, to leave slaves out of discussion of slavery in the political arena. Although a forthright speaker such as Lincoln used the word "despotism" in 1854 to describe the moral posture of a white man who held a black man without the latter's consent, most whites felt more comfortable thinking about the defense of the rights of their own race.[38] Thus conspiracy theories obscured slavery's injustice. Nonetheless, they revealed Americans' sense of the vulnerability of democracy to power-hungry factions.

Images of illicit designs to manipulate federal legislation also assumed that the government commanded significant power, so much so that some writers began to speak of the "state" as a political entity, with an agenda of its own, disengaged from the people. The New England transcendentalists most poignantly translated fears of minority oppression by the majority into concern that all individuals, whether or not allied with the mass, would be constrained by the state. Ralph Waldo Emerson opened his lecture on "Politics," delivered several times around 1840, with a reminder that "the State" was not "superior to the citizen," since it was created by single men and hence "alterable": "we may make as good, we may make better."[39] Although Emerson was sufficiently practical to see that government was a necessary expedient, he looked forward in a utopian mood to a time when individual moral character was the sole source of social order: "To educate the wise man the State exists, and with the appearance of the wise man the State expires."[40]

It was Henry David Thoreau (1817–62), Emerson's neighbor in Concord, Massachusetts, who turned this vision of progressive individualism into a tough program for conscientious political action in a lecture first published in 1849 as "Resistance to Civil Government" and reissued, after his death, under the title "Civil Disobedience." Writing during the Mexican War, a conflict that provoked angry debate about federal policy on slavery in the territories, Thoreau had a sharper sense than Emerson that government might not simply curtail personal freedom but might violate moral standards. Thoreau could tolerate imperfection in government since "all machines have their friction"; yet "when friction comes to have its machine, and oppression and robbery are organized," then "let us not have such a machine any longer."[41] Part of the reason that a state grew corrupt was that its bureaucratic, impersonal nature—conveyed by Thoreau's image of the "machine"—in effect dissuaded men from acting as moral agents: "The mass of men serve the state thus, not as men mainly, but as machines, with their bodies."[42] The solution was to provoke each man to distinguish himself from the crowd ("There is but little virtue in the action of masses of men") and to act according to his individual conscience.[43] Thoreau anticipated not merely self-purification but the kind of obstructionist tactics of nonviolent resistance used effectively by Martin Luther King, Jr., and the civil rights movement in the 1950s and 1960s. Thoreau wrote,

A minority is powerless while it conforms to the majority; it is not even a minority then; but it is irresistible when it clogs by its whole weight. If the alternative is to keep all just men in prison, or give up war and slavery, the State will not hesitate which to choose. If a thousand men were not to pay their tax-bills this year, that would not be a violent and bloody measure, as it would be to pay them, and enable the State to commit violence and shed innocent blood. This is, in fact, the definition of a peaceable revolution, if any such is possible.[44]

Thoreau had spent a night in jail for refusing to pay his taxes to a government that condoned the existence of slavery. His answer to immoral state power was a collective demonstration of conscience by individuals as committed as himself.

There was an ironic kinship between Thoreau's civil disobedience and Calhoun's concurrent majorities, because each thinker identified dissent by a minority as a way to block majority rule. The remaining ideological differences between the men were great: antislavery versus proslavery, individualism against hierarchy, and advocacy of moral standards in politics as opposed to secular republicanism. But both Thoreau and Calhoun, as men of definite principles, rebelled against the intellectual equivocation and yet unavoidable strength of majorities that increasingly acted through the ongoing civil apparatus of the state. If people as dissimilar as these sought new forms of resistance to majority rule, some Americans must have wondered how the nation's governing institutions would retain their authority. Alongside the visions of tyranny that appeared in public debate between 1830 and 1860 were images of imminent anarchy. People did not fear disorder simply because they heard strenuous calls for dissent like those of Calhoun and Thoreau, although such advocacy was one source of anxiety. More generally, uncertainty about political stability grew from experience with demonstrations of popular will that ignored the bounds of law.

From the nation's beginning, combinations of citizens interpreted republican liberty to include the right to act directly, without the mediation of political institutions, in their own interest. During the Whiskey Rebellion of 1794, for example, Pennsylvanians angry about high taxes congregated to harass government officials in the western part of the state.[45] Mobs became more common after 1830, however, for a number of probable reasons: democratic fervor deepened with the spread of white manhood suffrage, social impersonality grew with geographic mobility and made anonymous mass demonstrations a natural form of political action, and the diverging viewpoints present in an expanding society provoked volatile responses from ideological foes. Catholics, Mormons, abolitionists, and federal officials returning escaped slaves to southern masters were all objects of mob action.[46]

Among contemporaries, it was Tocqueville, once again, who most clearly identified the sources of the anarchic temper of democracy. Tocqueville saw that equality made the individual the fundamental political unit. This gave rise in turn to "individualism," a "word recently coined to express a new idea"—the disposition of "each citizen to isolate himself from the mass of his fellows."[47] When such inward-turning individuals did come together, they no longer united along established social lines of family or class. Rather, they joined each other as a mass bound by common allegiance to a cause, forming perhaps a political majority, an extrapolitical voluntary association, or an extralegal mob. Thus Tocqueville was struck by the atomized, unsettled, yet potentially overbearing quality of democratic freedom. He visited the United

States prior to the principal mob demonstrations of the antebellum decades. Later American political observers, though less attuned than Tocqueville to anarchy's underlying structural causes, were more interested in finding solutions to social disruption.

Young Abraham Lincoln revealed his Whig predilection for institutional answers when he proposed greater "reverence for the constitution and laws" as a cure for popular disorders in a speech delivered to the Young Men's Lyceum of Springfield, Illinois, in 1838, "The Perpetuation of Our Political Institutions."[48] Lincoln's address is significant for two reasons. It shows that concern about political discord grew in response to a wider range of events than sectional tensions over slavery, and it attempts to explain the origins of democratic unruliness. Lincoln was distressed that demonstrations of the "mobocratic spirit"—violent attacks on both blacks and whites—were everyday news. But he feared acutely for the country's safety because this civil instability coincided with the appearance of "men of ambition and talent" who, anxious to make their mark, did not care whether they were "emancipating slaves, or enslaving freemen."[49] This was the special problem of the sons and grandsons of the nation's founders. Base human motives of "jealousy, envy, and avarice" that were turned against the British during the Revolution now set Americans against one another.[50] More critically, leaders sought to win acclaim for themselves by finding a task that was as grand as creating the republic, even if their accomplishment was to destroy what their fathers had made.[51] In theory, Lincoln's call for the supremacy of law was a reasonable proposal for quelling democratic passions. What the rhetorical elegance of his address obscured, however, was that there were conflicting interpretations of laws and particularly of the Constitution. Proslavery conservatives and antislavery unionists were two crucial groups whose differing perceptions of civil disorder deepened political divisions.

To many Americans, north and south, the rise of radical abolitionism in the 1830s portended the triumph of irresponsibility and lawlessness in society as a whole. Tense reactions to abolitionism are not surprising. Abolitionist immediatism directly challenged the Constitution's compromise that slavery would be tolerated in existing slave states. In addition, abolitionists mailed quantities of antislavery polemics to the slaveholding South. Respected political leaders denounced abolitionism as insurrectionary. The aging Boston Federalist Harrison Gray Otis called the abolitionists "a *revolutionary society*" in a speech in 1835. John Tyler of Virginia, the future president, matched Otis's sense of crisis when he commented the same year on the "unexpected evil" that has "invaded our firesides, and under our own roofs is sharpening the dagger for midnight assassination, and exciting cruelty and bloodshed."[52] A conservative form of republicanism took shape across the nation in the 1830s in reaction to abolitionist agitation.[53] With an emphasis on social hierarchy, including slavery, and on gradual organic change, this set of values diverged from both the natural rights philosophy of the founding generation and the democratic individualism of the party system. Political conservatives were still sufficiently moderate to honor their republican heritage and participate in electoral politics, but they saw themselves as defending freedom by every available means in a disordered world. Although conservatives constituted a national minority, their ideas gained most coherence and dominance in the South.

As abolitionists agitated for total and immediate reform, slaveholders came increasingly to view free society as an alien and threatening landscape, filled with social disturbances, and to see themselves as guardians of order. In his open *Letter to an English Abolitionist* (1845), James Henry Hammond of South Carolina cataloged northern evils of which the South was happily free—riots, Shakers, Rappites, Dunkers, socialists, Fourierists, and "transcendental religion." He celebrated slavery as the source of his region's stability: "I endorse without reserve the much abused sentiment of Governor M'Duffie, that 'Slavery is the corner-stone of our republican edifice'; while I repudiate, as ridiculously absurd, that much lauded but nowhere accredited dogma of Mr. Jefferson, that 'all men are born equal.'"[54] A decade later George Fitzhugh of Virginia similarly depicted free-labor capitalism as the epitome of social chaos, because workers were exploited "slaves without masters." Fitzhugh voiced the southern sense of mission when he praised the South as "the only conservative section of civilized christendom," with the exception of Russia where serfdom remained intact until 1863.[55] These and other commentaries on the South's salutary conservatism were not mere statements of theory but one expression of a regional self-conception that influenced everyday life. After 1830 even the complex body of slave laws were tailored to protect social hierarchy by both limiting the ability of masters to free their slaves and restricting the owners' power to harm their laborers without legal reprisals.[56] Much like the writings of Hammond and Fitzhugh, southern slave law was a kind of document, though compiled by many men over a number of years, that voiced slaveholders' determination to create an orderly alternative to the anarchy they perceived elsewhere.

Despite the claim of southern conservatives that they held the solution to disorder, however, it is important to see that their self-conception was based on two deceptions, both of which concerned violence. First, although proslavery apologists wrote as if discontent was external to the South—a product of the democratic excesses of the free states— their search for social cohesion in fact grew as much from their experience of past slave insurrections and their fear of future uprisings as from their dismay at what they witnessed abroad. The plotted slave rebellion instigated by Denmark Vesey in South Carolina in 1822, the mass killings committed by followers of Nat Turner in Virginia in 1831, acts of individual violence directed at masters, as well as extralegal mobs of whites who effected reprisals (often lynchings) against offending blacks, all stood behind slaveholders' concern with stability, but also betrayed their contention that violence came from outside their borders to trouble their peaceful land. Second, conservative writers' image of well-managed plantations ignored the role of brutality in the day-to-day lives of masters and slaves. Ideologues liked to picture corporeal punishment as the result of the occasional breakdown of benevolent rule, but slaves knew that whippings and beatings were essential to involuntary labor extracted by all-too-human masters. Charlotte Foster, a former slave, recalled after the Civil War, "Just because they wanted to beat 'em; they could do it, and they did."[57] In sum, although white southerners offered their brand of republican conservatism as a critique of the troubling expressions of democracy's freedom, it is more accurate to say that these values, affirming liberty only so far as consistent with hierarchy, were a response to internal disorders as well.

Southern conservatives were not the only Americans caught in intellectual and, indeed, moral contradictions that grew from the prospect of political degeneration. Unionism, a predominantly though not exclusively northern perspective, was based on the idea that secession "is the essence of anarchy," as Lincoln said in his first inaugural address in 1861.[58] At the same time that southern conservatives, disturbed by antislavery initiatives, were formulating what they saw as a safer version of democracy, a number of northern spokesmen, particularly those of Whig or Republican leanings, brought new prominence to the idea of national unity in a way that denied local freedoms once taken for granted. This unionism was progressive in the sense that its advocates favored a strong federal government as a means to fortify the nation. But there was also an intellectual kinship between these advocates and southern conservatives: their common fears of disorder, their willingness to compromise some liberties to preserve a larger political good, and their problematic acceptance of violence as a means to keep the peace.

Ideas about the Union stretched back in time to the founding generation. Eighteenth-century Americans welcomed political confederation only as long as liberty was not compromised. Nineteenth-century unionists held the far less conditional view that the nation was, in Lincoln's words, "perpetual" in nature.[59] No longer seen primarily as the creation of free men, the Union was prized instead as the precondition of freedom. This transformation was not simply the result of emotional bonds to the nation that strengthened over time. Instead, self-conscious unionism emerged through confrontations with secessionist ideas. The northerners who rallied behind the Union were repelled by secessionist threats as wayward assertions of freedom, and they accepted restrictions on liberty because they feared anarchic excess. Daniel Webster's "Second Reply to Hayne," a Senate speech delivered in 1830 during the Nullification Crisis in reply to Senator Robert Hayne of South Carolina, concluded with the famous motto, "Liberty *and* Union, now and for ever [*sic*], one and inseparable."[60] True freedom, Webster told would-be secessionists, could be secured only through the order guaranteed by a civilized polity.

Two decades later Abraham Lincoln revealed his similar distrust of unregulated freedom during controversy over the admission of Kansas and

Nebraska as states. He declared in a speech on "The Repeal of the Missouri Compromise" that Stephen Douglas's doctrine of local self-determination in the extension of slavery was not "*declared* indifference" to bondage, as Douglas claimed, but "covert *real zeal* for the spread of slavery."[61] Affirming his wish to be "National" in all his positions, Lincoln in effect set himself in opposition to the "selfishness of human nature" that underwrote slavery in the South and, if given free reign in the territories through popular sovereignty, would expand slavery's influence as well.[62] Perhaps federal control of slavery policy curtailed freedom, Lincoln implied, but if the liberty to pursue self-interest was lost, the far more valuable prerogative to seek justice was gained. In much the same spirit as Webster, Lincoln endorsed only such freedom as was consistent with civilized principles.[63]

The wariness of liberty expressed by Webster and Lincoln sounded strangely like the position of proslavery advocates that social freedom would be best served through hierarchic order. Similarly, too, northern unionists were as willing as southern conservatives to protect their interpretation of freedom with force. "There can be no such thing as a peaceable secession," Webster said ominously in his famous "7th of March" speech in the Senate in 1850 on "The Constitution and the Union." He did not predict which side would initiate violence but professed to "see as plainly as I see the sun in heaven what that disruption itself must produce; I see that it must produce war."[64] On the eve of the Civil War a decade later, as delegates from the seceding states convened in Montgomery, Alabama, to form the Confederate government, Lincoln declared in his first inaugural that no state "upon its own mere motion" could leave the Union. Although he implied that the free states would not strike the first blow, "acts of violence" against the United States "are insurrectionary or revolutionary" and could expect to be met with retaliation in kind.[65]

These statements by political leaders reflected an increasingly widespread acceptance in the North in the 1850s of the legitimacy of coercion and violence. Antislavery demonstrators massed in Boston at the beginning of the decade to block the return of runaway slaves to southern masters by the federal courts. Northerners sent arms and men to "Bleeding Kansas" to defeat proslavery settlers and to guarantee Kansas's admission as a free state. In 1857 the Massachusetts Anti-Slavery Society, once the seedbed of nonresistance, passed a resolution that resistance to tyrants was obedience to God, thereby endorsing the slaves' right to rise up against their masters. When the abolitionist John Brown was hung in Virginia in 1859 for attempting to instigate a slave insurrection at Harpers Ferry, he was mourned as a martyr by the antislavery community.[66] Much as southern endorsements of stable paternalism rested uneasily on the real and threatened violence of slave society, northern unionism grew alongside a certain moral comfort at the prospect of using force to protect a different conception of order. Neither type of conservatism was simple traditionalism. Both were ideologies that reached out defensively to images of harmony in the midst of mounting civil stress.

What was the significance of these antebellum debates about democratic tyranny and anarchy overall? Three points may be made. First, although it might simplify historical analysis to be able to identify specific perspectives with tangible social groups such as Democrats and Whigs or southerners and northerners, it is more accurate to acknowledge that Americans of diverse backgrounds saw their society in strikingly similar terms as poised dangerously between oppression and anarchy. Different interpretations of the same concepts, such as order and liberty, deepened social divisions. It is also true, however, that dialogue using a common language, even when exchanges were acrimonious, remained a source of political unity as long a communication continued. Second, there was more intellectual coherence to political debate than the polar images of tyranny and anarchy might imply. Because the tyranny in question was that of popular government—of the majority, the mass, or manipulative special interests—the abuse of power implicit in this kind of domination consisted of imbalances of liberty among groups of citizens, all of whom had a voice in the state. For the Revolutionary generation, the intellectual dichotomy between power and liberty was unambiguous because the people were generally united against colonial authority. For antebellum Americans, however, the distinction between tyranny and anarchy tended to collapse into the single, self-created dilemma of democracy's excesses.

Third, the debate about democratic values demonstrated a distinctive pattern over time. The preeminent trend was to seek conservative remedies for popular government that involved adjustments in the design of the polity transcending the electoral process itself. Proposals for reform in the 1830s and 1840s, such as Lincoln's call for respect for law and Calhoun's ideas for restructured majorities, had a formalistic and legal tone. In contrast, hierarchical republicanism in the South and unionism in the North, both gaining momentum in the 1850s, assumed that the arrangement of the whole social fabric had political significance. At the same time, public discussion shifted toward greater concern with coherence and order. Southern conservatives sought material progress achieved through duty and deference, and northern unionists focused on geographic and economic expansion effected by self-regulating freeholders who were protected by a consistent national policy. Their common concern with disciplined change underscores the important kinship of trends in political discourse to the temper of Victorian Protestantism, with its commitment to gradualism and institutional means. Parties channeled individualism throughout the period in essential ways. The later ideologies, however, born of fears of democratic disorder, insisted that politics itself must be located in a society that regulated freedom. Yet it is clearly puzzling that a nation so interested in settling into steady routines in the 1850s should also find itself on the brink of civil war. This perplexing situation must be explored through the broader question of how antebellum political values related to contemporary social divisions.

Factions

Both the parties that American men joined and the language of debate about civic decline that political thinkers used worked to an important degree to obscure (though not cure) social differences. The polity endured, for example, because a southerner willingly identified himself as a Whig and because a northerner concurred with slaveholders that abolitionists were insurrectionary agents. Indeed, despite the substantial ideological differences represented by parties and by the varied perspectives on declension, there was a crucial point of intellectual convergence for most members of the political community: the benefits of democratic culture were reserved for white men of property. The limits of freedom were exposed in the thinking of social groups excluded from equal civic participation by this mainstream assumption. As the antebellum working class and women of the middle class came to see how inadequately their aspirations were represented by the dominant interpretation of democracy, they articulated dissenting versions of democratic values that lent intellectual power to their social campaigns. Northerners and southerners, the other principal factions of the period, allowed smoldering differences about the nature of property and man to enter the political arena and to stir opposing theories of democratic government. In sum, political ideology not only bonded Americans in some ways but demarcated boundaries between social interests, thereby accenting conflict rooted in differences of class, gender, and section.

An American working class was just beginning to gain coherence and self-consciousness in the decades after 1830, and working people entered electoral politics as a separate interest only modestly. But it is nonetheless true that a class-based reading of democratic values was instrumental in shaping workers' thinking about their common identity. In factory towns such as Lowell, Massachusetts, and in northeastern cities where artisan workshops were being transformed into capitalist-owned manufactures, workers expressed their views in periodicals, the manifestos of unions, and the platforms of political parties. The political philosophy voiced in these sources has been most thoroughly studied with reference to workingmen in New York.[67] The New York workers' version of republican theory contained three basic themes: egalitarianism, economic rights, and political declension instigated by capitalist greed. Whereas mainstream political dialogue on the perils of tyranny and anarchy was preoccupied with the problem of liberty, workers stressed the Revolution's heritage of equality as the goal toward which freedom should tend. Journeymen who met to consider a strike in 1829, for example, declared that "the Creator has made all equal," and some of their more radical leaders, including Thomas Skidmore and Robert Dale Owen, favored the equalization of property.[68] Implicit in the workers' focus on material rewards was the idea that government should guarantee economic as well as political rights. When unionized sailmakers asserted in 1835 that "we have the inherent right to dispose of [our labor] in such parcels as any other species of property," they claimed the prerogative to set their own wages.[69] These convictions about what democratic ideals should be were framed by familiar fears of degeneration owing to conspiracy. Capitalist entrepreneurs were plotting against working-class liberty, the workers believed, and politicians represented the owners' interests in the political arena as, in the words of the radical leader John Commerford, "agents of brokers and shavers."[70]

Thus working-class thinking took antebellum political theory in new directions with its emphasis on equality, economics, and class struggle. Yet workingmen still shared with their contemporaries a fundamental commitment to the values of the Revolution and an anxiety about evidence of declension in politics. A writer in the New York newspaper *The Man* looked back loyally to the founders' vision when he declared that "the time has arrived when the people of the United States must decide whether they will be a Republic in fact, or only a Republic in name."[71] His view that this was a time of decision reflected the workers' more general feeling that class conflict, though portended, might be averted if past ideals were honored. Both the ideological kinship of workers to the middle class and the strain of compromise in their outlook distinguished the antebellum working class from the more alienated industrial operatives, often influenced by socialist and anarchist ideas, who formed unions at the end of the nineteenth century. The earlier workers' conservative attitude toward women highlights their proximity to middle-class culture as well. It is noteworthy that the women who established the Ladies' Industrial Association in New York City in 1845 claimed that it was their "right" to "earn an honest livelihood" and determined to defend their liberty "against the unjust and mercenary conduct of their employers." The majority of workingmen, however, probably shared the opinion of the National Trades' Union that husbands needed fair wages for themselves so that their wives could stay home and "perform the duties of the household."[72]

Important as it is to recognize these elements of political moderation in the position of the pre–Civil War working class, their distinctive form of democracy was both a sign and an instrument of social conflict. Perhaps most revealing, because workers judged party politics as corrupted by capitalist designs, they generally sought to settle their grievances and to secure their interests by such extrapolitical means as strikes and producers' and consumers' cooperatives. Their strategy's underlying message was that class issues could not be resolved justly within normal political channels, a disturbing insight into one of antebellum society's deepening rifts.

The campaign for equal rights initiated by middle-class women at a meeting in Seneca Falls, New York, in 1848 involved much the same blend of loyalty to democratic ideals and discontent with their mainstream interpretation that informed working-class thinking. The women and men who gathered in a Methodist church modeled their "Declaration of Sentiments" on the Declaration of Independence. "We hold these truths to be self-evident," the manifesto began, "that all men and women are created equal," and the authors (Elizabeth Cady Stanton, Lucretia Mott, and others) listed among their grievances that women were denied control of their property, equal access to employment, and the "inalienable right to the elective franchise."[73] As women's rights advocates held numerous conventions in the following years, they were ridiculed in the press as "old maids," "badly mated" wives, and "mannish women."[74] These assessments reveal how unnerving the feminist doctrine of equal rights for the sexes was to a middle-class culture that believed the security of society depended on the presence of women at home.

Nonetheless, two characteristics of the women's rights movement indicate that it was less subversive of conventional political values than was the workingmen's perspective. First, the women (and their male supporters) demanded suffrage and, indeed, increasingly focused on the vote as the key to other reforms. This strategy reflected their faith that party politics was a sufficiently open and fair forum to accommodate women's ambitions. Not surprisingly, suffragists had little success in attracting working-class women, who shared workingmen's sense that the socioeconomic issues associated with class were too deeply rooted to be remedied by a possibly biased political process. Second, the language of political democracy functioned for many working-class activists as a set of secular concepts that displaced evangelicalism and reflected their religious skepticism. Still, most antebellum feminists remained close to the Christian beliefs that anchored middle-class society. This is not to say that the relationship of women's rights advocates to religion was simple. For the significant number who entered reform activity in the 1830s as abolitionists and who listened to Angelina Grimké's words that it was women's duty to aid the slaves, it was a significant intellectual leap toward a secular outlook to admit that their goal in the 1840s was no longer strictly altruistic but self-interested as well. In addition, many feminists after 1848 favored the containment of slavery by political means rather than the immediatist, conversion-oriented approach of the earlier radicals. Even so, antebellum feminists took moral issues seriously and commonly participated in a number of religiously inspired movements, such as antislavery and temperance, along with women's rights.[75] Their dissenting version of democracy coexisted with more traditional values, and this allegiance to moral conventions was one index of their determination to participate in, not transform, the political order.

Despite the justified charges of workingmen and activist women that they suffered social and political disadvantages, their entry into public discussion was facilitated by the basic openness of antebellum democracy. Literacy, sufficient wealth to publish one's views, and a political arena structured to admit competing arguments all helped to impel new voices into political debate. The issues that workers and women raised have persisted into the twentieth century. In contrast, divisions that grew from sectional conflict belonged more exclusively, and more tragically, to mid-nineteenth-century America. Although historians have offered numerous explanations for the transformation of sectional tensions into civil war, at least part of the answer lies in a democratic system where competing interpretations of political principles could be aired. The most basic question debated was whether it was morally possible and politically acceptable for Americans to hold property in man. This issue challenged the simplicity of the proposition that democracy was the prerogative of white men of property and thus jeopardized the existing boundaries of the polity. More broadly, three developments helped to bring discussion of slavery to political prominence: the transformation of antislavery from a religious to a political question, a crisis in major party alignments, and the formation of sectional views of democracy.[76]

Beginning in 1840, a succession of third parties—first the Liberty and then the Free Soil party—worked to present antislavery to American voters as a proposal consistent with social stability. As James G. Birney and others turned away from the snowballing radicalism of abolitionism, nonresistance, and feminism they embraced the promise of democratic politics—the chance to win a majority if one's issue appealed to the mass of voters. The approach taken by political opponents of slavery was to conceptualize their cause as a moral issue that could still be compromised. Rapid territorial expansion and western settlement during the 1840s, encouraged by victory in the Mexican War and by the California Gold Rush, focused national attention on the spread of slavery. In this context antislavery politicians blended indignation, moderation, and action. They denounced bondage as immoral yet vowed to honor the Constitution's silent compromises on slavery in the South. At the same time they committed themselves to opposition to servitude's unconstitutional expansion. Condemning the Kansas-Nebraska Act in 1854, Lincoln revealed a characteristic posture of self-righteousness mixed with conservatism. He vigorously denied that there could be "MORAL RIGHT in the enslaving of one man by another." Far from appearing to be a rabblerouser, however, Lincoln came across as a guardian of historical precedent when he claimed to defend the accord for regulating the extension of slavery contained in the Missouri Compromise of 1820 that would make the territories "the homes of free white people."[77] Lincoln was liberal in his determination to keep slavery out of "our own free territory" and in his hope, widely shared with others, that slavery would gradually disappear if restricted to the South. But he declined to challenge the social order when he bowed to "universal feeling" on the subject of black inferiority and agreed that freed slaves should be granted status as "underlings" rather than equals.[78]

The political expediency of such cautious views does not mean that they were insincerely held by Lincoln and other antislavery politicians. Indeed, men who genuinely respected the Constitution, the Union, and the process of political compromise played an essential role in transforming abolitionism into a popular doctrine by framing the radical abolitionists' moral insight in temperate political terms. The irony of the success of political antislavery was clear. Although the movement was based on a social philosophy more moderate than earlier abolitionism, it was more threatening to the South by virtue of the position's wider popular appeal.

The disruption of party politics in the 1850s augmented the influence of political antislavery. The year 1852 was the last time Democrats and Whigs faced each other in a presidential election and the effective end of the Second Party system. The Republicans emerged as a national party when they ran John C. Frémont for president in 1856. In 1860, when Lincoln won the presidency, they began a half-century's success as the majority party—a domination that had belonged to the Democrats during most of the antebellum years. How did party realignment affect sectional tensions? On both institutional and personal levels, Americans were forced to rethink their positions on slavery as one step in bringing a satisfactory conclusion to political uncertainty. Although historians long assumed that the divisive issue of slavery upset the stable competition between Democrats and Whigs, Michael Holt strongly argued that it was the prosperity of the early 1850s that eclipsed the importance of the economic issues that had structured Jacksonian party debate. As politicians scrambled to redefine party platforms, the question of slavery moved more prominently onto the confused political stage.[79] Whether slavery was the cause or consequence of the partisan crisis, however, there is little doubt that the issue of servitude's future gained unprecedented importance at a key moment in political reorganization and exerted so strong an influence on the emerging Third Party system that the containment of slavery was a leading Republican doctrine.

Individuals were as anxious as party organizers to find positions on slavery that were morally and politically acceptable. Their efforts to define their views helped to draw slavery toward the center of political debate. Lew Wallace of Indiana, a Union general during the war and later an active Republican, became successively a Whig, Free Soiler, Democrat, and Republican between 1848 and 1861, as he tried to find a political affiliation that would at once honor his opposition to slavery and his determination to preserve the Union. Zebulon Vance, governor of North Carolina during the war and after 1876 a Democratic senator, allied himself as a young man in the 1850s with the Whigs, Know Nothings, and Whigs again, all in an effort to establish public connections that reflected both his quiet support of slavery and his more vocal unionism.[80] These instances reveal how much private concern about slavery and the political questions it raised fueled the party realignment of the 1850s, as men struggled conscientiously to make alliances that matched their convictions. Overall, the mounting force of sectional issues caused the breakdown of ordinary partisanship to an extent, yet sectionalism also gained momentum in the absence of established terms of debate.

Seen in light of the tragic consequences of the Civil War, the turmoil of the 1850s is sometimes judged a moment of weakness in the development of democratic politics because parties failed to find a peaceable solution to the problem of slavery. Although there is some truth to this view, the transition from the Second to the Third Party system also demonstrated the strength of antebellum partisan culture. It was crucial to the long-term moral health of the republic that politics responded to the slavery issue, no matter how divisive in the short run the controversy proved. In addition, it is significant that Americans resolved the partisan crisis of the 1850s by accepting a new form of two-party competition, a system that gave the nation an important source of stability during the Civil War, Reconstruction, and into the twentieth century. In a way that John C. Calhoun would have understood, opposition between Republicans and Democrats worked, in effect, to curtail the minority rights of the postwar, largely Democratic, South. Yet ingrained habits of popular partisanship—the legacy of Jacksonian democracy—offered the South and other minorities the prospect that they might one day displace the reigning Republican majority. Commitment to the process of party competition thus survived the Civil War era.

Beyond the growing prominence of slavery in politics, sectional philosophies gained coherence in the 1850s. Northerners and southerners increasingly felt that they belonged to opposing cultures rather than different parts of a nation. Americans had been conscious of regional character since the country's founding. Thomas Jefferson supplied separate lists of northern and southern traits in a letter to a French correspondent in 1785: northerners were "cool," "laborious," "interested," and "jealous of their own liberties, and just to those of others," in contrast to southerners who were "fiery," "indolent," "generous," and "zealous for their own liberties, but trampling on those of others."[81] In the early republic and even into the antebellum decades after 1830, an awareness of distinctive sectional temperaments functioned as part of a national dialogue about social progress. Antebellum fiction written in the North depicted northerners, self-interested "Yankees," who worried about the unsettling consequences of capitalism and came to respect the gentlemanly "Cavalier" mores of the South. This southern ideal, as the historian William R. Taylor has explained, was characterized by "vestiges of an old-world aristocracy, a promise of stability and an assurance that gentility—a high sense of honor, a belief in public service and a maintenance of domestic decorum— could be preserved under republican institutions."[82] For at least part of the pre–Civil War era, this appreciative view of the southern personality was part of the nation's self-image.

By the mid-1840s and certainly after 1850, however, Americans were less able to picture the national character as a blend of regional traits. Each side's image of itself became less self-critical, more rigid, and more opposed to the other as the justice of slavery became an inescapable part of virtually every discussion of section. Time and again northern politicians observed that southerners were increasingly ready to defend slavery as a positive good. In the past the white South regarded servitude as an "evil" to be eventually removed, Webster told Congress in 1850, but now they viewed slavery as "an institution to be cherished."[83] The altered tone of southern statements, accurately described by Webster, involved justifications of social hierarchy. Proslavery spokesmen moved toward a distinctive kind of democracy when they argued that freedom for white men depended on mutual duties between superiors and subordinates and, most critically, between masters and slaves.

At the same time, northerners who by 1860 had made the Republican party an influential political voice embraced the far more egalitarian and aggressive social philosophy of "free soil, free labor, free men." No longer sufficiently disturbed by the changes of capitalism to seek balance in the South's Cavalier culture, Republicans set the small, independent entrepreneur at the center of their ideology. They were loyal to a set of values that Eric Foner calls "an affirmation of the superiority of the social system of the North—a dynamic, expanding capitalist society, whose achievements and destiny were almost wholly the result of the dignity and opportunities which it offered the average laboring man."[84] Most Republicans envisioned popular democracy as appropriate for white men only and favored restricted rights for blacks, immigrants, and women. By the 1850s, however, they judged the permanent subordination of slavery to be at odds with democratic ideals. Republicans valued property as much as did slaveholders. But they refused to allow property in man a role in America's future, and they defined goods as the inanimate products of capitalism—the fruits of free men's labor—in contrast to the very traditional view that a man might be assigned the status of a thing. Thus images of regional personalities changed gradually between 1830 and 1860 into conflicting programs for the nation's development. It was far less possible to compromise worldviews than party agendas.

Although sectional ideologies lent an undeniable rigidity to the nation's public life, the introduction of basic questions about social organization into civic dialogue nonetheless reflected Americans' high expectations for the political process. Whether or not slavery should be permitted in a free society was the most vexing moral problem faced by antebellum Americans. The fact that they in effect asked politics to resolve this intellectual and social dilemma was evidence of their faith in the vitality of representative institutions.

Yet if Americans' commitment to democratic politics persisted and even deepened during the antebellum period, the temper of public life was different in 1860 from what it was in 1830. Whereas Americans in 1830 were thrilled by the possibilities of partisan democracy as an agency of progress, three decades later there was a brooding quality to political dialogue as citizens wondered how the shifting coalitions of competitive politics related to the larger society. People's sights reached beyond the technicalities of partisanship—the party symbols, platforms, and struggles to gather majorities—to more troubling questions of civic identity that centered on the importance of sectional cultures to the Union. This change resembled the transformation in religion from revivalism to Victorian denominationalism. Much as the mood of exultant expectancy sitrred by personal conversion and collective millennial hopes gave way to a soberer view of faith as an experience nurtured by institutions, excitement at the promise of popular democracy changed into an understanding that the political process was part of a society with divisions that could not be healed in the next election. The fact that antebellum political culture gained what would prove to be a tragic sense of social complexity did not lessen Americans' commitment to democracy. But the new awareness did make them see that the effectiveness of politics would inevitably be qualified by conditions beyond the political sphere. Among those influences, perhaps the most decisive was the culture that took shape around capitalism.

three

The Languages of Capitalism

Nearly everyone in antebellum America, from city merchants to country housewives and even to slaves, must have been aware of the immense social changes that came with aggressive market expansion. People (and especially the young) were on the move to improve their fortunes. They left northern villages for cities or perhaps the frontier, and they quit southern farms in the coastal states for the promising cotton lands that ranged from Alabama to Texas. As railroad mileage increased from almost nothing in 1830 to nearly 35,000 miles of track by 1860, train travel encouraged migration, linked distant markets, and brought towns large and small into contact with new commodities and opinions. Better mail service also drew Americans toward a national culture. In contrast to the 4,500 counties with post offices in 1820, letters were delivered regularly in 13,500 counties by 1840. When the country's telegraph network expanded after 1845, the rapid transmission of information strengthened exchange, both commercial and intellectual, even more.[1]

Along with this movement of people, things, and ideas, the texture of daily life altered in turn. Particularly in cities, encounters with strangers, guided by new codes of manners, tended to replace the face-to-face relations among acquaintances that prevailed in traditional towns. Greater social distance opened, too, between husbands and wives. In the past, men and women shared the rhythms of labor on farms or in workshops adjacent to dwellings. But now more and more husbands left home each morning for the routinized world of business, while wives cared for houses and children at what seemed, by contrast, a pace that was slow and old-fashioned. All of these changes— ambition, mobility, worldliness, impersonality, and specialized roles—were most visible in the lives of an emerging middle class, the social group that left the deepest imprint on antebellum culture. As the middle class developed customs that distinguished it from more traditional and less prosperous Americans, divisions based on class appeared on the social landscape as well.

Capitalist development between 1830 and 1860 was on the surface exhilarating, but most Americans encountered progress with seriously divided feelings. On the one hand, they welcomed change. Although the tools of economic growth (surplus capital, available labor, international markets, and new technologies) impelled Americans toward expansion, capitalism was not the creation of impersonal forces but the result of many individual and collective decisions to use resources to increase private profits.[2] Not everyone was an eager entrepreneur. Yet the determination to enhance one's social standing and to acquire new comforts was widespread. When social change contested older ideals, on the other hand, Americans were less enthusiastic. Profit-seeking sorely challenged the attention to spiritual growth at the heart of evangelical Protestantism, and competition threatened to make the vision of a harmonious polity that had inspired the founders' classical republicanism obsolete. Anxious for prosperity as Americans were, conflicts such as these made many people view the spread of capitalism with reserve and even with fear. The society that took shape around the marketplace was one of unprecedented divisions. Rural and urban life, men and women, the middle class and its social subordinates, and even reason and imagination opposed each other in disturbing ways. Although the villages of earlier decades were not the peaceful communities sometimes pictured by romantic fantasies, market growth nonetheless brought new social strains.

Capitalist culture recorded and explained these tensions in ways that permitted progress to continue because anxieties were eased. Consider three examples. First, the rise of cities and their problems of poverty, crowdedness, and crime threatened to upset the nation's self-image as a garden in the wilderness. Literature and art, in turn, reaffirmed the pastoral ideal (even if now more elusive in practice), and landscape designers made sure that urban places retained at least patches of cultivated nature in the form of cemeteries and parks. Through words and images Americans used the commitments of the past to try to shape the future. Second, the personal anonymity of a mobile, mass society made Americans worry about the emotional detachment and social disorder threatened by the decline of traditional community life. Writers, at the same time, began to celebrate and encourage individualism—a new kind of temperament that promised to make autonomous men both self-sustaining and self-controlled. A population composed of such individualists erased the moral necessity of the close-bound towns of earlier times. Third, as the work of men and women grew increasingly dissimilar, social commentators explained that differing gender roles did not represent an unfortunate divorce of the sexes but instead ensured balanced material and moral progress. In all cases capitalist values mediated between Americans' hopes and fears and between their ambitions for change and attachment to tradition. The new outlook was a way to envision society that provided intellectual resolution, allowed emotional harmony, and sanctioned behavior considered by many contemporaries as essential for social peace.

This free-market ideology was not the deliberate creation of an articulate elite but the result of a series of ad hoc responses to troubling situations that were aired in the popular media and evolved through dialogue between thinkers and their audiences. In 1830 there was a remarkable fluidity, even indeterminateness, to attitudes associated with economic growth. Attached to neither specific institutions nor traditional beliefs as were Protestantism and democratic ideals, capitalist culture took shape preeminently in words, particularly the written words of mass-marketed fiction, advice literature, and periodicals. Over time the central tenets of capitalist thinking became increasingly clear. The struggle for individual success was legitimate if regulated by self-control and moderated by domestic attachments. Virtuous effort might be rewarded by the consumption of material luxuries and membership in the respectable middle class.

This process of intellectual definition simultaneously brought dissenting points of view into focus. At the center of free-market culture stood the middle class. To an extent, the new ideology reflected the concerns of these aspiring, progressive, and educated Americans from the first. But it is equally true that this code of prescriptions for morals and manners was a powerful instrument of middle-class formation. All who were ambitious for material and social success could reach out and acquire an outlook essential for respectability by merely listening, reading, and heeding the proper voices. As economic development continued, however, increasing numbers of Americans found that capitalism's rewards would not be equally shared, and their criticisms of middle-class culture replaced their desire for assimilation. By 1860 multiple languages of capitalism were heard, as country people, workers, social critics, and others withheld their assent from dominant middle-class ideals.[3]

This chapter analyzes the way capitalist values, both mainstream and dissenting, emerged through public discussions of three kinds of space—physical, social, and subjective. It looks at how antebellum Americans coped intellectually and emotionally with the growing distance between rural and urban life (the problem of physical space), between the sexes and social classes (social space), and between reason and imagination (subjective space). The answers they developed drew on the diverse resources for expression of the capitalist marketplace, not only literature, but the fine arts, architecture, technology, and social rituals as well.

The Changing Contours of the Landscape

By nearly every practical measure, country and city were more closely linked in pre–Civil War America than ever before. People, goods, and information flowed between farming communities and such commercial and industrial centers as New York, St. Louis, and New Orleans through the use of railroads, steamboats, telegraphs, and mail. Less than 9 percent of Americans lived in towns of more than 2,500 inhabitants in 1830, but nearly 20 percent did so in 1860, and many more were acquainted with city ways.[4] Thus it is noteworthy that these increasingly cosmopolitan Americans were preoccupied with the difference in life-style of rural and urban places, not with their ostensible convergence. These were the first decades when large numbers of individuals encountered the crowds, noise, and fast pace of cities, and their judgment was overwhelmingly negative. City attractions such as economic opportunities, consumer luxuries, and leisure entertainments were often overlooked in these critical assessments. Yet these were the lures that continued to draw country migrants. By 1860 most Americans still agreed that urban life was undesirable. But beneath this superficial consensus city dwellers had discovered ways to make their society more pleasant at the same time that country people were becoming more sure that the marketplace challenged their traditions. Bound by technology and commerce, inhabitants of the country and city were increasingly separated by ideas.

Intellectual responses to antebellum cities built on elemental emotional and moral reactions. Men and women accustomed to the quiet spaciousness of the country often found that cities assaulted their senses. In 1835 Lucy Larcom moved with her mother, then a widow, from the seacoast town of Beverly, Massachusetts, to the textile center at Lowell. Although she was just entering her teens, Lucy soon went to work in the mills. Writing her autobiography, *A New England Girlhood* (1889), 50 years later, Larcom still captured her feeling of enclosure in language that described the "confinement" of the mills, the "discords" of the machines, and the "disagreeable necessity" of functioning in crowds.[5] As if life in Lowell was a state of siege, Larcom concluded, "I defied the machinery to make me its slave."[6]

To make matters worse, the sea of faces of strangers made cities seem an incomprehensible, alien territory to village dwellers accustomed to mingling with acquaintances only. By choosing the title *Confidence Men and Painted Women* for her book on the development of urban middle-class culture, Karen Halttunen calls attention to the common impression among antebellum Americans that personal appearances in cities were duplicitous and threatening. The harm portended, she argues, was not simply the strangers' criminal intent, but far more seriously the impossibility of engaging in sincere relations in a mass society. The numerous books of etiquette published during this period—70 in America in addition to the many English manuals imported—were purchased by consumers anxious to know how to behave in social situations where traditional customs failed to apply. By the 1850s most middle-class Americans came to accept the kind of play-acting involved in using codes of manners to guide interpersonal relations.[7] But for some of urban society's most sensitive and concerned members, the blurring of personal identity brought on by the race for success, jostling crowds, and studied forms of address provoked more serious social criticism.

Perhaps the most disturbing portrayal of the moral dilemmas posed by cities was the story "Bartleby the Scrivener" (1857) by Herman Melville (1819–91). A resident of New York City for most of his life, Melville turned his observations on the failure of true human communication in the city into a fable he subtitled "A Story of Wall Street." Bartleby, a "motionless young man," is a scrivener or copyist for a prosperous lawyer, and he presents his employer with an ethical challenge. Utterly passive and will-less except in his stolid refusal to choose ("I would prefer not to," he repeats again and again), Bartleby declines to leave the lawyer's office even at night, almost literally becoming a fixture, until the lawyer's landlord finally has Bartleby removed to the Tombs prison where he dies of starvation.[8]

The tale is more about the lawyer, however, than about sad Bartleby himself. About 60 years old, unmarried, and by his own admission "the victim of two evil powers—ambition and indigestion," the unnamed lawyer should recognize in the blank personality of Bartleby an exaggerated image of himself. He is a success by common measures of business, but his accomplishments have been bought at the expense of his growth as a man. The limitations of the lawyer's human instincts and of the utilitarian ethic that curtailed their development are revealed in his treatment of Bartleby. The employer is not without pity for his scrivener. He tries to place him in new employment and even pays for his uneaten food at the Tombs. Yet the lawyer's gestures of caring are symbols without the substantial generosity necessary to save another human being. He would have liked a "sweet morsel for my conscience"; but in the end "business hurried me," and compassion gives way to the old "prudential feeling."[9] He is finally as morally passive as Bartleby is vacuous in all visible respects. Someone else takes Bartleby from the office to the Tombs while the lawyer is away, driving for days in his carriage through the countryside to escape the moral burden of taking responsibility for his fellow man.

Most troubling, "Bartleby the Scrivener" is a fable without a clear lesson for reform. Melville could see how the business ethic of the city, centering on ambition, application, and restraint, produced all aspects of the tragic situation: the lawyer's stunted personality; Bartleby's machinelike, routinized will-lessness that made him the perfect bureaucratic subordinate; and the absence of human bonds between them. But within the context of the story, Melville offered no real solution. Although few writers have understood the tragic aspects of antebellum city life as thoroughly as Melville, others devised ways to tolerate urban development better than he.

At the same historical moment when Americans began to fear that the growth of cities threatened the countryside, two intellectual movements gained influence that made nature their ideal: romanticism and pastoralism.

Romanticism celebrated nature's untamed free spirit. The vision of pastoralism, in contrast, focused on the image of the cultivated garden, where the best impulses of civilization tailored nature's gifts for human ends. Both perspectives had European antecedents, and neither originated in the decades after 1830. Nonetheless, antebellum Americans used these ideologies praising nature to retain a foothold in what they considered a purer world, while they simultaneously watched their society being dramatically transformed.

At its most basic, romanticism was expressed as a taste for breathtaking natural scenes. After the Erie Canal was completed in 1825, pilgrims trekked to Niagara Falls, for example, in search of inspiration. Margaret Fuller, Emerson's friend and one of the nation's leading women intellectuals, began her summer tour of the Great Lakes in 1843 with a stop at the falls. She wrote with excitement that the cascading water filled her with an "undefined dread," as if "naked savages [were] stealing behind me with uplifted tomahawks."[10] Landscape painters such as Thomas Cole (1801–48) and Asher Durand (1796–1886), the preeminent artists of the so-called Hudson River School, aimed to depict nature in all its moods from the awe-inspiring to the peaceful. In their writings, most painters agreed that American nature tended to "the picturesque, the sublime, and the magnificent," as Cole observed in 1835, and that viewing an artist's landscape might combat the age's "meager utilitarianism" by calling the mind to "the contemplation of eternal things."[11]

More adventurous painters journeyed to the western frontier in the years before railroads to record Indian life. George Catlin (1796–1872), who spent five years in the West in the 1830s, wrote in his "Letter from the Mouth of the Yellowstone River" that the "wilderness" is the "true school of the arts."[12] He celebrated the West in pictures and prose as a "romantic country" and painted young Indian men with "their long black hair mingling with their horses' tails, floating in the wind," riding with expressions of "bold defiance which man carries on his front, who acknowledges no superior on earth, and who is amenable to no laws except the laws of God and honor."[13] As magnificent and proud as Catlin believed the Indians were, he was also convinced that they were doomed by the advance of civilization. "I have flown to their rescue," Catlin concluded, by preserving "their looks and their modes" on canvas.[14]

It is uncertain whether Catlin had the self-awareness to see that his enthusiasm for Indian life grew from the pressure he himself felt from technological, industrial, and commercial progress—a sensitivity that underwrote a kinship between Catlin and his subjects. It is true, however, that all of these affirmations of nature's sublimity served white, urbanizing Americans in two ways. First, their forays into the wild to gather impressions worked emotionally as pilgrimages of personal renewal, much as a visit to the country does for city dwellers today, though with the difference that nineteenth-century Americans had higher expectations for religious inspiration. Second, romanticism transformed nature from a place into a value—that is, a concept that con-

George Catlin's *Osceola, the Black Drink, a Warrior of Great Distinction* is typical of the artist's elegant portrayals of American Indians. Catlin painted this oil on canvas in 1838. *Gift of Mrs. Joseph Harrison, Jr., National Museum of American Art, Smithsonian Institution.*

noted purity, simplicity, and elevation. This redefinition made the natural world available to inhabitants of cities as an ideal at the same time that the country grew more distant from their lives in fact.

Pastoral images acted similarly as a sort of leavening for urban culture, not reversing social changes but making them bearable. Pastoralism affirmed the preeminent importance of "a middle ground somewhere 'between,' yet in a transcendent relation to, the opposing forces of civilization and nature," in the words of the scholar Leo Marx.[15] The pastoral ideal had a long history in literature, first appearing in Virgil's *Eclogues*. From the time of America's discovery, pastoral language was used by both Europeans and Americans to describe a New World culture that seemed to combine the best of European civilization with America's stunning natural resources. Observers seemed to believe that America could be in reality, not just in literary fantasy, a garden in the wilderness. Yet in the antebellum decades, the advent of the railroad threatened America's pastoral self-image. City culture had always stood in opposition to country customs. But the new trains were mobile, and the urban mores they conveyed could invade the middle landscape and disrupt the tranquility of village life. Ironically, the result of these technological and social challenges to the nation's pastoral self-conception was a strengthening of the tradition in modified form. Americans succeeded in weaving reminders of the country into city routines.[16]

The incorporation of various kinds of "cultivated gardens" into cities grew from initiatives by urban elites that met with apparent popular acceptance. Landscaped cemeteries, cottage architecture, and wooded parks all functioned as pastoral enclaves. Whereas Americans before the 1830s buried their dead in plain graves next to churches, the opening of Mount Auburn Cemetery near Boston in 1831 marked the beginning of a "rural" cemetery movement that spread to New York, Baltimore, and elsewhere. Tree-lined lanes, artificial ponds, and artistic tombstones invited peaceful reflection from strolling citizens. Compared to the daily stress of urban life, death no longer seemed fearful but rather tranquil and uplifting. A walk or a drive in a cemetery promised an interlude of spiritual refreshment.[17] In housing design, the soft contours of the "cottage" homes advocated by the New York landscape gardener and architect Andrew Jackson Downing departed from the usual angular style and crowded pattern of urban residences. In theory surrounded by manicured lawns, shrubs, and flowers, Downing's homes were to be "picturesque" aesthetic objects that provided families with relief from the harsh city environment.[18] To gain the full benefit of these innovations required considerable financial means. Proprietors of cemetery plots, for example, often received special privileges for use of the grounds. But all could enjoy the studied beauty of urban parks. Following the creation of municipal parks in Germany and elsewhere in Europe from the 1820s on, New York became the first American city to set aside land in the mid-1850s for a city-owned natural expanse for public recreation. In 1858 and 1859 the design for Central Park was conceived and executed by Calvert Vaux and Frederick Law Olmsted. At a time when Manhattan's buildings still clustered in the southern part of the island, New Yorkers' anxiety about the quality of urban life inspired the preservation of an extensive tract of land dotted with woods, meadows, and a lake that became an invaluable resource for future generations of the city's inhabitants.[19]

American Country Life: October Afternoon (1855), a color lithograph made by Nathaniel Currier, pictured rural society as more genteel and prosperous than it often was. *The Harry T. Peters Collection, Museum of the City of New York.*

The appeal of the pastoral was ultimately so powerful that it colored the way Americans saw both country and city, acting as a subjective force to cast both images in similarly bucolic terms. A comparison of the country and city scenes produced by the New York lithographers Nathaniel Currier (1813–88) and James Ives (1824–95) suggests that many of the prints tended toward a single vision that blended attributes of rural and urban life. On the one hand, Currier and Ives's views of the country contained details in fact characteristic of the city: elegantly dressed men and women, stylish houses, and leisure time for sports. On the other hand, their New York scenes often pictured the city from a safe distance across a river, with the vegetation of the hinterland acting as a foreground frame and the city buildings so small that any disharmonies in their appearance were obscured.[20] Currier and Ives's consciousness of the social distance between country and city inspired their production of these separate series of American scenes. Nonetheless, their ostensibly distinctive subjects converged in an idealized vision that harmonized nature and progress, and tranquility and prosperity, creating a uniquely Victorian pastoralism.

There is so much evidence of a distaste for cities and a mounting attachment to nature among urbanizing Americans that two questions are raised. First, were value systems that focused on the moral worth of nature adequate ethical guides for cities? Second, didn't Americans have anything good to say about cities, opinions that might be seen as a proto-urban point of view? As Americans backed into city life by including often idealized images of the country among their baggage, a twentieth-century observer might wonder if they were disturbed by the apparent ill fit between their ideas and daily routines.

To listen closely to the voices of in-migrants who were confronted with crowds of "confidence men and painted women" or to watch Melville's lawyer try vainly to reach out to Bartleby, it seems that the fundamental problem of antebellum cities was the failure of intimacy and the frightening prospect of anonymity and, in a way, loss of identity. Neither romanticism nor pastoralism confronted this profound urban dilemma directly. Yet these philosophies of nature did allay the isolation of city dwellers in modest though important ways. Romanticism's emphasis on inner renewal through contact with the grandeur of nature, either in actual experience or as rendered in art, may have done little to foster human bonds, but it still helped to show uprooted individuals how to acquire a center of gravity and peacefulness in themselves. Pastoralism did not solve the difficulty of communicating with strangers, but it did provide the conditions in places such as homes or parks for small, selected groups of the city's inhabitants to deepen interpersonal ties. Under the aus-

View of New York from Brooklyn Heights (1849) made New York City aesthetically appealing by framing its crowded buildings with graceful ships and well-dressed, strolling observers. Lithograph by Nathaniel Currier. *The Harry T. Peters Collection, Museum of the City of New York.*

pices of anti-urban perspectives, new methods of creating identity that were appropriate to cities—self-communion, family intimacy, and neighborhood recreations—grew up to replace an older and broader sense of community. These strategies of adjustment were not available equally, however, since it often cost money to surround oneself with tokens of nature. The fact that some people benefited more than others from this urban culture of nature was one of a number of social conditions that tended to divide antebellum cities along class lines.

Beneath this backhanded urbanism was a nascent sense of excitement at the city's opportunities. In some private writings, positive attitudes about urban life began to edge aside small-town values. Thrill at the jostling variety of people and things overcame a preference for harmony, curiosity about the unusual replaced safe attachment to the familiar, and welcome of the crowded intensity of busy schedules prevailed over a taste for quiet days. The diary of George Templeton Strong (1820–75), who was born in New York City and practiced law there, spans 40 years, from his years as a student at Columbia College until his death. The diary reflects his passionate immersion in the city's life. He attended lectures, concerts, and séances; read about crimes, mobs, and scandals; worked on church vestries and private school boards; chased fire trucks to spectacular blazes; and experimented with hashish.[21] Yet the cosmopolitan views that Strong voiced still remained more the exception than the rule among city dwellers, since the village roots and modest incomes of many residents made their indulgence in city pleasures more tentative than his.

Even where self-conscious convictions of the city's worth appeared, thinkers could not seem to overcome either their lingering discomfort with urban life or the absence of established literary forms for its praise in order to express their new views in formal prose. Cornelius Mathews, a New York writer, argued in his capacity as a critic that American authors must portray American themes, including the city. He must have felt the awkwardness of his position when he produced a romance, *Behemoth: A Legend of the Mound-Builders*, in 1839. Mathews's subject was American, the prehistoric Indian peoples of the continent. But his treatment was far from the social realism he advocated in principle.[22] Two other authors who at one time wrote in New York—Edgar Allan Poe and Herman Melville—deliberately opposed romantic and pastoral conventions by highlighting the uncertainties, paradoxes, and even malevolence of nature. Yet neither one could clearly see or articulate an alternative ideology rooted in urban culture. Poe's cynicism about nature's goodness led him instead to Gothic melodramas. Melville wrote parodies of romances and a series of increasingly bitter fables, including "Bartleby," about the moral impossibility of urban society.[23] Their skeptical writings were provocative but failed to become focused examinations of a potential urban point of view.

More generally, a genre of reform fiction appeared, much of it also produced in New York, that graphically portrayed crime, prostitution, and intemperance, only to turn abruptly and condemn this lawless and indulgent behavior. In some ways these moralizing works, such as T. S. Arthur's popular temperance novel *Ten Nights in a Bar-room* (1854), depicted city activities with more liveliness and indeed sensationalism than did the self-conscious critics of ideals based on nature. But the minds of the reformers were as divided as the feelings of Mathews, Poe, and Melville, simply in a different way. Arthur instinctively grasped the temper of the city and yet condemned its vices. The critics of the philosophies of nature inclined toward urban subjects in principle but could not bring them to life in a positive way.[24] In the end all these intimations of an emerging urban perspective represented the attempts of city dwellers to understand their choice of society. That their efforts fell short of an adequate language for appreciation of urban mores reflected their deep-seated, persistent ambivalence.

While city people were struggling for positive self-conceptions, Americans who stayed in the country began to see that they must self-consciously formulate and defend rural ideals in order to protect tradition. In an age of commercial and industrial revolution, cities challenged village life most seriously by their aggressive cultural influence. Railroads in a sense brought entrepreneurship to the country by opening the possibility of urban markets and encouraging the establishment of wage relations between ambitious creditors, either prosperous farmers or local businessmen, and their agricultural laborers or tenants. With an insidiousness that must have been unnerving, the city's threat to the country was not simply material but intellectual and moral, as some local people began to behave according to the customs of the marketplace—"individualism, acquisitiveness, and deep adherence to private property," in the words of the historian Steven Hahn—and against older "habits of mutuality" of a "communal" and "egalitarian" tenor.[25] Whereas neighbors once helped each other in a noncompetitive spirit, the prospect of making money began to make relations in rural economies resemble those of Melville's lawyer and Bartleby.

Anger among yeomen farmers at the violation of traditional mores contributed to the rise of populism—that is, advocacy of political measures to help debtors such as the silver standard and public ownership of railroads, after the Civil War. But farmers did not translate their discontent into a coherent rural ethic during the antebellum period. Without the education, the access to publishers' capital, and the opportunity to do specialized labor of urban intellectuals, spokesmen of country people were slow to make cooperative principles into an ideology of protest. Besides, some aspects of urban culture were attractive to village dwellers, including novels, medical advice literature, and scientific tracts. Farmers' assimilation of selected aspects of city thinking must have deterred the formation of an independent rural point of view. Small-town Americans were torn between reliance on cities and resistance to them. It was their sense of the ambiguities of their dependence that stimulated reflection on the country's unique, and fragile, virtues.[26]

Few antebellum Americans, it seems, were altogether comfortable with the growth of cities, but the longing for individual success was a tempting lure that kept them moving cityward. The cultural strength of romanticism and pastoralism suggests that many coped with new sources of stress by seeking assurance that nature could be incorporated into urban life, so that progress could continue without losing touch with the past. There was a measure of self-deception to this intellectual strategy. But the philosophies of nature were even more problematic because they offered relief unequally. The urban poor had little time or means to enjoy reminders of the country, and rural people knew that neither set of natural images really addressed their social problems. Other ideologies that took shape under the force of advancing capitalism involved similar possibilities and limitations.

Conversations among Strangers: New Views of Gender and Class

Stories of the urban journeys of young men who entered cities in puzzlement and achieved enlightenment were told frequently in antebellum America. In "My Kinsman, Major Molineux" (1832) Nathaniel Hawthorne depicted the confusion of a country boy in an American city on the eve of the Revolution who, after searching vainly for his father's cousin, Major Molineux, witnesses the tar-and-feathering of a prominent Tory, the very kinsman Molineux, it turns out, who his father promised would help the boy to get a start in life.[27] On one level, Hawthorne's tale reaffirmed the common contemporary impression that cities presented problematic appearances that made them closed books, particularly to newcomers. But like Hawthorne's young traveler, those who grew accustomed to city ways could discern patterns of social identity beneath the perplexing mass of unfamiliar faces. The distinctions most easily seen were in the routines of men and women, on the one hand, and in the customs of the middle and working classes, on the other. Economic changes brought on by commercial growth were the most fundamental cause of widening distances between the sexes and classes. But it was culture that interpreted these social developments and imposed prescriptions for behavior that determined the way gender and class differences were finally expressed. Indeed, Americans who voiced their ideas in the intellectual marketplace handled these two problems of social space in strikingly different ways. They embraced the separation of the sexes as an instrument of social preservation yet nearly refused to acknowledge that class differences might exist. A common commitment to egalitarianism shaped these dissimilar responses.

It was hard for town and city dwellers to ignore the fact that men and women increasingly inhabited different workaday worlds and that the consequent differences in their outlooks threatened to block communication and heighten tension between them. Although husbands and wives in the past had performed separate agricultural tasks, both partners still worked at home at a pace determined by human needs and the forces of nature. Now, as growing numbers of men went to businesses and manufactures where insistence on productivity made time the most precious resource, their assimilation in a work culture based on routine, hurry, and output imposed new barriers, emotional and intellectual, between them and women.[28]

Many readers who picked up "Sweethearts and Wives," a story about these changes in families by T. S. Arthur that appeared in *Godey's Lady's Book* in 1841, must have seen the marital troubles of newlyweds Agnes and William Fairfield through a lens of self-recognition. Agnes, who thinks that genteel accomplishments such as piano playing are her principal duty in marriage, fails to understand that she must instruct her servant to provide punctual meals for William, a shopkeeper, to accommodate his business schedule. William's mounting anger at Agnes's thoughtlessness and Agnes's frustrated inability to understand what her husband expects finally explode in a distressing confrontation, followed by a reconciliation where the proper roles of wives and husbands become clear. Just as William must set his mind on business or risk "disorder" and "utter failure, instead of prosperity," Agnes, William concludes, must organize her "department, that I may feel home to be a pleasant place."[29] Men and women are "radically different," he continues: "He is stronger, and his mind is a form receptive of more wisdom; she is weaker, and her mind is a form receptive of more affection."[30] Their spheres should be separate yet must function similarly so that their common prosperity may continue and their mutual understanding be secured. Although William seems to have all the answers, T. S. Arthur does fault him for his failure to talk earlier with Agnes. He should have explained "to her rationally, calmly, and affectionately, her duty."[31] Just so, "Sweethearts and Wives" is most basically about the frightening prospect of alienation of the sexes—a lack of communication—in a capitalist economy where women remained at home.

Distance between private and public life and between women and men was not altogether new in the decades after 1830. In eighteenth-century Virginia, a setting where there had been little commercial development, gentry families became more woman-centered, refined, and private by 1790, according to the historian Rhys Isaac, as they seemed to turn away from a public "world that was now held to be impure and vulgar."[32] This suggests that wives were not simply left behind in the race for success but that they assumed the role of creators of domestic space through a kind of tacit agreement with husbands, as both partners sensed new dangers in a society divided by the political and religious movements of the Revolutionary era. Similarly, in New England around 1800 the work routines of women and men already diverged in a way that T. S. Arthur saw again in 1841. Nancy Cott concludes, after studying women's diaries and ministers' sermons from the period, that an ideology affirming that woman's place was in the family was widely accepted by 1835.[33] These evidences prior to 1830 of what historians have called the "cult of domesticity" help to explain why Agnes never thought to fill her idle time by seeking work outside the home. Not only did women's traditional tasks of providing clothing, food, and child care remain home-centered, but ideas about women's domestic nature were already influential by the time accelerated economic development drew more and more men into business and industry. What happened intellectually after 1830 was that the sense of crisis in gender relations grew more acute and prescriptions for the proper behavior of men and women became more elaborate.

Antebellum Americans looked at men in the marketplace with divided feelings. They respected ambition and welcomed prosperity yet worried deeply that men were morally at risk. While readers could take respectable William Fairfield seriously as a latter-day Benjamin Franklin, another part of their psyches suspected men in business of a "sordid prospensity which is continually driving [Americans] into all kinds of enterprise and money-making speculations," in the words an anonymous writer in the same *Godey's Lady's Book* in 1837.[34] In a culture with strong ties to traditional communities and to religion, a competitive temper that put self before others and an acquisitive hunger for material things above spiritual concerns seemed to portend imminent moral breakdown. When the health reformer Sylvester Graham warned of the growing incidence of "self-pollution," or masturbation, in his *A Lecture to Young Men, on Chastity* in 1834, his audience must have seen autoeroticism as merely one more sign of young men's moral weakness. Indeed, the causes of debilitating lust that Graham identified—rich and excessive food, lack of physical exercise, and feverish mental labor—were precisely the habits that distinguished the early white-collar work force.[35] Like the majority of reformers who addressed the moral dangers of the marketplace, Graham did not advise against the struggle for success but preached that personal advancement should be monitored by strict self-control. Graham advocated a diet of coarse food (including unbolted flour, the predecessor of the Graham cracker), abstinence from stimulants, and regular exercise.[36] In society at large, a variety of agencies appeared to help young men moderate their ambition through voluntary restraint. The most significant of these were temperance societies, lyceums, and lending libraries.[37]

So much public discussion of men's moral vulnerability and such widespread cooperative action to promote self-culture in a way obscures the fact that the fundamental problem, from the perspective of antebellum Americans, was that men in the marketplace were individuals acting alone. Men in established communities pursued their occupations under the watchful eye of male kin and village elders. Now cities offered the freedom to seek great success but also the space to harm the common interest and one's own physical and spiritual health. Anxiety about "self-pollution" epitomized this culture's discomfort with unregulated privacy. The dominant theme of the advice literature intended for young men was the necessity of nurturing inner control.[38] But observers also knew that aspiring men would most likely form at least one social attachment when they married. The idea that women would act as a moral anchor in a rootless society was central to contemporary understanding of both gender relations and social progress.

Among numerous writers, male and female, who voiced the doctrine of women's moral superiority and consequent ethical duties, few were more influential than Sarah Hale (1788–1879). Widowed in her mid-thirties and left to raise five children, Hale was asked to edit the *Ladies' Magazine* in Boston in 1828 on the basis of her reputation as the author of a novel, *Northwood* (1827). In 1837 she moved to Philadelphia to edit *Godey's Lady's Book* for the publisher Louis Godey, a position she retained until 1877. With 150,000 subscribers in 1850, *Godey's* had the largest circulation of any pre–Civil War American magazine.[39]

Hale's success at creating a respected position on domesticity owed much to her perseverance and tact. Without challenging the independence and social dominance of men, Hale consistently found ways to assert that women should freely exercise their influence. In an editorial in 1844, she characteristically flattered men and lobbied for the moral prerogatives of women: "We hope our American ladies will value the high privileges they enjoy as companions and equals of freemen, who, in throwing off the trammels of military power and hereditary rank, have elevated woman, by making the moral influence which she will always wield, the controling power of society and of government."[40] Strictly adhering to the idea that God created the sexes with distinct natures and that each should control a separate social sphere, Hale permitted the woman's role to expand subtly over the years. A mother's task of instructing her children, according to Hale, justified women's work as teachers and as writers of literature for children and of moralistic fiction for adults.[41] On a deeper level, Hale's own influence with the reading public depended less perhaps on her rhetorical skill than on the pressing need of Americans to understand how a society where men and women inhabited dissimilar social and ethical worlds could survive as a community. The "cult of domesticity" turned a problem into an asset. The isolation of the home in a capitalist economy became the guarantee of its moral purity, and women's ignorance of business values became the grounds of their spiritual power.

This vision of the mutual dependence of men and women appeared again and again in periodicals, advice literature, and popular fiction. Domesticity's intellectual force grew not only from its social and ethical message but from its political reassurance that inequalities magnified by economic development might be reconciled with a democratic commitment to egalitarianism. Although Americans expected a free economy to allow diverse abilities to produce different levels of individual achievement, they believed that inequalities imposed by society contradicted democracy's promise. Commercial expansion was worrisome because it seemed to increase involuntary and permanent subordination. Many suspected that wage earners were held to "a monotonous, stupefying round of unthinking toil," as the Unitarian minister William

Ellery Channing said in 1840.[42] Was the domestic confinement of women another inequity of the marketplace?

Catharine Beecher helped to formulate an answer that proved widely acceptable in her *Treatise on Domestic Economy* (1841). In no other country were "democratic institutions" so fully developed, Beecher wrote, because the "interests [of men and women] are regarded as of equal value."[43] "In civil and political affairs, American women take no interest"; but "in matters pertaining to the education of their children, in the selection and support of a clergyman, in all benevolent enterprises, and in all questions relating to morals or manners, they have a superior influence."[44] Beecher borrowed the notion of functional specialization from new methods of industrial production to replace old-fashioned language of hierarchy. The tasks of the sexes should be different in order to make society work efficiently, but men and women were equal nonetheless. It is possible that this neat answer gave Americans confidence in the egalitarian promise of capitalism overall. If domestic and market labor were similarly valued, in other words, perhaps blue- and white-collar work could be respected equally too. In significant ways, however, intellectual strategies for coming to terms with the appearance of distinctive social classes diverged from Americans' treatment of gender.

Whereas mainstream culture transformed the separation of the sexes from a troubling problem into a moral imperative, middle-class ideology confronted new distance between classes by denying the existence of permanent social divisions. Traditional villages had always contained people of diverse ranks. But in antebellum cities expanding middle and working classes increasingly labored in dissimilar settings, wore distinctive clothes, inhabited separate neighborhoods, and, most profoundly, participated in class-based cultures. Once master craftsmen, journeymen, and apprentices worked together in shops adjacent to their common dwelling. As the nineteenth century progressed, blue-collar (though still largely unmechanized) factories were set apart from white-collar offices, and social ties between workers and owners all but disappeared. The capitalist's drive for self-advancement initiated these changes. Yet the social result so seriously violated established values of community harmony and democratic opportunity that commentators defensively declined to acknowledge the possibility of enduring alienation. In the mainstream vision, mobility became the great equalizer in a fluid and hence classless society. "The labor of a single year gives to every laborer, if he choose to save his earnings, a very considerable capital," wrote Nathan Appleton, a textile manufacturer, in a treatise on *Labor* in 1844: "He takes at his pleasure a place in society."[45] Application, prudence, and ambition, all subject to control by the individual will, could defeat outward circumstances that conspired to restrict a man to a specific class.

This social vision did more than rationalize varying degrees of wealth. From an individual perspective, the optimistic picture of upward mobility became the success ethic, centering on the self-made man, and it shaped the way men viewed their work. Ambivalent about personal freedom as men in this generation were, they were also excited by the prospect of unprecedented wealth and virtually canonized the individual as the agent of his own destiny. Ralph Waldo Emerson became a key prophet of self-reliance through the mistaken way his audiences interpreted his ideas. A Unitarian minister who became a heterodox religious thinker, Emerson praised the self as a source of spiritual enlightenment and moral standards in numerous lectures and writings between the 1830s and 1870s. "Every man is a consumer, and ought to be a producer," Emerson told his listeners in Cincinnati in1852, so that the individual "not only pays his debt [to the world] but adds something to the common wealth": "He is by constitution expensive, and needs to be rich."[46] When a reporter for the *Cincinnati Gazette* summarized the lecture, the writer recast Emerson's words: "Man is an expensive animal and ought to be rich."[47] Gone was Emerson's sense of discharging an obligation to the cosmos by adding to a common stock of goods. The journalist's individual was an isolated "animal" who justifiably satisfied his considerable material needs. This clash of understanding between an intellectual and one listener indicates the strength of the wish to believe in the possibility and acceptability of individual success.

The cult of the self-made man also flourished despite its disharmony with social facts. Had aspiring Americans chosen to inquire into the truth behind the myth, they would have discovered at least two contradictions. First, although middle-class Americans praised the independent man as the instrument of progress, success in reality was a family enterprise. By the mid-nineteenth century couples deliberately produced fewer children, educated them better, and assisted them longer in order to help them achieve social status. Becoming middle class, according to Mary Ryan, was "not just a matter of self-creation" but "the culmination of a parental strategy."[48] Damaging as it might have been to a man's self-esteem to admit the importance of family support, Americans would have been at least as unnerved had they fully realized that mothers were not acting as moral breaks on their sons' ambition but coaches in the young men's race for material advancement. Second, although capitalist culture idealized autonomy, the business setting where white-collar workers had to expect to work was increasingly bureaucratic. Men sensed the conflict between their belief in individual enterprise and their actual jobs as white-collar subordinates. Mid-century employees of the federal government, for example, viewed wage labor as an undesirable and temporary expedient.[49] For growing numbers of men, however, working for a boss on a long-term basis was the only way to get ahead, or even to make a living. Daily routines stood in disconcerting conflict with individualistic ideals.

At least as important to social climbing as career advancement was the acquisition of symbols of status. Middle-class culture worked to erase class differences by offering instruction to the reading public on how to present oneself in respectable company. Capitalist society was much concerned with appearances—proper displays of ambition at work, refined manners in leisure, the right furnishings at home. Hardly of superficial importance, these gestures were used by men and women to create social identities for themselves. Customs of consumption worked together with the ethic of self-sufficient production as a route to middle-class status.

Before the nineteenth century Protestantism exhorted men to labor diligently as a way of honoring and improving God's gifts. Early American Protestants frowned on the self-centered acquisition of luxuries, although material advancement did inevitably occur and contributed to the classic dilemma of guilt-ridden prosperity.[50] After 1830 growing quantities of consumer goods seemed by their sheer mass to eclipse old-fashioned religious reservations. Homes in particular became places of comfort and self-expression for the rising middle class. "The bare floors, whitewashed walls, and scant furniture of middle-income eighteenth-century homes," explains the historian Sam Bass Warner, Jr., "gave way to wool carpeting, wallpaper, and all manner of furnishings."[51] Pianos, paintings, draperies, mirrors, ornamental vases, and ornate furniture contributed to the showy opulence of interiors that today are considered characteristically "Victorian." More rooms (and particularly more bedrooms, where each person had his or her own bed), as well as the introduction of conveniences such as running water and toilets, signaled rising standards of physical well-being. In all aspects of organizing a household, the middle class enjoyed unprecedented choice. Because homes and workshops were no longer adjacent, a family of means could select a residential street that reflected its sense of social identity. Popular magazines and manuals of architectural advice offered a wide array of housing fashions. One scholar has called the 1850s a decade of "stylistic anarchy," as home buyers could decide among Grecian, Gothic, Tuscan, or Byzantine houses, or a dwelling with an eclectic combination of historic themes.[52]

Customs of behavior inside middle-class households to an extent matched the demonstrative finery of the material setting. Even though the success ethic envisioned men in public as aggressive yet still rational and self-controlled, the mores of the household permitted both sexes an unrestrained emotionalism in private. A wide range of feelings could be indulged by a social class whose physical needs were adequately met. Perhaps in no aspect of middle-class life was sentiment expressed more freely than in romantic love. As marriage changed during the nineteenth century from a practical arrangement often initiated by parents to an affair of the heart brought about by young people acting alone, expressions of mutual feelings bonded courting couples. Men and women were allowed considerable privacy before marriage to weave their affections into an emotional edifice that became the basis of their lives together. Sometimes, one young woman wrote to her suitor in 1844, "I fancy in my dreams that you are by my side, and your arm around my waist and my hand in yours, and that you again lead me back to our old haunts of love and pleasures but when I awake I find it but a dream and the dear delusion flies from me, and I again sink back upon my bed and bedew the pillow with my tears."[53] Immersion in romantic love in middle-class homes was a kind of subjective luxury made possible by, and indeed displaying, a family's prosperity.[54]

Appealing as this culture of self-gratification was, it was as riddled with ambiguities as the doctrine of individual success. Two of the principal dilemmas involved hidden social restraints and the intimacy of the home and the market. First, although capitalism invited unprecedented self-display through the increasing availability of goods, wealth, and leisure, every step toward the creation of a desired impression also required the suppression of customs now thought to be unacceptable to one's anticipated peers. Middle-class Victorianism offered exciting opportunities for self-expression as a culture deliberately created from things, language, and gestures. Yet it was rooted, too, in yearnings for social acceptance that made a tyrant of neighbors' opinions. The elegance of parlors where families who aspired to gentility entertained acquaintances, for example, directed manners, particularly those of men, into narrow channels of respectability. Some men, according to Stuart Blumin, "either found it more difficult, or found themselves less inclined, to spit on the Brussels carpet than on the sanded floors of earlier middling homes, to drape their legs over the new parlor sofa, or to tell loud stories while their daughters (or their hosts' daughters) were at the piano."[55] Thus behind the new freedom of the middle class were class-defined limits of propriety. Second, the function of the household as an instrument of social climbing cast doubt on the image of the home as a moral refuge. Whereas the middle class embraced the dichotomized view of gender roles preached by the cult of domesticity, the consumerism so crucial to establishing a family's social position—the acquisition of the proper furnishing, fashions, and manners—was hard to reconcile with an otherworldly view of women.

A twentieth-century observer might wonder why people would entangle themselves in so many intellectual and ethical contradictions. One answer is that the ideology of early capitalism was preeminently a culture of apology, an intellectual system that allowed Americans to strive for economic advancement by explaining away their actions' undesired consequences. On the whole, they convinced themselves that they could live in cities without giving up nature, engage in enterprise without sacrificing morals, and achieve social mobility without undermining equality. In the specific case of middle-class formation, ambitious people embraced real prospects for independence, material acquisition, social self-creation, and membership in a new kind of community defined by class, and yet they chose to ignore the equally real constraints exerted by market forces and peer pressures. Although the manipulation of ideas needed to secure reassurance sometimes seems cavalier, mainstream capitalist attitudes were shaped at least as much by self-doubt as by self-confidence, as writers and audiences reviewed again and again, in an effort to build conviction, how their conflicting aspirations might be reconciled.

Here, it would seem, were unsettled conditions that might nourish dissent. To what extent did the ideologies of competing classes or the critiques of thoughtful individuals expose the tensions in middle-class thinking?

Not all who aspired to middle-class status achieved the prosperity they sought. But whether a working class with distinctive views emerged during the antebellum period is much less certain. Perhaps it is most accurate to say that many urban manual laborers were aware of their social distance from men in nonmanual occupations but that they had yet to develop a coherent, critical social ideology of their own. In religion, some working people registered their dissent by their skeptical rationalism. In politics, workingmen's parties gave an egalitarian emphasis to their democratic republicanism. Such evidence of a sense of class identity was not insignificant. Yet middle-class social arrangements were seductive, and workers quarreled less with opportunities for private ownership, consumption, and leisure than with the more abstract religious and political aspects of Victorian culture. Working-class families modeled their households after middle-class patterns to the extent that they were financially able. They tried to keep wives and children out of the labor force and to make their homes centers for the acquisition of consumer goods. Thus a comparison of the household furnishings of people of different ranks reveals a considerable range in buying power rather than dissimilar ideas about interior space. According to the items listed in one will registered in Philadelphia in 1861, a manufacturer of paper boxes, a man of modest means though still middle class, decorated his parlor sumptuously and his other rooms sparely. His attention to the impression he made on company reflected his social ambition. Further down the social scale, other Philadelphia probate records of the same year indicate that even poor artisans made some attempt at comfort and aesthetic display, because virtually all household inventories included carpeting and pictures.[56] Consumerism, as a matter of material and social aspiration, acted as a leveling force in a context of growing differences in the work routines of white-collar and blue-collar labor. Working people felt alienated, at least at times, by the snobbery of superiors who "despise that portion of their neighbors who obtain an honest livelihood in mechanical employments," in the words of the Philadelphia *Mechanic's Free Press*.[57] Nonetheless, the material rewards of capitalism were a persuasive lure that seemed to deter the formation of alternative working-class values.

Much the same relationship of semi-autonomy of capitalist culture characterized the ties of the traditional gentry to the rising middle class. Established merchants and professionals in the North and planters in the South may best be seen as regional elites rather than as a single class. Still, all who possessed wealth could take a critical view of the race for success, and the offspring of monied families produced some harsh social assessments. In the case of George Fitzhugh, the ne'er-do-well descendent of Virginia slaveholders, a sense of his own superiority became alienation from what he depicted as money-hungry northern society, a world of *Cannibals All!*, in his arresting title of 1857, a culture stripped of human bonds by the forces of greed and exploitation.[58] More generally, southern gentry built up a countervailing image of themselves as aristocratic "Cavaliers." In their mind's eye, theirs was a culture of honor, feeling, and manners.[59]

As traditional elites regrouped in the face of advancing capitalism around ideologies of reaction, however, their relation to the marketplace was ambiguous. Influential studies of slaveholders in the past several decades indicate that they were eager for profits and upward mobility, even if they were equally fearful of the possible upheaval in race relations that might follow commercial expansion. Fathers exhorted sons to work hard and prosper. More generally, southern politicians pictured the South as a white democracy because all of the "ruling race" could rise socially through the purchase of slaves.[60] In addition, slaveholders resembled free-market capitalists in their doubts as well as their ambitions. Fitzhugh's denunciation of the social consequences of profit-seeking echoed northerners' self-criticism. In *Uncle Tom's Cabin* (1852) Harriet Beecher Stowe, born in Connecticut, crystalized free society's anxiety about its capacity to produce greed and brutality when she made her depraved slaveholder, Simon Legree, a native of New England.[61] Thus southern gentry constructed a social critique based on aristocratic traditionalism and on an underlying fabric of acquisitiveness and uncertainty that strongly resembled the outlook of the northern middle class. This is not to say that southern exposés of free-labor capitalism were insincere or invalid; it does imply that the articulation of a coherent elite ideology was compromised by the nearly universal attraction of commerce.

In the North, social conditions fostered by market production encouraged some individuals to take on a new kind of dissenting social role, that of a reformer. Occupational upheaval, geographic mobility, and increasing education affected people drawn from all social classes to produce, at times, an explosive mix of discontent and freedom. Because religion remained a powerful force, social disaffection and Christian ideals blended together, too, to impel reform. The result of was a series of sharp critiques of the marketplace. The communal property of early Mormonism, the premillennialism of Millerism, and the unconventional social arrangements of communitarianism all worked not only as expressions of religious commitments but as indictments of capitalist culture. Two examples connected with the transcendentalist movement illustrate the way opportunity, frustration, and idealism combined to launch radical reform.

Fruitlands, a community in Harvard, Massachusetts, established in 1843 by Bronson Alcott (1799–1888), revealed the tendency of early capitalism both to inspire and limit reform activism. Like most communal experiments, Fruitlands attracted people in transition. Among the men who came to Fruitlands in search of spiritual peace were the former editor of a commercial magazine, a clerk in a countinghouse, and the owner of a bakery. Bronson Alcott himself had been disheartened by hostile public opinion that met his attempt to liberate children's capacity for spiritual growth at his experimental school in Boston in the 1830s. All of these reformers quarreled with the constraints of capitalist routines and middle-class morals. Fruitlands expressed this discontent by seeking to exorcise market activity altogether. With monastic rigor, community members drastically restricted their diet to fruit, vegetables, bread, and water, not only to purify their bodies but to free themselves from the necessities of labor and commerce. Here were ordinary Americans' suspicions of ambition, competition, and self-indulgence magnified to the point that economic activity was as much as possible denied.

The uncompromising temper of Fruitlands' critique of the market coexisted uneasily, however, with the reformers' thorough involvement in capitalist culture. It was their optimistic sense of opportunity, a feeling nourished by capitalism's movement of people and goods, that led them to quit constraining occupations and to travel from as far away as England to get a fresh start at Fruitlands. When the community disbanded after only nine months, the members' restlessness was again responsible for pushing the individuals apart. Fruitlands was typical of antebellum communities in the sense that it depended, in its inception and demise, on the unsettlement of the marketplace. Its transience did not make the theory of economic minimalism published by the participants in reform periodicals less valuable as social criticism but simply less credible as a social alternative. Whether readers agreed or, more likely, disagreed with Fruitlands' advocacy of abstinence as a solution to the spiritual bondage of exchange, capitalism had in effect invited comment on itself that pushed the reading public to reflect on commonplace economic decisions.[62]

Margaret Fuller (1810–50) similarly criticized social conventions and stood in an equally ambiguous relation to contemporary society. Fuller wrote the most fully developed argument for the freedom of women to appear during the antebellum period, *Woman in the Nineteenth Century* (1845). The document grew out of her impatience with the limitations of woman's sphere. "What Woman needs is not as a woman to act or rule," she wrote in her polemic, "but as a nature to grow, as an intellect to discern, as a soul to live freely and unimpeded, to unfold such powers as were given to her when we left our common ¹ ome."[63] Much as she chafed at her society's meager expectations for women, however, Fuller's writing depended on her prerogatives as a woman for leisure and reflection, the rewards, at least for unmarried women such as herself, of the cult of domesticity. The well-educated daughter of a lawyer from Cambridge, Massachusetts, Fuller taught school periodically to make a living after her father's death in 1835 and thus understood both market pressures and the vocational disabilities of women who needed to work. Even so, many of her days in the late 1830s and 1840s were spent studying, writing, and conversing with members of Emerson's circle. Her creativity was nourished by freedom from a consuming career. Fuller moved toward social criticism because the situation of women in the antebellum market culture blended liberties with restrictions. It was not an accident of social development that Fuller (and other women) asked radical questions about gender roles. Rather, the exclusion of literate, middle-class women from the consuming busyness of profit-seeking almost guaranteed that some would wonder about the justice of the status quo.

The dissenting voices of social classes and of individuals on the margins of mainstream culture indicate that antebellum capitalism gave rise to a brisk commerce in ideas as well as in things. In the end, however, consumers of values demonstrated preferences for some intellectual products over others. The vision most commonly approved was that of a society delicately poised between the consoling stability of gender divisions and the healing fluidity of upward mobility. This image not only rationalized social changes that were beyond any individual's control but actively shaped development as well. With unprecedented deliberation, a middle class created itself in the likeness of appearances and manners popularized by print culture. At the same time that diverse aspects of market culture gained coherence as ideology, however, new tensions appeared in the process of thinking itself.

Commercial Growth and the Fragmentation of Knowledge

It was a commonplace of antebellum thought that the head and the heart offered different ways of comprehending experience—through reason, on the one hand, and through intuition or imagination, on the other. In a review of Nathaniel Hawthorne's stories in 1850, Herman Melville proceeded from the characteristic assumption that a choice would be made between the faculties. It is "not the brain that can test such a man" as Hawthorne, Melville wrote, "it is only the heart."[64] Later in the essay Melville returned to the relationship between thought and sensibility. Hawthorne's greatness was his ability to combine "the largest brain with the largest heart."[65] Melville implied that such accord between the modes of consciousness was rarely found.

Americans of earlier periods assumed that human beings possessed potentially conflicting means of cognition. But by the antebellum decades there was a heightened sense of strain among ways of perceiving the world. During the early nineteenth century "real intellectual community collapsed," in the words of the historian Daniel Calhoun, and left two divergent modes of thought: the analytic, with an authority based on inner logic, and the personal, made compelling by the immediacy of individual experience.[66] Here once again was the problem of head and heart, no longer understood in Melville's sense as a conflict of unchanging human nature but as a cultural dilemma of a specific period in time. There is more than one way to state the antinomy between rational and emotional experience and more than one historical cause. This discussion focuses on the disjunction between practical reasoning, a process increasingly concerned with numbers, and imagination, a kind of creativity mainly involving words. The flourishing of these mental tools as separate modes of intelligence had roots in market growth during the antebellum decades.

There was significant continuity throughout the early nineteenth century in the assumptions about how people thought. The Scottish common sense philosophy, dominant among the educated public, asserted that the innate ideas of common sense supplemented knowledge acquired through the senses and revelation (the Bible) to allow inductive reasoning and, in the long run, progressive understanding of truth.[67] In practice, however, there were crucial shifts in the ways Americans used their minds that remained unregistered by formal epistomology. One key development was the change in focus of analytical reasoning from abstract speculation to practical problem-solving. As early as the mid-eighteenth century Benjamin Franklin memorably applied his down-to-earth inventiveness to such useful projects as the discovery of electricity and the design of bifocals. But logic used in scientific and mechanical projects was still subordinate in Franklin's time to theological reasoning, whether on the modest scale of sermons or in ambitious expositions such as Jonathan Edwards's *A Treatise concerning Religious Affections* (1746).[68] The balance began to tip the other way before the century's end. "After 1760," the religious historian Sydney Ahlstrom has concluded, "Americans were increasingly preoccupied by issues of government, law, trade, war, and nation-building—not theology."[69] The writings of the "New Divinity" ministers who followed Edwards in New England should probably be judged "intricate theological reasonings" rather than "a lifeless system of apologetics."[70] Even so, the real question was whether Americans had patience for religious speculation at all. The theological minimalism of the Second Great Awakening in the nineteenth century did not reverse this trend, and rational thinking became more closely identified with the solution of practical tasks.

Some of the impetus for the new direction in reasoning came from economic growth. Expanding opportunities encouraged innovations in technology and precision in the production and distribution of goods. From the 1820s on, mathematics played an increasing role in the education of boys, not only to train them to handle the calculations required of entrepreneurs but as an exercise in inductive reasoning, a mental tool valued as a means of getting ahead. Democratic ideals also inspired the push toward numeracy, as common schools worked to train rational citizens capable of sustaining their freedom.[71] Educators did not expect their pupils to produce reasonable treatises on political theory characteristic of the Enlightenment any more than they were interested in abstract theological speculations. Instead, the rise of numerical thinking was part of Americans' growing inclination to focus on social details without reference to theoretical questions, but with an eye to manipulating circumstances in a purposeful way.

Even reformers, more concerned than most people with moral issues, turned increasingly to statistics and pragmatic arguments to achieve their ends. In *The Cotton Kingdom* (1861) Frederick Law Olmsted used observation, numerical data, and induction to attack the institution of slavery. Based on his personal impressions of slave society gathered during two trips to the South between 1852 and 1854, Olmsted's document augumented its authority by the inclusion of statistics gathered from government, private agencies, and the press. Olmsted sincerely believed that slavery was immoral, but the thrust of his argument was that slave labor was less profitable than free labor. Slavery's violation of ethics had been an absolute question, impossible to compromise, for Olmsted's predecessor in the antislavery movement, William Lloyd Garrison. Olmsted, in a more utilitarian frame of mind, quarreled with slavery's measurable consequences—its inability to provide materially for its workers and socially for their owners, whose meager public culture betrayed, in Olmsted's view, the bestiality of the underlying system.[72] Here was antislavery adapted for a people attuned to firsthand observation and statistical proof, to analytical thinking that engaged the facts of the visible world.

Rising public interest in science reflected the same assumption that logic was a tool for gaining mastery of observable phenomena. Although most antebellum colleges were "rural and isolated," in the words of the historian of science Robert Bruce, they "strove valiantly to give science its due."[73] Pre-nineteenth-century teaching of "natural philosophy" and "natural history" became more specialized with course offerings in such fields as botany, chemistry, and mineralogy. Nearly half of a typical college faculty in 1850 taught mathematics or science. Only one in a hundred young men went to college during this period, but the wider public had access to technical information as well. Scientific lectures were popular, and mechanics' institutes in major cities sponsored annual exhibitions of inventions. The most grandiose showing was housed in the New York Crystal Palace in 1853, "a perfect fairy palace," in Mark Twain's words, filled with measuring equipment, dental tools, daguerreotypes, and much more.[74]

Certainly science may be valued as a source of abstract principles about the natural world as well as a guide to those laws' applications. In antebellum America, however, both intellectual and social pressures deterred the development of theory. Scottish common sense philosophy endorsed epistemological realism, the idea that sensory images were a true report of external objects, and this faith in people's ability to engage nature predisposed intellectuals to empiricism. Francis Bowen, the Alford Professor of Philosophy at Harvard from 1853 to 1889, revealed the anti-theoretical cast of mind nurtured by common sense premises when he rejected Charles Darwin's theory of natural selection, published in *The Origin of Species* in 1859, on the grounds that it strayed too much from observable facts. Bowen's dilemma, as explained by Bruce Kuklick, was that in order to accept Darwin "one had to admit [that] the workings of the natural processes in the past [went] far beyond the historical records, and one had also to allow that these same workings, at some time in the past, produced a world very different from that which we presently know, but which changed into this one."[75] This mental leap was too much for Bowen, whose test of principle was conformity to "everyday experience."[76]

Public preference for useful knowledge over pure science reinforced the suspicion of abstract thinking that grew from common sense ideas. After the Smithsonian Institution was chartered by Congress in 1846, its first director, Joseph Henry from Princeton, was determined that the organization should increase knowledge through primary research rather than simply diffuse information. He aided innovative work by sponsoring lectures and publications on advances in theory. But he knew that the Smithsonian was a public institution under Congressional control and, as he wrote privately in 1847, "in a country like ours . . . practical science must have a share."[77] Henry compromised by focusing on programs that both expanded scientific understanding and aided society, such as investigations in meteorology that assisted farming and maritime trade.

Overall, antebellum Americans expected reason to focus on society and nature in order to comprehend, with mathematical precision, how and why things worked. Their drive to grasp the principles of activity was closely related to their desire to make things work for them in turn. Profit-seeking was not the sole motive for wishing to manipulate objective relations, but capitalism did encourage an aggressive, optimistic faith in improvement if appropriate techniques were devised. Strangely, however, along with this search for regularity, certainty, and control, Americans exhibited equally strong passions for imagination, sentiment, and ornate verbal expression. Their taste was rooted in the social changes induced by capitalism as well.

Among many ways to document this flowering of imagination, perhaps the most dramatic is to trace Americans' changing literary tastes. In 1830 the Bible was still the centerpiece of family libraries and, particularly in rural areas, often the only book owned. Fiction by authors such as Sir Walter Scott and James Fenimore Cooper was widely read in the 1820s as well, but without the consuming hunger that led readers to wait eagerly for new stories in the decades that followed. By the 1850s new records in publishing history seemed to be broken repeatedly by the next best-seller. Susan Warner's *The Wide, Wide World* (1850) went through 14 editions by 1852, Maria Cummins's *The Lamplighter* (1854) sold 40,000 copies in eight weeks, and Harriet Beecher Stowe's *Uncle Tom's Cabin* (1852) reached sales of 100,000 in just five months.[78] From the point of view of readers, acquiring best-selling fiction was both a market and an intellectual event. As publishers well knew, part of the excitement of buying popular novels was the thrill of owning commodities made precious by critics' and neighbors' comments, a feeling relatively detached from the actual content of books. But it is equally important to interpret the stunning rise in sales of fiction as an index of Americans' desire to indulge in fantasy on a regular basis.

Although popular novels remained fairly close to the possibilities of everyday life, their deliberate sentimentality and florid language drew readers into self-contained and intense imaginative worlds. Much of the emotion elicited by

Uncle Tom's Cabin came from Stowe's decision to show that slavery was an integral and troubling part of American households, represented in the novel primarily by the Shelbys' home in Kentucky and the St. Clares' in New Orleans. Couched in terms of ordinary domesticity as the story was, however, it probed its readers' deepest feelings. Stowe was unashamed of sentimentalism, and she devoted five chapters, for example, to the death of Evangeline St. Clare (Little Eva), almost literally Tom's guardian angel.[79] Beyond her choice of an affecting plot, Stowe's dense language worked to heighten her readers' involvement:

> Uncle Tom was a sort of patriarch in religious matters, in the neighborhood. Having, naturally, an organization in which the *morale* was strongly predominant, together with a greater breadth and cultivation of mind than obtained among his companions, he was looked up to with great respect, as a sort of minister among them; and the simple, hearty, sincere style of his exhortations might have edified even better educated persons. But it was in prayer that he especially excelled. Nothing could exceed the touching simplicity, the child-like earnestness, of his prayer, enriched with the language of Scripture, which seemed so entirely to have wrought itself into his being, as to have become a part of himself, and to drop from his lips unconsciously; in the language of a pious old negro, he "prayed right up."[80]

Stowe's almost merciless piling of terms upon terms and thoughts upon thoughts in sinuous sentences discouraged readers from approaching her book critically and instead invited them to become lost in its streams of visible and subjective action. As nineteenth-century technology moved toward increased "precision," Daniel Calhoun has written, language became more "copious."[81] Americans expected analytic thinking to streamline functioning by identifying basic principles. In contrast, they wanted words to fuse disparate thoughts into an autonomous, imaginative world.

Antebellum Americans were not content to enjoy imagination simply as consumers of culture but insisted on becoming producers of texts as well. There were strong and widespread impulses toward self-expression and communication, as if storytelling held an irresistible fascination. Nathaniel Hawthorne, whose works sold modestly in comparison with the era's bestsellers, complained of the "d—d mob of scribbling women" who poured out poetry and fiction.[82] In his jealousy and frustration, Hawthorne probably overstated the proportion of women among aspiring authors. But he was right that there were enough literary hopefuls to form a "mob." One commentator writing in the *American Monthly Magazine* in 1831 agreed: "Ours is especially the golden age of Fiction, and the glancing and Protean shapes in which it appears, baffle all powers of classification."[83] At least as important, the desire to construct narratives was expressed in less formal ways than the crafting of publishable works. People wrote letters with a passion that revealed deeper motives than merely transmitting information. When couples exchanged hundreds of letters during courtship or when friends corresponded faithfully for decades, it seems clear that the writers took pleasure in framing their experience in language and, in effect, making their thoughts into objects that invited appreciation. Their determination to turn their lives into stories was as strong as their desire to consume fiction to enrich their experience.[84]

While it is easy to see why practical reason advanced with capitalist development, it may seem difficult to fit this enthusiasm for imagining into the same social landscape. Scholars are well aware, however, that in Western culture as a whole, the rise of modern society was accompanied by romanticism, a movement preoccupied not only with wild nature but with the rich possibilities within individuals for the development of the self, feeling, and creativity.[85] Three reasons may be suggested for the intense manifestation of the romantic mood in America after 1830. First, in a setting where traditional communities were disrupted by geographic mobility, social climbing, and class formation, individuals gained the responsibility and the freedom to shape their own identities. The ongoing exchange of creative visions, either privately in correspondence or through the literary marketplace, was one way of defining and repeatedly redefining who one was. Elaborate prose, effusive sentiments, and steady immersion in the products of imagination helped to give authority to inner lives no longer shared with one's neighbors and hence not validated by consensus. Second, as public life became more impersonal and as the urban landscape, subject to utilitarian demands, grew less nuanced, Americans looked for compensatory inner spaces and leisure times to enjoy the luxuries of deep feelings and integrated thoughts. In a distinctively modern frame of mind, people in these decades were able to compartmentalize separate kinds of experience. They accepted the rigors of logic as necessary for work yet welcomed the pleasures of fancy in leisure. Third, the cultivation of imagination complemented some aspects of middle-class social life as well as corrected others. There was a similarity between the demonstrative way middle-class Americans adorned their homes and persons and the ornate texture of literary culture. Outward and inward worlds were not simple opposites. Imaginative pursuits were supported by sufficient wealth to enable consumption and leisure. This prosperity was acquired by the hardheaded application of logic to market interests.

No matter how practical reason and imagination were woven together, it is puzzling that the divergence of these modes of thinking did not destabilize capitalist culture in dramatic ways. How could aggressive problem-solving and the enthusiastic pursuit of fantasy—or, indeed, both inclinations together—be part of a Victorian world that at other times seemed committed to systematic organization and gradual development? Part of the answer is that antebellum Americans, like practiced bureaucrats, carefully distinguished the functions of analysis and fancy. Men should think, and women should feel. Work should be rational, and leisure should be emotionally regenerating. Although these prescriptive boundaries were no doubt violated in real life, the existence of guidelines must still have reassured Americans that there was a rationale for the way they used their intelligence. Logic and fantasy were accommodated by Victorianism, too, because of the specialized manner in which this generation used each of these mental processes. If reason was directed at questions of political theory, it might be a tool of revolution. If imagination conceived social utopias, it might be a source of discontent and radical activism. But social thinking after 1830 tended increasingly away from a dangerously theoretical and visionary cast of mind. The passions for mechanical progress and literary entertainment that peaked in the 1850s, typified by technological exhibitions and record-breaking best-sellers, were consistent with the development of a free market that actually needed practical innovations and temporary release from social pressures. However disruptive it was for individuals and for society to swing between dissimilar kinds of mental experience, the kinds of analytic and synthetic thought used in this society supported the social status quo.

The rise of separate voices of reason and imagination was one expression of capitalism's tendency to stir multiple points of view. At its core, capitalist culture consisted of a compelling set of explanations and prescriptions that helped to determine the thinking of an emerging middle class. On the margins of society, however, many other voices—including country people, workers, gentry, and reformers—began to register their dissent. The exchange of unprecedented quantities of words, either to rationalize or criticize social changes, makes it easy to lose sight of the root cause of so much innovation, the desire to prosper in a free-market economy. Just as the majority of Americans wanted to be Christians and democrats, so they wanted to acquire property in a setting based on trade in commodities. When intellectuals set out to create a national literature and arts, their success depended on this popular culture.

four

American Renaissance

When Henry James, living in London, published his critical study of Nathaniel Hawthorne in 1879, he articulated assumptions about the relationship of intellectuals to American society that have continued to guide, and sometimes misguide, scholarly thinking on the social conditions of creativity in the antebellum decades. Hawthorne's history, James wrote, contained "a valuable moral":

> This moral is that the flower of art blooms only where the soil is deep, that it takes a great deal of history to produce a little literature, that it needs a complex social machinery to set a writer in motion. American civilization has hitherto had other things to do than to produce flowers, and before giving birth to writers it has wisely occupied itself with providing something for them to write about. Three or four beautiful talents of trans-Atlantic growth are the sum of what the world usually recognises, and in this modest nosegay the genius of Hawthorne is admitted to have the rarest and sweetest fragrance.[1]

James was shrewd to see that artistic excellence depended on a rich popular culture, itself a product, in his mind, of a people's accumulated historical experience. The truth of his accompanying premises—that America's resources for artistry were still limited and, implicitly, that the few creative individuals were isolated in a materialistic and pragmatic population—have been much debated among historians and critics of literature and the arts.[2] On the whole, however, James painted the situation of thinkers between 1830 and 1860 in excessively dreary terms. The aspirations and tensions of Christianity, democracy, and capitalism profoundly stimulated the national intelligence and underwrote a widespread, self-conscious determination to fashion a native culture. Rather than struggle in solitude, writers, painters, philosophers, and scientists formed communities among themselves and established audiences for their work. Justly called the American Renaissance, the years before the Civil War were a time of extraordinary flourishing of intellectual expression.

This chapter looks at culture and intellectuals from a different perspective from that used earlier in the book. In the discussions on religion, politics, and society the term "culture" connoted the ideas that constituted the worldview of antebellum Americans. Culture was the frame of reference through which people interpreted events and tried to control future developments. Here "culture" refers more specifically to the deliberately crafted products of intelligence, objects commonly associated with "cultivation."

A similar adjustment in viewpoint will help to highlight the changing social role of intellectuals. Articulate individuals have been cited time and again in this study for their contributions to national debate on numerous issues. They commonly spoke as ministers, politicians, reformers, or other kinds of community leaders. Now for the first time in American history, however, some intellectuals created an identity for themselves as a distinct social type without relations or responsibilities to the public except through their works. To explore the change this chapter shifts attention from what intellectuals said to the social settings they created to facilitate their thinking. The analysis centers on artistic communities and their audiences, linked by the marketplace, an approach that in itself registers the degree to which thinking was no longer carried on as part of traditional, more personalized leadership. Part of the creative power of the American Renaissance came precisely from the self-awareness and pride of intellectuals.

Even so, the impressive achievement of this intellectual movement grew most fundamentally from the connection between the two kinds of culture—culture as ideology and culture as artistry—just as Henry James saw. Intellectuals set themselves in a delicate relationship to popular culture: they sought sufficient distance to ensure creativity but were determined to engage American materials as well. This dual purpose helps to explain why the American Renaissance was concurrent with dramatic religious, political, and cultural transformation. Antebellum artistry gained vitality from the dynamic debates that led to the formation of new centers of cultural stability. The gradual definition of mainstream religion, the entrenchment of political partisanship, and creation of middle-class ideology in the end closed off discussion of some issues. But the process of seeking resolution was invigorating to all levels of intellectual life, and the firmer institutional and ideological foundations that emerged gave thinkers support and confidence conducive to experimentation. The dissenting works of intellectuals who belonged to ethnic and racial minorities—the subject of the next chapter—flourished, too, because of conditions hospitable to cultural production. The central story told in this chapter is of the creation of an artistic mainstream through the deliberate establishment of purposes, social arrangements, and genres that together made thinking possible by grounding it securely in society. Literature was the premier achievement of the American Renaissance, but people involved in the fine arts and in science formed organizations and established styles in much the same way as did imaginative writers.

Making a Native Culture

Periodicals and orations after 1830 were filled with declarations of intentions to create a national literature and distinctly American arts. In the years following the Revolution a few writers and artists achieved significant technical excellence and international recognition, including Washington Irving, James Fenimore Cooper, and the painter Washington Allston. But persuasive factors worked against development of the country's creative potential during the early decades of the century: suspicion of luxury as a corrupter of morals fostered by republican ideology, inattention to deep feelings owing to the influence of Enlightenment rationalism, imitation of British models growing from a provincial nation's desire for artistic acceptance, poorly capitalized literary markets, and small audiences for ideas that departed from familiar religious and political themes. After 1830 Americans moved toward the kind of independence and security that Henry James thought essential for intellectual experimentation. Lively commerce in texts and artifacts as well as widening access to education were preconditions for a flourishing culture. Perhaps more important, however, were the intellectual self-assurance and adventurousness that grew with the nation's deepening sense of identity. These attitudes informed the ambitious plans for an American culture repeatedly presented to the public.[3]

Assessments of the state of the national literature typically combined grandiose expectations with gloomy judgments of current deficiency. In the fourth edition of his popular anthology, *The Prose Writers of America* (1854), Rufus Wilmot Griswold, the ubiquitous literary promoter, wrote that the arts were essential to "a people's glory and happiness." With more leisure, better transportation, active publishers, and widespread interest in self-improvement, "we cannot doubt that the Progress of Civilization in the coming age will be rapid and universal."[4] Americans must seize the opportunity, Griswold implied, since until now they had been slaves to English tastes: "We have no confidence in ourselves, . . . [and] instead of giving a free voice to the spirit within us, we have endeavored to write after some foreign model."[5]

Nearly every commentator concurred with Griswold's assumption that artistic success was connected with sturdy national character. When the *Democratic Review* issued its first number in 1837, the editor simply reversed Griswold's premise (that great literature must draw on native virtues) by asserting that art should protect national values. "Our mind is enslaved to the past and present literature of England," a dangerous situation in his view, since the "high and holy DEMOCRATIC PRINCIPLE" is "darkened and confused by the arts of wily error." To protect the republic, "the vital principle of an American national literature must be democracy," and the *Democratic Review* vowed to lead the way in its advocacy.[6] Thus in arguments for the promotion of native culture, the dual goals of creative excellence and national prosperity stood side by side.

These were not simply abstract principles, because publicists knew that the appeal to patriotism implicit in this logic was one device to help sell the products of American intelligence. The high-sounding ideals of the campaign for native expression may have been voiced sincerely by literary promoters, but these were also practical men who knew that to flourish in a democracy the arts must also pay. Interrelated arguments for a copyright law and for the establishment of literature as a profession backed up the exalted rhetoric about art and national character. Because there was no international copyright in effect until 1892, antebellum writers not only lacked artistic protection for their work and assured financial rewards from its sale but were forced to compete with pirated (and immensely popular) editions of fiction by such European authors as Charles Dickens. In one of numerous appeals aimed at Congress, Edgar Allan Poe reasoned that without copyright protection for aspiring writers, only "gentlemen of elegant leisure" could afford to pursue literary careers. "Obstinately conservative" and enamored of "British models," this privileged class, Poe concluded, would spread "monarchial or aristocratic" values "fatal to democracy."[7]

Advocacy of copyright protection was commonly linked with what the *American Monthly Magazine* called, as the title of an article in 1829, "The Profession of Authorship." Although the essay's anonymous author worried that the prospect of money-making in literature might encourage "a mercenary view" and "deaden the inspiration of feeling," he felt even more strongly that establishing writing on a paying basis was the only way to "bring [our literature] to maturity."[8] Overall, literary partisans were more successful at encouraging financial rewards for creative efforts than in their fight for copyright laws. Book royalties and payment for magazine contributions were rare in 1830, but in later decades publishers began to compensate writers sufficiently to make professionalism possible. Few were paid as handsomely as Henry Wadsworth Longfellow, who once received $3,000 for a single poem.[9] Still, the rewards were respectable enough to allow capable men and women to take literature seriously as a life's work.

Painting, sculpture, and architecture were often mentioned along with literature by advocates of American culture. The case made for their encouragement paralleled the justifications offered for the development of native writing. Obstacles to the establishment of the arts were substantial: general unfamiliarity with art objects because virtually all collections were in Europe, the small number of patrons who could afford expensive pieces, Protestant suspicion of potentially idolatrous images, and, once again, republican anxiety about luxury. Yet despite difficulties, the argument was successfully made that the health of the fine arts would speak well of the nation's freedom and, conversely, that a democratic culture was the best safeguard of political liberty. In the early republic, the historian Neil Harris has written, promotion of the arts was "not argumentative but stylistic," as the introduction of the pure lines of neoclassicism in practical projects disarmed critics.[10] Just as discussion of the uses of literary culture intensified after 1830, however, so did debate on the arts, until, in Harris's words, "a swollen mass of intellectual and emotional justifications was allowed to balloon up unrestrained, as every American artist became a fighter in the war for patriotism, prosperity and religion."[11] The rise of American art involved this irony: as the public came to value the fine arts and the need to justify the arts in reality declined, the rhetoric of culture's defenders became more extravagant.[12] In fact, feverish discourse on the arts' social uses may at some point have begun to smother creativity rather than encourage it. The danger of intense popular involvement in the nurture of the arts was a situation of which contemporaries were aware.

In contrast to the prevailing organicism of theories of artistic development, some observers sensed that inspiration did not spring spontaneously from the people but that the options open to writers and artists were influenced, if not controlled, by market demand. Perhaps in the best of all possible worlds a virtuous people would support a wide range of artistic experiments. In antebellum America, however, aspiring professionals found that the need to court popularity, expressed in dollars, might restrain artistic freedom. Alongside the smooth rhetoric about culture as the flower of national character, the problem of how intellectuals should relate to audiences was hotly debated in the popular press.

As early as 1829 an anonymous magazine commentator on the state of the "National Literature" argued that questions about the American character should be distinct from the issue of native letters because "national literature is the embodied fancy and reason of a chosen few raised by nature, or elevated by their own strenuous exertions above the vulgar level."[13] The writer hoped to encourage the production of literary "treasures" rather than works that were "limited, local, transient." He advised authors to disdain "popular favor" in order to pursue "that unappeasable longing after something higher and better than this world affords."[14] In the view of this critic, acquiescence to market pressures was deadly to literary excellence.

Edgar Allan Poe took the opposite side in 1842. In a review of Nathaniel Hawthorne's *Twice-Told Tales*, Poe registered his awareness of the distance between serious writers and popular readers when he said that Hawthorne's reputation was so far confined to "literary society." Still, he criticized Hawthorne for his failure to win wide readership and affirmed his faith that it was the "popular mind which most keenly feels the original." Poe advised Hawthorne that the best way to realize his artistic potential was to leave his transcendentalist friends and speak directly to the people: "Let him mend his pen, get a bottle of visible ink, come out from the Old Manse, cut Mr. Alcott, hang (if possible) the editor of 'The Dial,' and throw out of the window to the pigs all his odd numbers of 'The North American Review.'"[15] Perhaps mass tastes would curtail Hawthorne's freedom to dally with such unpopular and, Poe believed, second-rate literary devices as allegory. But by attending to public opinion, Hawthorne would gain the more valuable reward of finding his true literary mark.

Such exchanges of views on precisely how artists should relate to democratic audiences continued throughout the antebellum decades. One trend evident on both sides was the increasing use of authorial personas or masks. Writers seemed to sense the distance between themselves and the mass of readers and devised rhetorical strategies that facilitated communication—all the while keeping their sincere feelings in reserve. This ambiguously engaging yet defensive posture framed even the flamboyantly democratic message of Walt Whitman. In the preface to his first major poem, *Leaves of Grass* (1855), Whitman proclaimed the American writer's intimacy with society: "Of all nations the United States with veins full of poetical stuff most need poets and will doubtless have the greatest and use them the greatest."[16] Without questioning Whitman's intellectual honesty, however, it is hard to miss the stylized quality of the identity he created for himself as a popular poet, as he asked his language to swell to encompass the democratic masses in one part of the *Leaves of Grass*, "Song of Myself":

> I am of old and young, of the foolish as much as the wise,
> Regardless of others, ever regardful of others,
> Maternal as well as paternal, a child as well as a man . . .
> Of every hue and caste am I, of every rank and religion,
> A farmer, mechanic, artist, gentleman, sailor, quaker, Prisoner,
> fancy-man, rowdy, lawyer, physician, priest.[17]

Perhaps Whitman vindicated the capacity of serious writing to stay in touch with the people. But the tax he imposed on his literary resources to do so revealed that the intellectual's ability to communicate with the wider public was not as effortless as his theory suggested.

Two other major writers, Herman Melville and Nathaniel Hawthorne, were less sanguine than Whitman about their reception by a popular audience. Each voiced his opinion through a fictitious persona in separate essays in 1850. In an anonymous review published in the New York *Literary World* of Hawthorne's stories, *Mosses from the Old Manse*, Melville chose to speak as "a Virginian spending July in Vermont" who found Hawthorne's work perfectly suited to his "seclusion."[18] Perhaps Melville meant this image of a vacationing southerner to connote simply the literary enjoyments of leisure. Still, the speaker's nonurban and nonlaboring traits also reflected, more negatively, Melville's sense of the marginal social role of thoughtful writers such as himself. Melville was in fact uncertain about what authors could expect from readers and how they should respond. "Let America then prize and cherish her writers" and particularly those "who breathe that unshackled, democratic spirit of Christianity," he wrote hopefully in the review. Yet in virtually the same breath he asserted that "failure is the true test of genius." It is "better to fail in originality, than to succeed in imitation."[19] Melville's skepticism about the marketplace lacked the tone of elitism and moralism of the 1829 critic who disdained the "vulgar." Instead, he phrased his frustration in democratic terms as a conflict between the individual genius and mass audience, where the issue was less artistic superiority than free expression. However conceived, the problem of reception remained. Melville judged that Hawthorne coped with his anxiety by "hoodwinking the world," hiding his dark meanings under simpleminded titles such as "Young Goodman Brown" that passed a tale of guilt off to unsuspecting readers as "a supplement to 'Goody Two Shoes.'"[20] In Melville's eyes, restraint and subterfuge were unavoidable components of democratic authorship.

Melville had also read Hawthorne's preface to *The Scarlet Letter* (1850), a sketch titled "The Custom House," and thus must have known that Hawthorne was even more wary of general readers than he. Hawthorne devised his account of his novel's genesis to distance himself from his manuscript, to the point that the story of Hester Prynne seemed nearly to lack an author. He told his readers that he found notes on this tale of Puritan times during his tenure as a politically appointed (Democratic) custom officer in the superannuated port of Salem, Massachusetts. Jonathan Pue, one of his predecessors as surveyor of the revenue, was the author of the account taken down from the recollections of colonial eyewitnesses. Now the narrator (a fictionalized version of Hawthorne, who had really worked in the Salem Custom House) had been swept from office by the recent Whig victory. *The Scarlet Letter* should be read as "the posthumous papers of a decapitated surveyor."[21] Image upon image of ineffectiveness, decay, and death reflected Hawthorne's shaky self-esteem as an author and his ambivalence about the marketplace. After two decades as a writer, Hawthorne professed to be reconciled to the fact that "the author addresses, not the many who will fling aside his volume, or never take it up, but the few who will understand him, better than most of his schoolmates or lifemates."[22] To imagine that such friends were listening, he said, loosened his tongue enough to write. Yet Hawthorne was sufficiently cautious of the public to maintain "a native reserve" and to "keep the inmost Me behind its veil."[23]

In fact, the publishing records of Melville and Hawthorne did not altogether correspond to these authors' feelings of failure and consequent reserve. Melville was an acclaimed author of romances about the South Seas in 1850 and Hawthorne a well-known writer of stories.[24] Their statements about lack of esteem by the public and their use of fictional masks in the end conveyed less information about literary conditions than about their states of mind. As intellectuals who wished to experiment with themes and styles, Melville and Hawthorne must have chafed at popular tastes and market pressures. They could write to please readers, but they did not wish to feel that they had to. Their unhappiness with the public grew as well from a more benign desire for intellectual company. As writers and artists gained professional self-aware-ness, they sought one another's companionship in a frame of mind not unlike Hawthorne's search for spiritual intimates. It was as if they spoke more easily to the public when supported by artistic communities. American culture flourished in the antebellum decades in part because intellectuals created social circumstances conducive to dialogue among themselves. In February 1851 Melville drove through the snow from his temporary home in Pittsfield, Massachusetts, to meet Hawthorne in the neighboring town of Lenox. This was the beginning of a friendship that brought the two authors together in a privileged intellectual space conceived by Melville as "an aristocracy of the brain."[25] Far from a unique event, the formation of bonds among writers and artists was the social vehicle that pushed forward their creative intentions.

Intellectual Communities

In 1931 Constance Rourke wrote a path-breaking study of American folk cul-ture called *American Humor*. Based on the premise that Americans were an intrinsically "theatrical race," Rourke described the nearly spontaneous appearance, in legends and in the productions of traveling players, of arche-typical native characters including the Yankee, backwoodsman, and comic "Jim Crow" figure of blackface minstrelsy.[26] Rourke's image of the collective artistry of common people is appealing, and it is altogether true that through-out the nation, no matter how sparsely populated the area, neighbors gathered to sing, dance, and tell stories. In contrast to Rourke's romanticized vision, however, much of this popular culture was not produced by the "folk" but by individual artists whose work was assimilated by the people. Quite typically, "Jim Crow" was the creation of the actor Thomas D. Rice, who was white, and minstrelsy, with its imitation of black self-expression, apparently got its start in New York.[27] This market-oriented artistry was nurtured by intellec-tual communities that were distinct from ordinary towns. Cities, colleges, spe-cial towns that drew intellectuals, and European centers of art and learning all played important roles in providing a rising class of intellectuals with social foundations for their ambitions.

If an antebellum American sought a career in the arts, the most common first step was to move to a city. Each urban center—most significantly Boston, New York, Philadelphia, and Charleston—developed its own cultural institu-tions and distinctive intellectual temper. No city was better prepared to sup-port serious thought in 1830 than Boston. With strong traditions in education, publishing, and literary clubs, Boston offered aspiring intellectuals a hos-pitable setting in which to work. Two of the popular "parlor poets," Henry Wadsworth Longfellow and James Russell Lowell, were helped by teaching positions at Harvard. The Lowell Institute commanded $25,000 a year to pay for lectures on science. The Town and Country Club in the late 1840s and the Saturday Club in the 1850s offered thinking men a monthly forum for the exchange of ideas. Behind these highly visible institutions that facilitated discourse among the city's premier intellectuals were numerous other lecture series, self-improvement associations, and informal coteries that helped to stimulate the creative efforts of their less distinguished members.[28]

Boston's artistic life was moralistic and genteel, perhaps betraying the Puritanism of the city's seventeenth-century founders and the cultural influence exercised by people of wealth. Even so, intellectual activity centered increasingly less on religious subjects after 1830, and writers and artists perceived themselves in more secular terms as people open to critical thinking and experimentation. In tune with this trend, it is revealing that while more than half of those in an intellectual circle called the Transcendentalist Club in the 1830s were ministers, there were no clergy in the Saturday Club begun in 1855. Instead, there were four poets, two lawyers, and one historian, essayist, biologist, geologist, mathematician, astronomer, classical scholar, music critic, judge, and banker.[29] Participation in the Saturday Club and in similar organizations both reflected and reinforced intellectuals' sense of themselves as a distinct social group with few ties to churches or theology.

In a study of New England literature, Lawrence Buell has said that by 1850 the values of Boston thinkers favoring moral growth, human improvement, and the control of passion by reason formed the "hegemonic literary culture" of the region.[30] Powerful as the city's influence was, however, smaller places could offer intellectuals social resources similar to Boston's, though on a modest scale, and perhaps the chance to articulate views that diverged from those of the metropolis. Cities throughout the Connecticut River Valley, an area long dominated by the conservative Congregationalism taught at Yale, nurtured their own intellectual elites through local colleges, lyceums, and literary clubs. The novelist John William DeForest began to write in New Haven in the 1850s, as did Emily Dickinson in Amherst, Massachusetts. The poet Lydia Sigourney, the theologian Horace Bushnell, and, for a time, Harriet Beecher Stowe belonged to Hartford's intellectual community. As Buell shows, the lure of secular thinking tended to blur long-standing doctrinal differences between eastern and western New England and thus to deter the formulation of a dissenting perspective in the hinterland to contest the dominance of Boston.[31] Emily Dickinson's religious opinions were, after all, nearly as heterodox as Emerson's. From a social perspective, however, it is important to see that, in a region deeply committed to culture, both large cities and small provided conditions for the emergence of local literary classes.

Cities outside New England had distinctive cultural personalities when compared with either Boston or its satellites. In New York writers and artists congregated much as they did in Boston, but the tone of the city's culture was more bohemian and risqué. Although neighborhoods that housed painters and sculptors also formed in Boston and Philadelphia, lower Broadway in New York eclipsed their importance by 1860, so that "decisions which artists agonized about in the 1830s and early 1840s were no longer necessary," Neil Harris has said, and "either they stayed in their native community or they moved to New York."[32] In two buildings in particular, the old New York University building on Washington Square and the Studio Building on West 10th Street, galleries and adjacent studios offered artists unusual intimacy. Editorializing in *Harper's Magazine* in 1859, George William Curtis satirized the demonstrative flaunting of unconventional manners by the city's artists and writers. "Bohemia is the realm of vagabondage," Curtis wrote, "the modern sphere of the spirit that formerly coursed the world for adventure—but now prefers to explore the universe in microcosm, and finds a metropolis the best place of all."[33] The pioneering role of New York publishers in popularizing the sensational penny press—newspapers such as James Gordon Bennett's *Herald* that catered to the public's appetite for stories on crime, sex, and chicanery—attests further to New York's receptiveness to more unrestrained creativity than was welcome in Boston.[34] Without Boston's tenacious religious heritage and established professional classes, New York was populated by ambitious entrepreneurs and independently minded working people who patronized an adventurous culture. "New York had become the nation's leading art center not merely because of its wealth and numerical superiority," Harris concludes, "but by its openness and energy, and the eager enthusiasm its newly made businessmen took in the success of local art."[35]

Did intellectuals from Boston and New York relate to each other with kinship or rivalry? To what extent did they see themselves as members of a single intellectual class? Significant regionalism characterized the artistic life of antebellum America. Although young people born in New England might bypass small cities for Boston, probably only one in four New England authors eventually moved to New York, and once there they formed a self-promoting enclave of transplanted Yankees.[36] Still, this persistent localism coexisted with a rising sense of participation in a national culture. Nearly all intellectuals voiced their support for the development of broadly American arts and letters. The mass marketing of literature and the establishment of a nationwide lecture circuit deepened ties among thinkers. Even today cities retain specific intellectual and artistic strengths that do not preclude their absorption of ever more homogenized national values. Overall, antebellum intellectuals balanced particular urban loyalties with nascent professional identification with others working in their crafts.

Philadelphia developed an intellectual ambience descended from the tolerant and practical mood Benjamin Franklin found congenial when he ran away from Boston to this "City of Brotherly Love" in 1723.[37] In the antebellum decades Philadelphia became the national publishing center for home magazines— periodicals aimed particularly at women and children that avoided provocative or controversial themes. *Godey's Lady's Book* (1830–98), *Peterson's*

Magazine (1842–98), and *Graham's Magazine* (1828–58) preached an implicit doctrine that intelligence should be cultivated only to the point that thinking was socially useful. Thus during the Civil War Sarah Hale argued in *Godey's* that the magazine's domestic focus provided a beneficial respite from strife, "a quiet, cultured garden" in which "the teaching of the Savior" were protected from "the burning lava" outside.[38] This utilitarian view of culture might have seemed restrictive to New York and most Boston intellectuals. The creativity of the Philadelphia writers who produced for a national market was indeed channeled by entrepreneurial decisions about what would sell the most by offending the least. Evidence of excitement about thinking for its own sake, manifested perhaps in literary clubs or bohemian coteries, was slim in Philadelphia. The workaday approach to the arts in antebellum Philadelphia highlights the power of democratic convictions and mass-market pressures to tie intellectual life to practical ends.[39]

One reason for the intellectual caution of family magazines was that many of their readers lived in the slave states. The success of Philadelphia writers at building southern markets once again reveals how a national intellectual community began to emerge from regional bases. Yet southern cities also hosted indigenous cultures. The South closely resembled the North in the importance of urban centers for encounters among intellectuals. Charleston had its Conversation Club, college (the College of Charleston), and circle of thinkers, including at different times John C. Calhoun, William Gilmore Simms, Francis Lieber, and Hugh Legaré. Richmond took pride in publishing the *Southern Literary Messenger* (1834–64), as did New Orleans in supporting *De Bow's Review* (1846–67).[40] Nonetheless, southern intellectuals established themselves less securely as an independent class than did their counterparts elsewhere. Professionals who wrote in the context of such traditional vocations as the ministry did much to stimulate thought. Those who wished to break free of established audiences, including churches and denominations, seemed to feel more isolated than did northern writers and artists. Drew Faust argues that southern thinkers conceived themselves as "geniuses" in the romantic tradition, alienated from their contemporaries by their originality and yet yearning for a "sacred circle" of spiritual kin among themselves.[41] From a national perspective, this outlook was not unprecedented (consider Hawthorne and Melville), but it was far more common in the South. The region's small publishing industry and the consequent difficulty of creating audiences probably contributed to intellectuals' sense of solitude. One result of their insecurity was that there was greater mobility out of the South by thinkers than of any other region. Washington Allston, John Pendleton Kennedy, Edgar Allan Poe, and others migrated northward in search of a social atmosphere more congenial to creativity.

Overall, the formation of social networks of intellectuals in antebellum cities offered thinkers essential support for individual creativity. Urban enclaves of artists were not utopias, however, and could pose difficulties as well. Financial opportunities for writers and artists often lagged behind enticing communal enthusiasm. City culture, too, was oriented toward entrepreneurship and mass-marketing, and some intellectuals did not work well in an atmosphere of conformity and haste. Both of these dilemmas troubled the career of Edgar Allan Poe (1809–49). From the early 1830s until his death, Poe, who grew up in Richmond, was seduced by the literary life of cities. Moving restlessly among Richmond, New York, Philadelphia, and Baltimore, he gained sufficient reputation to find work as an editor of periodicals: Richmond's *Southern Literary Messenger* (1835–37), Philadelphia's *Burton's Gentleman's Magazine* (1839–40) and *Graham's Lady's and Gentleman's Magazine* (1841–42), and New York's *Broadway Journal* (1845–46). Yet despite Poe's professional visibility in the nation's cultural hubs, he was tormented by frustration. Poe gravitated toward editorial positions because supervising the production of magazines was one of the only kinds of salaried work available to writers. Authors of short fiction such as himself otherwise received almost no remuneration for stories and poems. His brief tenure at these jobs, on the other hand, must have been due in part to the constraints that the routines of the magazine business placed on an imagination capable of crafting tales of malice, terror, and despair. Poe's experience as a writer in the antebellum city thus consisted of recurrent cycles of professional activity followed by depression and poverty. This instability suggests how much the benefits of urban artistic communities—camaraderie, market access, and public acceptance of the legitimacy of creative endeavors—cloaked real and sometimes persistent problems, including restricted career choices and pressures toward conventionality.[42]

In twentieth-century America, the main professional alternative for intellectuals to reliance on the popular marketplace is support by colleges and universities. Providing thinkers with a steady livelihood, collegiality, and libraries and other resources needed for research, institutions of higher education are now perhaps the nation's most important intellectual communities. Universities were just beginning to play this cultural role in the decades before the Civil War. Becoming a professor remained an unappealing choice for many creative people owing to burdensome teaching methods that emphasized rote learning, administrators' lack of interest in graduate education, and suspicion within college communities of intellectual diversity. Even at Harvard, probably the country's most progressive university, eminent scholars spent hours each week in the classroom listening to undergraduate recitations, student-by-student recitals of material from obligatory texts in a narrow range of subjects. It was not until Charles William Eliot (1834–1926) became president of Harvard in 1869 that educational policies were revolutionized: lectures and discussions replaced recitations, the elective system and departmental organization invited flexibility and specialization, and the creation of the Graduate School of Arts and Sciences reflected a commitment to research. Not surprisingly, too, the faculty of Harvard Divinity School (founded in 1819) remained exclusively

Unitarian until the open, experimental administration of Eliot.[43] Thus antebellum Harvard, on the whole, was traditional and homogenous in its intellectual orientation. It is hard to imagine the scholarly giants of its postwar faculty—among them William James, Josiah Royce, Henry Adams, and George Santayana—accepting a teaching post at Harvard before the Civil War.[44]

Still, academic changes in the antebellum decades, though less dramatic than Eliot's sweeping innovations, encouraged some intellectuals to choose university life. Universities gradually added teaching positions and programs to the core curriculum of classical languages, mathematics, and moral philosophy. Thinkers who were lucky enough to work on the margins of established subjects enjoyed considerable liberty. Cornelius Felton, a professor of Greek at Harvard from 1829 to1859, was virtually locked into the recitation format in what was considered an essential subject. But Henry Wadsworth Longfellow, who became a professor of modern languages in 1836, and Jared Sparks, the McLean Professor of Ancient and Modern History after 1838, were able to tailor their teaching to serve their broader careers. Although Longfellow (1807–82) often chafed at his university obligations, he at least economized his teaching efforts by giving lectures and managed to establish a national reputation as a poet by publishing *Evangeline* and other works before leaving Harvard in 1855. Sparks (1789–1866), perhaps best known for his *Life of George Washington* (1839), arranged to teach only four months a year and to devote the other eight to archival research.[45]

Expanding the college curriculum contributed to intellectual freedom in other ways as well. While in the crucial subject of theology Harvard Divinity School remained Unitarian, the growth of the university overall produced a faculty with a variety of religious beliefs. An 1831 pamphlet reported that Harvard's teachers and administrators included not only six Unitarians but three Roman Catholics and one Calvinist, Lutheran, Episcopalian, Quaker, and Sandemanian.[46] Most likely, it was several European émigrés who taught Romance languages around 1830 who brought Catholicism to the Harvard faculty. To an intellectual such as Longfellow, intrigued by medievalism and Dante though he never formally left the Unitarian church, the chance to have Catholic colleagues might have enhanced the appeal of a university community.[47] Thus Longfellow and other thinkers, particularly in fields just gaining legitimacy, became academics because they found that college conditions forwarded their professional goals.

Perhaps no group of intellectuals gained as much from the expansion of universities as did scientists. Most major cities during this period hosted at least one scientific society, an organization supported by amateur scientists that sponsored lectures and publications. But the professionalization of technical fields required a sustained commitment of institutional resources, including funding for laboratories, expeditions, and collaborative work. The founding of Yale's Sheffield Scientific School in 1846, Harvard's Lawrence Scientific School in 1847, and similar programs elsewhere resulted from the convergence of the public's interest in progress (and profits) and scientists' eagerness to work in their particular fields of interest. Although science was legitimized in this pre-Darwin era by the belief that the study of nature would reveal the wonders of God's creation, a practical desire for technological improvement was the more immediate motive behind scientific education. Thus Harvard's Lawrence School was named for its principal benefactor, Abbott Lawrence, the textile manufacturer, and the first courses taught were in applied subjects such as industrial chemistry and civil engineering.

Resourceful faculty were able to circumvent institutional pragmatism, however, in order to pursue their own intellectual agendas. In an entrepreneurial spirit anticipating modern grantsmanship, Louis Agassiz, Harvard's Swiss-born professor of geology and zoology, raised $220,000 from private donors during the 1850s to set up a Museum of Comparative Zoology as a base for his global work of collection and classification. Even without such extraordinary personal successes, college-based scientists benefited from the national network of active researchers that began to take shape. Mobility of faculty among universities both reflected and reinforced the existence of this broad scientific community. Elias Loomis, for example, a meteorologist trained at Yale in the 1820s, taught successively at Western Reserve College, New York University, Princeton, and NYU again before returning to Yale in 1860. Yet whether contact among scientists was the result of career moves or, alternatively, collaboration and publications, it was clear that university-sponsored science transcended its practical origins by the start of the Civil War.[48]

There was suspicion among some intellectuals, however, that such showplaces of a modern society as cities and colleges were inimical to creativity. Drawing on widespread anxieties about the social and spiritual costs of capitalist development, the impulse of writers and artists to withdraw from the mainstream led to the formation of intellectual communities deliberately insulated from the stresses of progress. The town of Concord, Massachusetts, effectively nurtured literary talent at home, while European cities, particularly Rome and Florence, offered havens to American artists abroad.

By 1860 Concord was well known as the residence of major American writers: Ralph Waldo Emerson, Henry David Thoreau, Nathaniel Hawthorne, Bronson Alcott, and, just beginning her career, Alcott's daughter, Louisa May. To an ambitious author such as William Dean Howells, just 22 when he came east from Ohio in the spring of 1860 in hopes of furthering his career, a pilgrimage to Concord was obligatory. Howells spent a day calling on Hawthorne and Emerson.[49] The Concord literary community had come together more or less spontaneously following Emerson's decision to settle in the town, 20 miles from Boston, in 1835. Although Emerson's ancestors were among Concord's seventeenth-century founders, only Thoreau of the principal nineteenth-century writers was a native of the place. It was the perceived advantages for literary work that induced intellectuals to gather there: seclusion from the city without isolation, time to reflect and write, and the company of fellow spirits. Concord seems "a desirable residence," Alcott wrote just before his move in 1838, "as being near to Boston, healthful, and affording the society of my friend Mr. Emerson."[50] In the decades before the Civil War life in Concord remained impressively true to this vision of easy conviviality and intellectual exchange. Highbrow conversations on prearranged topics, held in private homes, were the most formal encounters that punctuated otherwise self-determined days. The chief disadvantage of Concord was the absence of local sources of financial support. Among strategies for money-making, Emerson toured widely to give lectures, Hawthorne left town periodically to take government jobs, and Alcott tried day labor in the fields. Yet the uncertainty of securing an income was probably no worse an affliction for intellectuals than the consuming routines of magazine editing or college teaching. Concord writers traded security for freedom, and the quality of their literary output attests to the wisdom of the exchange.[51]

For American painters and sculptors, the pleasures of leisure and sociability afforded by cultural enclaves were heightened by proximity to great works of art. Artist colonies grew up during the pre–Civil War era in Rome, Florence, and, to a lesser extent, Paris, Düsseldorf, and Munich.[52] These European cities offered numerous galleries, inspiring architecture, and a tradition of respect for the fine arts. In an era before the endowment of American museums, artists had to go to Europe, in part, simply to study the masters. But the same impulse that sent writers to Concord—the desire to find a way of life that nourished creative passions—made artists seek Europe's atmosphere of tradition and cultivation, which was so different, in their eyes, from the money-hungry hustle of their republic. In 1903 Henry James, a later expatriate, published an appreciative account of antebellum artistic circles in Rome and Florence titled *William Wetmore Story and His Friends*. Story (1819–95), a sculptor from Boston, began his first extended stay in Europe in 1847. From 1856 until his death he lived permanently abroad. As Story moved in the early years among Italian residences, he met American artists and writers settled in several communities: Horatio Greenough and Hiram Powers, both sculptors, Charlotte Cushman, an actress, and Margaret Fuller, Emerson's friend. The Americans interacted with European (mainly British) intellectuals as well. Story and his wife became intimate in Italy with the poets Robert and Elizabeth Barrett Browning. Although the political and social life of nineteenth-century Europe was hardly idyllic, foreign artists were generally insulated from cycles of revolutionary upheaval and authoritarian repression. In addition to their work, the Storys indulged a range of pleasures still suspect in comparatively puritanical America, including opera, plays, and dancing, as well as more benign donkey rides, walks, and shopping.[53] Thus American intellectuals used the cultural heritage and tolerance of Europe to build communities that furthered their aspirations.

Yet some artists who reflected sincerely on the calls to create an indigenous American culture pointed out that a sojourn abroad would distance a painter

Hiram Powers's *The Greek Slave* (1846) was one of the most popular works of art produced by an American living in Europe. Despite the uneasiness of many Americans about the marble statue's nudity, U.S. audiences acclaimed the sculptor's work as a major American accomplishment. *Gift of William Wilson Corcoran, Corcoran Gallery of Art, Washington, D.C.*

William Sidney Mount's *The Bone Player* (1856; oil on canvas) depicts an ordinary American man. Mount's choice of subject and the bone player's informal pose contrast sharply with Powers's *Greek Slave*, a work strongly influenced by European artistic conventions. *Bequest of Martha C. Karolik for the Karolik Collection of American Paintings, 1815–65, courtesy of the Museum of Fine Arts, Boston.*

or sculptor from native materials and values. William Sidney Mount, a genre painter of everyday American scenes, chose not to study in Europe on the patriotic principle that "originality is not confined to one place or country," as he wrote in a letter in 1850.[54] Mount's criticism raises questions about intellectual communities that have implications beyond the special case of Americans living abroad. How could thinkers who communicated with each other more than with the people at large produce works that captured the essential spirit of the nation? More broadly, did participation in intellectual circles encourage creativity, as anticipated, or rather pressure individuals to conform to artistic orthodoxies, perhaps at odds with the people's interests? Mount's position, in short, draws attention to the perplexities hidden in two key cultural issues: the social responsibility of intellectuals in a democracy and the reasonableness of their expectation of artistic freedom. To understand these questions more fully, it is helpful to consider women writers precisely because they were not generally part of the emerging groups of intellectuals. Their professional success or failure serves as a measure of how much the activity of thinkers became insulated from popular culture during the pre–Civil War era.

Women in fact wrote some of the best-selling fiction in antebellum America, and yet few participated in literary communities. The distinctive pattern of their careers underscores the continuing lack of centralization and consequent openness of the nascent cultural marketplace. Mary Kelley's book on 12 best-selling female authors, active between the 1820s and 1870s, suggests why women were comparatively isolated from professional circles.[55] Commonly married to men whose careers determined the couple's place of residence, women writers with families were not free to move to New York, Concord, or Rome. Instead they worked in small towns such as Brockport, New York, and Florence, Alabama, or, if they married professors, in provincial college communities such as Brunswick, Maine. They had the support of friends and perhaps of local societies devoted to culture, but they could not immerse themselves in a social milieu conducive to literary production.

The fact that Harriet Beecher Stowe and her contemporaries sold staggering numbers of books despite these cultural disadvantages leads to several conclusions about the importance of intellectual coteries in antebellum society. First, the company of other writers was not essential to women's productivity, nor did a small group of insiders so tightly control what was published that talented women could not be heard. Women writers were rooted intellectually in the female world of home, church, and benevolent associations—an essential part of the democratic landscape—and they spoke persuasively to both women and men through the undiscriminating mass market. Perhaps some thinkers were more in touch with the tastes of kindred spirits than with public moods, but the success of women writers was one sign that the alienation of intellectuals in this period was not the rule. Second, it seems that the contribution of artistic communities was to encourage independent thought, because in the absence of ongoing dialogue with intellectual peers, women tended to follow set formulas in their writing. Even if women's prose is judged carefully on its own terms of sentimentality and moralism, and not by the literary conventions established by men, most authors still depicted domestic subjects in a fairly standardized way.[56] It was the minority of women who participated regularly in informal debate who most often went beyond an adept manipulation of accepted values to contest their validity. Margaret Fuller, a strong personality in the Concord circle, almost surely was impelled in part by her friends' critical spirit to produce her stirring appeal for women's freedom, *Woman in the Nineteenth Century* (1845).[57]

The lesson to be learned from the women writers is that the bounds of intellectual life remained permeable in antebellum America. Communities of thinkers encouraged experimentation and supported individualism. But these coteries were neither so powerful nor so rigid that they put intellectuals out of touch with popular thought.[58] The success of communication between intellectuals and audiences depended in part on the evolution of artistic forms that conveyed Americans' preoccupations as a people.

Genres

The world has become too "matter of fact," complained William Gilmore Simms, the South Carolina writer, at the beginning of a ghost story entitled "Grayling" in 1843.[59] Simms determined instead to explore the "romantic" and proceeded to tell a tale about a mysterious apparition in Revolutionary times. Yet he could not get away from the issue of realism—the story's truth to the laws of the visible world—and finally framed the narrative in debate among the narrator, his father, and his grandmother about its credibility. Simms was typical of antebellum intellectuals in his fascination with facts and their meaning. In nearly all the forms to which writers and artists turned, they built outward from meticulous presentations of detail toward organizing terms of interpretation, as if anxious to know the significance of so much sensory information. Perhaps this was the preoccupation of a capitalist society where unprecedented quantities of numbers and words were exchanged in the intellectual marketplace. More disturbingly, because the kinds of knowledge processed by reason and imagination diverged in antebellum culture, intellectuals seemed to feel impelled to reestablish connections between them in their work. Characteristically, Simms turned to romance because of his distaste for the narrow utilitarianism of "that cold-blooded demon called Science."[60] Whatever the psychological roots of American artists' interest in probing appearances, the relationship between the real and ideal was one theme that recurred in the cultural products crafted in nascent intellectual communities: photographs, short stories, histories, and essays. Other genres than these might also be considered representative of antebellum intelligence. These four artistic modes merit special attention, however, because they gained currency between 1830 and 1860 and because they serve as points of entry into the intellectual worlds of producers and consumers of culture.[61]

It is easy to see why the introduction of daguerreotypes in America in 1839 produced tremendous excitement. In this process brought from France by a follower of its inventor, Louis Daguerre, a machine fixed an exact image of the subject on glass. A technique easy to master, cheap to execute, and avidly sought by consumers, daguerreotypes transformed Americans' visual landscape from a place with few likenesses to catch the eye into a world full of artistic stimulation and provocative of speculation on the meaning of appearances. The word "photography," the generic term for both the daguerreotype process and the wet-plate method developed in the 1850s to reproduce images on paper, literally means writing with light.[62] Americans were indeed awed by photography's nearly miraculous quality. Beyond this fascination, however, photography propelled discussion about the connections between the visible world and the ideal, physiognomy and character, and technology and art.

Commentators on daguerreotypes and, later, on photographs were impressed by the accuracy of representation and, beyond simple precision, by the way flawless visual detail gave viewers access to a higher realm of truth. Edgar Allan Poe praised the daguerreotype in *Alexander's Weekly Magazine* in 1840 as "*infinitely* more accurate in its representation than any painting by human hands," making the "variations of shade, and the gradations of both linear and aerial perspective . . . those of truth itself, in the supremeness of its perfection."[63] Oliver Wendell Holmes, Sr., writing in the *Atlantic Monthly* two decades later, similarly focused on photography's technical proficiency and visionary power. Not only do photographs capture the "infinite complexity which Nature gives us," Holmes observed, but they accomplish the "greatest of human triumphs over earthly conditions, the divorce of form and substance."[64] The views of Poe and Holmes reflected a widespread impulse among Americans to explain their infatuation with photography in culturally constructive terms. Rather than emphasize that photographs were machine-made and, with the invention of negatives, mass-reproducible images concerned with surfaces only, these writers stressed the capacity of exact impressions to serve as avenues to a transcendent sphere. To a generation ambivalent about technological change and materialism, this was a consoling view.

A similar strategy to link surface with substance guided the assumptions Americans made about whether photographs revealed inner character. The question of how much might be known about a person from appearances was a vexing concern in a mass society and, in a way, a special case of the uncertainty about the relation of accurate images to invisible truths. The majority of photographs made before 1860 were portraits. In the process of sitting for one's picture, an individual not only acted as a subject and consumer but as an artist, too, having some control over the impression of personality conveyed. Antebellum Americans who chose to be photographed assumed that genuine

Daguerreotype of Edgar Allan Poe made in 1849. Poe believed that photography revealed the inner truth about the subject, and his haunting expression in this daguerreotype might make a viewer think that the picture offered insight into Poe's consciousness. *Rare Book Department, Free Public Library of Philadelphia.*

character should and could shine through. One scholar attributes the severe look of faces in daguerreotypes less to the physical trial of enduring a long exposure than to the "mood-ridden introspection" of people determined to have the camera record their true selves.[65] The way they displayed photographs reinforces the conclusion that they believed that pictures were windows on character. Either to put one's likeness on a calling card (the formal *carte-de-visite*) or to hang photographs of family members on the walls of a home must have rested on the faith that the camera evoked and communicated some part of a person's essence.[66] Thus for the most immediate producers of photographic portraits, the subjects themselves, as well as for the intellectuals who wrote about photography such as Poe and Holmes, these technically adept images wonderfully resonated to reveal hidden meanings.

The implication of widespread faith in the ability of pictures to penetrate surfaces was that photography was a new form of art. Rather than value the camera as an intriguing piece of technology, most Americans approached photography as a process marvelously combining objectivity and depth. To contend that an interpretation of nature by an artist would yield a more satisfying understanding than a photograph became a contested, though not an abandoned, position. Thomas Cole, the painter, defended the superiority of the human eye in a letter in 1840. Although photographs might help an artist to remember his subject's appearance, Cole conceded, "the art of painting is a creative as well as imitative art, and is in no danger of being superseded by any mechanical contrivance."[67] Yet the popular tide was against Cole's humanistic conception of artistry. As photography studios opened in major American cities, galleries of finished works were commonly part of a series of elegantly furnished rooms, and patrons viewed photographs with a respect once reserved for paintings. Prominent photographers were treated not as technicians but as serious contributors to a rising national culture. Ironically, however, through the legitimacy gained by photography's reputation for unbiased exactitude, photographers who were inventive and enterprising increasingly turned their craft toward interpretation. Mathew Brady (1823–96), for example, perhaps the leading photographer of the period, published *The Gallery of Illustrious Americans* in 1850, 12 portraits of famous men rendered as lithographs. His book seems inspired less by an aesthetic honoring objectivity than by a shrewd awareness that his carefully posed and assembled faces were a persuasive instrument of patriotism and, not incidentally, of profits. This is not to say that Brady played deceptively on the public's trust; but he relied on Americans' enthusiasm and rationale for photography to explore the medium's potential as a means of personal statement and social influence.[68]

The establishment of photography as a valued part of culture thus casts light both on Americans' expectations for art and on the dynamics of intellectual communities. Widely shared democratic loyalties and utilitarian inclinations may have stood behind the acclaim of photography's down-to-earth realism, but a Christian nation could not rest content with the representational accuracy of photographs without assurance that they also illumined ideals. This implicit understanding emerged through a kind of dialogue that occurred mainly in cities. The public communicated its viewpoint through its use of photographs, intellectuals commented in the print media, and photographers actively projected an image of themselves and their art. This exchange was one sign of the openness of antebellum intellectual life.

Short pieces of fiction were another art form that flourished in this cultural atmosphere. They also served authors and readers as vehicles to investigate meanings behind observable facts. So important are short stories to the national culture that they have been called America's distinctive contribution to modern literature.[69] Tales and sketches gained currency as part of the dramatic expansion of magazine literature in the 1830s and functioned well in a capitalist democracy: they could be produced by a wide sample of writers with little literary training, turned out quickly, and consumed with even greater haste by a time-conscious people. If the 1850s may be seen as the point when American novel-writing reached maturity (*The Scarlet Letter, Moby-Dick, Uncle Tom's Cabin*), the 1830s and 1840s were a golden age for stories. Edgar Allan Poe published 78 pieces before his death in 1849, for example, and Nathaniel Hawthorne wrote most of his stories (totaling about 100) before he issued *The Scarlet Letter* in 1850.[70]

This body of literature is often criticized by scholars for its romantic quality. Not only are the settings of action removed from "everyday" (middle-class) life, but, more seriously in the eyes of some commentators, characters are unchanging and allegorical, and dramatic conflicts are too simple to admit ambiguity.[71] It is possible, however, to argue that this view mistakes the purpose of antebellum short fiction. Perhaps story writers did not seek to imitate social life, laying out problems in an expansive one-dimensional landscape, but rather to trace lines of connection between human activities and ideal values, allowing shadowy essences to play around the edges of visible detail. If their writing thus aimed at layered meanings that created an illusion of depth, then it makes sense that they wrote stories instead of novels, since length—the literary equivalent of real-life time—served little role in developing themes. Examples taken from two of the period's most skilled writers of tales—Poe and Hawthorne—may illustrate this perspective.

Poe curiously combined an interest in factuality with habitual inattention to ordinary situations. His stories were dense with information that, as one critic has said of contemporary romances, created "a veneer of surface realism."[72] "The Murders of the Rue Morgue" and other so-called tales of ratiocination meticulously presented the evidence pertinent to mysteries or crimes. Tales of terror such as "The Pit and the Pendulum" recorded the minute-by-minute perceptions of their fevered narrators.[73] Yet Poe's camera-eye method was almost never directed toward common scenes, focusing instead on tormented eroticism or, perhaps, perverted ill will. A realist in technique, he had little interest in mundane events and was hardly a realist, in the usual sense, in intent. One way to explain Poe's strange yoking of scrupulous observation to his fascination with disordered consciousness is to point out that he valued knowledge only as connected with minds. In his fictional conversations between characters beyond the grave, such as "The Colloquoy of Monos and Una," Poe insisted that thought became constructive only as it lost its abstraction and came in touch with sensation, intuition, and taste. His poetic theory, centering on the idea that a poem ought to create a unified effect on the reader, similarly contained an implicit disregard of facts (or, in this case, words) in themselves and turned on their relation to consciousness.[74] These principles help to explicate the role of realistic technique in Poe's tales. He used details to build impressions about the mental world of each story's main subject or narrator. Behind the history of "Ligeia" looms her tormented husband, behind the pounding of "The Tell-Tale Heart" lurks the guilty killer, and behind these fictional minds evoked by indirection sits the affected reader. Unconcerned about drawing out social fables in time, Poe manipulated precise observations to force readers to enter his characters' states of mind.

Hawthorne, who outlived Poe by a decade and a half, had time to reflect on the similar kind of double vision he required of the readers of his tales. When he reissued *Twice-Told Tales* (1837) in 1851, he dismissed his earlier preference for "allegory" as one characteristic of the "Dreamland of [my] youth."[75] It is likely, however, that Hawthorne's self-criticism was partly disingenuous, perhaps offered to protect himself from shifting tastes in the 1850s toward straightforward narratives.[76] In fact, Hawthorne's stories, particularly the historical tales written between 1825 and 1842, were constructed with disciplined attention to accuracy as well as care in constructing avenues for readers to move from one level of meaning to another.

Consider the intricacy of perhaps the best of Hawthorne's Puritan tales, "Young Goodman Brown" (1835). The story of a "silly fellow," in the Devil's words, who keeps a "covenant" with Satan one night in the woods near Salem, Massachusetts, at the turn of the eighteenth century, "Young Goodman Brown" had less to do with social relationships in the usual sense than with Hawthorne's questions about penetrating appearances.[77] How could the reader (or Brown) be sure that Brown's traveling companion, ostensibly the Devil in the shape of the young man's father, hadn't simply fabricated spectral apparitions of upstanding Puritans at a witch's sabbath in order to test the faith of his naive and wavering friend? How could anyone know that Brown, perhaps falling asleep in the forest, hadn't just "dreamed a wild dream?"[78] Was it even certain that this subtle parable of self-righteous presumption, mixed with gnawing self-distrust, really happened outside even the waking torments of Brown's mind? Was it possible that this was a typical tale of Puritan consciousness, not a sketch of an insignificant young man, and that we should thus question the Devil's dismissal of Brown as a "silly fellow" and, more broadly, wonder about the necessary truthfulness of words?

Notwithstanding these provoking doubts that made readers distrust the face value of the story's facts, Hawthorne scrupulously incorporated Puritan language and issues into his text. Words that resonated with meaning in seventeenth-century New England—such as "faith," "justification," and "errand"—gave "Young Goodman Brown" the texture of historical realism.[79] Contemporaries of the Salem witch trials in 1692 had publicly debated the reliability of spectral evidence. So attentive was Hawthorne to Puritan materials that Michael Colacurcio has argued that Hawthorne was a "moral historian."[80] Hawthorne did not simply use history for literary effect, but aimed to make the past his theme, approaching enduring human issues through the moral dilemmas of particular eras. This view of Hawthorne's seriousness about history is compelling. Yet despite his immersion in an earlier society, the passage of time—the dynamic aspect of history—was insignificant to Hawthorne. Behind the carefully rendered Puritan world of "Young Goodman Brown" played a series of interpenetrating theological and psychological meanings, but the Puritanism of the tale never changed in itself. Hawthorne's sole concern was the relationship of this historical world, statically conceived, to the invisible truths.

It might seem that reading Hawthorne and Poe required considerable intellectual agility, but antebellum audiences were well prepared to discern hidden meanings because of their intimacy with Christian literature. Whether they listened to sermons that explicated biblical passages or read domestic fiction that used home-centered occurrences to convey moral lessons, readers of stories expected texts to be symbolic. Many times the message was simple to decipher because it was conventional. In "Uncle Lot," the opening story in Harriet Beecher Stowe's collection, *The May Flower* (1843), the exemplary piety and inspiring death of a young preacher converts his friend, who becomes a minister in turn and marries the sister of the saintly man.[81] Few readers could miss Stowe's allusion to Christ's sacrifice, her evangelical directive to seek conversion, or, in a theme characteristic of domestic prose, her affirmation of marriage as a seal of faith. Poe and Hawthorne more or less abandoned Christian metaphysics and, free to pose difficult questions, vastly complicated the ideas implicit in their tales. Nonetheless, contemporary readers who were accustomed to probing the surfaces of prose were familiar with the method of their writing.

In "Young Goodman Brown" Hawthorne may have counted on his audience's interest in history to draw them toward deeper themes. This was a clever strategy in the pre–Civil War decades. One expression of Americans' fascination with facts was their passion for history. They liked to collect and preserve information. While only 14 local or state historical societies were formed between 1790 and 1830, 52 appeared during the next 30 years.[82] People enjoyed reading about past times as well. On a small scale, towns commissioned local histories. More grandly, the first professional historians, such as George Bancroft and Francis Parkman, produced multivolume accounts of the growth of the nation.[83] Americans' involvement with history was not disinterested and scientific. Facts caught their attention because they provoked thoughts and feelings about the transcendent importance of events. For this reason the major historians have often been considered "romantics." Building from bases of thorough research, they emphasized the exotic and panoramic, pictured heroes and villains, favored ornate and moving narratives, and assumed that the past held moral lessons. Their method requires that their works be read with a skeptical eye as to the accuracy of their records, but this approach enhances the value of their histories as products of a particular culture. So-called romantic history was fully in tune with the taste of antebellum Americans for densely textured, real-life detail and with their insistence on exploring their observations' significance.

Precisely because antebellum histories were not mere compilations of facts but instead instruments of debate about values, reading about the past was a means for Americans to reflect on, and to an extent control, their future. One of the most enthralling stories of a dramatic historical moment—that on a deeper level functioned as a nationalist jeremiad—was William Prescott's *History of the Conquest of Mexico* (1843). Blind as an adult, Prescott (1796–1859) nevertheless traveled from his home in Boston to undertake extensive research in Spanish archives, determined to observe "the severe rules of historical criticism."[84] The resulting three-volume history of the 1520 expedition led by Hernando Cortés was based on impressive use of sources. But on the surface, the *Conquest* had all the appeal of "romance," as Prescott knew: the "knight-errant" Cortés clashed with the melancholic Aztec ruler, Montezuma, in the "subversion of a great empire by a handful of adventurers," even finding passion along the way in his affair with the Indian translator who the Spanish named Marina.[85] Prescott's expansive descriptions of physical landscapes, Aztec customs, leaders' characters, and battles all engaged the sensibilities of his readers.

More serious themes informed the text as well. Prescott focused discussion on whether the Spanish invasion and the conquistadores' cruel methods were morally justified. Was it possible that the legitimacy of a modern-day incursion played in the back of his mind, since the *Conquest*, though far more than a political polemic, was published just four years before U.S. troops landed in Vera Cruz during the Mexican War? In a more introspective mood, Prescott's book was a tract on the survival of nations. The Aztec empire fell, according to Prescott, because of its leaders' indulgence in luxury, their neuroses and passivity, disregard of the popular will, and acceptance of human sacrifice.[86] A cross between a Puritan jeremiad and a discourse on republican virtue, the *Conquest* asked North American readers to ponder their own vices lest they, like the Aztecs, make themselves vulnerable to subversion. In sum, the *History of the Conquest of Mexico* typified the dominant school of antebellum historiography in its mixture of fantasies and fears with insistence on factual accuracy.

Even when antebellum readers did not pick up works of nonfictional history, they often gravitated toward stories that were faithful to true-life conditions of the past. They seemed to like the aura of human possibility in historical fiction, as well as the implicit connection of tales about their ancestors to themselves. Many of the period's historical narratives were regional in orientation and, not surprisingly, helped to consolidate regional cultures in the face of increasing national communication.[87] In 1835, the same year Hawthorne published his New England tale, "Young Goodman Brown," William Gilmore

Simms issued his far more popular book, *The Yemassee*, a novel about eighteenth-century South Carolina. Populated by Cavaliers, evangelicals, loyal slaves, and rebellious Indians, the fictional world of *The Yemassee* (taking its name from the Muskogean-speaking Indian tribe, the Yamassee) dealt with themes nearly identical to Prescott's *Conquest*: territorial expansion, fitness for governing, and, more centrally than Prescott's book, race relations. Noble and doomed, the Yemassee disqualified themselves for a place in a harmonious and, in Simms's eyes, necessarily hierarchical interracial society because of their use of violence to protect their lands. The novel closed with the Indians' crumbling siege of Charleston. Simms's story of interracial violence was based on the historical uprising of the Yamassee in 1715, but it also called to mind the far more recent alleged slave conspiracy against Charleston in 1822 under the leadership of the slave Denmark Vesey. In his fiction Simms resolved complex and troubling historical circumstances to the satisfaction of his white readers. The novel's aristocratic governor, his trusted slave, and his backcountry allies looked forward in the end to peace in the city and on the frontier.[88]

The Yemassee was more a work of simple self-justification than Prescott's searching inquiry into ethics and national fates. But the historicity of Simms's novel was an essential part of its power. By setting his story in colonial South Carolina, Simms ensured its credibility and connection with current issues, as well as established the sense of distance and resolution needed for his readers' psychological comfort. Both Simms and Prescott wrote books that answered the reading public's taste for a blend of factual and ideal truth. Curious in a down-to-earth way about what society was really like in the past, antebellum consumers of history and historical fiction at the same time expected authors to search out the moral implications of events.

The last form of cultural expression helpful in reconstructing the perspective of antebellum intellectuals and audiences is the essay. Short pieces of expository prose, such as those developed by sophisticated craftsmen including Ralph Waldo Emerson and James Henry Hammond, had an anachronistic quality because they depended for effective communication on personal voice. Photographs, stories, and histories all seemed in tune with mass-market conditions. These machine-produced images, intricately constructed tales, and compilations of facts conveyed their significance to audiences without much need for direct commentary by their creators. But essays cultivated the impression that they were a form of speech between intimates and relied on the creation of a credible speaker to ground a series of abstractions. With an affinity to a world of face-to-face relationships, it is not surprising that the essay as a literary medium predated the 1830s (think, for example, of *The Federalist Papers*). In the antebellum years, however, essays enjoyed renewed life as a sort of dissent from impersonal exchange. The best essayists belonged to cloistered intellectual communities, most notably Concord, Massachusetts, and the more amorphous "sacred circle" of southern thinkers. Perhaps attuned to the potential of the spoken word to enliven these enclaves, they adapted the strategies of speech to writing. Here the realism of the presentation consisted neither of exact images nor accurate facts, but of convincing sounds.[89]

Conversation was the staple intellectual nourishment of antebellum Concord. Thinkers moved to the town in part so that they could talk frequently with one another, and their reasons were not altogether pragmatic. Although they lived in a culture still rich in oral forms of art, including sermons, lectures, and orations, they seemed to sense the threat to spoken expression posed by mass-distributed written prose and to savor, instead, spontaneous interpersonal discourse. Emerson, Thoreau, and Margaret Fuller excelled as essayists. The conversational quality of works such as Thoreau's "Resistance to Civil Government" and Fuller's "The Great Lawsuit" came in part from the origin of many written pieces in formal presentations such as lectures or group discussions.[90] But the essayists' decisions to anchor abstract propositions about governing or equality of the sexes in first-person narratives also grew from their attachment to personalized language. Emerson's thoughts about the preparation of *Essays: First Series* (1841) and the strategy of the collection's exemplary piece, "Self-Reliance," underscore the importance of voice in the works of the Concord writers.

Writing in his journal before the publication of *Essays* in March 1841, Emerson used a variety of artistic and literary metaphors to describe his sense of his failures and successes. The essays were no more than "a cold exhibition of dead thoughts," Emerson wrote in the mood of one obliged to stroll through a drafty gallery. How much better would they be if he could imagine himself composing "a letter to anyone whom I love."[91] When he judged his efforts less harshly, he turned to figures of speech that alluded to sound. "I have scarce a day-dream on which the breath of the pines has not blown," Emerson reflected. "Shall I not then call my little book Forest Essays?"[92] To the reader who opened to "Self-Reliance," Emerson made clear that listening to the voice of his speaker was essential to an appreciation of the text. Thus his opening paragraph contained a torrent of phrases about conversing: "speak your latent conviction," "the soul always hears," "the voice of the mind."[93]

Why was voice so important? On the simple level of readability, Emerson relied on the personality of his narrator to introduce his audience to abstract assertions. Without the speaking "I" who occasionally dipped into his past ("I remember") or reflected on his peaceful routine ("In this pleasing contrite wood life which God allows me"), Emerson's major themes would have been reduced to a collection of aphorisms.[94] Readers were asked to take moral imperatives seriously—"Whoso would be a man, must be a nonconformist"— because the ideas were recommended by a thoughtful voice. In the course of the essay, too, readers found themselves transformed from mere listeners to participants in dialogue. "Suppose you should contradict yourself; what then?," Emerson asked to provoke self-questioning, until speaker and readers came together in common experience: "We lie in the lap of immense intelligence, which makes us receivers of its truth and organs of its activity."[95] For

Emerson, the sounds of language seemed to provide the vibrant human foreground of transcendent truths. It was as if conversation had the power to evoke inspiration all-the-while available, but silent unless coaxed to expression.

In the South, essays emerged as a genre as they became a vehicle of proslavery arguments. When prominent thinkers such as William Gilmore Simms, James Henry Hammond, and George Fitzhugh defended slavery in southern periodicals, their choice of the essay as a form of expression reflected their ideology. The thematic core of the proslavery position was that traditionalism was superior to reform, as was paternalism to the indifference of the marketplace. In keeping with these values, these writers' polemical essays cultivated a tone of reasoned discourse between gentlemen, much in the mode of prose pieces published in eighteenth-century British magazines. Although the southerners would have shuddered at a comparison of their essays to the works of the Concord authors—idealists who, in their view, wrote with a romantic's pernicious faith in direct inspiration—both groups of essayists did adopt an assertively personal style in a spirit of dissent against the smooth prose of the marketplace.[96]

In "Letter to an English Abolitionist" (1845) James Henry Hammond, politician and writer from South Carolina, made assumptions about writing not unlike those of Emerson. The most basic similarity was the use of an individualized narrative voice to carry abstract argument. Indeed, Hammond chose to personalize a neutral situation. Having received from a friend a copy of a circular letter addressed to northern Christians by Thomas Clarkson, the British abolitionist, Hammond decided to reply to Clarkson directly, "since you have thrown down the gauntlet to me."[97] Rather than verbal conversation, correspondence was the literary model for this closely reasoned, hard-hitting tract. Still, Hammond cultivated an impression of informality. He claimed to write as a "recreation" in his "abundant leisure," as if the polemic was the continuation of a private talk between honorable men.[98] Much as Emerson's first-person narrator mediated a series of propositions for readers, Hammond's voice made it seem that the truisms presented in the essay had immediate human significance. Hammond did have a talent for brilliant turns of phrase, such as this affirmation of his basic conservatism: "This world was made for man, and man for the world as it is."[99] Yet had he not punctuated his arguments with plain and sincere statements of conviction, readers, though enlightened, would not have been moved and convinced. "I might say that I am no more in favor of Slavery in the abstract, than I am of poverty, disease, deformity, idiocy," Hammond began with disarming bluntness. But, he continued as he steered toward resolution, it is "well for us to leave the Almighty to perfect his own works," and "on Slavery in the abstract, then, it would not be amiss to have as little as possible to say." "Let us contemplate it," he concluded with authority, "as it is."[100] Thus in Hammond's essay, as in Emerson's, individual personality as conveyed by the sounds of words give texture to fundamental doctrines. This was not simply a literary device to heighten the interest of readers, but one expression of the inclination of antebellum Americans to imitate the details of life in art. Intellectuals and their audiences approached general statements of values through richly sensible evidence.

The development of serviceable artistic genres furthered the creation of a national culture in unanticipated ways. Proponents of native arts seemed to expect that cultural products would be marked as American by displaying characteristic themes, perhaps reflecting Christian or democratic values, or by drawing on recognizable personality types and physical settings. This did occur. But beyond the substance of art, the availability of popular forms of expression—photographs, short stories, histories, and essays, among others—facilitated the process of self-exploration for Americans as a people. These characteristic products of antebellum America were neither created spontaneously by folk culture nor imposed on the people by intellectuals. Rather, they emerged through dialogue between artists and audiences, which, like most discussions, consisted neither of total agreement nor unqualified dissent. Thus there was a relationship, even if not a simple one, between popular interest in photography or in history and the aspirations of professional photographers and historians. As each genre took definite shape, these conventional styles continued to facilitate communication between producers and consumers of ideas because they provided familiar common ground, without a suffocating rigidity. Indeed, established forms of expression not only left room for intellectual experimentation but, by providing a sophisticated cultural language, actively encouraged creativity. It is by no means surprising that the literary masterpieces of the American Renaissance were produced in this setting.

Masterworks

There has been lively debate among scholars in recent years about which antebellum literary works deserve a place in the canon, the list of exemplary texts, and, even more problematically, about the intellectual validity of distinguishing extraordinary from ordinary writings at all. One thing that is clear is that critical judgments have changed over time. Commentators around the beginning of this century gave highest honors to such authors as Longfellow, Lowell, and Emerson. Later modernist critics, including F. O. Matthiessen in *American Renaissance* (1941), favored writers of more brooding temperaments or experimental inclinations, among them Melville, Hawthorne, and Whitman. Today scholars question implicit terms for judging greatness that have excluded whole groups of writers, such as women and African Americans, simply because their work was different from that produced by white, middle-class men. To observe so much flux in literary reputations underscores how much a critic's decisions about value reflect the preoccupations of his or her time.

With the caution instilled by these critical questions in mind, it is still possible to identify works that reflected the preoccupations of antebellum society

An Imaginary Gathering: Washington Irving and His Friends at Sunnyside, 1864 represents a genre of fictitious group portraits of American authors that reflected the nation's pride in its literary accomplishments. *Collection of the New-York Historical Society.*

and incorporated the established modes of literary expression in an unusually powerful way. This discussion of masterworks of the American Renaissance looks closely at Harriet Beecher Stowe's *Uncle Tom's Cabin* (1852), Nathaniel Hawthorne's *The Scarlet Letter* (1850), Herman Melville's *Moby-Dick* (1851), Henry David Thoreau's *Walden* (1854), and Frederick Douglass's *Narrative of the Life of Frederick Douglass* (1845). The criterion for their selection is historical. Each book examined a crucial question in the culture of this era using ideas and language of wide currency. All may be seen as symbolic narratives. They were produced by writers with more than an ordinary self-awareness and control of their craft. The authors were adept much less because they were geniuses by nature than because they could draw on established genres. It is not accidental that most of these works were published around 1850. They represented the fruition of the drive for an indigenous culture and were the work of self-conscious intellectuals. These texts, in short, grew from the new-found stability of the American arts. They are not offered here as a new canon but as works that reveal the intellectual potential of the American Renaissance.[101]

When Harriet Beecher Stowe (1811–96) published *Uncle Tom's Cabin* in 1852, she was already an acclaimed author of short domestic fiction. Part of her novel's ability to engage her audience came from the creation of a landscape and characters familiar to readers accustomed to Christian symbolism. But the book was arresting, too, because it took the evangelicalism articulated by women writers out of the home and into the public arena of antislavery activism. By combining conventionality and innovation, Stowe coaxed ante- bellum readers toward bolder moral views in a way only available to a person intimate with prevailing ideas and tastes.[102]

Like most domestic fiction, *Uncle Tom's Cabin* offered moral lessons through images of home life. Although Stowe's language could draw readers toward moments of intense emotion, she chose a pedestrian surface for her story as a reliable groundwork for flights of feeling and reflection. To win the sympa- thies of northerners who had never visited a slave dwelling, she introduced her black characters in a recognizable domestic scene at Uncle Tom's cabin: Aunt Chloe, Uncle Tom's wife, is a proud cook (her corn cakes are "a sublime mys- tery") and a conscientious housekeeper, who decorates her walls with prints of biblical scenes and a portrait of George Washington.[103] Only the fact that this picture of Washington is shaded black distinguishes Uncle Tom's household from a white middle-class home. Behind this veneer of domestic realism played the kind of moral drama equally familiar to Stowe's audience. Nearly every character represented some value. Self-sacrificing Little Eva is a pure and redemptive influence in the midst of a society corrupted by lassitude (her parents) and greed (Simon Legree). The perfect motherly love of Eliza, the escaped slave, and the industriousness of her husband, George, qualify them

Authors of the United States (1866), another imaginary group of writers, included women authors. The value judgments inherent in canon building were already being made in decisions about the composition of these pictures. Engraving by Alexander Hay Ritchie, after Thomas Hicks. *National Portrait Gallery, Smithsonian Institution.*

to colonize and Christianize "my glorious Africa," in George's words, as a new Adam and Eve.[104] Readers of domestic fiction expected stories to carry evangelical messages, and consumers of short stories, more generally, were prepared to probe narratives for allusions to ideals. Thus *Uncle Tom's Cabin* fully conformed to literary conventions in a way that ensured that the novel would be widely and appreciatively read.

Yet Stowe also took considerable risks. For a woman to address the themes of slavery and race in 1852 was a radical step. Stowe in effect confessed that she violated the tacit rule that domestic fiction should be limited to discussion of private life when she explained that she wrote to protest the injustice of the fugitive slave law included in the Compromise of 1850.[105] Once she crossed the line to confront public issues, Stowe wove startling assertions into her story: blacks were as human as whites, northern whites were as responsible for slavery as were slaveholders, and Christianity was the only true solution to political problems. Blacks and whites were among Stowe's heroes, most prominently Uncle Tom and the Harris family (George, Eliza, and their son, Harry). Although some modern critics have interpreted the self-effacing meekness of Uncle Tom as a sign of Stowe's racism, Tom's spiritual composure may be seen more accurately as a mark of his high achievement in a novel informed by evangelical beliefs. Stowe's African Americans were not simply human but exemplary Christians. In a similarly bold choice, the novel's moral geography implicated all white Americans as perpetrators of slavery. The cold-hearted acquisitiveness and rigid righteousness of New England (Legree and Miss Ophelia, respectively) combined with the weak-willed selfishness of the border states (Mr. Shelby) and the amoral indulgence in luxury of the deep South (the St. Clares) to support the institution of slavery. Only the sacrificial deaths of Eva and Tom, along with the voluntary emigration of the Harrises to Africa, could bring some peace to the middle ground, Kentucky, where the young George Shelby finally freed his father's slaves. Was it true, then, that political measures alone would inevitably fail to end slavery without Christianity? In Stowe's view the nation's well-being rested on the spiritual resources that women nurtured privately and expressed, occasionally, in fiction. Moral drama was the norm for women's fiction, but this portrayal of struggle over principles, favorably depicting the involvement of women in questions of politics and race, was exceptional.

Stowe's criticism of society and aesthetics, though real and forceful, was limited in the end. She questioned neither evangelical Protestantism in itself nor free-labor capitalism, only the divorce between them. Nor did she have second thoughts about whether prose fiction ought to function as moral allegory. On all levels, the ability of *Uncle Tom's Cabin* to stir opposition to or defense of slavery grew from the novel's precarious balance between respectability and protest.

Nathaniel Hawthorne's *The Scarlet Letter* similarly began with ideas familiar to antebellum readers and moved toward searching questions about gender and family, on the one hand, and the moral consequences of creating symbols, on the other. As a novel about New England's Puritan history, the book conformed to the conventions of historical fiction. Hawthorne tried to give his narrative the texture of truth by claiming to have found a manuscript about Hester Prynne in the attic of the Salem Custom House. He tacitly asked his readers, too, to use their knowledge of history when he alluded to the seventeenth-century antinominan martyr, Ann Hutchinson, in the novel's opening pages.[106] Perhaps Hawthorne wished his audience to compare Hester's unlawful passion to Hutchinson's heterodox religious ideas. Certainly the suppressed and tortured guilt of Hester's lover, Arthur Dimmesdale, resembled the theological complicity of the Reverend John Cotton with Hutchinson's radical Puritanism in the 1630s.[107] Hawthorne may have placed the historical controversy centering on Hutchinson in the background to reinforce his own theme—the psychology and costs of rebelliousness. Indeed, beneath Hawthorne's careful adherence to the mores of Puritan times was a series of symbolic meanings. Although the novel is less precisely allegorical than *Uncle Tom's Cabin*, Hawthorne still wished readers to approach his book as moral drama: the luxuriant, artistic nature of Hester struggles with the cold, mechanistic temperament of Roger Chillingworth for influence over the delicate spirituality of Dimmesdale, all against the background of a society so conventional as to seem incapable to have produced such characters.[108]

The Scarlet Letter was more than an intricate example of standard historical fiction, however. Hawthorne's quiet skepticism about his culture's too easily accepted faiths raised open-ended questions. Consider the way Hawthorne wondered about domesticity and symbolism—a set of values and a method, respectively, that were central to the thinking of antebellum Americans. In one sense, *The Scarlet Letter* was simply a domestic novel, with domesticity gone tragically awry. Suppose women's feelings did not incline them naturally to peaceful family life, Hawthorne seemed to ask, but were wild and free as the woods outside Hester's Boston and hence created conflict instead of harmony. Hawthorne entertained the disturbing thought that human nature was far less predictable than the cult of domesticity assumed. He asked if middle-class society's romanticized social vision, which depended on women's inherent purity, might not need to be redrawn to include sexuality, repression, guilt, and sadness. In a world that contained such involuntary limitations, perhaps language no longer bodied forth meaning in flowing allegories but distorted intended significance and imperfectly communicated one person's idea to another. This is the effect of the symbolic "A" that Hester wears by order of the Puritan court. When she puts the letter back on her dress in the forest after a clandestine meeting with Dimmesdale, it works "a withering spell" that eclipses the "richness of her womanhood."[109] As the author of many stories, Hawthorne had created symbols whose sense, even if not transparent, was not altogether obscure. Now, in his first novel, he circled back to the suspicion voiced in "Young Goodman Brown" about the credibility of the Devil's words.

Hawthorne did not despair, however, about the possibilities of self-expression and human interaction. Although his narrator professes uncertainty about the future of Pearl, Hester's illegitimate child, he thinks she marries a man of means in Europe.[110] Some society, even if not Puritan Boston, could understand Pearl's passionate vibrancy. In the next generation, Hester's sad fate might be reversed. Thus the appeal and depth of *The Scarlet Letter* lay in its combination of questioning and, in a soberer spirit than many of Hawthorne's contemporaries, hope. Hawthorne drew readers toward unsettling views by manipulating the genre of historical fiction.

Herman Melville (1819–91) worried about the same issues—the reliability of symbols and the humanity of American society—in *Moby-Dick*, a novel he dedicated to Hawthorne. Melville began with well-established modes of expression. Indeed, he took his contemporaries' fascinations with facts and their significance to unconventional lengths. This was a tale of a whaling voyage, and time and again Melville interrupted the plot with chapters of information about whales: biological classifications of whales, fossils of whales, pictures of whales, foods made from whales. He even began his book with a long series of quotations about whales, extending from the Book of Genesis ("And God created great whales") to a popular Nantucket song. Although he poked fun at his encyclopedic mind-set by calling the extracts the contribution of a "sub-sub librarian," it seems clear that Melville was aroused by the wealth of information available in the intellectual marketplace of his cosmopolitan culture.[111]

Like his contemporaries, Melville wondered about the meaning of so many facts. Far more unconventionally, he was finally unsure that symbols signified anything at all. In *Moby-Dick*, human beings (the crew of the whaling ship *Pequod*) were clearly pitted against nature (the whale "Moby Dick") in a struggle to achieve understanding and control. Yet even while creating this allusive narrative, Melville speculated that people form their own unique perceptions of things. Captain Ahab sees Moby Dick as the personification of malice, but no other crew member shares his view of the whale.[112] Melville even approached the thought that nature contains no inherent message but simply stimulates a variety of human reflections. This was a radical view in a Christian culture that normally considered the material world an embodiment of God's design. Is the white color of Moby Dick, Melville asked apprehensively, "not so much a color as the visible absence of color, and at the same time the concrete of all colors; is it for these reasons that there is such a dumb blankness, full of meaning, in a wide landscape of snow—a colorless, all-color of atheism from which we shrink?"[113] Probably only an author deeply in touch with his society's habit of finding imperceptible ideas behind visible facts—the hand of God in creation—could have thought through the implications of this common outlook to the point of doubting its validity. In this sense Melville was much less a prescient skeptic than a man of his time.

Indeed, *Moby-Dick* was not simply a book about metaphysics but also a commentary on Melville's society. Much as Stowe explored the dilemma of slavery and Hawthorne questioned prevailing beliefs about gender, Melville worried about the social and moral consequences of the nation's enterprising spirit. Men cooped up all week in Manhattan offices, Melville began, "tied to counters, nailed to benches, clinched to desks," spend the sabbath gazing out at the sea in "ocean reveries."[114] The sea lures these white-collar captives with the prospect of a tranquility born of the cessation of ambition. Yet when Ishmael, Melville's narrator, signs on to go whaling to cure the "drizzly November in my soul," it is not clear if he and his shipmates escape modernity's self-created restraints or act out, with nightmarish exaggeration, the obsessions of driven men. The sea is a strange blend of liberating dreams growing out of a metaphysical mood and enterprise stripped of civilized manners, and it is populated by a wide variety of men. The South Seas islander Queequeg, the American Indian Tashtego, black Dagoo, Nantucket Quakers, and the rootless captain, Ahab, all crowd on the *Pequod* as a microcosm of Melville's America.

Was the nation's quest, beneath so much talk of improvement and progress, no better than Ishmael's nighttime vision of the "rushing Pequod, freighted with savages, and laden with fire, and burning a [whale's] corpse, and plunging into that blackness of darkness, [which] seemed the material counterpart of her monomaniac commander's soul"?[115] What could these men learn from the unexpected circle of "enchanted calm" they encounter at sea, where "nursing mothers of the whales" spiritually nourish their young on "some unearthly reminiscence"?[116] Melville examined the key dichotomies of pre–Civil War culture: enterprise and domesticity, masculine and feminine, head and heart. When Ishmael alone survives the final contest with Moby Dick, he is buoyed by the coffin made by his homely companion, Queequeg, until another ship, the *Rachel*, picks him up as she searches for her lost children. Human feeling saves Ishmael. But the heart still could not satisfy the unsettling curiosity and desire for possession that Melville identified with Ahab's mind, and the result is nearly wholesale destruction. Like his friend Nathaniel Hawthorne, Melville doubted that the supposed balance between public entrepreneurship and private domesticity, so often praised by their contemporaries, could really be achieved.

Whereas *Moby-Dick* had the expansive quality of a mythic quest (though with critical anti-mythic intentions), *Walden* unfolded as a one-man pastoral in a miniaturist framework. Henry David Thoreau told about his experience living alone for two years near Walden Pond, outside Concord, Massachusetts. Without a full cast of characters, an ordinary plot, or an obvious interest in national issues, *Walden* might well seem an unlikely choice as a major text of the American Renaissance. But even on the level of style, Thoreau's narrative was an elegant example of one genre of contemporary writing, the essay. Professing self-consciousness about the "egotism" of speaking throughout his book as "I," Thoreau turned his use of the first-person voice into a sign of sincerity: "I should not talk so much about myself if there were any body [*sic*] else whom I knew as well."[117] The reader never learns as much about the external facts of the speaker's life as about his sensations and thoughts. This is a man who, after building his cabin, listens to the whistle of a train in the woods, studies his growing beans, and watches a battle between red and black ants.[118] It was this voice that Thoreau's audience was asked to trust and follow from his meticulous record of particular details to his general conclusions.

Walden was not in fact a microscopic study of one man's views but a searching jeremiad on the spiritual costs of modernization. In this sense Thoreau's questions were similar to Melville's, though less expansively stated. Anyone who has ever felt harried by pressures toward status-seeking, consumerism, and haste will appreciate the poignancy of Thoreau's social criticism:

> The mass of men lead lives of quiet desperation. What is called resignation is confirmed desperation. From the desperate city you go into the desperate country, and have to console yourself with the bravery of minks and muskrats. . . . When we consider what, to use the words of the catechism, is the chief end of man, and what are the true necessaries and means of life, it appears as if men had deliberately chosen the common mode of living because they preferred it to any other. Yet they honestly think there is no choice left.[119]

By exposing the fetishes of his countrypeople for fashions, news, and inventions, all of them "improved means to an unimproved end," Thoreau asked his readers to rethink their goals—indeed, to realize most basically that they were free to choose them.[120] This was the example he meant to set: "I went to the woods because I wished to live deliberately, to front only the essential facts of life, and see if I could not learn what it had to teach, and not, when I came to die, discover that I had not lived."[121] Satisfying his needs for shelter, clothing, and food with studied economy, Thoreau advanced "in the direction of his dreams," observing nature, entertaining guests, and simply thinking.[122]

Perhaps Thoreau saw from the start that his success depended not only on making his life a symbol of self-reform but on transforming his actions into a literary text capable of inspiring others. Thoreau labored from the time of his return to Concord in 1847 until the publication of *Walden* in 1854 to make the particular incidents of his experience into symbolic steps in an odyssey past the "invisible boundary" of common life toward "new, universal, and more liberal laws."[123] Every one of his observations drew him toward deeper reflections. The train's whistle impels him to consider the encroachment of civilization, his bean field spurs him to contemplate the care needed to harvest superior men, and the ant war brings him around to thoughts of hostility among races of men. Creating this densely allusive narrative, Thoreau seemed suspended between Emerson's faith that nature was a series of readable symbols and Melville's suspicion that the writer arbitrarily attached meanings to facts. Compounding this ambivalence about the source of values, Thoreau sensed that he had to make his "I" narrator, inevitably afflicted in a mass society by anonymity and insignificance, into a voice convincing enough to carry his point of view. Perhaps these very challenges made Thoreau work with special care and even exhilaration in a literary medium that depended on resonance of voice. The first-person speaker of *Walden*, more affectingly than the "I" of most other antebellum essays, offered readers one person's observations as an avenue to usable principles.

Thus Thoreau, along with Stowe, Hawthorne, and Melville, raised essential social questions in forms of expression familiar to their contemporaries. Together, these authors addressed an impressive range of issues: slavery, domesticity, capitalist enterprise, and middle-class values. They worked within the prevailing mind-set of yoking realism to searching curiosity about the significance latent in facts. More than most writers, however, they wondered about the possibilities and limitations of their tools of expression. Could domestic fiction serve as a political weapon? What if language obscured human intentions? What if words capriciously ascribed meaning to things, and people had to decipher a variety of competing usages? Could a solitary person create a set of symbols from his (or her) single experience that made sense to others? The way these writers explored and stretched the terms of contemporary thinking shows that there was considerable room for experimentation within the antebellum intellectual community. Still, it is important to ask if there were boundaries in the era's artistic life. Suppose all of the intellectual habits so far described were unique to major writers and consumers of their works, the "reading public," who in social terms belonged primarily to the white, Protestant middle class. Perhaps racial, ethnic, and other minorities talked about the world in other ways. The next chapter measures the distance between the dominant artistic culture and minority speakers. Yet these categories were not mutually exclusive. Writers who belonged to social minorities participated in the literary marketplace and shared many prevailing ideas and styles. Indeed, Frederick Douglass's *Narrative of the Life of Frederick Douglass* may well be judged a masterwork of the American Renaissance.

Douglass's *Narrative*, published in 1845, has riveted generations of readers by its stark and brutal simplicity. In an unembellished "I" narrative, Douglass told his own story. Born in Maryland to a slave mother and an unidentified white father, Douglass's life in slavery consisted of uncertainty, lack of self-determination, separation from kin, physical cruelty, and, on his part, determined struggle for freedom.[124] No less than *Walden* or any classic text of the period, the *Narrative* led readers from these historical facts to their underlying connotations. Among many symbols, Douglass made his uncertainty about his birthdate a sign of the slave's enforced lack of identity, his separation from his mother a token of slavery's inhumanity, and his fight with the slaveholder, Covey, the turning point in his struggle for selfhood.[125] Douglass took this symbolic approach because he was a literary craftsman in touch with mainstream perspectives. He spent the years between his escape from slavery in 1838 and the publication of his *Narrative* as an abolitionist lecturer. He hoped now that his book would appeal to white audiences, as well as black readers, through this familiar and provocative allusive mode of speech. More deeply, Douglass was intimately acquainted with black and white Christianity, in the South and in the North, and understood the typological mind-set of traditional religion.[126] As an artist thus attuned to contemporary culture, Douglass made his narrative into a myth of self-initiated liberation.

Douglass was not Thoreau, however, and his account would have achieved far less power had he assimilated a white viewpoint altogether. One key difference between his story and other masterworks of the period was his final impatience with symbols and his slim interest in metaphysics. It is hard to imagine a chapter in Douglass's book such as Thoreau's extended discussion of "Higher Laws." Nor did he choose to contemplate a multifaceted symbol such as the whale, Moby Dick. Douglass deliberately invested the events of his life with a message that gave them an overall coherence: his story represented the fight for freedom of the spirit waged against an institution whose intent was human degradation. Yet Douglass restricted the narrative's allegorical dimension. As a spokesman for a race that was socially as well as spiritually dispossessed, Douglass skirted the temptation to get lost in reflection. He must have respected himself as a thinker to write with such care, but he was far less content to be simply an intellectual than were other major writers. Probably that option did not seem responsible for a former slave in a country that too easily acquiesced in the perpetuation of slavery. Douglass's comparatively flat narrative was a clean instrument to move readers to action.[127]

The differences between dissenting and mainstream culture are important and merit additional discussion. Yet it is also true that all of the intellectuals involved in the flowering of aesthetic expression in the pre–Civil War decades drew support from common cultural possessions. Christianity encouraged a taste for symbolism, democracy endorsed artistic treatment of public subjects, and capitalism harnessed art to the work of addressing social anxieties. The artistic triumphs of the era depended on the vitality of these three popular cultures. More immediately, achievement was possible because of the legitimacy and stability that intellectuals won for cultural activity. Thinkers had articulated rationales for artistry in a democracy, supported one another in communities, and developed genres that facilitated communication with American audiences.

The American Renaissance did not prosper without tensions, however. This was an artistic movement in a capitalist society, and market mechanisms strained relations between intellectuals and audiences. How could a writer develop her talent if she depended on the unsophisticated tastes of a mass audience to make her living? If an artist sought a community of his peers, a kind of buffer for thinkers in a democracy, might he not lose touch with the everyday mores he needed for inspiration? Intellectuals dealt repeatedly with the difficult choices between conformity and freedom, public commitments and professional interests, and making a living and making time for thought. Outside of the white, Protestant mainstream, thinkers who belonged to ethnic and racial minorities faced the additional question of how their efforts would relate to the Anglo-Protestant works that dominated the marketplace. The energy and success of minority intellectuals in addressing this issue further opened American culture to a range of new voices.

five

The Flowering of Minority Cultures

About 1850, at almost the precise moment that the masterworks of the American Renaissance appeared in print, members of America's ethnic and racial minorities began to produce significant bodies of imaginative literature. Irish, Jewish, African, and Native Americans wrote autobiographies, histories, and poetry that self-consciously cast each group's social and moral experience into written forms. Novels, however, were the most popular genre. Mary Anne Sadlier chronicled the life of Irish immigrants in 1850 in her best-selling book, *Willy Burke; or, The Irish Orphan in America*. Rabbi Isaac Mayer Wise, the pioneering leader of Reform Judaism, serialized fiction in his magazine *The Israelite* beginning in 1854. William Wells Brown transformed his widely read narrative of his escape from slavery, issued in 1847, into the preface of a full-length antislavery novel, *Clotel; or, The President's Daughter*, published six years later. John Rollin Ridge, a Cherokee journalist, attacked racial prejudice through his sensational story of 1854, *The Life and Adventures of Joaquín Murieta: The Celebrated California Bandit*.

These works were part of an intellectual renaissance that stood in an intimate yet ambiguous relationship to the artistic achievements of the predominantly white, Anglo-Saxon, and Protestant cultural mainstream. The decision of minority thinkers to issue works in English involved both betrayal and empowerment. In order to claim a place in an intellectual world demarcated by English prose, they moved away either from other European languages and heritages, in the case of Irish and Jewish authors, or from the oral traditions of African and Native Americans. Writing for the mass literary market thus challenged long-established customs of communication within minority communities. Yet linguistic assimilation was also a means to advance a new kind of selfhood in American society. Minority writers were inevitably aware of the intellectual communities, genres, and themes that after 1830 increasingly centered the Victorian mainstream, and they, too, used the available tools of culture to state their points of view. Nonetheless, the power of minority expression grew as much from a troubled impulse to resolve the meaning of cultural differences as from a simple eagerness to adopt new routes to intellectual self-assertion. The literatures of Irish, Jewish, African, and Native Americans defined and often celebrated the distinctiveness of each social group from the Anglo-Protestant majority. But the cost of this achievement was much struggle to come to terms with each people's half-involuntary, half-voluntary marginality. The term "minority" is used throughout this discussion to designate these groups' problematic and often disadvantaged states rather than simply a small segment of the population.

The most important effect of the flowering of dissenting literatures transcended the minority communities themselves. Although these bodies of works grew up in the shadow of Anglo-Protestant letters, their success shifted the balance of cultural power toward greater ideological and artistic pluralism. The voices of ethnic and racial minorities changed the overall shape of antebellum intellectual life.

It has only become possible in the past several decades to analyze the lives and works of minority intellectuals in a comprehensive and satisfactory way. Henry Louis Gates, Jr., tells a story of his discovery of *Our Nig* (1859), a novel by the black writer Harriet Wilson, that underscores how recent our appreciation of minority literature is. Despite Gates's work as a critic of African-American writing, he was unaware of *Our Nig* until he ran into the text in a bookstore in 1981. *Our Nig* is now considered a pioneering black novel—"a seminal contribution to black letters," in Gates's words—and has invited much commentary by literary critics and cultural historians.[1] This account dramatizes the escalating interest in the cultural expression of social minorities.[2] Still, there has been little attention so far to synthetic questions. How did minority expression relate to the imaginative works produced by the white Protestant majority? Did the efforts of intellectuals of one minority group affect the cultural activities of other writers in similar situations? Did minority thinkers evolve a distinctive artistic vision?

This chapter explores such comparisons and emphasizes three themes that help to establish connections between minority and mainstream cultures. First, intellectuals who belonged to ethnic and racial minorities were tied more closely to their communities than were the significant number of white Protestant thinkers who had begun to see themselves as writers or artists, disengaged from specific civic roles. Freedom and creativity were less important to minority writers, in other words, than were social responsibility and advocacy. Second, minorities often expressed themselves in genres similar to those current in the mainstream. Yet they used popular forms to answer questions of social identity more than to resolve philosophical meanings. Irish Catholics and Jews wrote histories, and blacks and Indians extended first-person narratives into full autobiographies. In neither case, however, was the principal concern the relationship of visible facts to informing ideas but the comparatively down-to-earth issue of who the subjects of the texts were as people. Third, minority writers commonly shared systems of ideas with the majority culture and spoke in terms associated with Christianity, democracy, and capitalism. Yet not surprisingly, they criticized prevailing intepretations, pointing to the hypocrisy implicit in the distance between mainstream ideals and practice, and restated these values in ways that advanced the interests of their particular ethnic or racial group. All three of these generalizations suggest that minority intellectuals were in close communication with white Protestant culture. Relations, however, were marked by tension. Both sides shared an orientation recognizably "American," though precisely what that meant shifted repeatedly in the course of continuing debate.

Writing in English

Antebellum minority literatures can seem deceptively familiar to twentieth-century readers. It is easy to choose a pair of novels—one written by a minority author and the other by a white Protestant man—and find similarities perhaps attributable to their common cultural milieu. The heroine of *Our Nig*, a black girl named Alfrado, resembled Hester Prynne of *The Scarlet Letter*, for example, because both women were misunderstood, oppressed by prevailing mores, and socially marginalized. In what appears to have been a like frame of mind, Harriet Wilson and Nathaniel Hawthorne created female characters who dramatized the victimization possible when prejudice was the acceptable norm.[3] Yet it would be surprising if these novels of the 1850s—produced, respectively, by a poor black New Hampshire woman and a college-educated popular author—were not also different. The very act of using written language must not have had the same emotional impact and social intent for black writers, who struggled to overcome illiteracy enforced by bigotry and law in an effort to promote reform, as it did for a man thoroughly intimate with prose in a relatively secure private and professional life. Modern readers must approach mid-nineteenth-century minority writing with a cautious sense of the distinctiveness of this body of works. Specific accounts of Irish, Jewish, African-American, and Native-American expression may helpfully be prefaced with comments on the signficance of writing for minority intellectuals, their self-image as authors, and the social composition of their audiences.

The titles of autobiographies by African Americans and Native Americans commonly included the phrase "Written by Himself." On the surface the words gave each narrative a seal of authenticity. More deeply, they called attention to the special meaning that writing had for these minority groups. It would be hard to underestimate the intellectual and emotional importance that writing had for subordinate peoples in a highly literate society. Henry

Louis Gates, Jr., does not exaggerate when he says that fugitive slaves, deemed "things" by federal law, used autobiographies to *"write themselves into being,"* performing "an act of self-creation through the mastery of language."[4] Native-American cultures lacked alphabets and hence texts, and Indians who produced autobiographies did so in a spirit of asserting selfhood similar to that of blacks. George Copway of the Ojibwa tribe vigorously condemned whites' virtual theft of Indian lands in his autobiographical narrative, *The Life, History, and Travels of Kah-Ge-Ga-Gah-Bowh* (1847). Yet he sadly conceded the diminished power of traditional Indian society, and he looked instead to "the Gospel and to education as my only hope" for his people.[5] Copway placed his faith in literacy, along with the Christian message, as an instrument for Native Americans to achieve parity with Americans of European background.

Copway understood, however, that writing involved loss as well as gain for Indian authors. Written prose could not reproduce and thus preserve the intricate oral traditions of Native Americans. Gesture and intonation were essential parts of oral performances, so that "the act of speaking," in the words of one scholar, was "creative and not merely descriptive, sacred."[6] Early Indian authors did not even try to transcribe oral narratives, perhaps because of their sense of the impossibility of the task. Instead, they gravitated toward literary forms comprehensible to white audiences. The autobiographies produced by antebellum Indians and blacks belonged to a highly conventionalized, and in that sense restrictive, genre. Minority autobiographies contained such standardized elements as an opening account of the author's birth and a testimony about how he or she became literate. Authenticating documents, usually letters by white sponsors attesting to the author's truthfulness and character, framed the writer's narrative. Beyond formal structure, the English words themselves could distort the speaker's voice. George Copway swore in "A Word to the Reader" that the friend who helped him with style made only small revisions. But some sentences recast facts in suspiciously ornate prose: "I poised my gun and fired; hearing no noise, I concluded my game was sure."[7] In sum, adopting English prose offered a realistic means for peoples with exclusively oral traditions to create cultural identities in antebellum America, but the compromises were also clear.

For transplanted Europeans of Jewish or Catholic background, the challenge was posed not by writing itself but by writing in English. Consider the decision in favor of acculturation implicit in the production of English texts by Isaac Mayer Wise (1819–1900), the most influential American Reform rabbi of the nineteenth century. Educated primarily in Prague, at the time a part of Bohemia, Wise read and wrote Hebrew, Yiddish, Czech, German, Latin, and Greek when he arrived in New York in 1846. By the early 1850s, however, Wise began a long and fertile career of publication in English, including one journal that he edited, *The Israelite* (established in 1854), as well as works of history, fiction, and theology. Wise did not turn away altogether from the languages of his childhood and scholarly training, founding a German-language

Isaac Mayer Wise in 1854. *American Jewish Archives, Hebrew Union College–Jewish Institute of Religion, Cincinnati.*

weekly called *Die Deborah*, for example, in 1855. Yet the principal thrust of his initiative was to construct a cultural identity for American Jews in English, thereby obscuring perhaps divisive customs of their varied European pasts for the sake of asserting a united Jewish presence in Victorian society.[8]

Later in the century, the retention of European languages became a far more passionately contested issue, a development that underscores the intimate connection between forms of expression and deep-seated questions about ethnicity. Increasing diversity within both the Catholic and Jewish communities fueled controversy. The hegemony of Irish Catholics, many of whose cultural leaders published works in English before they left Ireland, was bitterly challenged after 1880 by recent German-Catholic immigrants who wished to use German in their churches, schools, and writings. Among Jewish Americans, the desire for accommodation of progressive Ashkenazic (northern European) Jews such as Wise, in conjunction with the continuing influence of the small and assimilated Sephardic (Iberian) Jewish communities of the Atlantic coastal cities, were contested by the massive immigration of more traditional Ashkenazic Jews from lands between Germany and Russia, who were united by spoken Yiddish and who brought Yiddish literature to America. These internal debates among Catholics and Jews at the turn of the twentieth century might have been predicted by an observer of pre–Civil War ethnic writers. Despite the movements toward Americanization of Isaac Mayer Wise and his Irish Catholic contemporaries, English was no more a value-free tool for mid-century ethnic writers than it was for African and Native Americans. It was perhaps only a matter of time before conservative immigrants took the assimilationists to task for their concessions to Anglo-Protestant culture.[9]

One final word may be said about the mixed burden and promise of writing in English for intellectuals who belonged to racial and ethnic minorities. These communities, often lacking effective institutions because of their recent formation or the restrictions imposed by the white Protestant majority, relied to an unusual extent on written communication for a sense of coherence. What Jay Dolan has said of Catholics in early nineteenth-century America was generally true for all marginal groups: "Many Catholics lived in towns or villages devoid of clergy and church, and thus religion necessarily became a very domestic and private affair, with the book as the focal point."[10] The effectiveness of writing and reading as a source of shared commitments depended on literacy. By the 1850s there were Catholic and Jewish middle classes who were sufficiently educated to sustain an exchange of ideas and to provide cultural leadership.[11] Communities of free blacks and Native Americans, less literate overall than the ethnic minorities, could not use original works in English by their members to forge a unified perspective to the same degree. Yet the circular influence of authorship and literacy should be kept in mind. The availability of books of special interest to minorities must have induced men and women to learn to read, just as the growth of minority reading publics must have encouraged the efforts of writers. Both producers and consumers of minority texts must have known, most basically, how essential intellectual activity was to their success as peoples. Unable to trust the fairness of churches, schools, and courts of the majority culture or to take the strength of their own institutions for granted, members of cultural minorities turned to language as a key instrument of social advancement.

This was a setting in which authors must have felt a heavy social responsibility, and the communal emphasis of minority beliefs reinforced the pressure of circumstance to make these writers less intent than mainstream thinkers on seeking individual distinction. In the capitalist literary market the acceptable objectives for authors were creativity, recognition, and profits. The competitive ethic encouraged each writer to produce a unique product that appealed to consumers by its inventiveness. Stories circulated in the antebellum decades about Edgar Allan Poe's drunkenness and Nathaniel Hawthorne's reclusiveness. To the extent that these images were myths, they grew from a value system that honored individual—even if unstable and solipsistic—genius.[12] The traditional cultures of antebellum minorities prized selfhood much less. In the oratory of Native Americans, for example, tribal identity overshadowed the importance of individual expression. One critic of this literature explains that "the Indian poet does not consider himself the originator of his material but merely the conveyor," receiving ideas either from his elders or from "a supernatural power," and "Indian poetry, then, is usually attributed not to an individual but to his culture."[13] Early American minority writers must thus be viewed in the context of community-oriented artistry: Indian storytelling in prose and verse, the oral traditions of slavery, the disputatious exchanges of Talmudic scholarship, and the church-centered corporatism of Catholicism. Members of racial and ethnic minorities necessarily acted as individual authors when they wrote in English for the public. But their work was nonetheless rooted in a series of worldviews that held personal effort in less esteem than did Anglo-Protestant culture.

Minority authors in this generation, in sum, probably did not write in the same spirit of independence that motivated the emerging class of white Protestant intellectuals who began to gather between 1830 and 1860 in cities, colleges, and expatriate communities abroad. Creativity was closely connected with advocacy for thinkers such as Isaac Wise, who wrote several inspirational novels about ancient Israel in the 1850s, and Mary Anne Sadlier (1820–1903), the most prolific chronicler in fiction of the Irish experience in America.[14] Not surprisingly, this literature succeeded better at social criticism of Anglo-American culture than at the kind of searching self-criticism occasionally achieved by an individual such as Herman Melville, who, as a man of few loyalties, was willing to look with a skeptical eye on most prevailing beliefs. The point is not to judge the comparative virtues of these two bodies of imaginative writing, however, but simply to explain the authors' diverging purposes.

Communicating with readers also posed special dilemmas for minority intellectuals. Should writers aim their work at members of their own ethnic or racial group, or should they seek a wider readership at the risk of evading their immediate responsibility and encountering prejudice? The problem of audience was most troubling for black writers. First-person stories of escaped slaves contained images of blacks as intelligent, resourceful, and moral, and the authors must have intended, at least in part, to inspire African-American readers with pride in their race. In 1859 Harriet Wilson wrote with a sense of hope that a black audience existed for *Our Nig*: "I sincerely appeal to my colored brethren universally for patronage, hoping they will not condemn this attempt of their sister to be erudite, but rally around me a faithful band of supporters and defenders."[15] Yet realistically, African-American authors knew that the black audience was small, poor, and with insufficient power to work successfully for social reform alone. Rather than aim primarily to energize fellow blacks, writings by and about African Americans sought to enlist the aid of whites. Thus a letter appended to *Our Nig* by Margaretta Thorn, who was apparently white, appealed to the sympathy of readers who "call themselves friends of our dark-skinned brethren."[16] Whether these diverging statements about the anticipated audience of *Our Nig* reflected Wilson's divided mind or signaled her manipulation by white sponsors, it was clear that this literature of advocacy had to carry its message across racial lines.

Black writers were almost inevitably misunderstood in the process. Narratives of fugitive slaves were widely reviewed in northern journals, as increasing numbers of whites became committed to antislavery. White reviewers grasped the stories' basic argument—that slavery was unjust—but they otherwise praised the accounts for qualities that betrayed their own racial bias. The *New Englander* approved Kate Pickard's decision to make no "offensive attempt at fine writing" when, acting as a white amanuensis, she recorded the recollections of two escaped slaves in *The Kidnapped and the Ransomed* (1856). The *Christian Examiner*, published in Boston, seriously evaluated several slave narratives in 1849 but also noted the element of "romance" in the fugitives' escapes.[17] Thus African-American writers faced the difficulty of being heard appreciatively by whites who expected blacks to restrict themselves to simple thoughts and diverting tales. This mixed message from their audience could not have unambiguously encouraged the development of sophisticated black prose.

Probably few antebellum writers, of whatever social background, were lucky enough to find loyal and comprehending readers who encouraged an author's creativity by promising an intelligent reception. Original thinkers in particular often struggled with mass tastes. Still, intellectuals who belonged to racial and ethnic minorities faced additional problems, the most important of which were small reading publics among their peers and the prejudices of mainstream consumers. The creation of minority literatures involved not only obstacles and frustration, however, but excitement and the prospect of cultural power. As Irish, Jewish, African, and Native Americans stood suspended between traditional cultures and a mainstream worldview defined by written English, they must have been enlivened by the challenge of turning the English language to their own purposes, thereby creating a distinctive place for themselves in a more heterogeneous intellectual milieu.

Ethnic Literatures in America

Just as the artistic renaissance of the white Protestant mainstream flourished because of the vitality of intellectual communities, Jews and Irish Catholics in antebellum America began to create original literatures as their respective social identities were strengthened. Each group's sense of peoplehood grew primarily from shared religion but also from common customs and, for the Irish, a homeland that distinguished them from other Catholics. More deeply, the influences of ethnic societies and literatures were reciprocal. Growing communities nurtured creativity at the same time that works articulating what it was like to be Irish or Jewish in America reinforced social bonds. In all, the successful use of English for ethnic writing depended on three circumstances: the contact of ethnic minorities with the Anglo-Protestant mainstream, an accented sense of their differences, and effective cultural leadership.

American Jewish communities in 1830 were balanced between autonomy and acculturation, a situation highly favorable to their participation in the broad-based national movement to expand the cultural marketplace. Nearly all Jewish Americans lived in coastal cities where the Jewish population numbered, at most, several hundred. German-Jewish immigrants to America joined established Sephardic families throughout the antebellum decades, and the members of the communities overall were well educated and prosperous. The papers of two influential women, Rebecca Gratz of Philadelphia and Penina Moïse (1797–1880) of Charleston, suggest both the familiarity of sophisticated Jewish Americans with Anglo-Protestant letters and yet their commitment to a separate cultural identity. Gratz straddled the worlds of Christian and Jewish benevolence as a founding and sustaining member of the Philadelphia Orphan Society, a predominantly Christian charity established in 1815, and the Hebrew Sunday School Society, the first in the United States, begun in connection with Congregation Mikveh Israel in 1838.[18] Authors mentioned by Gratz in her correspondence with her large family (she had 11 brothers and sisters) show that she kept up with current literary tastes. In letters in the early 1830s to her sister-in-law, Maria, of Lexington, Kentucky, Gratz spoke of books by best-selling Protestant authors.[19] Penina Moïse, a poet who began her public career when she issued *Fancy's Sketch Book* in 1833, was similarly in touch with Protestant letters as well as Jewish culture. Her poems appeared, for example, in both *Godey's Lady's Book* and *The Occident*, a periodical edited by Isaac Leeser, the rabbi of Philadelphia's Mikveh Israel.[20] In the poem "An Alphabet of Authors," written as an exercise for the girls enrolled in her niece's school in Charleston, Moïse connected the 26 English letters with such names as Addison, Boswell, and Dickens.[21] Moïse clearly felt intimately linked with the great writers of British and Continental literature. Both the reading and writing of Rebecca Gratz and Penina Moïse indicate that these Jewish women identified, to a significant extent, with works associated with the Christian cultural tradition.

The comfort of Gratz and Moïse in a preeminently Christian society did not lessen their attachment to Judaism, however, but stood side by side with a parallel commitment to beliefs that made them different. When a neighbor tried to convert Rebecca Gratz in 1834, she stood firm in her faith. "Thank God I have the law & the prophets," she wrote to Maria, "and am willing to hear them."[22] Similarly, although she was on intimate terms with the successive Gentile wives of her brother, Benjamin, first Maria and then Ann, Rebecca herself remained single, it was said, to avoid intermarriage, a strong temptation given the small numbers of eligible Jewish men.[23] Her letters to her sisters-in-law were filled with patient explanations of Jewish observances that had meaning for Rebecca but that she did not try to force on her correspondents. On the eve of Yom Kippur, "the day of Atonement," in 1833, she told Maria that "'tho I believe the Eye of God is upon us every day with the same unerring judgment—the same pardoning Mercy—it is well when we search our own hearts, and desire to acknowledge our sins."[24]

In Charleston, Penina Moïse likewise chose spinsterhood over intermarriage and in her writing honored Jewish themes. She composed nearly 200 hymns for use in Jewish worship and wrote poems that chronicled contemporary Jewish events, including "The Rejection of the Jew Bill, By the House of Lords," "Lines, on Beholding the New Synagogue, 1840," and "Lines, on the Persecution of the Jews of Damascus."[25] The quality of doubleness in the characters of Gratz and Moïse—their Christian-tinged Americanness and their persistent Jewishness—was the cultural foundation on which Jewish literature in antebellum America emerged. Jewish prose and poetry were works of opposition but not of alienation. They reflected the subtle mixture of cosmopolitanism and traditionalism in the Jewish community.

These promising intellectual conditions required a catalyst to change Jewish-American self-awareness into more active production of ethnic writings. In the decades after 1830 rabbis were the moving force. Isaac Leeser (1806–68), born in Germany, and Isaac Mayer Wise were principal figures. Although in liturgical matters Leeser favored orthodox practices, in contrast to Wise who welcomed reforms, in the sphere of literature both encouraged the creation of Jewish texts suitable to American circumstances. During his tenure as the religious leader of Congregation Mikveh Israel in Philadelphia from 1829 to 1850, Leeser laid essential groundwork for Jewish thought by improving education and communications. He translated or wrote catechisms and prayer books, edited the monthly magazine *The Occident, and American Jewish Advocate* beginning in 1843, helped to establish the American Jewish Publication Society in 1845, and recruited book agents and rabbis to distribute Jewish texts because there was no established network of Jewish publishers.[26]

Isaac Wise broadened the content of American Jewish writing in the 1850s from the religious themes that occupied Leeser to more inclusive ethnic issues. When Wise moved from Albany to Cincinnati in 1854 to become rabbi of Congregation B'nai Yeshurun, he wrote or translated novels for his new periodical, *The Israelite*. With titles such as *The Jewish Heroine* (1854) and *The First of the Maccabees* (1860), Wise's fiction commonly combined Jewish history and romantic literary conventions to create engaging images of an idealized Jewish identity. After the Civil War Wise turned away from didactic stories for a popular audience and instead concentrated on theological and ethical subjects, probably a more appropriate intellectual outlet for a pioneering thinker.[27] In sum, although nineteenth-century rabbis did not produce a diverse Jewish-American literature on their own, they articulated goals and established means for ethnic expression in their role as community leaders. Arriving in antebellum Jewish enclaves where people were ready to appreciate imaginative writing, the rabbis lit the spark of a cultural movement.

Irish-American writers similarly produced a body of literature, yet only by overcoming obstacles not encountered by Jewish thinkers. Although the Irish were the largest group of Catholics in antebellum America, they were not the only community that wished to interpret Catholicism. They competed most directly with a small but articulate Anglo-Saxon Catholic minority composed of recent Protestant converts to Catholicism, who, on the whole, advocated the rapid assimilation of immigrants in a church that blended Roman doctrines and American mores. Orestes Brownson, who aimed to have a determining voice in defining American Catholicism after his conversion in 1844, approved neither of the Irish nor of works of fiction. "I do not like in general our Irish population," Brownson wrote to Isaac Hecker, another convert, in 1845.[28] Nor could *Brownson's Quarterly Review* be expected to support Irish-American imaginative writing when Brownson, its editor, commented in a review that "we set our face against all novels."[29] Irish Americans thus had to contend for cultural space with largely unsympathizing Yankee Catholics. In addition, the Catholic clergy was wary of writings whose purpose was not strictly devotional. They declined throughout the nineteenth century to sponsor either a Catholic publishing house or a Catholic publication society. Only in the last years of the century did church leaders overcome long-standing anxieties that fiction might secularize and individualize doctrine and instead sanction the use of literature as a didactic tool.[30] Most members of the American priesthood were of Irish background, but they declined to exercise the cultural influence that the rabbis had in the Jewish community. Irish-American intellectuals who wished to explore ethnic values could not count on the church for leadership.

The means of self-expression were provided to Irish Americans by Irish publishers who not only issued books but made their social presence felt as supporters of Catholic organizations. Mathew Carey (1760–1839) of Philadelphia, a man of multiple literary and reform commitments, was a model for the growing numbers of Irish-American publishers who flourished after 1830, among them Patrick Donahoe of Boston, John Kenedy of New York, and Denis and James Sadlier of New York and Montreal. The efforts of

Patrick Donahoe (1810–1901) epitomized the way these literary entrepreneurs helped to shape Irish-American culture. Born in Ireland, Donahoe was 19 years old when he began his first periodical in Boston, the *Jesuit; or, Catholic Sentinel*. In 1836 he established his influential journal, the *Boston Pilot*, which, together with his book-publishing business, provided a forum for Irish-American writers such as Anna Dorsey, Thomas D'Arcy McGee, John Boyce O'Reilly, and Louise Guiney. Nearly as important for Irish-Catholic self-awareness, Donahoe participated in public causes involving benevolence, religion, and civic affairs. He founded an immigrant aid service, contributed to the American College in Rome to train American priests, and recruited Irish troops for the Union army.[31] The ethnic culture grounded in the initiatives of Donahoe, along with the approximately 60 other Catholic book publishers who were active in the republic before 1850, was more lay-centered and market-oriented than were the literary activities of the Jewish community. Like Jewish cultural leaders, however, Irish-American publishers effectively opened avenues for ethnic expression.

These publishers were not necessarily intellectuals themselves, at least in the sense of being producers of texts or art. The success of Irish-American letters depended on thinkers who were able to voice a minority perspective because they stood on a margin between mainstream and immigrant societies. The best Irish-American writers borrowed from the strengths of Protestant culture at the same time that they designed their work to answer its weaknesses. John Gilmary Shea (1824–92), who has been called the "father of American Catholic history," was familiar with the conventions of antebellum Protestant historical writing and yet applied prevailing methods to the task of chronicling Catholic achievements. Born in New York City, Shea was the son of an instructor in English at Columbia College. Perhaps his middle-class background and superior education won Shea acceptance by Protestant historians, including his friend, Jared Sparks, one of several presidents of Harvard in the 1850s. Shea was elected to the New-York Historical Society in 1846 and earned his living during most of his career as an editor of Protestant magazines such as Frank Leslie's *Popular Monthly*.[32] Nonetheless, being Catholic anchored Shea's identity. Between 1848 and 1852 he studied for the Jesuit priesthood, and although he left the order before his ordination, his most memorable books as a layman dealt with Catholic subjects. Shea wrote Catholics into the history of western expansion in his first major work, *Catholic Missions among the Indian Tribes of the United States* (1855). "The American Catholic missions are unparalleled," he explained in a tone of high moral drama, "for heroic self-devotedness, energy of purpose, purity of motive, or holiness of design."[33] Indeed, they were far more effective than Protestant missions that were "purely individual; . . . isolated and unsupported," and "necessarily evanescent."[34] In sum, Shea combined professional expertise and a dissenting religious commitment, making his work a critical commentary on Protestant assumptions.

He was an effective minority spokesman because he was sufficiently familiar with conventional scholarship to define the Catholic position in relation to mainstream thinking.

Essential social conditions for the development of ethnic literatures thus existed among Jewish and Irish Americans after 1830: communities ready to enter into dialogue with a wider public and intellectual leaders eager to articulate ethnic viewpoints. A comparison of the content of writings by minority authors with the themes that preoccupied Protestant culture is also important. Did Jewish and Irish thinkers, like Protestant intellectuals, dwell on the relationship of facts and meanings, a question that seemed to be posed by the challenge of coming to terms with unprecedented quantities of information available for exchange in the intellectual marketplace? Or did antebellum Jews and Irish Catholics approach their literature in a different frame of mind?

Intellectuals who belonged to ethnic minorities resembled their Protestant peers in their taste for texts that joined facts, realistically presented, to informing ideas. But they also brought to their writing a unique emphasis on corporate identity. Isaac Wise's novel, *The First of the Maccabees*, and John Shea's history, *Catholic Missions among the Indian Tribes of the United States*, may illustrate these points of comparison and contrast. Both books were works of history and thus part of the fascination with the past widespread among antebellum Americans. Both, too, used historical details to convey moral messages. Wise's novel recast the history behind the Jewish festival of Chanukah in fictional form. He wove a love story between minor characters through the standard account of how the hero, Judah Maccabee, overthrew the Syrian conqueror in 165 B.C.E. to restore the Temple in Jerusalem to Jewish worship. As a text closely linked to Jewish tradition and ritual, *The First of the Maccabees* summoned Jewish readers to reflect on ideas near the heart of their religion: the meaning of persecution and the duty to struggle for freedom.[35]

John Shea similarly intended that his *Catholic Missions among the Indian Tribes* not be read dispassionately but in a spirit of awe and rededication consistent with its underlying theme: "The discovery of America, like every other event in the history of the world, had, in the designs of God, the great object of the salvation of mankind."[36] Although he acknowledged that neither the American missionaries nor their converts were officially sanctified by the Catholic church, he nonetheless felt the presence of the "supernatural" in this history and prepared his readers for his use of terms "implying sanctity, martyrdom, or the like."[37] This was a history of heroes of faith, designed to instill in readers renewed loyalty to their religion.

Like contemporary Protestant historians, ranging from authors of panoramic narratives such as William Prescott to a miniaturist such as Nathaniel Hawthorne, Wise and Shea chronicled events heavily weighted with moral overtones. Just as clearly, however, neither of the ethnic authors wrote an as individual voice for an undefined audience. The corporate framework of minority history distinguished these works from mainstream accounts. Wise and Shea wrote as self-conscious spokesmen for particular social groups. Jews and Catholics, respectively, would be each one's principal readers, and the collective achievements of each social body would be the writer's main theme. Certainly antebellum Protestant historians did not see their subjects with objectivity and disinterest. Even so, their work generally lacked the deliberate social purposes that motivated Isaac Wise and John Shea.

Beyond these scholarly efforts to define ethnic identity, popular writers in touch with a broader audience wrote fiction that contained the archetypal story of immigrant life, the threats and seductions that American culture posed to traditional customs. These narratives about coming to America incorporated themes that were standard in Western literature: the loss of innocence through experience, the metaphor of a journey as a sign of inner growth, and, with special meaning in an expanding market society, the dangers of cities to the characters of young people who had recently arrived from the country. Yet new issues also appeared that were specifically related to immigration to America. Ethnic authors warned readers of the challenge of Protestantism to inherited religions and, more insidious, of the spiritual corrosion effected by the immigrant's own desire for material success. Mary Anne Madden Sadlier, who married the publisher James Sadlier in 1846, played a leading role in establishing the immigrant Catholic novel as an American genre in the 1850s. Born in Ireland, Sadlier was sufficiently well-to-do and educated to publish in English-language magazines before she emigrated to New York in 1844, after her parents' deaths. During 14 years in Montreal, where her husband managed the Canadian branch of the New York publishing house, D. and J. Sadlier, Mary Anne Sadlier wrote numerous stories and novels that blended nostalgia, sentimentalism, and didacticism. Among them were *Willy Burke; or, The Irish Orphan in America* (1850), *New Lights; or, Life in Galway* (1853), and *The Blakes and Flanagans: A Tale Illustrative of Irish Life in the United States* (1855). As an experienced author, a fervent Catholic, and an ambitious woman who was prominent in Catholic social circles after her return to New York in 1860, Sadlier was well prepared to voice the aspirations and tensions of Irish-American life. *Willy Burke*, a book that sold 7,000 copies within weeks of its publication, illustrates the essential qualities of Sadlier's novels.[38]

Willy Burke powerfully drew readers as a myth of Irish trials and triumphs, centering on themes of abandonment, temptation, and redemption. Andy and Briget Burke, the parents of the virtuous protagonist, Willy, both die either during or soon after their family's passage to America. The hazards of Protestant culture then beset their orphaned children. Mr. and Mrs. Watkins, scheming Methodists, "artfully and insidiously" argue that accepting Protestantism is the only sure means to economic success.[39] Mr. Weimer, an employer prejudiced against Catholics, falsely accuses Willy of stealing money. Willy's fellow workers taunt him for saying the Litany of the Blessed

MARY A. SADLIER.

MRS. MARY A. SADLIER was born in Cootehill, County
Cavan, Ireland, where her father, Francis Madden, Esq.,
was a highly respected merchant. Miss Madden began
her literary career by poetical contributions to *La Belle
Assemblée*, a London Magazine. Shortly after her emigration to America, Miss Madden was married to Mr. James
Sadlier, the publisher. From this time forth, she embarked
upon a literary career which lasted with but little interrup-
tion for almost half a century. She edited for some years
the *New York Tablet*, being fortunate in such co-laborers

This photograph of Mary Anne Sadlier appeared in *A Round Table of Representative
American Catholic Novelists* (New York, 1897). *Courtesy of the Archives of the University of
Notre Dame, Notre Dame, Indiana.*

Virgin. At the same time, Willy's ambitious brother, Peter, nearly becomes a Protestant because of his greed for advancement, and his sisters risk being sent to live with Protestant ladies instead of learning honest trades.[40]

With miraculous swiftness, however, Sadlier transformed this narrative of Irish vulnerability into a story of Catholic success, both spiritual and temporal. Mr. Weimer converts to Catholicism on his deathbed, leaving $5,000 and his business to Willy and the rest of his fortune to the bishop of New York. Rather than, with Protestant selfishness, keep this windfall for himself, Willy goes into business with Peter and his new brother-in-law, another American convert to Catholicism.[41] With helpful Irish neighbors and kind priests in the background, *Willy Burke* affirmed values of piety, family, community, and, as a reward for faithfulness to those ideals, economic mobility. *Willy Burke* was not a simple apology for status-seeking. Sadlier's plot hinged on Weimar's conversion, making the novel every bit as much an evangelical celebration of Catholicism's spiritual power as a recipe for worldly comfort. It was probably the novel's blend of Catholic piety, Irish pride, and cautious approval of American opportunities that determined its appeal to Irish Americans.

Willy Burke epitomized the ambivalent embrace and rejection of Anglo-Protestant values that supplied the fertile force behind the development of antebellum ethnic cultures. Much as mainstream society was anchored by an adherence to Protestantism, democracy, and capitalism, Jewish and Irish-Catholic spokesmen praised religious observance, defended their right to freedom, and outlined the acceptable terms of success for their communities. Yet along with these kindred priorities, ethnic writers felt imperiled, like Willy and his orphaned siblings, and they used their writing to reaffirm their differences from the majority. Their successful achievement of a voice in antebellum society depended on the support of the Jewish and Irish communities. Ethnic religious organizations, schools, publishing firms, and reading publics supported the intellectual efforts of writers. The same process of cultural consolidation that facilitated the artistic accomplishments of the American Renaissance appeared among Jewish and Irish-Catholic Americans. Racial minorities, in contrast, were subject to added disadvantages in Protestant America: histories of involuntary immigration, non-European cultural backgrounds, weak communities, and race prejudice on the part of whites.

Literary Cultures of African and Native Americans

During the 1850s black and Indian authors turned increasingly from autobiographical narratives and expository prose to works of fiction and history. These more complex forms of expression were made possible by the growing intellectual sophistication of African-American and Native-American writers and readers. Novelists, for example, had to establish a critical distance from their characters, balance disparate narrative elements, and be willing to explore ambiguity. Thus when William Wells Brown listed his occupation as "author" on his marriage registration in Cambridgeport, Massachusetts, in 1860, it was a sign of how far his career—and his thinking—had progressed since his days as an antislavery lecturer in the 1840s.[42] Following the success of the story of his escape from slavery, *Narrative of William W. Brown* (1847), Brown produced a travel narrative, two plays, and a novel during the next decade. The achievement of William Wells Brown and of all contemporary intellectuals who belonged to racial minorities stands out all the more sharply against a social background where marginality clearly meant inequality. Black and Indian writers struggled far more painfully than did ethnic authors with ill-defined audiences, questions about their public role, and sponsorship by white reformers.

African-American writing in the antebellum decades was produced almost exclusively in the free states, as well as abroad, and it is helpful to begin with consideration of the communities in which black thinking developed. By the 1830s blacks who lived in northern cities had their own cultural resources, and they continued to create new organizations and literary organs in the following years. Examples may be taken from journalism, schooling, and reform. African Americans understood the importance of communication and advocacy to the advancement of their collective rights, and this perspective inspired a significant number of black periodicals. Beginning with *Freedom's Journal*, established in New York City in 1827, approximately 40 magazines were published by black journalists before 1865.[43] A more immediate sense of social community at times emerged through schooling. Although many black intellectuals were self-taught and the few who attained higher education attended white colleges, the African Free School in New York was one institution that demonstrated the potential of schooling to shape a network of black leaders. Henry Highland Garnet (1815–82), born in slavery, and Alexander Crummell (1819–98), born a free man in New York, were two of a number of African-American spokesmen who first met and formed lifelong friendships at the African Free School.[44] In addition, black voluntary associations anchored local and regional black societies by the 1840s. William Wells Brown, the future novelist, founded a black temperance association in Buffalo around 1840, and in 1847 he attended a convention in Troy, New York, where African Americans passed resolutions in favor of a national black press and a network of black colleges.[45] All of these efforts built on foundations of black neighborhoods, businesses, and churches to provide, overall, a social and cultural base for African-American literature.

Yet black communities were also subject to sources of stress that influenced their members' creative ambitions. Prejudice, alienation, and, more positively, aspirations for reform kept intellectuals from settling comfortably into free black northern enclaves. White racism introduced elements of chronic imbalance into black society, precluding the unimpeded growth of black institutions and virtually demanding the attention of black leaders to issues of social reconstruction. Inequality prevented William Wells Brown, for one, from pursuing a career of authorship in an atmosphere of peace and stability. When Brown moved from Buffalo to Boston in 1847 he found that the public schools were segregated, and he sent his two daughters to live in New Bedford, Massachusetts, to attend an integrated school. Soon the Fugitive Slave Law of 1850 made Brown himself feel as vulnerable as he thought inferior education made his girls. Like many former slaves who had gained prominence in the antislavery movement, Brown lived in England during the early 1850s to ensure his safety.[46]

Brown's sense of perpetual contest with white society was one sign of a deep-seated alienation from American culture that must have haunted most free blacks and, on a pragmatic level, resulted in unstable leadership. African-American spokesmen who fled to Europe were tempted to stay abroad in societies freer of racism than America. In a dramatic instance, Alexander Crummell of New York, who received a bachelor's degree from Cambridge University in 1852, spent much of the next two decades in Liberia, only returning to the United States in 1872.[47] No matter what the shifting—and, for black communities, disruptive—choices of black intellectuals, nearly all stayed close to the riveting issues of antislavery and black rights. But advocacy required still another kind of distance from fellow blacks, as writers moved into the biracial world of antislavery reform.

The immediate social context in which most African-American authors worked was the antislavery movement. The rise of Garrisonian abolitionism in the 1830s and political antislavery in the 1840s brought white reformers and black fugitives into close contact. White opponents of slavery were eager to have former slaves speak and write about their experience, and blacks who wished to resist slavery publicly must have seen the value of having articulate and fiercely committed white allies. Among scholars, there is continuing debate about the consequences of the intimacy with reformers of former slaves. Writing in 1946, Marion Starling argued that white interest in fugitives, a new development in the 1830s, benefited men and women who were once enslaved by changing their slave status from a "humiliating secret" to "an actual asset."[48] In contrast, many recent analyses stress the way sponsorship by whites cast free blacks into dependent roles.[49] There is truth in both of these positions. Reform alliances with whites both aided and constrained blacks. From the perspective of culture, however, the most immediate issue concerns the consequences of interracial social connections for African-American writing.

Not all antebellum black thinkers were born slaves. But many African Americans who issued texts after 1830 did begin their writing careers by composing narratives about their lives in bondage and had contact with the network of northern antislavery societies. The pattern of involvement of William Wells Brown and Frederick Douglass reveals the impetus that white-sponsored reform lent to black expression as well as the potential restraints that antislavery placed on black intellectuals. Following their respective escapes from slavery in 1834 and 1838, Brown and Douglass worked at manual-labor jobs. Brown was a crew member of a lake steamer based in Cleveland, and Douglass was a caulker in New Bedford, Massachusetts.[50] Although both men had ties with local black communities, it is not hard to see why each was drawn to radical abolitionism, or why white reformers anxiously recruited the men as speakers. Douglass became a traveling agent for the Massachusetts Anti-Slavery Society in 1841, as did Brown for the Western New York Anti-Slavery Society in 1843.[51] Issuing autobiographical accounts of their lives as slaves and their escapes from bondage was an extension in written prose of the kind of polemical testimony each gave on the lecture platform. White abolitionists appended documents to the *Narrative of the Life of Frederick Douglass* (1845) and the *Narrative of William W. Brown* (1847) to certify their authenticity and importance, and it was probably white readers, increasingly curious about slavery if not dedicated to its abolition, who made each book a best-seller.[52]

For former slaves who were less adept with language than Brown and Douglass, publishing a first-person reminiscence, sometimes dictated to a reformer, was the limit of their creative activity. Douglass and Brown were people of ambition and talent, however, and they seemed to need to put distance between themselves and the world of white-dominated antislavery in order to develop independently as authors. Thus Douglass left Boston and settled in Rochester before he serialized his novella, *The Heroic Slave*, in his own journal, *Frederick Douglass' Paper*, in 1853. Brown blossomed as a writer during five years in England between 1849 and 1854. Neither moved geographically simply to achieve intellectual space. There were complicated ideological and circumstantial reasons behind their decisions as well.[53] Nonetheless, whatever Douglass and Brown gained through a sort of apprenticeship on the abolitionist circuit—including facility with language, a sense of purpose, and confidence in their abilities—they had to cast off the relationship of black dependency subtly woven through the antislavery cause before venturing into imaginative literature.

This was not only a social and perhaps a psychological problem but also a dilemma of language. Abolitionist prose about blacks, whether written by white or black reformers, tended to develop as a single genre, and it was not easy for African-American thinkers who moved through antislavery circles to achieve independent forms of expression. The issue was more complex than how fugitives might escape the intellectual terms provided by white sponsors. Rather, the task for African-American authors was to incorporate narrative conventions of biracial origin into more self-consciously black writing.

The web of literary connections between antislavery fiction by whites and autobiographical accounts by former slaves epitomized the situation facing black writers. In 1836 Richard Hildreth, a white Massachusetts abolitionist, anonymously published a fictional, first-person account of slavery, *The Slave, or Memoirs of Archy Moore*. Hildreth's aim was to give life to standard abolitionist arguments by casting them in dramatic terms. Thus Archy Moore, so light a mulatto that Hildreth subtitled the novel "The White Slave" when he reissued it in 1856, tells of planters' lusts, religious hypocrisy, the prohibition of slave education, and the separation of slave families, all framed in a narrative where the main theme was Archy's struggle for freedom.[54] The fact that Hildreth judged the tragedies of slavery appropriate material for fiction, as well as anchored the novel in the voice of a slave, may be interpreted as the product of his generous feelings about blacks, more open-minded views than those held by most of his white contemporaries. As abolitionist polemics and fiction began to conceptualize slavery in certain ways, however, fugitives who spoke or wrote about their histories in antislavery forums probably fell into emerging conventions.

It is equally true that the life experiences and convictions of blacks shaped these narrative patterns, along with the priorities of white reformers. *The Fugitive Blacksmith* (1847), by James W. C. Pennington, a black Presbyterian minister living in New York City, added a stirring account of his religious conversion to the usual catalog of slavery's evils. Writing from his personal experience of faith, Pennington wove the language of evangelical testimony into his slave narrative and, no doubt like other individual voices, contributed to the design of the genre.[55] Slave accounts, moreover, could have a reciprocal influence on white fiction. Harriet Beecher Stowe read the *Narrative of the Sufferings of Lewis Clarke* (1845), interviewed Clarke more than once, and acknowledged that her character, George Harris, in *Uncle Tom's Cabin* was modeled on the author of the narrative.[56] Perhaps the intellectual impact of white and black writers on stories involving slaves was uneven. Perhaps Stowe listened to Lewis Clarke to gather firsthand material without reflecting that Clarke might construct his perceptions differently from herself. What is clear is that this important narrative form—the account of the fugitive's experience—thoroughly mixed white and black points of view.

Two of the earliest works of fiction by African Americans, Douglass's *The Heroic Slave* and Brown's *Clotel*, grew directly from this ambiguous literary heritage. Both appeared in 1853, and they were most likely produced because of the convergence of several circumstances: their authors' artistic maturity, the inviting activity of the literary marketplace, and, most immediately, the huge popular success of *Uncle Tom's Cabin*, issued the year before, which must have made reformers think more seriously than ever about fiction as an agent of social reform. Each text retained strong links to slave narratives. *The Heroic Slave* consisted of a series of conversations between Mr. Listwell of Ohio and Madison Washington, a Virginia slave. Washington, in effect, delivers an extended narrative about his escape that centers on the theme that a man cannot be converted into "merchandise" without violating "decency or humanity."[57] *Clotel* moved beyond convention just as cautiously. The first chapter of the book was a third-person version of Brown's autobiography, published as a first-person narrative six years before.[58] Whether Brown hoped to attract

Frederick Douglass, ca. 1850, daguerreotype by an unidentified photographer. *National Portrait Gallery, Smithsonian Institution.*

readers by including his popular story or aimed to prove his reliability as an observer of slavery or simply felt most comfortable writing about himself, his literary strategy attested to the power of the slave narrative as a genre. Personal, direct, and provocative, these stories of the slaves' struggles invested early black fiction with emotional depth. Yet Douglass and Brown also succeeded in controlling the ideological implications of their accounts of slavery and thereby transcended the constraints of abolitionist-sponsored writing.

Ordinary slave narratives were designed to evoke sympathy and antislavery commitments. *The Heroic Slave* and *Clotel*, in contrast, made broad statements about the role of slavery in American society.

The common theme of *The Heroic Slave* and *Clotel* was the significance of slavery in a democracy. Both books insisted that slavery was an essential problem of the polity, not simply a moral dilemma of involving individual slaveholders and slaves. Frederick Douglass's novella conveyed a simple and optimistic message. Based on the historical records of a mutiny led by a slave named Madison Washington on the ship *Creole* in 1841, *The Heroic Slave* shifted the focus of writing about blacks from slavery to race and from individual to collective resistance. Douglass portrayed a black man who, "fairly worshipped" by fellow slaves, was capable of leading them to freedom in the West Indies. Douglass seemed hopeful that the potential of black people could be developed within the American republic. He indicted the state of Virginia, the "mother of statesmen," for conceiving so talented a man as Madison Washington as no more valuable than "a horse or an ox."[59] But he allowed Washington to bear the name of two presidents proudly, and because he pictured Washington's mutiny as successful, he implied that the nation in the future would offer an equal chance to black and white heroes.

William Wells Brown also politicized the slave narrative by making his heroine, Clotel, a mulatto daughter of Thomas Jefferson. When Clotel dies by suicide, jumping from a bridge outside Washington, D.C., to avoid recapture, Brown commented with bitter understatement on the political meaning of the tragedy: "Thus died Clotel, the daughter of Thomas Jefferson, a president of the United States; a man distinguished as the author of the Declaration of American Independence, and one of the first statesmen of that country."[60] Brown's pained sense of the corruption and despair brought on by slavery pervaded *Clotel*. In contrast to Brown's introductory autobiography, which ended happily with his escape and his antislavery career, the novel itself chronicled a seemingly endless series of separations, abandonments, and deaths. After the sale of Clotel's mother (Jefferson's mistress) and her sister, Clotel and her new master, Horatio Green, fall in love and have a child. But his affection turns to cruelty, and Green sells Clotel away from Mary, their daughter.[61] At another point in the novel, Clotel's sister, Althesa, marries a white man, Henry Morton, who buys her but neglects to free her. After the couple's deaths, their two daughters, who look white, are shocked to discover that their mother was a slave and that they will be sold with the rest of their father's estate. One daughter, Ellen, poisons herself rather than become her master's concubine, and Jane, the other child, dies of a broken heart after her master kills her lover.[62] With thoughts probably similar to Brown's own, Morton, before his death, condemns as "despots" all the "free citizens" of the United States who continue to tolerate slavery.[63] Perhaps in theory these people could renounce oppression, but Brown's instincts instead made *Clotel* move fatefully toward nearly wholesale tragedy. All of the major characters achieve only "death's freedom," the title of the chapter on the suicide of Clotel. Only Mary, Clotel's daughter and Thomas Jefferson's granddaughter, survives and finally marries George, a mulatto son of George Washington, in England.

The way Douglass and Brown were able to frame and rework slave stories is clear. Despite the emotional power of the memoirs of escaped slaves, the narratives made a limited ideological statement that was consistent with the objectives of most white reformers. The fugitives' accounts focused on the inhumanity of southern slavery, and although the duty to abolish the institution was implicit, the texts portrayed the role of blacks to be merely individual flight. *The Heroic Slave* and *Clotel* looked at slavery in a broader political perspective and took more seriously the complexity and resourcefulness of black Americans. Especially in the intricate and brooding events of *Clotel*, William Wells Brown arrived at a pessimism out of tune with the fervency and often millennial hopefulness of antislavery. Capable of loving first Horatio Green and then her daughter, Clotel is victimized by racial attitudes that control Washington, the scene of her death, every bit as much as they do Richmond. Brown critically surveyed white society in a far-ranging and systematic way.

The tragedy of racism was also the theme of a very different kind of African-American novel that came from outside the antislavery world, *Our Nig* (1859). The author, Harriet E. Adams Wilson, was born a free woman in New Hampshire in 1827 or 1828. She was probably an indentured servant before she moved to Massachusetts in 1851. While working as a domestic, she married a fugitive slave, Thomas Wilson, and bore a son, George, in 1852. Thomas Wilson abandoned Harriet shortly before the birth of George. Poor and in ill health, she placed George in a foster home and moved to Boston to work as a dressmaker. In 1859 she wrote *Our Nig* to make money so that she might regain custody of her child. Sadly, George died in 1860. Harriet Wilson was listed in the *Boston City Directory* of 1863 but cannot be traced thereafter in public records.[64]

Our Nig reads very differently from the narratives and fiction produced by former slaves. Strongly autobiographical, the novel is not about slavery in the South but instead presents one woman's view of black life in the North. Wilson's dominant theme was racism. Reflecting on the experience in the antislavery community of her heroine, Alfrado, after Frado's marriage to a fugitive slave, Wilson wrote, "Watched by kidnappers, maltreated by professed abolitionists, who didn't want slaves at the South, nor niggers in their own houses, North. Faugh! to lodge one; to eat with one; to admit one through the front door; to sit next to one; awful!"[65] Abuse by self-styled reformers seemed the inevitable climax of Frado's early years. Frado is the mulatto child of a destitute white woman, "lonely Mag Smith," and Jim, the kind black man who marries Mag. But Jim dies, and Mag marries Seth, another black man, who persuades Frado's mother to abandon her child by ruse at the home of the well-to-do, white Bellmont family, as Mag and Seth sneak away. The novel centers on the mean-spirited tyranny, physical and mental, that Mrs. Bellmont exercises over Frado throughout her childhood and adolescence. Perhaps Harriet Wilson had read sentimental novels about afflicted servant girls and sensed how those literary conventions might help to give voice to events from her own past. But because Wilson tied Frado's oppression to her heroine's race, *Our Nig* was more focused ideologically than other tear-provoking stories. Is "there a heaven for the black?," Frado wonders sadly after a savage beating by Mrs. Bellmont.[66] It must have been clear to Wilson that her life, represented in the story of Frado, was a kind of enslavement as inhumane as its southern counterpart. She used her title, "Our Nig," to capture the demeaning opinion of blacks that limited their opportunities and contributed to their trials in the ostensibly free states.

There is a temptation to see *Our Nig* as a more genuine expression of black consciousness than writings linked to slave narratives because Wilson's novel was less influenced by the values of white reformers. It is true that Harriet Wilson offered a poignant and distressing image of northern racism virtually unique in antebellum black fiction. But most imaginative writing by African Americans nonetheless emerged in the social context of biracial antislavery reform. The border of white mainstream culture occupied by black literature was complicated by the crusading of white antislavery advocates. To the extent that the works of black writers articulated these tangled interracial bonds and, at least in the cases of Douglass and Brown, self-consciously examined their significance, these writings were no less genuine than *Our Nig* as expressions of the African-American experience.

The social situation of Native Americans was somewhat different from that of blacks, although there were important similarities as well. The formal enslavement of blacks both heightened the racial prejudice that white Americans felt about people of color and meant that African languages and traditions were disrupted by involuntary immigration. In contrast, Indians during this period were treated by the national government as autonomous nations, at least in theory. The oral cultures of tribes that had survived the initial settlement by whites of the Atlantic seaboard states retained much of their integrity. Indian oratory involved highly ritualized presentations requiring mastery of conventions and feats of memory, and orations by tribal leaders continued to mark ceremonial occasions after 1830.[67] Whatever the apparent advantages that Native Americans had over blacks, however, Indians were also subject in practice to white racism and violence. More positively, both African Americans and Native Americans gained facility at written expression in English because of their contact with white reformers—antislavery advocates or, in the case of Native Americans, Christian missionaries.

The importance of familiarity with white culture as a spur to Native-American writing may be illustrated by the early lives of two Indian authors, Kah-Ge-Ga-Gah-Bowh (1818–63), an Ojibwa known as George Copway, and John Rollin Ridge (1827–67), a Cherokee who wrote under the name of Yellow

Bird. Education by missionaries and intermarriage were key influences in the assimilation of both writers. Copway, who published *The Life, History, and Travels of Kah-Ge-Ga-Gah-Bowh (George Copway)* in 1847 and a history of his tribe in 1850, first encountered Protestant missionaries in 1827 in his home community on the Canadian side of Lake Ontario. Most of Copway's family soon converted to Christianity, and George himself left home as a Methodist missionary in 1834 after several years of schooling. Around 1840 Copway married Elizabeth Howell, a white, English-born Methodist. They subsequently worked together as itinerant preachers to Indian tribes in Canada and the United States.[68]

John Rollin Ridge, probably the first Native American to write a novel, *The Life and Adventures of Joaquín Murieta* (1854), grew up in Georgia as a member of the slaveholding gentry of the Cherokee nation. The Ridge family, Cherokee chiefs, had intermarried with whites at least as far back as the grandparents of John Rollin Ridge. His father, John Ridge, attended a school run by the American Board of Commissioners of Foreign Missions (ABCFM) in Cornwall, Connecticut, that was officially designated for "foreign youth." John Rollin Ridge's earliest teacher in Georgia was an ABCFM missionary, and, like his father, he was later educated in New England, although not in a mission school. Both the father and son married white women.[69]

It is not surprising that Ridge and Copway, people thoroughly exposed to Anglo-Protestant values, would be among the first Native Americans to publish works in English. Yet this cultural assimilation progressed against a social background of conflict between Indians and whites based on white challenges to Indian rights. Sadness, anger, and desire for reform impelled Copway and Ridge to write, as much as did the intrinsic fascination of crafting literature. A central theme in Copway's *Life, History, and Travels* was the downfall of the Ojibwas at the hands of unscrupulous whites. "I was born in *nature's wide domain,*" Copway began in a romantic tone, but he grew up to see distressing changes. Much of the Ojibwas' land was sold to the British in Canada for a fraction of its worth, and the tribe succumbed to "King Alcohol."[70] In the American South, the childhood of John Rollin Ridge was shattered by the forced emigration of the Cherokees from Georgia to present-day Arkansas, the notorious "Trail of Tears" initiated by the policies of Andrew Jackson. After Cherokee leaders split over the issue of whether to obey or resist the federal government's directive, John Rollin Ridge witnessed a rival faction murder his father, a spokesman of accommodation, in 1839. They also killed his grandfather and his uncle, Elias Boudinot, the editor of a periodical published in both English and transliterated Cherokee, the *Cherokee Phoenix.*[71] From an intellectual perspective, George Copway and John Rollin Ridge reacted dissimilarly to their personal experience of injustice by whites. For neither man, however, were the consequences of contact with whites unambiguous.

George Copway's first book belonged to a genre that was used widely by both antebellum African-American and Native-American authors: autobiography. Both groups made first-person memoirs into polemics to expose wrongs and urge reforms. Perhaps with more consistency than slave narratives, however, the Indians' stories were shaped by Christianity, the system of beliefs brought to them by white missionaries. *A Son of the Forest* (1829), by William Apes, a Pequod and a Methodist itinerant, set a precedent for Copway's *Life, History, and Travels* nearly two decades later. The literary model for both books was the conversion narrative. In the hands of Native-Americans authors, the genre conveyed a social as well as a spiritual message. At the same time that Copway condemned whites' land hunger and their unscrupulous profits from selling liquor, he embraced their religion, Christianity, as the solution to Native-American problems. He portrayed the Ojibwas' past as socially Edenic. Yet inwardly, those were "days of our darkness."[72] Copway offered the story of his own conversion not only as an example of the spiritual benefits of Christianization but of the progress an acculturated man might make in education and the performance of duty. Copway borrowed the language of white, middle-class moralism when he said that Christianity would make Native Americans "industrious, intelligent, and useful citizens." He reported the achievements in that direction of some Indians, in contact with missionaries, who already had "good farms, dwellings, school houses, meeting houses, and a saw mill."[73] Copway's embrace of Victorian values may seem like a betrayal of Native-American culture, but his narrative was also informed by anger at white injustice and the insistence that attention be paid to Indian problems. Although he believed that Protestant Christianity was the only possible answer to his tribe's decline, Copway did not ignore the responsibility of whites for the condition of Native Americans.

Behind this intellectual resolution, social and literary difficulties persisted for Copway. On a personal level he encountered prejudice as a man of color. When he brought his white wife along on a trip to Buffalo, New York, to lecture to Methodists on missions, his hosts asked, "'How did you obtain your wife?' 'Where were you married?' 'Did her father consent?' 'How many of your people have married our white women?'"[74] A common religion, Methodism, united Copway, Elizabeth, and his audience; but shared beliefs did not preclude these insults growing from racial bias. In Copway's professional life, multiple commitments made the audience for his prose uncertain. Was he writing to evangelize the minority of Native Americans who read English, to win favor with white Protestants who supported missions, or to influence government policy? The dilemma of addressing several sets of readers simultaneously was far different from the situation of Jewish and Irish-Catholic writers, who were assured of an intelligent and sympathic reception among their own people. The Ojibwas were in fact suspicious of writing as an instrument that would reveal tribal secrets to outsiders, and Copway complained in his autobiography of the "unwillingness on the part of the Indians to communicate many of their traditions."[75] Copway must have seen his work as a combination of preservation, evangelism, and defense of Indian rights. Yet his precarious status in both communities—Indian and white—could not have eased his efforts.

John Rollin Ridge was the first Native American to sustain a career as a writer. His success was built on elements of alienation, however, as troubling as the deracination of George Copway. Along with a number of other literate and ambitious Cherokees, Ridge moved from Arkansas to northern California during the Gold Rush. He worked for a succession of periodicals, including the Sacramento *Daily Bee* and the Marysville *California Express*, between 1852 and his death in 1867.[76] Ridge achieved literary fame despite the racial prejudices of white Californians. Indigenous "Digger" Indians, Mexican Americans, and Chinese immigrants were all the objects of legal action and personal violence initiated by white settlers. But the transplanted Cherokees, literate in English and familiar with Anglo-Protestant customs, did well professionally in California, a region still more fluid economically and socially than the East. Ridge did not embark on his new life, however, without feelings of betrayal. "Instead of writing for my living here I should be using my pen in behalf of my own people and in rescuing from oblivion the proud names of our race," Ridge wrote home to his uncle, Stand Watie, in 1854.[77] Yet he never returned to the Cherokee Nation in Arkansas to establish the Cherokee newspaper his letter proposed. In California, Ridge did defend the rights of the state's Indians and Mexicans, but he never became a consistent champion of minorities. Like many Cherokees, he remained loyal to slavery well into the Civil War. A convert to the idea of progress, he believed that social groups more advanced on the evolutionary ladder should enjoy superior privileges, and, in that spirit, joined a nativist organization called the Knights of the Golden Circle in 1860.[78] Overall, Ridge belonged to white society but had continuing Cherokee loyalties, spoke for some minority interests but added the biases of Anglo-American culture to the prejudices of slaveholding Cherokees. No longer bound by the Christianity of the ABCFM, Ridge still composed a popular, pantheistic poem in praise of God as a creator, "Mount Shasta," in 1852.[79] These strands of a complex personality all appeared in Ridge's widely read novel, *The Life and Adventures of Joaquín Murieta*.

The Life and Adventures of Joaquín Murieta: The Celebrated California Bandit combined at least three literary genres: the sensational crime novel, the travel narrative, and reform fiction. This unlikely combination of elements—the bloody, beautiful, and polemical—corresponded to varied parts of the experience of a divided man. John Rollin Ridge told the story of a Mexican, Joaquín Murieta, whose mining claim was attacked by whites because of "prejudice of color."[80] After they rape his mistress and hang his half-brother, Joaquín's "soul" becomes "darkened," and he lives only for "revenge."[81] The novel documents crime after gory crime against scenic backgrounds across the state—Mariposa, Marysville, Mount Shasta—until finally a posse returns with the head, preserved in alcohol, of this "extraordinary man."[82]

Ridge justified his book on historical and moral grounds. He did not write "for the purpose of ministering to any depraved human action, but rather to contribute my mite to those materials out of which the early history of California shall one day be composed."[83] He wished to drive home the lesson, too, "that there is nothing so dangerous in its consequences as injustice to individuals—whether it arises from prejudice of color or from any other source; that a wrong done to one man is a wrong done to society and to the world."[84] Coming from a man who had seen his father murdered, who had adopted California, and who understood race prejudice at firsthand, a novel that moved from violence to social reporting to ideological message reflected the jarring elements in Ridge's own life. Natural, too, in the writing of a person who seemed to stand as a perpetual outsider was the way Ridge distanced himself from his hero, Joaquín. Rather than defend Indian rights directly, Ridge approached the issue of racism through his Mexican character. Thus *The Life and Adventures of Joaquín Murieta* was a sinuous work of fiction, built on internal tensions of style and theme. Beneath its fast-paced action, the book told the subtler story of the precarious, patchworked identity of its pioneering Native-American author.

Perhaps not surprising in light of Ridge's overlapping loyalties, *Joaquín Murieta* may at last be read as an affirmation of democracy and capitalism, seen from a minority perspective. Much as Mary Sadlier's *Willy Burke* recast the myth of the self-made man in terms acceptable to Catholics, Ridge's fable of Joaquín the bandit at once criticized and appropriated mainstream Anglo-American principles. The novel's political vision centered on freedom for all, without the impediments to the liberty of minorities imposed by race prejudice. In socioeconomic terms, Ridge subtly praised Joaquín as a clever entrepreneur, despite his character's wicked purposes. Joaquín is determined, resourceful, and lucky enough to be one of few men "who bear charmed lives" until they meet with "a silver bullet." He even sounds like a business executive when he tells his men that he heads "an organization" of 2,000 followers throughout the state that will "kill Americans by 'wholesale.'"[85] A Sunday crowd of ladies at Stockton further attests to Joaquín's virile prowess when they ignore their "very prosy minister" to swoon at the sight of the outlaw.[86] In sum, John Rollin Ridge used *Joaquín Murieta* to attack the injustices born of white settlers' greed but not to impugn the underlying drive for success. When Ridge claimed traits of independence and self-assertion for his Mexican hero, he worked to expand capitalist ideology enough to assure racial minorities a place in the free-market system.

This affinity between minority and mainstream values raises two general questions about the relationship of the literatures of marginal cultures to the writings of the Anglo-Protestant majority. First, did minority intellectuals perceive common interests among themselves? Even more, did they share a social vision that diverged from the perspective of the majority? Second, how homogeneous in outlook was the white, Protestant center? Were there differences within the mainstream that require twentieth-century observers to approach the dichotomy between majority and minority viewpoints, no matter how useful this distinction for academic analysis, with intellectual caution? Both of these issues require reflection on the overall shape of antebellum cultural boundaries.

Toward a Vision of a Diverse Society

The rise of dissenting literatures in antebellum America proceeded as a series of separate efforts. Each body of works was shaped by one ethnic or racial group's independent attempt at self-definition in relation to white, Protestant values. A combination of prejudice and simple human shortsightedness kept minorities from achieving a clear view of their shared liabilities and potential. John Rollin Ridge built *Joaquín Murieta* around his sense of kinship, as a Native American, with Hispanic Californians. At the same time, however, he dismissed other ethnic and racial groups with crass stereotypes, including epithets about "peddling Jews" and "pitiful" Chinese.[87] In contructing the plot of *Our Nig*, Harriet Wilson understood that poverty—or, more broadly, social class—brought together Alfrado's white mother and black father. But Wilson left other minority relationships, such as bonds between women, unexplored, in fact making the antagonism between Frado and her mistress, Mrs. Bellmont, her novel's pivotal conflict. At this early stage in the development of ethnic and racial pluralism in American culture, it is not surprising that marginal peoples had a limited perception of their mutual interests. From a modern perspective, however, it is possible to see the outlines of a common literary approach that distinguished minority from mainstream writing.

The distinctive mark of literature produced on the margins of the Anglo-Protestant mainstream was attention to the social traits of characters and to the influence of social identities on the dynamics of plot. Minority authors were profoundly aware of the individual and collective consequences of membership in a particular ethnic or racial group. Their lives were shaped not simply by characteristics of their private personalities but by how white, Protestant Americans responded to their color, speech, and customs. In their texts there was a corresponding concern with social detail. Much more than to enhance literary interest through intricate social texture, minority writers aimed to show clearly the determining social forces in their characters' histories. George Copway's *Life, History, and Travels* carefully situated his own people, the Ojibwas, in relation to Hurons, Sioux, British, and Americans. William Wells Brown's *Clotel* could not be comprehended without paying attention to Brown's explanations of miscegenation, racial identity, and slave law. The plot of Mary Sadlier's *Willy Burke* was determined by the hardships of Irish immigration and the evangelical pressures on Catholics in workplaces controlled by Protestants. In all cases, social characteristics and structure were integral to the fiction's message.

Certainly the literature of Anglo-American authors also commented on social identity, but the writings of the American Renaissance focused primarily on metaphysical depth, not social breadth. Mainstream thinkers invited readers to penetrate surfaces more than to observe the interplay of visible forces. This is not to say, for example, that the Puritan materials were insignificant in Hawthorne's *The Scarlet Letter*.[88] Even so, it was the flawed personalities of the principal figures—Hester, Dimmesdale, Chillingsworth—that impelled the dramatic development of Hawthorne's novel. At least in comparison with the works of minority writers, *The Scarlet Letter* did not depend for its meaning on its characters' social traits. The result of this social emphasis in minority fiction was a literature that was unusually sensitive to the variety of peoples who composed antebellum American society. Minority writing was racially colorful, linguistically polyglot, and temperamentally polemical, situated more firmly than Anglo-Protestant texts in the empassioned conflicts that inevitably arose in an increasingly diverse and articulate culture.

Yet there were also divisions within the white Protestant mainstream. Whereas the concept of a majority culture and minority cultures is valid for antebellum America, it is important to keep in mind that what may be termed a "mainstream" was not altogether unified and that the boundary beween cultural insiders and outsiders was fairly permeable. Consider the cases of writers who were either white, Protestant women or spokesmen of the native-born working class. Judged by race, religion, and customs, they belonged to and helped to create the Anglo-Protestant mainstream. Yet the writings of these women and working-class men at the same time offered distinctive perspectives on antebellum America attuned to each one's experience. Two best-selling novels—Susan Warner's *The Wide, Wide World* (1850) and George Lippard's *The Quaker City; or, the Monks of Monk Hall* (1845)—underscore the complexities of antebellum intelligence.

Susan Warner's novel on the whole affirmed, yet in part criticized, middle-class Protestant beliefs. From the viewpoint of sales, there was nothing marginal about *The Wide, Wide World*. Readers, probably men as well as women, bought 40,000 copies of the novel within a year of its publication. Ultimately, *The Wide, Wide World* was reprinted 67 times.[89] The popularity of *The Wide, Wide World* was guaranteed by its simple and sympathic presentation of convictions near the heart of the self-conception of the native-born middle class. The story of a spunky child, orphaned Ellen Montgomery, Warner's novel defended the superiority of country life over cities, simple manners over social pretensions, balanced labor and sociability over exclusive devotion to work, and, most crucially, pious submission over angry rebellion. Taking place primarily in the American country town of Ventnor, *The Wide, Wide World* depicted characters and events outside of Anglo-American culture in almost exclusively negative terms. An insensitive Catholic priest refuses to conduct the funeral of an Irish boy who had called a Protestant minister to his deathbed.[90] Similarly, Ellen discovers toward the end of the book that her relatives in Scotland, where she has gone to live, value status above goodness. Through this portrayal of European corruption, Warner summoned her readers back to America's honest, Christian virtues.[91]

Despite these middle-class commitments, *The Wide, Wide World* was unmistakably the statement of a woman and, explicitly and implicitly, criticized the priorities of men. Captain Montgomery, Ellen's father, is ambitious, restless, and unsentimental, the prototypical rising man. Ellen fears, after her mother's death, that he will make Ellen, too, "a wretched wanderer from everything good and pleasant," and readers cannot blame the heroine for greeting her father's death with "relief."[92] More subtly but no less persuasively, Warner located the action of *The Wide, Wide World* almost exclusively in the social world of women. She traced Ellen's movements through a recurring routine of housework, visiting, churchgoing, and shopping, as if business, politics, and material progress were tangential to life's true meaning. In sum, *The Wide, Wide World* belonged to the white, Protestant mainstream and still contained powerful elements of dissent. The Anglo-Protestant center of the antebellum decades may better be seen as a patchwork of ambivalently loyal and disloyal texts than as a seamless fabric based on unquestioning consensus.

The writings of George Lippard (1822–54) similarly provoke a needed skepticism about the coherence of Anglo-American culture. Along with other novelists such as Ned Buntline, George Thompson, and Mike Walsh, Lippard produced fiction that was urban in orientation, characterized by sensationalism and scandal, and intended for a popular audience. Lippard in particular combined a literary interest in eroticism and violence with a commitment to working-class reform. The son of a man who was a grocer and minor politician in Philadelphia, Lippard organized and headed the Brotherhood of the Union, a body established in 1850 to oppose the division of capital and labor and to promote the brotherhood of men.[93] Despite Lippard's adversarial relationship with middle-class commitments, his fiction stopped short of outright rebellion against respectable society. Like *The Wide, Wide World*, Lippard's book *The Quaker City* alternatively rejected and embraced the beliefs of the Anglo-Protestant majority.

A first reading of *The Quaker City; or, the Monks of Monk Hall* leaves an impression of the novel as a strident work of social criticism, a viewpoint to which there is a signficant measure of truth. In a Gothic mood, Lippard created "Monk Hall" as a labyrinthine home-away-from-home of respected Phildadelphians, where they indulge their penchant for seductions, illicit affairs, and crime. Lippard's aim was to expose genteel hypocrisy, and even the texture of the narrative chafed at the limits of propriety in its graphic descriptions of sensuality and, at other times, violence: "The libertine felt her heart throbbing against his breast as he held her in his arms." He "flung back the night gown [*sic*] from her shoulders. Her bosom, in all its richness of outline, heaving and throbbing with that long pulsation, which urged it upward as a billow, lay open to his gaze."[94]

In the end, however, Lippard declined to transform his critical impulses into radical moral and social alternatives. His plot and language led readers toward the prospect of free expression of passion, but he finally closed off the possibility of new sexual standards. By presenting *The Quaker City* as a reform novel to warn citizens against seduction as "*the assassination of the soul*," Lippard leashed his wayward thoughts within the bounds of conventional morals.[95] Society's leaders, he implied, although seriously depraved, were ultimately redeemable. In addition, the novel contained undertones of anti-Catholicism and anti-Semitism—messages that worked indirectly to endorse Protestantism. Lippard identified the corrupted residents of Monk Hall as "monks," conjuring the contemporary nativist image of the Catholic church as a secretive, manipulative, and ill-intentioned organization to serve as his metaphor for human sinfulness. Just as negatively, Gabriel, a forger and an extortionist who speaks in dialect, had "Jew . . . written on his face as clearly and distinctly as though he had fallen asleep at the building of the Temple at Jerusalem, in the days of Solomon, the rake and moralist [and woken up] in the Quaker City, in a state of Perfect and Hebraic preservation."[96] Overall, Lippard's sincere and angry quarrel with middle-class respectability coexisted uneasily with his willingness to accept the dominance of Protestant culture. Here was one more sign of tensions within the Anglo-American mainstream.

The existence of dissenting voices among white, Protestant intellectuals serves as an essential reminder of the fragility of mainstream culture. Even among the most firmly rooted groups in antebellum society there were important differences in their interpretation of shared beliefs in Christianity, democracy, and capitalism. Yet it is no less true that an intellectual marketplace, dominated by texts in English that were produced by people of Anglo-Protestant background, became a powerful social force in the decades before the Civil War. The way ethnic and racial minorities worked to define their identities through language was profoundly affected by the existing terms of mainstream writing. Nonetheless, as Jewish, Irish, African, and Native Americans created voices for themselves, they effectively, if not intentionally, challenged the preeminence of Anglo-American thinking by establishing alternative points of view. It is ironic that the strength of white, Protestant discourse, by spurring social minorities to self-expression through their tangled motives of imitation and resistance, led in the direction of a reduced influence for Anglo-Protestant convictions simply because culture became more pluralistic. This process of intellectual diversification was one critical line of development in the 1850s as the nation moved toward civil war.

six

America at a Crossroads: The 1850s

America's mood at mid-century was characterized by high-pitched feeling and a taste for dramatic effects. Americans were exuberant about the arts, infatuated with technological progress, enthusiastic once again about personal salvation, and, far more ominously, passionately divided over the nation's political future. This was a culture that thrived on spectacle and courted excess. Crowds across the country clamored to hear the "Swedish nightengale," Jenny Lind. Patrons of the First International Exposition in New York toured a shimmering replica of London's Crystal Palace. Readers made literary history by buying out successive editions of best-selling novels. Public leaders made self-congratulatory speeches to celebrate the completion of the transatlantic telegraph. Revivals that swept northern cities in 1857 and 1858 were marked by lay initiative and centered emotionally on the testimonies of the converted. The politics of the sectional crisis evoked recurring demonstrations that, all too often, tended toward violence: the mobbing in northern cities of federal agents charged with returning fugitive slaves, the quasi-military pagentry of Republican "Wide Awakes" who marched throught streets before elections, and the public beating of Senator Charles Sumner on the floor of Congress by his colleague from South Carolina. Whether Americans were celebrating their achievements or hotly registering their differences, they expressed themselves with an excitement that gave their culture a feverish intensity.[1]

Certainly the tone of public life in the 1850s owed much to broad economic, social, and political conditions. But the consistently fervent spirit of the many dialogues among Americans grew more immediately from the successful establishment of the cultural marketplace. By 1850 intricate networks within the religious, political, literary, and artistic communities made possible

J. W. Orr, after S. Wallin and W. Wade, *A Beautiful Representation of the New York Crystal Place* (1853), wood engraving from *Gleason's Pictorial Drawing-Room Companion. Eno Collection; Miriam and Ira D. Wallach Division of Art, Prints, and Photographs; the New York Public Library; Astor, Lenox, and Tilden Foundations.*

a wide range of intellectual expressions. No longer tentative and experimental, cultural activity was distinguished by mastery: politicians were adept at maneuvering partisan contests, writers manipulated tested genres, and the aspiring middle class showed off symbols of their social identity. The assertive enthusiasm of Americans at mid-century typified a society that, in terms of cultural institutions and languages, had arrived.

But there were also notes of nervousness in the sometimes frantic exchange of ideas. The Victorian marketplace achieved stability through mainstream Protestantism, the two-party system, and the coherence of the middle class. Yet cultural life remained democratic, and wide access to the tools of self-expression invited statements of differences that shaded toward acrimonious dissent. New voices on the margins of the Anglo-Protestant center—including those of Jewish, Irish, African, and Native Americans—accented the complexity of public discourse. At the same time, there were deepening rifts within the Victorian mainstream. The sectional conflict between the North and South was the most pressing and explosive question, but there were also strains along new lines that anticipated the struggles of the post–Civil War era. Predecessors of later Protestant fundamentalists and modernists began to speak about religion in diverging ways. Critics of a new, pretentious upper class sensed that an elastic middle-class self-image could not indefinitely absorb social differences among Americans. Class conflict seemed increasingly certain in future years. Advocates of regional cultures set out to record their areas' unique traits and histories when they realized how much the national marketplace threatened local distinctiveness. These tensions provoked by emerging patterns in religious, class, and market relations were muted in the 1850s compared with the escalating crisis over slavery. Yet they gained importance after the Civil War as challenges to Victorianism.

In the midst of unprecedented means of cultural communication, Americans in the 1850s thus wondered about the direction of their nation's development. Debate about slavery impelled both speakers and listeners to reexamine their political heritage. More broadly, people were more aware than ever of the diversity in the nation's intellectual life. They savored the variety of cultural products but also sensed the unsettling implications of pluralism: all perspectives were limited, competition among them was inevitable, and perhaps no value was immune to challenge and revision. The integrative and idealistic outlook that shaped the American Renaissance began to yield to a new way of thinking that was more tolerant of diversity, conflict, and change.

Our Common Heritage

It became increasingly difficult during the 1850s to avoid discussion of slavery and the prospects of the Union. Beginning with the Compromise of 1850 and ending with Lincoln's election to the presidency, Americans were forced repeatedly to rethink their political assumptions in light of a disconcerting series of events: the Kansas-Nebraska Act (1854), the dissolution of the Whig party and the formation of the Republicans (1852–56), the Dred Scott decision (1857), and John Brown's raid (1859). The immediate issue was the role of slavery in the nation's future, particularly in the West, but the temper of debate was often retrospective, as public figures probed the Constitution and other historical documents both for honest guidance and self-justification. The swelling volume of congressional oratory, campaign speeches, and printed polemics on sectionalism provided a vast—and often confusing—public forum for considering the contemporary relevance of the founders' statements on liberty and union.

There were as many interpretations of the Constitution, in fact, as there were partisan positions. Stephen Douglas of Illinois, for example, the Democratic advocate of popular sovereignty, denounced Lincoln's belief that "a house divided against itself cannot stand" by using the Constitution as his weapon. The convention of 1787 "made this government divided into free States and slave States," Douglas told an audience during the Lincoln-Douglas debates of 1858, "leaving each State perfectly free to do as it pleased on that subject of slavery."[2] Jefferson Davis of Mississippi agreed with Douglas to an extent when he argued for the preeminence of states' rights over federal policy. But speaking to a crowd in 1860 in the town of Corinth, Davis went further to insist that it was erroneous to think "the States to be the *creatures* instead of the *creators* of the Federal Government."[3] Davis's view of history potentially challenged Douglas's vision of diverse states under a tolerant national government and set the stage for secession. If the states made the Constitution, they could as legitimately reject its authority, regardless of whether its power was applied in a benign or restrictive way. Davis must have thought his listeners appreciated constitutional analysis because he made it a prominent part of his speech. He "referred to the debates in the convention for the formation of the Constitution," the Corinth *True Democrat* reported, and "denounced in strong language the craven wretch that could countenance the coercion of a sovereign State by Federal authority."[4]

These invocations of the Constitution were by no means unprecedented. At least as far back as the Nullification Crisis and the beginnings of abolitionism in the 1830s, politicians and reformers stated their positions on slavery and union in light of their readings of the Constitution's intentions.[5] Yet the 1850s was a time of particularly fierce political controversy. When nearly all advocates made the Constitution their ally, arguments about the founders' designs, so variously interpreted for such obviously partisan purposes, perhaps lost credibility as a result of overuse. In his first inaugural address, Abraham Lincoln skirted the issue of the Constitution in an effort to find firmer ground for the Union than the hotly contested document. "The Union is much older than the Constitution," Lincoln declared, "formed in fact, by the Articles of Association in 1774" and simply reinforced by the Constitution, whose stated goal was "'*to form a more perfect Union.*'"[6] Lincoln's approach suggests that he still thought historical analysis was valuable and potentially persuasive even at this moment of national crisis. Still, his caution about relying on the Constitution perhaps also reflected his fear that incessant polemical battles had nearly reduced the founders' words to mere rhetoric. Public leaders in the 1850s knew which figures of speech to use to arouse their audiences. But the crossfire of highly charged language made it difficult to listen seriously to an opponent's ideas and easier simply to take and defend one side.

Behind the arguments about history, themes appeared in the sectional debates that clearly voiced concerns of the present. The role of African Americans in the nation's future was one question that preoccupied northern whites. Slavery, Stephen Douglas told an Illinois audience, was not the most crucial current political issue: "The question is far more important to you. What shall be done for the free negro?"[7] In an atmosphere of cheers from the crowd of "Good for you" and "Douglas forever," Douglas stated his opinion: "I believe [this government] was made by white men for the benefit of white men and their posterity forever, and I am in favor of confining the citizenship to white men—men of European birth and European descent, instead of conferring it upon Negroes and Indians, and other inferior races."[8] Not all white public figures were as crudely racist or categorically dismissive of the possibility of black political equality as was Douglas. Lincoln, for example, conceded "a physical difference" between the races but believed blacks had an equal right to the life, liberty, and pursuit of happiness promised by the Declaration of Independence.[9] Even so, racial prejudice among northern whites was nearly universal. Theodore Parker, Unitarian minister and abolitionist, argued in 1859 that slavery must end in order to stop the "Africanization of America." By a biological mechanism he did not explain, enslavement according to his calculations, encouraged black fertility. An "Anglo-Saxon with common sense" must want "the superior race to multiply rather than the inferior."[10]

Parker's logic is unsettling to twentieth-century readers not only because of his unashamed racism but because his views are so contrary to our image of the abolitionists as friends of African Americans. Yet there is a brighter side to discussions in the 1850s of the future of American blacks. Douglas's question, "What shall be done for the free negro?," acknowledged the humanity of African Americans and assumed they would occupy some position in free society. Slaves had appeared in the Constitution merely as a footnote to provisions for taxation and representation, even though this was an addendum of understated importance. Never identified explicitly as slaves, they were nonetheless to be counted as "three-fifths of all other Persons." By the 1850s the legacy of decades of controversy about slavery, in which African-American abolitionists played a prominent role, was the realization that blacks, slave and free, had to be talked about as men and women rather than chattel and, more specifically, as Americans. The introduction of theories of racial inferiority into the sectional controversy thus had both pernicious and redeeming effects. The assumption of innate racial differences acknowledged blacks' humanity at the same time that it denied their equality.[11] As social issues such as race relations entered public debate, it was clear how much the conflict over slavery had to do with Americans' visions of their future as well as their interpretations of the past.

Partisan speeches that examined public events in light of the Constitution and social policy were in fact the decade's standard form of political expression. Time and again newspapers reported crowds of hundreds and even thousands of people who responded with enthusiasm to these orations. Yet a few polemicists threw the intellectual conventions of politics to the winds. Their new kinds of arguments underscore that much more was at stake in the slavery controversy than settling old scores unresolved in 1787.

For George Fitzhugh of Virginia and Frederick Law Olmsted of New York, the key issue was the comparative moral value of socioeconomic systems. Flying in the face of the historical temper of the decade, Fitzhugh in effect dismissed constitutional precedent as a guide in the current crisis when he wrote in *Cannibals All!* (1857), "Times change, and men change with them."[12]

Fitzhugh believed that the solution to conflict would not be found by study-ing past political compromises. On the contrary, Americans must recognize that the real problem was free labor capitalism, the "White Slave Trade" that exploited workers and epitomized anarchy because of the absence of all authority.[13] Olmsted matched Fitzhugh's concern with political economy in *The Cotton Kingdom* (1861). Although the two men held diametrical opinions on free and slave labor, they agreed that the main criterion for resolving sec-tional tensions should be which economic arrangement most effectively encouraged virtue and suppressed vice. Virtue, in Olmsted's eyes, meant ambition, hard work, and productivity, and he concluded that slavery dis-couraged all of these traits in both blacks and whites. On a visit to Virginia, "I was satisfied, after a few weeks observation, that most of the people lived very poorly; that the proportion of men improving their condition was much less than in any Northern community; and that the natural resources of the land were strangely unused, or were used with poor economy."[14] On the eve of the Civil War, here were writers who declined to discuss the constitutional design of the Union. They inquired instead into the comparative benefits of compet-ing labor systems. Unusual in their inattention to standard political rhetoric, Fitzhugh and Olmsted nonetheless raised social questions that must have been on many people's minds.

The Civil War was such a momentous event in American history that mod-ern observers are tempted to look back on the 1850s as a simple prelude to war. But the appearance within the sectional debates of issues concerning race rela-tions, economic progress, and social order indicates that slavery in a narrow sense was not the sole preoccupation of mid-century Americans. In fact, Victorian culture offered Americans additional perspectives on experience that often had little to do with sectionalism. Not surprisingly, however, Victorianism was as vulnerable to tensions as was the political union.

Our Common Culture

By the 1850s Americans who adhered to the beliefs of the Anglo-Protestant mainstream had drawn toward several points of consensus: Protestant gradu-alism, political nationalism based on partisan contests, and the desirability of middle-class virtues. But broad areas of agreement began to yield to stress and imbalance before the Civil War. Subtle differences between religious groups, social classes, and geographic regions emerged alongside the conflicts of the sectional controversy. These dialogues within the Victorian center contained important seeds of the cultural pluralism that flourished after the Civil War.

For American Protestants the 1850s was a decade of realignment. Millennialism and utopianism on the religious left and sacramentalism and reaffirmations of hierarchy on the right became less visible than they had been during the tumultuous 1840s, a time of apocalyptic expectancy, radical social initiatives, and tormented personal decisions. In their place, a practical faith, based on belief in the compatibility of spirituality and institutional life, gained influence.[15] But this Victorian Protestantism was a precarious blend of other-worldliness and compromise and threatened to divide along new lines. During the 1850s the perfectionism of Phoebe Palmer and the liberalism of Henry Ward Beecher gained currency as dissimilar choices available to Americans.

The Methodist perfectionist theology of Phoebe Palmer (1807–74) anticipated key positions of post–Civil War fundamentalism: a firm attachment to the Bible, a dispensational view of history, and the possibility of charismatic experience.[16] Taken together, these commitments signaled a rejection of compromises between Christianity and middle-class mores. *Entire Devotion to God* (1845) articulated the premises that guided Palmer's long career as an itinerant evangelist from 1837 until the year of her death. Writing in personalized language to a fictional "beloved Christian friend," Palmer dismissed the "traditions of men" in favor of the authority of the Bible.[17] As a dense series of biblical passages anchored her thoughts, she redirected her reader's attention from a secular view of time to a sacred vision of history. She contrasted the "old covenant dispensation," under which God required outward obedience, with the "new covenant dispensation," where God asked that faith be offered in exchange for redemption.[18] This was not the elaborate interpretation of historical stages, framed by apocalyptic predictions, proposed by fundamentalists around 1900. Still, Palmer's reassertion of the old Puritan idea of successive covenants recalled the readers of her popular book to a biblical (and implicitly transcendent) perspective of human events.

Palmer promised ceaseless gifts of the spirit to the converted as well. The soul "experiences *constantly* the all-cleansing efficacy of the blood of Jesus" and, in consequence, "triumphant ecstacies" and "perfect love."[19] Like later Pentecostal and charismatic Christians, Palmer pictured the reward for "entire surrender of the world" to be intimacy with the divine.[20] Palmer did not directly confront the increasingly cautious and decorous churches of the Protestant mainstream; nor were most of her followers sufficiently disaffected to leave established denominations. But her ideas nonetheless contained a critical affront to worldliness based on a return to biblical Christianity. Along with her rapturous vision of God's love, Palmer betrayed feelings of disappointment at society's—and Christianity's—apostasy. Her discontent links her with the rebellious antimodernism of later fundamentalism.

The persistence of a unifying center in Protestantism is suggested by the participation of both Palmer and Henry Ward Beecher in the last great revival of the antebellum era: the international series of awakenings that spread through the United States, Canada, and Britain beginning in 1857. Palmer, a passionate and tireless itinerant, undertook preaching tours on both sides of the Atlantic. Beecher, a son of Lyman Beecher and since 1847 the pastor of the Plymouth Church in Brooklyn, New York, held daily prayer meetings that brought 350 new members into his church in the spring of 1858 alone.[21] Yet the heart of neither Palmer nor Beecher was really in traditional revivalism. Although Palmer continued to seek converts in interdenominational gatherings until the end of her life, her thinking shifted the focus of Protestant teaching away from the single, saving experience of justification and toward the sustained ecstasies of sanctification. The Christian life, understood not simply as the performance of good works but joyous immersion in spiritual blessings, offered believers a more constant and comprehensive piety than did the ordinary process of conversion followed by church membership. Henry Ward Beecher was moved by a similar impulse to turn seasons of awakening into uninterrupted religious experience. But whereas Palmer sought to subordinate secular to sacred interests, Beecher nearly collapsed spirit into nature.

In anticipation of post–Civil War Protestant modernists, Beecher was willing to adapt Christianity to contemporary secular culture because he trusted the beneficence of the human and natural worlds. Beecher's actions and his language tended to close the distance between religion and everyday life. Not only did he affirm his belief in gradual character formation in lieu of sudden conversion after the revival of 1858, but he increasingly bypassed the church as an institution in his efforts to bring his message to society. On weekdays Beecher lectured on the lyceum circuit, and on Sundays he preached in church. In the words of one biographer, he saw "sermons and lyceum lectures in the same light—both helped to improve the character of the common people."[22] When he wrote for newspapers and magazines, his essays were short (usually five to ten pages) and anecdotal. *Star Papers; or, Experiences of Art and Nature* (1855) was a typical book-length collection of pieces published originally in periodicals. It contained a miscellany of topics, including "A Sabbath at Stratford-on-Avon," "New England Graveyards," "Trouting," and "Christian Liberty in the Use of the Beautiful."[23] Beecher's words were more often moralistic than specifically Christian. Farms have a "*moral* beauty" because they are made by industrious men and because they nurture good character in turn.[24] The rich may be "benefactors of their race" if they display their luxuries in view of "the ignorant," who need to be uplifted.[25] In the pulpit Beecher's untheological cast of mind struck one eminent listener, Horace Bushnell, as "unspeakably crude and naturalistic." But Bushnell concluded his private observations to his wife by saying that "I was greatly moved notwithstanding, and, I trust, profited."[26]

Overall, Beecher exploited the potential power of taking religion out of the church and into the world. He gained immediacy and relevance for Christianity even though he also put religion's ability to inspire self-reflection and social criticism at risk. However one judges Beecher and Palmer, the essential fact is that each began to transform Victorian Christianity in distinctive ways. After the Civil War the fundamentalist and modernist positions articulated by their successors came increasingly into open conflict.

Americans in the 1850s, and particularly those living in cities, were at least as aware of the growing division between social classes as they were of the distance between Protestant viewpoints. In previous decades inequalities in wealth and power were explained away, as much as possible, by the reassuring thought that middle-class status was available to all. Private virtues of industriousness and self-control, if faithfully cultivated, would bring domestic comforts and public esteem.[27] Yet the literature of the 1850s suggests that this intellectually satisfying solution diverged more than ever from social facts. Social critics lamented that the rich did not enjoy their rewards in a spirit of modesty and benevolence but adopted attitudes of pretentiousness, superficiality, and callousness. To an extent, these critiques were latter-day jeremiads, overstating any evidence of self-indulgence and pride. But mid-century society did offer well-to-do people unprecedented opportunities for visible consumption—fine clothing, houses, and furnishings within close view of one's neighbors—and it is likely that the successful were indeed status-conscious and materialistic, at least by established standards. In the 1850s the most important aspect of the appearance of a new elite was the easygoing response of their articulate contemporaries. In contrast to both the moralistic sermons on wealth preached to earlier generations and the anxious prescriptions for class conflict formulated in later industrial cities, the characteristic style for examining society's ills was humorous satire. Light-hearted treatment of social climbing was an indication that writers and readers, including the genteel, could still laugh at this challenge to public integrity and perhaps, through comic self-reflection, reform themselves.

One of the decade's most popular satires of snobbery was *The Autocrat of the Breakfast Table* (1858) by Oliver Wendell Holmes, Sr. Pretentiousness, with its components of narrow-mindedness and a smug assumption of superiority, must have been a common character trait in an intensely status-conscious society. Holmes critiqued the habit of self-inflation by showing how little pride suited the small abilities of a minor literary man (the "autocrat") who shares meals with modest fellow boarders, among them a schoolmistress, a divinity student, and an actor. Relentlessly opinionated, the "autocrat" tries to impose his views on the company—that puns are unacceptable, family pedigree is preferable to self-made achievement, short weapons are superior to long— only to be met by the skeptical queries, jokes, and hasty exits of his audience.[28] Holmes never deviated from a spirit of fun in transcribing the "autocrat's" rambling lectures, but by calling his speaker the "autocrat" he acknowledged that an impulse to dominate was part of the presumed omniscience of this man of letters. When other satirists turned to the foolish ambitions and self-deceiving illusions of the rich themselves, they sensed that foppery was similarly related to questions of social power.

George William Curtis's *The Potiphar Papers* (1853) accomplished the difficult task of being consistently amusing and at the same time depicting the assault of genteel self-promotion on humane values. This series of sketches about the Potiphar family first appeared in *Putnam's Magazine*, a New York journal that Curtis edited. In these funny essays, exaggerated to the point of the ridiculous in their portrayal of social climbing, Curtis chronicled the self-willed transformation of the respectable middle class into an American aristocracy. Few heroines could be more ambitious, superficial, or patronizing than Mrs. Potiphar (called "Polly" by her husband, betraying their commonplace social origins). In one narrative, "Our New Livery, and Other Things," Mr. Potiphar thinks that Mrs. Croesus is his wife's friend "because," in Mrs. Potiphar's words, "we call each other 'dear.'" But Polly knows better than her husband that fine words cloak ruthless competitiveness.[29] In her relations with her social subordinates, on the other hand, Mrs. Potiphar is consistently insulting. When Mr. Potiphar wonders whether dressing their servants in livery is not a "peacock absurdity" and, for the servants, "a menial badge," Polly counters, "'Why,' said I, 'is not an American servant a servant still?'"[30] She insists on calling Henry, her prospective footman, by the name of "James," because "the name of my footman is always James."[31] As her interview with Henry continues, she asks, after much embarrassment, to inspect his legs to see how he will look in breeches. "I hope you won't insist" on livery, Henry replies, "for I am very anxious to get a place." But, he concludes, turning down the job with democratic pride, "I cannot put on those things and make a fool of myself."[32] The central lesson of *The Potiphar Papers* was that Polly could not abide social equals. Whether scrambling ahead of her prosperous neighbors or acquiring trappings of greatness at the expense of her employees, Mrs. Potiphar instinctively advanced a hierarchical view of society at odds with the earlier homogenizing vision of an inclusive middle class.

Although humor remained the dominant literary device of these portraits of social ambition, the brutal facts of poverty occasionally crept into these pieces and transformed them from diverting amusements into more serious warnings for the ambitious bourgeoisie. "Nothing to Wear," an immensely popular poem published in *Harper's Magazine* in 1857, was one work that underscored the admonitions of satire with a cold look at the life of the urban poor. As a narrative written in spirited verse by William Allen Butler, an attorney as well as an author, this tale of the trials of fashion that afflict "Miss Flora M'Flimsey, of Madison Square" explored the values and pressures of an appearance-conscious, consumer-oriented culture. "'Why Harry, *mon cher*,'" replies Flora to her fiancé's request that she go to the "Stuckup's" party, "I should like above all things to go with you there; / But really and truly—I've nothing to wear."[33] The crisis, Butler explained in a tone of mock distress, touched other girls in addition to Flora:

> Researches in some of the "Upper Ten" districts
> Reveal the most painful and startling statistics,
> Of which let me mention only a few:

In one single house, on the Fifth Avenue,
Three young ladies were found, all below twenty-two,
Who have been three whole weeks without any thing [*sic*] new
In the way of flounced silks, and thus left in the lurch
Are unable to go to ball, concert, or church.[34]

The elegant young lady satirized by William Allen Butler in his 1857 poem "Nothing to Wear," *Harper's New Monthly Magazine.*

A poor woman who really had nothing to wear. The drawing appeared at the end of Butler's poem "Nothing to Wear" (1857), *Harper's New Monthly Magazine*.

106 Yet the tone of "Nothing to Wear" shifted from lilting humor to slow-metered pathos. The illustrations that *Harper's* chose to frame the text warned readers of Butler's darker message. The poem was introduced by a drawing of Flora dressed in layers of fabric and lace, accompanied by decorous pet dogs. In stark contrast, a sketch followed the text showing a barefoot woman in rags, surrounded by her ill-clad, despondent children. The image depicted the sobering turn of Butler's last two stanzas:

Oh ladies, dear ladies, the next sunny day
Please trundle your hoops just out of Broadway,
From its whirl and its bustle, its fashion and pride,
And the temples of Trade which tower on each side,
To the alleys and lanes, where Misfortune and Guilt
Their children have gathered, their city have built;
Where Hunger and Vice, like twin beasts of prey,
Have hunted their victims to gloom and despair;
Raise the rich, dainty dress, and the fine broidered skirt,
Pick your delicate way through the dampness and dirt,
Grope through the dark dens, climb the rickety stair
To the garret, where wretches, the young and the old,
Half-starved and half-naked, lie crouched from the cold.[35]

Moving toward a class-conscious literature willing to speak in favor of changes in social relationships, Butler retreated to a moralistic diagnosis and cure for society's ills. If Flora and the other "foolish virgins" were only "clothed for the life and the service above"—in "purity, truth, faith, meekness, and love"—then goodness would heal this world's wounds and guarantee that when the "daughters of Earth" reached heaven, they would not be rudely awakened to find that, without virtue, they had "nothing to wear!"[36]

These satires concerned with the cultural dimensions of class distinctions were mild compared with such uncompromising later assessments of social inhumanity as Stephen Crane's *Maggie: A Girl of the Streets* (1893) and Edith Wharton's *The House of Mirth* (1905), as well as graphic nonfictional writings by advocates of Progressive reform, the Social Gospel, and socialism.[37] Still, the light pieces of the 1850s betrayed a resigned understanding that an elastic middle-class culture could not long contain social tensions. Along with more pronounced distinctions of wealth would come class-based conflicts of values that would challenge the integrity of a unifying mainstream.

The most threatening division among Americans was based neither on religion nor wealth, however, but on place. North and South visibly struggled over slavery in the West. Yet from a cultural perspective it is important to explore the relation of this political sectionalism to a broader regionalism—defined as an attachment to part of the country because of the area's distinctive customs and mores. Both attitudes grew along with national expansion and consolidation. Sectionalism moved toward crisis over the future of slavery in the territories. Regional loyalties took root, in a defensive mood, in the face of increasing contact with strangers and the homogenizing influence of expanding markets. The Civil War brutally resolved the dilemma of political sectionalism. Regional consciousness, in contrast, strengthened in the postwar era. So-called local colorists in fiction made physical place—and the traits of character to which geography seemed to give rise—a major theme of their writing. Some of the best-known later authors who wove social details into intense evocations of localities were Bret Harte, George Washington Cable, Sarah Orne Jewett, and Hamlin Garland.[38] In the decade before the Civil War polemics aimed at defending sectional causes stood side by side with literature shaped by regional awareness.[39] This antebellum regional prose anticipated long-term dissent against the power of mass-circulated ideas.

For decades, Americans had read fiction that incorporated regional color, including the Puritan tales of Nathaniel Hawthorne and the historical romances about South Carolina of William Gilmore Simms. Over time, place gained prominence as a subject, not simply as literary background, and literature worked increasingly as a tool for the assertion of regional self-consciousness.[40] Henry Wadsworth Longfellow's narrative poem, "The Courtship of Miles Standish" (1858), was one widely read composition that exemplified this changing attitude toward regional material. On the one hand, Longfellow was concerned specifically with evoking the New England character. He drew on a well-established genre of historical writing about New England that commonly eulogized its early settlers. The love triangle of Miles Standish, the Pilgrim leader, John Alden, Standish's proxy in courtship, and Priscilla, the object of both men's affection, is played out heroically against the background of the New World "desert," a physical setting more challenging than the "garden" of England they left behind.[41] New Englanders who read "Miles Standish" as a tale of the Pilgrims found a message of pride in their heritage. On another level of interpretation, however (and there may be more), the poem contains a debate about the nature of manly virtue. Standish, the physically dark and muscular warrior who chooses to read Julius Caesar instead of the Bible, contends for the hand of Priscilla against the scholarly Alden, "fair-haired, azure-eyed, with delicate Saxon complexion."[42] To an extent, this contest between opposites—force and faith, hand and mind, even swarthy and light-skinned races—is a struggle for control of New England, with implications for the future as well as the past. But the moral questions that Longfellow so unmistakably posed also transcended his immediate neighborhood. Moving in the direction of later local colorists, Longfellow typified the outlook of the 1850s by balancing advocacy of regional interests against a commitment to broader issues, including those of religion, gender, and race.

Southern writing offers an equally strong case for a deepening regional awareness. Fiction depicting southern customs steadily gained popularity, among northern as well as southern readers, throughout much of the nineteenth century. Attention to the region's idiosyncrasies of speech and sensibility shaped many works of humor, including A. B. Longstreet's *Georgia Scenes* (1835), George Washington Harris's "yarns" about "Sut Lovingood" in the 1850s and 1860s, and Joel Chandler Harris's stories of "Uncle Remus" in the 1880s and 1890s.[43] Yet self-portrayal by southerners was increasingly barred from a tone of simple praise, first by conflicted feelings about slaveholding and, after the war, by a tormented awareness that the South was a defeated culture. *Beulah* (1859), a best-selling novel by Augusta Jane Evans of Alabama, illustrates the perplexities of southern regionalism on the eve of the Civil War.

Nearly every biographical detail about Augusta Evans (1835–1909), later known by her married name Wilson, would make a reader expect her novel about the struggles of the orphan Beulah Benton to be rich in local color. Evans was a vocal sectionalist in the late 1850s and a passionate Confederate during the war. Within months following the publication of *Beulah*, she wrote a defense of southern literature for the Mobile *Daily Advertiser*. She established a hospital in 1861 near her home in Mobile called "Camp Beulah" and wrote a patriotic novel to rally the Confederacy, *Macaria*, that appeared in 1863.[44] Thus it is puzzling that *Beulah* contains almost no hint that the story takes place in the South. A reviewer for the Baltimore *Daily Exchange* criticized the novel as a poor imitation of Charlotte Brontë's *Jane Eyre* (1847), and there is truth in the critic's comparison, if not in his dismissive appraisal of *Beulah's* quality.[45] Like the heroine Jane Eyre, Beulah is an intelligent and independent young woman who must reconcile her insistence on self-respect with her love for a possessive yet finally honorable man. Beyond a reference to the characters' "sunny southern home," a short plea for southern literature, and a critique of Virginia-born Edgar Allan Poe as the writer who lured Beulah into the troubling path of religious skepticism, Evans apparently chose not to develop a sense of place in her novel.[46]

Even so, *Beulah* may be read a southern counterpart to regional works such as "Miles Standish," although shaped in addition by southern self-doubts. Like Longfellow's poem, *Beulah* addressed some themes that simply had little to do with the customs of a particular area, the most important of which were the conflict between skeptical philosophy and Christian faith and the relationship of the sexes. Part of the story's detachment from place was due, too, to the romantic focus on the characters' inner dilemmas. Yet Evans's deemphasis of southern manners may also have been a backhanded argument in favor of the South's cosmopolitanism and, implicitly, its cultural maturity. Beulah herself remains in the South throughout the novel, but she travels widely in imagination through her acquaintance with great authors in the Western tradition. Other characters actually go abroad, either to study in Europe or to tour as far away as Asia. Southerners, Evans subtly informed her readers, were as worldly as anyone else. Indeed, no slaves appeared in the novel. In all, *Beulah* may be seen as a curious instance of regional writing. Evans recorded southern idiosyncrasies with a light hand because those differences, in the eyes of the South's critics, were marks of shame. Precisely because she was sensitive to the opinions of a national audience, Evans presented regional mores in a careful and self-conscious way.

Americans on the eve of the Civil War were thus in possession of a culture that included sources of disagreement as well as a core of Victorian commitments to which many, if not all, citizens ascribed. Did growing intellectual differences mean that after the war Americans would share less common cultural ground? The stunning variety of postwar ideas indicates that to an extent this was true. But it is also possible that a new and at least partly unifying intellectual framework emerged that gradually displaced mid-century Victorianism. The lives and works of young writers in the 1850s contained signs of a rising worldview attuned to variety, irony, and transience.

Meetings of Young and Old

The dominant culture of the 1850s tended toward aesthetic self-indulgence. Americans at mid-century luxuriated in an unprecedented range of artistic pleasures—books, music, plays, and architecture—where the prevailing note was enjoyment of a profusion of ideas and emotions. This was a culture of cel-ebration, grounded in feelings of self-congratulation at having formed institu-tions and languages capable of sustaining public discussion.[47] Yet in the shad-ow of this vibrant style, new forms of writing began to gain currency that thrived on elements of humor, satire, and social realism. Although these genres were not identical with one another, all focused on limited, human themes that were presented with acceptance, even appreciation, of the inconsistencies of common life. The use of symbols to tie visible facts to philosophical messages, the distinguishing mark of creativity of the American Renaissance, was not the new writers' chosen technique. The tense encounters of three young realists— William Dean Howells, Mark Twain, and Rose Terry Cooke—with their liter-ary predecessors illustrates the appearance on the literary scene of intellectuals who set out to portray down-to-earth complexities. To the extent that these changing literary tastes reflected shifting intellectual orientations, the stories of these writers point to the beginnings in the 1850s of a fresh point of view.

William Dean Howells (1837–1920) is remembered by twentieth-century critics as a pioneer of a genteel kind of literary realism, a standard for American prose that insisted on the portrayal of ordinary lives but equated the commonplace with middle-class routines and conventional morality. Although novels such as *A Modern Instance* (1882) and *A Hazard of New Fortunes* (1890) have a limited intellectual boldness from a modern perspective, Howells's goal to make literature a faithful record of the day-to-day ambitions and troubles of average people represented a determined break with fiction based on a principle of depth, the habit of probing meanings hidden behind perceptions.[48] Thus it is not surprising that when Howells traveled as a young man from Ohio to New England in 1860, he was disconcerted by his meetings with acclaimed authors. "My First Visit to New England," published in *Harper's New Monthly Magazine* in 1894, must be read cautiously as a retro-spective account; still, Howells's essay reveals the new intellectual tempera-ment of successors to the American Renaissance.

Howells pictured himself as a "passionate pilgrim from the West" to "his holy land" of Boston, "our literary centre" before the Civil War.[49] The final and most important stages of his journey, a trip that wound through Quebec and Portland, Maine, took him to Boston itself and Concord. Each place seemed to nourish a distinctive frame of mind. The centerpiece of Howells's stay in Boston was an intimate dinner at the Parker House "at the old-fashioned Boston hour of two" with James Russell Lowell, the editor of the *Atlantic Monthly*, James T. Fields, the magazine's publisher, and Oliver Wendell Holmes, Sr. A model of fine manners and witty conversation among cultivated men, the meal, in Howells's recollection, possessed a "dramatic perfection."[50]

Howells's days in Concord were less satisfying. He approached Hawthorne with a "devotion" based on veneration of the older man's novels, but he found Hawthorne in person to be shy, able to extend only "shadowy kindness" and to engage in conversation of a "desultory and unfinal character."[51] Howells's conclusion that "I entirely liked Hawthorne" hid a note of insincerity, because in the same breath he nearly dismissed Hawthorne by praising his "quaintness."[52] His discussion of literature with Emerson cast him even deeper into "confusion."[53] Emerson "praised extravagantly, and in the wrong place, especially among the new things, and he failed to see the worth of much that was fine and precious beside the line of his fancy."[54] Howells fled back to Boston and found relief for his dashed expectations in Fields's perception of the episode as humorous rather than tragic. He felt better as he watched Fields "lying back in his chair and laughing and laughing, till I thought he would roll out of it."[55] Writing three decades after this trip to New England, Howells probably tailored his memories half-consciously to underscore the lesson of his experience: he was comfortable with the self-confident wit and artistry of the genteel writers he identified with Boston, but he felt equally impelled to dismiss the "dark repose," the quality of inward reflection, that he saw in Concord in Hawthorne's face.[56] Based in his genuine dismay as a young author that his heroes were inadequate to his tastes and ambitions, Howells used his intellectual antecedents selectively to take American fiction toward his vision of realism.

Mark Twain's trip to the East in 1853 was filled with similar tensions. Almost an exact contemporary of Howells and, like Howells, raised in the Midwest, Twain (1835–1910) began to experiment with comic sketches when he was still in his teens. "The Dandy Frightening the Squatter" (1852) and fictional letters by "Thomas Jefferson Snodgrass" (1856–57) thrived on humorous reversals of foolish expectations and, more broadly, on literary devices of discontinuity and upset—techniques that departed from the dominant romantic impulse of the American Renaissance to harmonize clashing elements. Even so, Twain did not rebel against his predecessors altogether. Humor was an important part of antebellum popular writing, and satire drew a wider, more respectable audience beginning in the 1850s through the efforts of the light-handed social critics as well as a group of writers known by their pseudonyms, among them "John Phoenix," "Petroleum Nasby," and "Artemus Ward." Indeed, Twain's piece about the "Dandy" was published in a Boston humor magazine, *The Carpet-Bag*. Thus when he left Missouri for New York in 1853, he must have approached eastern literary culture in a mood of wide-eyed expectancy, mixed perhaps with half-formed doubts.[57]

Twain was impressed by the East, but he did not find an intellectual home. As a young man from Hannibal, Missouri, he could not help but be excited by theatrical performances in New York and by patriotic monuments in Philadelphia and Washington, enthusiasm he communicated in his letters.[58] Yet none of his fiction of the late 1850s showed "the author-to-be discovering his métier," in the words of Everett Emerson, a recent critic of Twain.[59] Twain wrote sporadically for midwestern newspapers during four years as a riverboat pilot on the Mississippi just before the Civil War. But it was only after he moved to Carson City, Nevada, in 1861 and gravitated toward the publishing world of San Francisco that he developed a comic style, demonstrated most memorably in "The Notorious Jumping Frog of Calaveras County" (1865), that helped to fix him in a literary vocation. This western market was the intellectual setting that had inspired John Rollin Ridge's *Joaquín Murieta*. It was an atmosphere that was unrestrained, irreverent, and experimental, and yet a place where artistry was still prized. The "authentic Mark Twain," Emerson concludes, "was a product of Nevada."[60]

The problem of professional commitment in Twain's early career was created to an extent by conflicting regional tastes. The midwestern humorist instinctively shied away from eastern conventions of humor as well as serious prose. But Twain's irresolution grew as well from changing intellectual standards. Uninterested in his early career in nuanced symbols carrying metaphysical meanings, Twain sketched limited characters, dramatized quick turnabouts, and sought a hearty laugh to disrupt an ordinary train of thought. His fictional world was centered in ambiguity and instability, qualities that pre–Civil War Victorianism tried hard to master and control. It is no wonder that Twain failed to respond on a deep level in 1853 to eastern literary culture.[61]

Not all of the new directions in taste came from outside the East. Some young writers who gained popularity after the Civil War for their blunt style and commonplace themes—traits associated with realism—grew up near old literary centers and published alongside established authors in prestigious antebellum magazines. Rose Terry Cooke (1827–92), remembered for her masterful regional sketches, was connected socially with eminent New Englanders. Her father was a distant relative of Longfellow, and her mother was the daughter of a famous shipbuilder. Born in Connecticut, Cooke was educated at Hartford Female Seminary, founded by Catharine Beecher. Cooke's earliest fiction in the mid-1850s oscillated between romantic and realistic styles. "Maya, the Princess," appearing in the first volume of the *Atlantic Monthly* in 1857, had a delicate, mythic quality, a tone that might be expected of a woman writer of Cooke's background. The story of a princess given a "spark" at birth by a fairy, "Maya" tells of the ambiguous consequences of the girl's passionate restlessness, both intellectual vigor and bitter loneliness, because Maya found no one able to respond to her gift.[62] The readers of the *Atlantic* were educated people accustomed to hearing social criticism, but they were also genteel enough to appreciate Cooke's circumspect handling of her commentary on women. Her future stories in the *Atlantic* were far less guarded.

"The Ring Fetter," published in the *Atlantic* in 1859, squarely faced social ills by taking on the subject of unhappy marriages. Cooke vowed to subvert "the usage of novel-writers" who commonly conclude their books with marriage, an event that "brings a woman's legal existence to an end when she merges her independence in that of a man," but all too often does not secure fairy-tale bliss.[63] At the heart of Cooke's story stood the crippling loneliness of Mehitable Hyde, the daughter of a prominent family of Greenfield, Massachusetts. After the death of her parents, preceded by many years spent nursing her invalid father, Hitty Hyde is courted in her middle age by Abner Dimock, a man who seeks only her fortune. Bereft of all emotional nourishment, Hitty risks everything for a last chance at love and deceives herself about her suitor's character. The tale unwinds in a predictable but anguished spiral of psychological cruelty and physical abuse, including Abner's killing of their son, and ends with Hitty's suicide. Here again was the theme of "Maya, the Princess," literally the fetters that society placed on women. But Cooke's treatment was socially graphic, brutal, and direct, with her meaning displayed close to the surface. She used the *Atlantic*, an influential channel of literary expression, to turn New England writing in the direction of the terse, emotionally riveting tragedies of everyday life.[64]

Howells, Twain, and Cooke were all young writers in the 1850s, just beginning their careers. The popular styles of the decade had little in common with the compact social themes and streamlined language that would characterize these authors' mature fiction but instead favored luxuriant and nuanced expression. Yet perhaps the true test of the intellectual power of the antebellum marketplace was the space it allowed for rising thinkers who would ultimately subvert prevailing tastes. In the postwar decades Howells and his contemporaries crafted a literature that was less leisured, resonant, and curious about hidden implications than the Victorianism of the 1850s. Nonetheless, they inherited from their predecessors a cultural milieu that offered them the means of experimentation and a path to independence. This market-oriented system of intellectual production and exchange was the accomplishment of the antebellum decades. It was instrumental in changing the nation's intellectual experience in sweeping ways.

Individuals in the Marketplace

In 1830 fewer than 10 percent of Americans lived in towns large enough to be considered urban by the standard of the U.S. Census (2,500 inhabitants), and the majority's exposure to ideas was correspondingly modest. The reading public had access to published sermons and religious tracts as well as growing numbers of newspapers, magazines, and books. Fourth of July celebrations, traveling theater companies, and occasional lecturers brought stimulation and entertainment to communities. Yet experiences that most Americans took for granted in 1860 were simply not possible 30 years before. There was no two-party system, because the Whigs did not organize on the national level until the mid-1830s. Daguerreotypes and photographs were not yet invented, and few people lived in homes displaying images on the walls. Magazines included illustrations only infrequently, and when they did the pictures consisted of black-and-white drawings. Most native-born Americans knew no language except English. If they read foreign books, they stuck to British authors such as Walter Scott. On the whole American culture in 1830 was centered in the use of written words of a familiar sound to readers. Most contemporaries did not encounter visual representations, art objects, or dramatic events on a daily or even weekly basis.[65]

Oral traditions were also strong in this setting. In contrast to later mass-marketed ideas that came to individuals from a distance in an easily transmitted and purchasable form, intelligence in 1830 often traveled from person to person. Literate citizens read the newspapers to their illiterate neighbors who gathered at a local store. Parents, in tacit recognition of the educational mission of families, read the Bible and other books aloud with their children at home. For perhaps a majority of Americans, preaching was the most important source of public culture. Whether people heard ministers during weekly services, protracted revivals, or meetings of benevolent societies, Protestants listened with attention and comprehension to the nuances of doctrine. In 1830 the language of Christianity remained the primary means used by many Americans to explain their individual and common purposes. The struggles of politics and the activity of the market engaged the American imagination, yet the fascination of secular contests and communication still did not match the intellectual and emotional power of the drama of salvation.[66]

In 1860 basic elements of American culture remained the same. Fewer people in a religious environment now attentive to the gradual spiritual nurture of children anxiously awaited a sudden conversion, once standard in the evangelical tradition. But most people thought of themselves and their nation as Christian, just as Americans had in the past. The languages of democracy and capitalism, both components of American values in 1830, were now dense and sometimes conflicted sets of ideas, a sign of their growing importance to Americans and their intensive use. Victorian politics was anchored by a faith in the controlled competition of party contests. Middle-class mores focused on a vision of individual self-improvement and upward mobility. Around this intellectual center, however, public discourse had developed in complex ways. Distinctive sectional, gender, and class interpretations of democratic ideals made political life a forum for multiple, concurrent debates. The culture of capitalism strove to reconcile divisions that came with social development—

between city and country, rich and poor, men and women, head and heart—and in the process produced compelling prescriptions and myths, including the cult of domesticity and the notion of the self-made man. This middle-class vision, providing the newest vocabulary to Americans for speaking about themselves, was the distinctive contribution of the antebellum generation to the nation's intellectual life. On the eve of the Civil War, Americans relied more strongly than ever on these secular modes of thinking about society and politics to describe and indeed to try to control their culture.

Even with these points of continuity with the past, culture in 1860 had a texture that was far more varied and challenging than was the nation's intellectual and aesthetic experience three decades before. Now one-fifth of Americans lived in towns and cities of at least 2,500 people, and inhabitants of smaller places could keep up with the latest ideas by means of mass-marketed literature, better mail service, and increasing railroad mileage. Face-to-face communication was still important, as listeners came together to hear preaching, lecturing, and stump speaking. But print culture had virtually exploded over the years in terms of quantity and genres, among them poems, stories, novels, polemics, histories, and scientific tracts. Much of this writing had an argumentative edge or imaginative luxuriance that stirred readers' passions. The popularity of *Uncle Tom's Cabin*, a novel combining these strains of advocacy and evocation, was one indication of Americans' eagerness to have words touch deep personal sources of sensibility and conviction. The reading public understood the potential for stimulation and reflection offered by writing, and they consumed the literary products of the marketplace without inhibition.

Central to this society as language was, Americans also encountred a feast of images and pageantry. By 1860 magazines commonly illustrated prose with color pictures. Houses of the aspiring and prosperous classes were designed to incorporate architectural fashions and, in their interiors, displayed furniture, carpets, and wall decorations as opulent as their owners could afford. Plays, exhibitions, and concerts, most of which traveled from place to place, gave public culture a theatrical tone. Compared with Americans in 1830, people in 1860 lived in a setting that was visually and sensibly rich. There was much more to see and enjoy than was available to Americans in the past.[67]

New uncertainties accompanied this intensification of cultural activity, however. Just as tensions along sectional, religious, class, and regional lines appeared during the 1850s in public expression, private individuals experienced conflicts that were endemic to a diversified, fast-paced society. Private and public identity diverged to the point that individuals must have felt at times that they were leading fragmented lives. In homes the trend in domestic architecture was to divide houses into many rooms that provided family members with personalized spaces, an unprecedented affirmation of the value of individuality. But how would this private person relate to society at large if, as a man, he went to work, church, and political meetings, or, as a woman, she gave time to benevolence, shopping, and obligatory social calls? The variety of cultural opportunities in 1860, in some ways so enticing, jeopardized the integrity of the self and required that Americans find what comfort they could in a plurality of public roles.[68]

Likewise, Americans felt divided in time between memories of the past and ambitions for the future. Sentimentality and aspiration conspired to crowd out their ability to appreciate the present moment. As the pace of change accelerated, interest in history correspondingly rose, and the 1850s in particular included evidence of growing historical awareness: the campaign to restore Washington's home at Mount Vernon, the formation of numerous historical societies, the strengthening of regionalism in literature, and the intense discussions of the Constitution.[69] The underlying cause of much of this mounting nostalgia was the desire for individual success and the faith in social progress virtually canonized by the culture of capitalism. Americans hastened from modest origins to visions of individual and national splendor only to have second thoughts about their dreams and regrets about the simpler life they left behind. Thus torn between the future and past, they had little energy to savor the present. One message of Henry Thoreau's *Walden* (1854) was the need to take time to note the details of everyday life. This was an important thought for Thoreau's contemporaries but one, given the book's small readership, that most of them had no time to hear.

Hard as it was for Americans in 1860 to live with divided energies and commitments, the most difficult lesson taught by the cultural marketplace was the limitation of each individual's point of view. There are two ways to tell the story about the proliferation of means of expression in antebellum America. One account emphasizes communication, exposure to ideas, and the empowerment of rising social groups through their access to language. But a soberer version suggests that the diversity of voices heard must have impressed each speaker with the thought that his or her set of convictions was only one among many. Probably white, middle-class Protestants still commanded sufficient cultural power and subscribed to Victorian values of enough coherence to cloud their perception of increasing pluralism. To an important extent, however, Americans in 1860 did see that there were abiding differences among them. This consciousness produced no single reaction. In the painful context of the sectional crisis, the clashing beliefs of the free and slave states led finally to the abandonment of persuasion and the embrace of violence to secure each side's distinctive principles. In a mellower mood, young realistic writers such as Howells, Twain, and Cooke approached cultural idiosyncrasies with curiosity and an interest in faithfully rendering individual and regional peculiarities. Whether Americans in 1860 responded to their differences with dogmatism or toleration—or perhaps both feelings at separate times—they must have been aware of the appearance of many diverging viewpoints since the beginning of the antebellum era and grasped the way debate contested the preeminence of any single perspective.

The establishment of a national marketplace of ideas thus contained unprecedented opportunities for expression along with an equally great risk of conflict. The availability of powerful languages of communication, the formation of communities of intellectuals, and the determination of minorities to participate in public discussion were some of the developments that produced a culture inspiring to individual talent and yet portending division. It is equally understandable that the American Renaissance of literature and art emerged as the era's most sophisticated achievement and that the Civil War ended the mid-nineteenth-century period. This dual antebellum legacy of cultural accomplishment and controversy continued in later decades to shape the intellectual life of an increasingly diversified American people.

Chronology

1830   Joseph Smith's *Book of Mormon* published.

1831   William Lloyd Garrison begins publishing *The Liberator*. Nat Turner slave revolt in Virginia. First American-built steam locomotive ("Best Friend of Charleston") begins regular service in South Carolina.

1832   Andrew Jackson reelected president. High point of the Nullification Crisis.

1833   Penny press begins when two New York newspapers, the *Sun* and the *Morning Post*, issue dailies at a cost of a penny per day. General Trades' Union organized in New York City (as were similar unions in Philadelphia, Baltimore, and Washington). Oberlin established as the first coeducational college in America. Publication of *Tracts for the Times* begins at Oxford University (England).

1834   Whig party formed.

1835   Alexis de Tocqueville publishes the first two volumes of *Democracy in America* in Paris (the last two volumes appeared in 1840). Lyman Beecher, *A Plea for the West*. Charles Grandison Finney, *Lectures on Revivals of Religion*. Cherokee removal ("the Trail of Tears") from Georgia to Arkansas.

1836   Popular nativist exposé published under the alleged authorship of Maria Monk, *Awful Disclosures of the Hotel Dieu Nunnery of Montreal*. Ralph Waldo Emerson, *Nature*.

1837   Financial panic. Abolitionist Elijah Lovejoy murdered by a proslavery mob in Alton, Illinois. Sarah J. Hale becomes editor of *Godey's Lady's Book*. Nathaniel Hawthorne, *Twice-Told Tales*.

1838   Ralph Waldo Emerson delivers the "Divinity School Address" at Harvard. Abraham Lincoln speaks on "The Perpetuation of Our Political Institutions" at the Springfield, Illinois, lyceum. Sarah Grimké, *Letters on the Equality of the Sexes and the Condition of Women*.

1839   Daguerreotypes introduced in America.

1840   Liberty party formed.

1841   Catharine Beecher, *Treatise on Domestic Economy*. Brook Farm community established.

1842   Trade unions and collective bargaining declared legal by the Massachusetts Supreme Court in *Commonwealth v. Hunt*.

1843   Rabbi Isaac Leeser begins publication of *The Occident, and American Jewish Advocate*. Completion of the model of Hiram Powers's statue, *The Greek Slave*.

1844   Methodist Episcopal church divides into northern and southern branches over the slavery issue. Conversion to Roman Catholicism of Orestes Brownson and Isaac Hecker. Anti-Catholic riots in Philadelphia. First domestic telegraph line completed. Robert and Richard Hoe's rotary cylinder press speeds the printing process.

1845   Baptist church splits into northern and southern branches over the slavery issue. Frederick Douglass publishes *Narrative of the Life of Frederick Douglass, an American Slave*. Margaret Fuller, *Woman in the Nineteenth Century*. Phoebe Palmer, *Entire Devotion to God*.

1846   Beginning of the Mexican War. Beginning of the "potato famine" in Ireland. Smithsonian Institution established by Congress. American Union of Associationists (Fourierists) established. School of Science (later the Sheffield Scientific School) established at Yale.

1847   Horace Bushnell publishes *Christian Nurture*. Frederick Douglass begins publication of the *North Star* in Rochester, New York. Lawrence Scientific School established at Harvard.

1848   Treaty of Guadalupe Hidalgo ends the Mexican War. Women's Rights Convention at Seneca Falls, New York, issues its "Declaration of Sentiments." Henry David Thoreau delivers "Resistance to Civil Government" at the Concord, Massachusetts, lyceum.

1849   California Gold Rush begins.

1850   Compromise of 1850. Daniel Webster's "The Constitution and the Union" ("7th of March" speech) delivered in the U.S. Senate. Susan Warner, *The Wide, Wide World*. Mary Anne Sadlier, *Willy Burke; or, The Irish Orphan in America*.

1851   Posthumous publication of John C. Calhoun, *A Disquisition on Government*. Herman Melville, *Moby-Dick*.

1852   Harriet Beecher Stowe, *Uncle Tom's Cabin*. Publication of *The Pro-Slavery Argument; as Maintained by the Most Distinguished Writers of the Southern States*. First Plenary Council of the Roman Catholic Church in America held in Baltimore.

1853   New York Crystal Palace Exhibition.

1854   American or "Know-Nothing" party established. Rabbi Isaac Mayer Wise begins publication of *The Israelite*. Henry David Thoreau, *Walden*. John Rollin Ridge ("Yellow Bird"), *The Life and Adventures of Joaquín Murieta*.

1855   Walt Whitman, *Leaves of Grass*.

1856   Republican party runs its first presidental candidate, John C. Frémont. Construction of New York's Central Park begins. Saturday Club begins meeting in Boston.

1857   Financial panic. Revival begins and continues into 1858. George Fitzhugh, *Cannibals All!; or, Slaves without Masters*. James T. Fields begins publication of the *Atlantic Monthly*. Nathaniel Currier and James M. Ives, New York lithographers, form partnership.

1858   Transatlantic telegraph completed. Lincoln debates Stephen Douglas.

1859   John Brown's raid at Harpers Ferry, Virginia. Charles Darwin publishes *The Origin of Species* in London.

1860   Abraham Lincoln elected president. Shoemakers' strike, Lynn, Massachusetts.

Notes and References

Introduction

1. This perspective may be seen as a revision of John Higham's classic argument that American society moved in the antebellum decades "from boundlessness to consolidation." I agree with Higham that a process of social and intellectual definition occurred, but I propose that this firmer institutional base facilitated intellectual activity and encouraged the expression of dissent. For Higham's view, see *From Boundlessness to Consolidation: The Transformation of American Culture, 1848–1860* (Ann Arbor, Mich.: William L. Clements Library, 1969). Many of the terms that convey the exuberance of pre–Civil War culture are so widely used by scholars that it is impossible to trace them to individual sources. Still, influential interpretations associated with the phrases cited include Arthur M. Schlesinger, Jr., *The Age of Jackson* (Boston: Little, Brown, 1945); Van Wyck Brooks, *The Flowering of New England, 1815–1865* (London: J. M. Dent & Sons, 1936); and F. O. Matthiessen, *American Renaissance: Art and Expression in the Age of Emerson and Whitman* (1941; rpt., New York: Oxford University Press, 1972).

2. Sydney E. Ahlstrom, *A Religious History of the American People* (New Haven: Yale University Press, 1972), 437.

3. On the changing patterns of denominationalism, see Winthrop S. Hudson, *American Protestantism* (Chicago: University of Chicago Press, 1961), 97, and Sidney E. Mead, *The Lively Experiment: The Shaping of Christianity in America* (New York: Harper & Row, 1963), 106–7. Nathan O. Hatch makes the important point that despite Methodism's internal bureaucracy, the denomination (along with other popular religious groups) represented a route for ordinary people to register their religious views in society at large. See *The Democratization of American Christianity* (New Haven: Yale University Press, 1989), esp. 81–93. On *The Ladies' Repository*, see Nina Baym, *Novels, Readers, and Reviewers: Responses to Fiction in Antebellum America* (Ithaca: Cornell University Press, 1984), 17.

4. Donald M. Scott, *From Office to Profession: The New England Ministry, 1750–1850* (Philadelphia: University of Pennsylvania Press, 1978).

5. Donald M. Scott, "Abolition as a Sacred Vocation," in Lewis Perry and Michael Fellman, eds., *Antislavery Reconsidered: New Perspectives on the Abolitionists* (Baton Rouge: Louisiana State University Press, 1979), 51–74.

6. Kathryn Kish Sklar, *Catharine Beecher: A Study in American Domesticity* (New Haven: Yale University Press, 1973), chap. 12.

7. Despite the prohibition of a state church on the national level effected by the First Amendment, the disestablishment of tax-supported religious organizations in individual states was a process that continued for many decades after 1787. One of the most thorough studies of disestablishment is William G. McLoughlin, *New England Dissent, 1630–1833: The Baptists and the Separation of Church and State* (Cambridge, Mass.: Harvard University Press, 1971), esp. vol. 2.

8. Carroll Smith-Rosenberg, *Religion and the Rise of the American City: The New York City Mission Movement, 1812–1870* (Ithaca: Cornell University Press, 1971), chap. 4.

9. This estimate for adult white literacy is cited in Michael T. Gilmore, *American Romanticism and the Marketplace* (Chicago: University of Chicago Press, 1985), 4. For a good discussion of the changing significance of literacy, see David D. Hall, "Introduction: The Uses of Literacy in New England, 1600–1850," in William L. Joyce et al., eds., *Printing and Society in Early America* (Worcester, Mass.: American Antiquarian Society, 1985), 1–47.

10. This political procession is described by Charles E. Payne in *Josiah Bushnell Grinnell* (Iowa City: State Historical Society of Iowa, 1938), 8.

11. Kenneth S. Greenberg, *Masters and Statesmen: The Political Culture of American Slavery* (Baltimore: Johns Hopkins University Press, 1985), esp. chap. 7.

12. Richard Hofstadter, *The Idea of a Party System: The Rise of Legitimate Opposition in the United States, 1780–1840* (Berkeley: University of California Press, 1969), chap. 6.

13. Among the vast literature on particular parties, one essay that explains the basic assumptions and rituals of this democratic political culture is Jean H. Baker, "The Ceremonies of Politics: Nineteenth-Century Rituals of National Affirmation," in William J. Cooper, Jr., Michael F. Holt, and John McCardell, eds., *A Master's Due: Essays in Honor of David Herbert Donald* (Baton Rouge: Louisiana State University Press, 1985), 161–78.

14. These rates of electoral participation are cited in Michael E. McGeer, *The Decline of Popular Politics: American Politics from the Age of Jackson to the Progressive Era* (New York: Oxford University Press, 1986), 5–6. On changes in suffrage laws, see James Oakes, *The Ruling Race: A History of American Slaveholders* (New York: Vintage, 1982), 139.

15. McGeer, *Decline of Popular Politics*, 24–27.

16. Among numerous studies of this socioeconomic transformation, monographs on particular regions and social groups are especially helpful. See especially Steven Hahn, *The Roots of Southern Populism: Yeoman Farmers and the Transformation of the Georgia Upcountry, 1850–1890* (New York: Oxford University Press, 1983); Sean Wilentz, *Chants Democratic: New York City and the Rise of the American Working Class, 1788–1850* (New York: Oxford University Press, 1984); John Mack Faragher, *Sugar Creek: Life on the Illinois Prairie* (New Haven: Yale University Press, 1986); and Christopher Clark, *The Roots of Rural Capitalism: Western Massachusetts, 1780–1860* (Ithaca: Cornell University Press, 1990).

17. Baym, *Novels, Readers, and Reviewers*, 14. On this cultural transition see esp.

Mary Kelley, *Private Woman, Public Stage: Literary Domesticity in Nineteenth-Century America* (New York: Oxford University Press, 1984), chap. 1; Lawrence Buell, *New England Literary Culture: From Revolution through Renaissance* (Cambridge: Cambridge University Press, 1986), chaps. 2 and 3; Richard D. Brown, *Knowledge Is Power: The Diffusion of Information in Early America, 1700–1865* (New York: Oxford University Press, 1989); and William J. Gilmore, *Reading Becomes a Necessity of Life: Material and Cultural Life in Rural New England, 1780–1835* (Knoxville: University of Tennessee Press, 1989).

18. 27 November 1861, *Mary Chesnut's Civil War*, ed. C. Vann Woodward (New Haven: Yale University Press, 1981), 245.

19. Donald M. Scott, "The Popular Lecture and the Creation of a Public in Mid-Nineteenth-Century America," *Journal of American History* 66 (1980): 791–809.

20. Ruth E. Finley, *The Lady of Godey's: Sarah Josepha Hale* (Philadelphia: J. B. Lippincott, 1931); Justin Kaplan, *Walt Whitman: A Life* (Toronto: Bantam, 1982), 15–16, 106, 181.

21. On Fields, Barnum, and Bonner, respectively, see Nathan Irvin Huggins, *Protestants against Poverty: Boston's Charities, 1870–1900* (Westport, Conn.: Greenwood, 1971), 163–65; Neil Harris, *Humbug: The Art of P. T. Barnum* (Chicago: University of Chicago Press, 1973); and Kelly, *Private Woman, Public Stage*, chap. 1.

22. Baym, *Novels, Readers, and Reviewers*, 49–50; Carl Bode, *The Anatomy of American Popular Culture, 1840–1861* (Berkeley: University of California Press, 1959), 20–21.

23. Baym, *Novels, Readers, and Reviewers*, 50; Claudia D. Johnson, "That Guilty Third Tier: Prostitution in Nineteenth-Century American Theaters," in Daniel Walker Howe, ed., *Victorian America* (Philadelphia: University of Pennsylvania Press, 1976), 111–20.

24. Daniel Howe provides a basic definition of American Victorian culture in "Victorian Culture in America," in Howe, ed., *Victorian America*, 3–28. I explore the usefulness of the concept of "Victorianism" to describe the culture of mid-nineteenth-century America in *Victorian America and the Civil War* (Cambridge: Cambridge University Press, 1992), esp. 7–9. *Victorian American and the Civil War* emphasizes the tensions and conflicts in middle-class Victorian society that were obscured by the points of consensus identified here.

1. The Transformations of Faith

1. The membership figures cited are found in Jay P. Dolan, *Catholic Revivalism: The American Experience, 1830–1900* (Notre Dame, Ind.: University of Notre Dame Press, 1978), 25–26, and Nathan Glazer, *American Judaism*, 2d rev. ed. (Chicago: University of Chicago Press, 1972), 23.

2. Essential surveys on American religion include Ahlstrom, *Religious History of the American People*; Jay P. Dolan, *The American Catholic Experience: A History from Colonial Times to the Present* (Garden City, N.Y.: Doubleday, 1985); and Jacob Rader Marcus, *United States Jewry, 1776–1985* (Detroit: Wayne State University Press, 1989–94), esp. vols. 1–2. This chapter concentrates on Protestantism because of the pervasive and dominant influence of Protestant Christianity in society during this period. Further discussion of Catholic and Jewish thought appears in Chapter 5.

3. *The Life of the Mind in America: From the Revolution to the Civil War* (New York: Harcourt, Brace & World, 1965), 7.

4. Ibid., 73–77.

5. Mary P. Ryan, *Cradle of the Middle Class: The Family in Oneida County, New York, 1790–1865* (Cambridge: Cambridge University Press, 1981), 110–27. On Baltimore, see Terry D. Bilhartz, *Urban Religion and the Second Great Awakening: Church and Society in Early National Baltimore* (Rutherford, N.J.: Fairleigh Dickinson University Press, 1986), 96.

6. *Slave Religion: The "Invisible Institution" in the Antebellum South* (Oxford: Oxford University Press, 1978), 153–54. On revivalism and voluntary associations in the South, see *Slave Religion*, esp. 152–80, and Donald Mathews, *Religion in the Old South* (Chicago: University of Chicago Press, 1977), chaps. 3 and 4.

7. One version of this argument is made by Paul E. Johnson, *A Shopkeeper's Millennium: Society and Revivals in Rochester, New York, 1815–1837* (New York: Hill & Wang, 1978). For a critique of the social control hypothesis, see Lawrence Frederick Kohl, "The Concept of Social Control and the History of Jacksonian America," *Journal of the Early Republic* 5 (1985): 21–34. Nathan Hatch has made an important counter-argument that Protestant evangelicalism in the early nineteenth century was a genuinely popular movement, in *Democratization of American Christianity*.

8. On the influence of Scottish common sense ideas, see Sydney E. Ahlstrom, "The Scottish Philosophy and American Theology," *Church History* 24 (1955): 257–69, and Mark A. Noll, *Princeton and the Republic, 1768–1822* (Princeton: Princeton University Press, 1989). On Methodist theology, see Robert E. Chiles, *Theological Transition in American Methodism, 1790–1935* (New York: Abington Press, 1965), 26–31. Information on the sales of Palmer's books appears in Timothy Smith, *Revivalism and Social Reform: American Protestantism on the Eve of the Civil War* (New York: Harcourt, Brace & World, 1965), 117. See also Phoebe Palmer, *Phoebe Palmer: Selected Writings*, ed. Thomas C. Oden (New York: Paulist Press, 1988). For a discussion of Methodism as an exemplary early nineteenth-century popular denomination, see Hatch, *Democratization of American Christianity*, esp 49–56, 81–93, 201–6.

9. "What a Revival of Religion Is," in Finney, *Lectures on Revivals of Religion*, ed. William G. McLoughlin (Cambridge, Mass.: Harvard University Press, 1960), 9. The italics that appear in this and subsequent quotations are found in the original texts.

10. Ibid., 9, 13.

11. "A Plea for the West," excerpted in Conrad Cherry, ed., *God's New Israel: Religious Interpretations of American Destiny* (Englewood Cliffs, N.J.: Prentice-Hall, 1971), 120.

12. Ibid., 121.

13. See Anne M. Boylan, *Sunday School: The Formation of an American Institution, 1790–1880* (New Haven: Yale University Press, 1988), chap. 5.

14. *Christian Nurture* (New Haven: Yale University Press, 1947).

15. "The Peculiar Responsibilities of American Women," excerpted from *Treatise on Domestic Economy*, in Nancy F. Cott, ed., *Root of Bitterness: Documents of the Social History of American Women* (New York: E. P. Dutton, 1972), 175. For a discussion of the *Treatise*, see Sklar, *Catharine Beecher*, 151–67. Beecher's argument betrayed her assumption that Anglo-Saxon Protestants composed the most important group of American citizens. For more information on religious conceptions of women's role and the participation of women in reform, see Nancy F. Cott, *The Bonds of Womanhood: "Woman's Sphere" in New England, 1780–1835* (New Haven: Yale University Press, 1977), chap. 4; Colleen McDannell, *The Christian Home in Victorian America, 1840–1900* (Bloomington: Indiana University Press, 1986); Carroll Smith-Rosenberg, "The Cross and the

Pedestal: Women, Anti-Ritualism, and the Emergence of the American Bourgeoisie," in her *Disorderly Conduct: Visions of Gender in Victorian America* (New York: Knopf, 1985), 129–64; and Lori D. Ginzberg, *Women and the Work of Benevolence: Morality, Politics, and Class in the Nineteenth-Century United States* (New Haven: Yale University Press, 1990).

16. Smith-Rosenberg, *Religion and the Rise of the American City*, 203–22.

17. Lori Ginzberg suggests that the women who remained active in benevolent organizations did not think of their work in religious terms after the Civil War but rather as a secular and class-oriented effort. Among many factors, the women's perspective may have been shaped by the increasingly restrictive meaning of religious concepts concerning gender. See *Women and the Work of Benevolence*, esp. chaps. 4–6.

18. For a concise explanation of this view of American Victorianism, see Daniel Walker Howe, "Victorian Culture in America," in Howe, ed., *Victorian America*, 3–28. For a broader cultural history of Victorianism in America, see my *Victorian America and the Civil War*. While my interpretation acknowledges the importance of institutional formation, I emphasize the spiritual and emotional disequilibrium that was obscured by the Victorians' apparent stability and self-assurance.

19. Quoted in Anne C. Rose, *Transcendentalism as a Social Movement, 1830–1850* (New Haven: Yale University Press, 1981), 13.

20. Smith, *Revivalism and Social Reform*, chap. 6. On Unitarian voluntary efforts and a slightly different definition of "evangelical Unitarianism," see Rose, *Transcendentalism as a Social Movement*, 28–37.

21. *A New England Girlhood: Outlined from Memory* (Boston: Houghton Mifflin, 1889), 164, 209–10.

22. Johnson, *Shopkeeper's Millennium*, 118.

23. *A Discourse on the Wants of the Times* (Boston: James Munroe, 1836), 18. The judge's opinion of Kneeland may be found in "Charge of Judge Peter O. Thacher, Municipal Court of Boston, Jan., 1834," in John D. Lawson, ed., *American State Trials* (St. Louis: Thomas Law Book Co., 1921), 13: 508. On Paine, see Eric Foner, *Tom Paine and Revolutionary America* (New York: Oxford University Press, 1976), 246–49.

24. Quoted in Ahlstrom, *Religious History of the American People*, 562, and Cherry, *Religious Interpretations*, 120. On the similarity in organization of nativist and other voluntary agencies, see Ahlstrom, *Religious History of the American People*, 560.

25. Ibid., 560–64. For a selection from Monk's *Awful Disclosures*, see Edwin S. Gaustad, ed., *A Documentary History of Religion in America to the Civil War* (Grand Rapids: William B. Eerdmans, 1982), 462–63.

26. "I Like to See It Lap the Miles," in Cleanth Brooks et al., eds., *American Literature: The Makers and the Making* (New York: St. Martin's, 1973), 2: 1239. Although the Irish were the largest group of antebellum Catholic immigrants, they were not the only Roman Catholics to come to America during the period. The next largest group consisted of more prosperous Germans who settled mainly in the midatlantic states and the Midwest. See Dolan, *American Catholic Experience*, 127–31.

27. *Imminent Dangers to the Free Institutions of the United States through Foreign Immigration*, excerpted in Gaustad, ed., *Documentary History*, 461.

28. See Dolan, *American Catholic Experience*, esp. 159, 166–67, 211–13, and chap. 11. On Catholic missions and devotions, respectively, see Dolan, *Catholic Revivalism*, and Ann Taves, *The Household of Faith: Roman Catholic Devotions in Mid-Nineteenth-Century America* (Notre Dame, Ind.: University of Notre Dame Press, 1986).

29. "Some Themes of Counter-Subversion: An Analysis of Anti-Masonic, Anti-

Catholic, and Anti-Mormon Literature," in David Brion Davis, *From Homicide to Slavery: Studies in American Culture* (New York: Oxford University Press, 1986), 137–54.

30. *Walden and Civil Disobedience* (New York: Penguin, 1983), 59.

31. For a good discussion of postmillennial and premillennialism for the viewpoint of later developments, see George M. Marsden, *Fundamentalism and American Culture: The Shaping of Twentieth Century Evangelicalism, 1870–1925* (New York: Oxford University Press, 1980), 48–55.

32. On Mormon premillennialism, see Kenneth H. Winn, *Exiles in a Land of Liberty: Mormons in America, 1830–1846* (Chapel Hill: University of North Carolina Press, 1989), esp. 38–39, 49–50, 86–87, 236. On the Mormon conception of time as it developed in the later nineteenth century, see Jan Shipps, *Mormonism: The Story of a New Religious Tradition* (Urbana: University of Illinois Press, 1985), chaps. 6 and 7.

33. Ruth Alden Doan, *The Miller Heresy, Millennialism, and American Culture* (Philadelphia: Temple University Press, 1987), 34, 39–53.

34. "The Divinity School Address" (1838), in *Selections from Ralph Waldo Emerson: An Organic Anthology*, ed. Stephen E. Whicher (Boston: Houghton Mifflin, 1957), 112.

35. *Selections from Emerson*, ed. Whicher, 50.

36. For a brief analysis of spiritualism, see Ahlstrom, *Religious History of the American People*, 483–90. For an extended discussion, see R. Laurence Moore, *In Search of White Crows: Spiritualism, Parapsychology, and American Culture* (New York: Oxford University Press, 1977), pt. 1.

37. 16 June 1850, 26 November 1855, *The Diary of George Templeton Strong*, ed. Allan Nevins and Milton Halsey Thomas (New York: Macmillan, 1952), 2: 15–16, 245. Moore examines clerical opposition to spiritualism in *In Search of White Crows*, chap. 2. Lay people, in contrast, had divided views on spiritualism, such as those of Strong, but did not act on their misgivings to the extent that some had in relation to Mormonism, for example, a decade before.

38. I use the term "abolitionism" to connote the religiously oriented philosophy of opposition to slavery that emerged in the 1830s. The word "antislavery" usually refers more broadly to all proposals for the liberation of slaves. Chapter 2 discusses the political antislavery movement that gained momentum in the 1840s and 1850s. For an analysis of the usage of the terms "abolition" and "antislavery," see David Brion Davis, "Antislavery or Abolition?," *Reviews in American History* 1 (1973): 95–99.

39. For a general view of abolitionism, see Lawrence J. Friedman, *Gregarious Saints: Self and Community in American Abolitionism, 1830–1870* (Cambridge: Cambridge University Press, 1982). On Garrison, see James Brewer Stewart, *William Lloyd Garrison and the Challenge of Emancipation* (Arlington Heights, Ill.: Harlan Davidson, 1992). On the involvement of free African Americans in abolitionism, see David E. Swift, *Black Prophets of Justice: Activist Clergy before the Civil War* (Baton Rouge: Louisiana State University Press, 1989) and Peter C. Ripley, ed., *The Black Abolitionist Papers*, vols. 3–5 (Chapel Hill: University of North Carolina Press, 1991–92), esp. 3: 3–69; Jean Fagan Yellin, *Women and Sisters: The Antislavery Feminists in American Culture* (New Haven: Yale University Press, 1989), esp. 46–48, 77–96; Carol V. R. George, "Widening the Circle: The Black Church and the Abolition Crusade, 1830–1860," in Perry and Fellman, eds., *Antislavery Reconsidered*, 75–95. The estimate of black subscribers to the *Liberator* is cited in Truman Nelson, ed., *Documents of Upheaval: Selections from William Lloyd Garrison's "The Liberator," 1831–1865* (New York: Hill & Wang, 1966),

xvi. On the radical impulse behind African-American Protestanism more generally, see Hatch, *Democratization of American Christianity*, 102–13.

40. "The *Liberator* and Slavery: Introductory Remarks," 7 January 1832, in Nelson, ed., *Documents of Upheaval*, 42.

41. Davis makes this point in "The Emergence of Immediatism in British and American Antislavery Thought," in his *From Homicide to Slavery*, 255–57.

42. "Appeal to the Christian Women of the South," in Alice S. Rossi, ed., *The Feminist Papers: From Adams to de Beauvoir* (New York: Bantam, 1973), 300–1.

43. "The *Liberator* and Slavery," in Nelson, ed., *Documents of Upheaval*, 44. Donald Scott makes a point of the abolitionists' drive for self-purification in "Abolition as a Sacred Vocation," in Perry and Fellman, eds., *Antislavery Reconsidered*, 51–74.

44. "What Shall Be Done?," 30 July, in Nelson, ed., *Documents of Upheaval*, 11.

45. On the denominational schisms, see C. C. Goen, *Broken Churches, Broken Nation: Denominational Schisms and the Coming of the American Civil War* (Macon, Ga.: Mercer University Press, 1985), esp. chap. 3. Two examples may suggest how complicated these religious divisions were. In the case of the Presbyterian split into New School and Old School factions, Goen observes that "differing views of slavery figured significantly if not decisively" (67). Also at issue was the use of aggressive evangelical techniques—the "new measures"—that implied that human beings could control the conversion process to an extent unacceptable to more traditional Christians. In the case of the Baptist schism, the precipitating cause of the secession of southern churches was a statement of denominational neutrality on slavery issued by the northern majority (95). Slavery was the issue, but most northern Baptists were not abolitionists. On violence aimed at abolitionists, see Leonard Richards, *"Gentlemen of Property and Standing": Anti-Abolition Mobs in Jacksonian America* (New York: Oxford University Press, 1970).

46. The foregoing discussion is based mainly on Lewis Perry, *Radical Abolitionism: Anarchy and the Government of God in Antislavery Thought* (Ithaca: Cornell University Press, 1973).

47. See Aileen S. Kraditor, *Means and Ends in American Abolitionism: Garrison and His Critics on Strategy and Tactics, 1834–1850* (New York: Vintage, 1967), chap. 3. On Tolstoy, see Perry, *Radical Abolitionism*, chap. 1.

48. "A Pastoral Letter, 'The General Association of Massachusetts (Orthodox) Ministers to the Churches Under Their Care,'" in Rossi, ed., *Feminist Papers*, 305, 306.

49. "Appeal to the Christian Women," in Rossi, ed., *Feminist Papers*, 297.

50. *Letters on the Equality of the Sexes*, in Rossi, *Feminist Papers*, 308. Capitals that appear in this and subsequent quotations are found in the original texts.

51. Ibid., 307.

52. Macdonald's list appears in John Humphrey Noyes, *History of American Socialisms* (1870; rpt., New York: Hillary House, 1961), 10–12.

53. Louis J. Kern, *An Ordered Love: Sex Roles and Sexuality in Victorian Utopias—the Shakers, the Mormons, and the Oneida Community* (Chapel Hill: University of North Carolina Press, 1981), esp. 209, 213, 224, 238, 246–51.

54. Ripley to Isaac Hecker, 18 September 1843, quoted in Rose, *Transcendentalism as a Social Movement*, 143; my discussion of Brook Farm is based on pp. 130–61.

55. These totals are cited in *Transcendentalism as a Social Movement*, 151–52. Carl J. Guarneri arrives at slightly different totals in his excellent study *The Utopian*

Alternative: Fourierism in Nineteenth-Century America (Ithaca: Cornell University Press, 1991), 407–9. Whatever the exact number of these sometimes elusive social experiments, there is no question that Fourierism was popular in America, particularly during the 1840s.

56. This analysis of the relation of dissenting and mainstream positions is offered by Ruth Doan in *Miller Heresy*, 215–28.

57. Ahlstrom, *Religious History of the American People*, 548.

58. *The Mystical Presence*, in Sydney E. Ahlstrom, ed., *Theology in America: The Major Protestant Voices from Puritanism to Neo-Orthodoxy* (Indianapolis: Bobbs-Merrill, 1967), 404.

59. Ibid., 382–85.

60. Ahlstrom, *Religious History of the American People*, 620–21.

61. *Apologia Pro Vita Sua*, ed. David J. De Lauria (New York: Norton, 1968), 50–54. For discussion of the historical background of the High Church movement of the 1830s and 1840s, see Robert Bruce Mullin, *Episcopal Vision/American Reality: High Church Theology and Social Thought in Evangelical America* (New Haven: Yale University Press, 1986).

62. 9 April 1839, 21 January 1844, *Diary of Strong*, ed. Nevins and Thomas, 1: 101, 224.

63. 31 October 1841, 25 December 1841, 17 June 1844, ibid., 1: 169, 171, 238.

64. 4 June 1843, ibid., 1: 204.

65. Ahlstrom, *Religious History of the American People*, 548.

66. For accounts of Brownson's religious development, see his autobiography, *The Convert* (1854), in *The Works of Orestes A. Brownson*, ed. Henry F. Brownson (Detroit: Thorndike Norse and H. F. Brownson, 1882–87), vol. 5, and Henry F. Brownson, *Orestes A. Brownson's Early Life: From 1803 to 1844* (Detroit: H. F. Brownson, 1898).

67. *New Views of Christianity, Society, and the Church*, in *Works*, ed. Henry Brownson, 4: esp. chap. 9.

68. "No Church, No Reform," *Brownson's Quarterly Review* 1 (1844): 183.

69. Gratz to Miriam Cohen [15 October 1840], Rebecca Gratz Papers, American Jewish Archives, Hebrew Union College, Cincinnati, Ohio. The original copy of this letter is located in the Southern Historical Collection, University of North Carolina Library, Chapel Hill, North Carolina. On Protestants' curiosity about Judaism, mixed with an undercurrent of anti-Semitism, see my *Victorian America and the Civil War*, 45–46.

70. Jacob Marcus notes that the identification and characterization of Sephardic versus Ashkenazic Jews may be complex. For example, some eighteenth-century Ashkenazic Jews, who were not actually from the Iberian peninsula or Mediterranean lands, had accepted the dominant Sephardic ritual in America and considered themselves Sephardim. With respect to liturgy, the later wave of Ashkenazic Jews was more open to liberalizing ideas. But it was the Sephardic congregations that were English-speaking and the Ashkenazic synagogues whose members spoke German. See *United States Jewry*, 1: 231–32. In addition, not all of the Ashkenazic rabbis of the nineteenth century, including Isaac Leeser of Philadelphia, favored reforms. See Chapter 5 for further discussion of Leeser and Wise.

71. Gratz to Miriam Cohen [15 October 1840], Rebecca Gratz Papers. Gratz's letters to her niece, Miriam Cohen of Savannah, were written between 1836 and 1867 and contained passionate discussion of Jewish themes. They stand in contrast to other sets

of her correspondence that largely predated the antebellum period and slighted Jewish subjects, particularly letters to her Gentile friends such as Maria Fenno Hoffman and to her Gentile relatives by marriage, including the successive Christian wives of her favorite brother, Benjamin. Exemplary letters of Gratz to Cohen include 1 March 1838, 9 November 1840, 29 March 1841, 20 June 1842, 28 March 1854, and 11 October 1855, Gratz Papers. Jacob Marcus estimates that intermarriage ranged from 10 to 50 percent of American Jews prior to 1840, depending on place of residence, in *United States Jewry*, 1: 608. On the assimilation of Jews into American Christian culture prior to 1840, see ibid., esp. chap. 15.

72. *Narrative of the Life of Frederick Douglass, an American Slave* (1845; rpt., New York: New American Library, 1968), 74.

73. Eugene D. Genovese, *Roll, Jordan, Roll: The World the Slaves Made* (New York: Vintage, 1974), 70–75 (quotation on p. 75). Sylvia R. Frey shows that these ideas had strong roots in the early national era, in her *Water from the Rock: Black Resistance in a Revolutionary Age* (Princeton: Princeton University Press, 1991), chap. 8.

74. Quoted in Genovese, *Roll, Jordan, Roll*, 77.

75. My thinking about how to evaluate slavery has benefited from Robert William Fogel, "Toward a Modern Indictment," in his *Without Consent or Contract: The Rise and Fall of American Slavery* (New York: Norton, 1989), 393–406.

76. *Slave Religion*, 318.

77. Ibid., 314. On the relation of black and white Christianity in the first decades of the nineteenth century, see Frey, *Water from the Rock*, chap. 9. It is also important to keep in mind that not all black religion was that of slaves. See Wilson Jeremiah Moses, *Alexander Crummell: A Study of Civilization and Discontent* (New York: Oxford University Press, 1989).

78. Quoted in Raboteau, *Slave Religion*, 292.

79. On the controversies that involved the Mercersburg theology and High Church Episcopalianism, see Ahlstrom, *Religious History of the American People*, 619–20, 626–32.

80. This simplified statement does not do full justice to sophisticated arguments. Scholars who have developed this line of thinking include Ann Douglas, *The Feminization of American Culture* (New York: Knopf, 1977); James Turner, *Without God, without Creed: The Origins of Unbelief in America* (Baltimore: Johns Hopkins University Press, 1985); and Richard Rabinowitz, *The Spiritual Self in Everyday Life: The Transformation of Personal Religious Experience in Nineteenth-Century New England* (Boston: Northeastern University Press, 1989). A version of this theory is also the basis of my *Victorian America and the Civil War*, esp. chap. 1. Other scholars have proposed, in contrast, that religious commitment in fact increased over the course of American history. See, for example, Jon Butler, *Awash in a Sea of Faith: Christianizing the American People* (Cambridge, Mass.: Harvard University Press, 1990).

2. The Struggles of Political Loyalties

1. *Democracy in America*, ed. J. P. Mayer (Garden City, N.Y.: Doubleday, 1969), 15, 9, 12.

2. Among works that document the inequalities of Jacksonian America, the most synthetic is Edward Pessen, *Jacksonian America: Society, Personality, and Politics*, rev. ed. (Homewood, Ill.: Dorsey Press, 1978).

3. There is much discussion among historians about the terms "republicanism,"

"democracy," and "liberalism." On republicanism, see Daniel T. Rodgers, "Republicanism: The Career of a Concept," *Journal of American History* 79 (1992): 11–38. See also the special issue of the *American Quarterly* devoted to "Republicanism in the History and Historiography of the United States," ed. Joyce Appleby, 37 (1985), and esp. articles by Jean Baker, "From Belief into Culture: Republicanism in the Antebellum North," 532–50, and James Oakes, "From Republicanism to Liberalism: Ideological Change and the Crisis of the Old South," 551–71. For two other syntheses on the use of "republicanism" by historians, see Robert E. Shalhope, "Republicanism and Early American Historiography," *William and Mary Quarterly*, 3d ser. 39 (1982): 334–56, and Shalhope, "Toward a Republican Synthesis: The Emergence of an Understanding of Republicanism in American Historiography," *William and Mary Quarterly* 3d ser. 29 (1972): 49–80. Some of this literature uses the term "liberalism" to designate the more individualistic political culture that displaced community-centered classical republicanism. But I have chosen the word "democracy" to underscore the connection between antebellum politics and Tocqueville's compelling analysis.

4. *The Federalist Papers* (New York: New American Library, 1961), 77, 78.

5. Jean Baker cites this phrase as a favorite antebellum description of parties, in "From Belief into Culture," 545. On the growing acceptability of parties, see Hofstadter, *The Idea of a Party System.*

6. The term political "culture" signifies a people's overall political orientation and customs. The word calls attention to the social and institutional means of trans-mitting civic ideas, such as patriotic gatherings and schools, that make beliefs an inte-gral part of a people's behavior and feelings. Political "ideology" refers more narrowly to the concepts of government held by a particular social group. Although there is a degree of overlapping in the ordinary meaning assigned to these terms, this chapter assumes that the political ideas—"ideology"—of the revolutionary generation became a complex political "culture" during the early nineteenth century. For theoretical dis-cussions of "ideology" and political "culture," see Karl Mannheim, *Ideology and Utopia: An Introduction to the Sociology of Knowledge* (1936; rpt., New York: Harcourt, Brace & World, 1968), esp. pt. 2, and Sidney Verba, "Conclusion: Comparative Political Culture," in Lucian W. Pye and Sidney Verba, eds., *Political Culture and Political Development* (Princeton: Princeton University Press, 1965), 512–60. For use of the con-cept of ideology in the Revolutionary setting, see Bernard Bailyn, *The Ideological Origins of the American Revolution* (Cambridge, Mass.: Harvard University Press, 1967).

7. *Patricide in the House Divided: A Psychological Interpretation of Lincoln and His Age* (New York: Norton, 1979), 36, 40.

8. Neil Harris, *The Artist in American Society: The Formative Years, 1790–1860* (New York: Simon & Schuster, 1966), 44–45.

9. *Unquiet Eagle: Memory and Desire in the Idea of American Freedom, 1815–1860* (Ithaca: Cornell University Press, 1967), 136. Lafayette's tour is described in chap. 4.

10. Forgie, *Patricide in the House Divided*, 168–72.

11. The text of the "Concord Hymn" can be found in *Selections from Emerson*, ed. Whicher, 415.

12. Faragher, *Sugar Creek*, 219 and chap. 20. On the trend toward nostalgic patrio-tism in the 1850s, see also Forgie, *Patricide in the House Divided*, chap. 5. Michael Kammen discusses the balance between antebellum Americans' attention to the future and the past, in *Mystic Chords of Memory: The Transformation of Tradition in American*

Culture (New York: Knopf, 1991), chaps. 2 and 3. See Chapter 4 for discussion of ante-bellum Americans' interest in history.

13. Jean Baker agrees in part with Tocqueville's assessment that Americans were too self-interested and pragmatic to think deeply about political philosophy, in "From Belief into Culture," 536–37. Arthur M. Schlesinger, Jr., interprets Jacksonian political statements as true reflections of underlying ideology in his classic work, *The Age of Jackson*. Lawrence Frederick Kohl offers a new reading of Jacksonian parties that identifies their true orientation as quite different from their professed beliefs, in *The Politics of Individualism: Parties and the American Character in the Jacksonian Era* (New York: Oxford University Press, 1989). For a review of historiographic literature on antebellum parties that suggests how complex they were, both socially and institutionally, see Ronald P. Formisano, "Toward a Reorientation of Jacksonian Politics: A Review of the Literature, 1959–1975," *Journal of American History* 63 (1976): 42–65.

14. This discussion of Jackson is based on John William Ward, *Andrew Jackson: Symbol for an Age* (New York: Oxford University Press, 1962).

15. *The Political Culture of the American Whigs* (Chicago: University of Chicago Press, 1979), 211. For further discussion of Webster, see Irving H. Bartlett, *Daniel Webster* (New York: Norton, 1978).

16. On the Democrats' communitarian emphasis, see Baker, "From Belief into Culture," 532–34. On the emergence of the Democratic outlook more generally, see Jean H. Baker, *Affairs of Party: The Political Culture of Northern Democrats in the Mid-Nineteenth Century* (Ithaca: Cornell University Press, 1983). On Stephen Douglas, see Robert W. Johannsen, *Stephen A. Douglas* (New York: Oxford University Press, 1973). On Republican ideology, see Eric Foner, *Free Soil, Free Labor, Free Men: The Ideology of the Republican Party before the Civil War* (Oxford: Oxford University Press, 1970).

17. On the Lowell to Concord trip, see Gay Wilson Allen, *Waldo Emerson: A Biography* (New York: Viking, 1981), 360. On the Boston and South Carolina Whigs, see Ward, *Jackson*, 94. On Legaré, see also Michael O'Brien, "Politics, Romanticism, and Hugh Legaré: 'The Fondness of Disappointed Love,'" in his *Rethinking the South: Essays in Intellectual History* (Baltimore: Johns Hopkins University Press, 1988), chap. 3. For an excellent discussion of the Whigs' decision to adopt popular images, see Ward, *Jackson*, chap. 5.

18. On the importance of military images to antebellum culture and politics, see Marcus Cunliffe, *Soldiers and Civilians: The Martial Spirit in America, 1775–1865* (Boston: Little, Brown, 1968), esp. chaps. 3 and 9. On the more specific role of the Mexican War in American thinking, see Robert W. Johannsen, *To the Halls of the Montezumas: The Mexican War in the American Imagination* (New York: Oxford University Press, 1985), esp. chap. 5.

19. Allen, *Emerson*, 360.

20. Jean Baker comments on this pattern of choosing names in "The Ceremonies of Politics," 166.

21. "Farewell Address, March 4, 1837," in David Brion Davis, ed., *Antebellum American Culture: An Interpretive Anthology* (Lexington, Mass.: D. C. Heath, 1979), 193.

22. Editor's commentary on "The Repeal of the Missouri Compromise and the Propriety of Its Restoration: Speech at Peoria, Illinois, in Reply to Senator Douglas, October 16, 1854," in *Abraham Lincoln: His Speeches and Writings*, ed. Roy P. Basler (Cleveland: World Publishing Co., 1946), 323.

23. Letter of 2 July 1833, in *The Life and Writings of Major Jack Downing* (1833), quoted in Mary Alice Wyman, *Two American Pioneers, Seba Smith and Elizabeth Oakes Smith* (New York: Columbia University Press, 1926), 43. Variant spellings and punctuation appear in the original text.

24. See Walter Blair, "Six Davy Crocketts," *Southwest Review* 25 (1940), 443–62; Johanna Shields, "A Sadder Simon Suggs: Freedom and Slavery in the Humor of Johnson Hooper," *Journal of Southern History* 56 (1990): 641–64; and Johnson Jones Hooper, *Adventures of Captain Simon Suggs* (1858; rpt., Tuscaloosa: University of Alabama Press, 1993).

25. Among numerous works on the evolution of "woman's sphere," the most concise and persuasive is Cott, *Bonds of Womanhood*. See Chapter 3 for further discussion of the cult of domesticity.

26. Beecher is quoted in Howe, *Political Culture of the American Whigs*, 157. Antipartisan attitudes were particularly strong among Whigs and southerners. See, respectively, Howe, ibid., esp. 50–55, and Greenberg, *Masters and Statesmen*, esp. chap. 3.

27. Historians who are perhaps most sensitive to the connections between religion and politics are those of the so-called "ethno-cultural" or "ethno-religious" perspective, a viewpoint that identifies differing religious values as the basis for choice of party affiliation. See, for example, Paul Kleppner, *The Third Electoral System, 1853–1892* (Chapel Hill: University of North Carolina Press, 1979).

28. On the ideology of the Revolution, see Bailyn, *Ideological Origins of the American Revolution*, esp. chap. 1.

29. *Democracy in America*, ed. Mayer, 252.

30. Ibid., 264.

31. One such Whig cartoon of Jackson and a relatively sympathetic lithograph of the inaugural crowd appear in Bernard Bailyn et al., *The Great Republic* (Lexington, Mass.: D. C. Heath, 1977), 486, 475.

32. For the theoretical argument of Calhoun's text of the *Exposition and Protest*, see *The Papers of John C. Calhoun*, ed. Clyde N. Wilson and W. Edwin Hemphill (Columbia: University of South Carolina Press, 1977), 10: 496–532 (even pages only; odd pages supply the South Carolina legislature's version). For a collection of essays on Calhoun, see John L. Thomas, ed., *John C. Calhoun: A Profile* (New York: Hill & Wang, 1968).

33. *A Disquisition on Government and Selections from the Discourse*, ed. C. Gordon Post (Indianapolis: Bobbs-Merrill, 1953), 22–23.

34. Ibid., 33.

35. Ibid., 36–40. A good selection from the *Disquisition* appears in David A. Hollinger and Charles Capper, eds., *The American Intellectual Tradition* (New York: Oxford University Press, 1989), 1: 337–47.

36. A selection from Julian's speech appears in David Brion Davis, ed., *The Fear of Conspiracy: Images of Un-American Subversion from the Revolution to the Present* (Ithaca: Cornell University Press, 1971), 123.

37. A selection from Hunter's speech appears in ibid., 145. The italics in this and all subsequent quotations appear in the original texts. On the theme of conspiracy, see also David Brion Davis, *The Slave Power Conspiracy and the Paranoid Style* (Baton Rouge: Louisiana State University Press, 1969).

38. "Repeal of the Missouri Compromise," in *Lincoln: Speeches and Writings*, ed. Basler, 303.

39. *Selections from Emerson*, ed. Whicher, 241.

40. Ibid., 249.

41. *Walden and Civil Disobedience*, ed. Michael Meyer (New York: Penguin, 1983), 389.

42. Ibid., 388.

43. Ibid., 392.

44. Ibid., 399. For Martin Luther King, Jr.'s view of nonviolent resistance, see, for example, "Letter from the Birmingham Jail" (1963), in Cherry, ed., *God's New Israel*, esp. 349–50.

45. John C. Miller, *The Federalist Era, 1789–1801* (New York: Harper & Row, 1960), 155–62.

46. Among the substantial literature on these incidents, see, for example, Richards, *"Gentlemen of Property and Standing"*; Ray Allen Billington, *The Protestant Crusade, 1800–1860: A Study of the Origins of American Nativism* (Gloucester, Mass.: Peter Smith, 1963), chaps. 3 and 9; Leonard Levy, "Sims' Case: The Fugitive Slave Law in Boston in 1851," *Journal of Negro History* 35 (1950): 39–74; Harold Schwartz, "Fugitive Slave Days in Boston," *New England Quarterly* 27 (1954): 191–212; Samuel Shapiro, "The Rendition of Anthony Burns," *Journal of Negro History* 44 (1959): 34–51; and Davis, "Some Themes of Counter-Subversion: An Analysis of Anti-Masonic, Anti-Catholic, and Anti-Mormon Literature," in his *From Homicide to Slavery*, 137–54.

47. *Democracy in America*, ed. Mayer, 506.

48. *Lincoln: Speeches and Writings*, ed. Basler, 84–85.

49. Ibid., 80, 82, 83.

50. Ibid., 83.

51. George Forgie interprets this address as an expression of Lincoln's anxiety about his own ambitions as well as those of his generation, in *Patricide in the House Divided*, chap. 2.

52. The citations from Otis's speech at Faneuil Hall, Boston, on 22 August, and Tyler's address at Gloucester Courthouse, Virginia on the same day are included in Davis, ed., *Fear of Conspiracy*, 139, 141.

53. Larry E. Tise, *The Proslavery Argument: A History of the Defense of Slavery in America, 1701–1840* (Athens: University of Georgia Press, 1987), esp. 323.

54. "Letter to an English Abolitionist," in Drew Gilpin Faust, ed., *The Ideology of Slavery: Proslavery Thought in the Antebellum South, 1830–1860* (Baton Rouge: Louisiana State University Press, 1981), 176. Denunciations of the radical groups cited are found on 179, 181, and 175.

55. "Southern Thought" (1857), in Faust, ed., *Ideology of Slavery*, 282, 281. "Slaves without masters" was not only a phrase in this article in *DeBow's Review*, but the subtitle of Fitzhugh's book-length proslavery argument published in 1857, *Cannibals All!; or, Slaves without Masters*, ed. C. Vann Woodward (Cambridge, Mass.: Harvard University Press, 1960).

56. This discussion of slave law is based on Genovese, *Roll, Jordan, Roll*, 25–49.

57. Quoted in Dickson D. Bruce, Jr., *Violence and Culture in the Antebellum South* (Austin: University of Texas Press, 1979), 140. There is much scholarly debate about the meaning of violence in southern society. But virtually all historians acknowledge that force, and the threat of force, were an essential part of the culture of slavery. In addition to Bruce's book, see Sylvia Frey, *Water from the Rock: Black Resistance in a Revolutionary Age* (Princeton: Princeton University Press, 1991), esp. chap. 2;

Herbert Aptheker, *American Negro Slave Revolts*, rev. ed. (New York: International Publishers, 1969); Genovese, *Roll, Jordan, Roll*, 587–98; and Bertram Wyatt-Brown, *Southern Honor: Ethics and Behavior in the Old South* (New York: Oxford University Press, 1982), esp. chap. 15. On the rape of slave women by masters, see esp. Melton A. McLaurin, *Celia: A Slave* (Athens: University of Georgia Press, 1991). On racial violence in the North (Pennsylvania), see Thomas P. Slaughter, *Bloody Dawn: The Christiana Riot and Racial Violence in the Antebellum North* (New York: Oxford University Press, 1991).

58. *Lincoln: Speeches and Writings*, ed. Basler, 585.

59. "First Inaugural Address," in ibid., 582. Much of this discussion of unionism is based on Paul C. Nagel, *One Nation Indivisible: The Union in American Thought, 1776–1861* (New York: Oxford University Press, 1964). For an interpretation that emphasizes the importance of a tradition of compromise to unionism, see Peter B. Knupfer, *The Union as It Is: Constitutional Unionism and Sectional Compromise, 1787–1861* (Chapel Hill: University of North Carolina Press, 1991).

60. *The Papers of Daniel Webster: Speeches and Formal Writings, 1800–1833*, ed. Charles M. Wiltse (Hanover, N.H.: University Press of New England, 1986), 1: 348.

61. "Repeal of the Missouri Compromise," in *Lincoln: Speeches and Writings*, ed. Basler, 291.

62. Ibid., 283, 309.

63. This qualified conception of liberty had deep roots in American political thought. In John Winthrop's famous speech to the General Court of Massachusetts in 1645, he distinguished unrestrained "natural" liberty from the freedom of "civil" society, that is, the "liberty to [do] that only which is good, honest, and just." See Perry Miller and Thomas H. Johnson, eds., *The Puritans*, rev. ed. (New York: Harper & Row, 1963), 1: 207.

64. *Papers of Daniel Webster, 1834–1852*, ed. Wiltse (1988), 2: 547.

65. *Lincoln: Speeches and Writings*, ed. Basler, 582–83, 583.

66. On the Boston mob that attempted to free the escaped slave Anthony Burns, see Shapiro, "The Rendition of Anthony Burns." On the abolitionists' official acceptance of force as a tactic for slaves, see "Annual Meeting of the Massachusetts Anti-Slavery Society, February, 13, 1857," in Nelson, ed. *Documents of Upheaval*, 219–33. On John Brown as a northern hero, see George M. Fredrickson, *The Inner Civil War: Northern Intellectuals and the Crisis of the Union* (New York: Harper & Row, 1965), 36–44.

67. Wilentz, *Chants Democratic*. On the ideological orientation of antebellum workers, see also Edward Pessen, *Most Uncommon Jacksonians: The Radical Leaders of the Early Labor Movement* (Albany: State University of New York Press, 1967), and John R. Commons et al., *History of Labor in the United States* (New York: Macmillan, 1918), vol. 1.

68. The quotation appears in Wilentz, *Chants Democratic*, 191; on Skidmore and Owen see 194, 201.

69. Quoted in ibid., 242.

70. Quoted in ibid., 245; see also the discussion of fears of a capitalist conspiracy on 200.

71. Quoted in ibid., 237.

72. The statement of the Ladies' Industrial Union appeared in the New York *Evening Post*, 7 March 1845 and is quoted in Christine Stansell, *City of Women: Sex and Class in New York, 1789–1860* (New York: Knopf, 1986), 146; the workingmen's position

represented that of the National Trades' Union in the 1830s and is quoted in Stansell, 138.

73. "Declaration of Sentiments," in Rossi, ed., *Feminist Papers*, 416. On women's rights, see also Ellen Du Bois, *Feminism and Suffrage: The Emergence of an Independent Women's Movement in America, 1848–1869* (Ithaca: Cornell University Press, 1978).

74. These epithets appeared in the New York *Herald* in 1852. The article is included in Aileen S. Kraditor, ed., *Up from the Pedestal: Selected Writings in the History of American Feminism* (Chicago: Quadrangle Books, 1968), 189–90.

75. Alice Rossi documents the connections between religiously inspired reform movements and women's rights in her essay "Social Roots of the Woman's Movement in America," in *Feminist Papers*, 241–81 and esp. 276. It is important to recognize, however, that the comparatively secular orientation of women's rights distanced some feminists from religion as time went on. In 1895, for example, Elizabeth Cady Stanton published *The Woman's Bible* (New York: European Publishing Co.), a critical commentary on the Christian scriptures that reviewed all statements that Stanton judged to be unjust to women.

76. For a survey of interpretations of the Civil War's causes, see Eric Foner, "The Causes of the American Civil War: Recent Interpretations and New Directions," in his *Ideology and Politics in the Age of the Civil War* (Oxford: Oxford University Press, 1980), 15–33. For a long-term view of interpretations over the last century, see Thomas J. Pressley, *Americans Interpret Their Civil War* (Princeton: Princeton University Press, 1954).

77. "Repeal of the Missouri Compromise," in *Lincoln: Speeches and Writings*, ed. Basler, 313, 290–91, 306. The capitalization in the quotation appears in the original text. On the emergence of political antislavery from radical abolitionism, see Kraditor, *Means and Ends in American Abolitionism*.

78. On Republican attitudes toward race, see Foner, *Free Soil, Free Labor, Free Men*, chap. 8. Foner argues that although Republicans were not generally willing to grant blacks equal rights, their racial attitudes were still more liberal than those of many contemporaries since they acknowledged blacks' basic humanity (261). Indeed, Jean Baker (*Affairs of Party*, chap. 5) explains that Democrats in the 1850s were moving toward the theory that there was more than one act of divine creation of mankind and as a result, that blacks belonged to an inferior species. On white racial views in general, see George M. Fredrickson, *The Black Image in the White Mind: The Debate on Afro-American Character and Destiny, 1817–1914* (New York: Harper & Row, 1971), chaps. 1–5.

79. *The Political Crisis of the 1850s* (New York: John Wiley & Sons, 1978). William E. Gienapp similarly argues that the slavery issue was not the sole determining factor in the politics of the 1850s in *The Origins of the Republican Party, 1852–1856* (Oxford: Oxford University Press, 1987).

80. On Wallace and Vance, see Lew Wallace, *Lew Wallace: An Autobiography* (New York: Harper & Brothers, 1906), 1: chap. 28, and Glenn Tucker, *Zeb Vance: Champion of Personal Freedom* (Indianapolis: Bobbs-Merrill, 1965), chaps. 5 and 6. For a more general discussion of how moral self-scrutiny affected the politics of the sectional crisis, see my *Victorian America and the Civil War*, chap. 5.

81. Jefferson to Chastellux, 2 September 1785, in *The Portable Thomas Jefferson*, ed. Merrill D. Peterson (New York: Viking, 1975), 387.

82. *Cavalier and Yankee: The Old South and American National Character* (New York: Harper & Row, 1961), 18.

83. "The Constitution and the Union, March 7, 1850," in *Papers of Daniel Webster*, ed. Wiltse, 2: 545.

84. *Free Soil, Free Labor, Free Men*, 11.

3. The Languages of Capitalism

1. On railroad expansion, see Stuart Bruchey, *Enterprise: The Dynamic Economy of a Free People* (Cambridge, Mass.: Harvard University Press, 1990), 270–71. On mail and telegraph communication, see Brown, *Knowledge Is Power*, 218, 15.

2. For an overview of economic development in pre–Civil War America, see Bruchey, *Enterprise*, chaps. 1–8, and W. Elliot Brownlee, *Dynamics of Ascent: A History of the American Economy*, 2d ed. (New York: Knopf, 1979), pt. 2.

3. There is more than one way to define the crucial concept of the "middle class." If a historian uses social criteria to identify this group, then the "middle class" might consist of antebellum Americans who pursued nonmanual occupations with the expectation of upward mobility and who lived in urban areas. If a scholar adopts cultural standards to demarcate this class, however, then "middle class" might more broadly include all people who ascribed to values associated with market capitalism. The cultural aspect of the definition is important because it acknowledges that being middle class was a matter of aspiration as well as achievement and that goals in addition to wealth were instrumental in the ongoing changes in the group's composition. In this chapter I attempt to blend these approaches by using the term "middle class" to connote ambitious Americans involved in market activity who were committed to principles of self-determination and upward mobility. The most synthetic effort to define who belonged to the middle class is Stuart M. Blumin, *The Emergence of the Middle Class: Social Experience in the American City, 1760–1900* (Cambridge: Cambridge University Press, 1989). Blumin favors a social concept of "middle class" as those people who occupied an intermediate position between the working class and the gentry. Other works on the middle class include Burton J. Bledstein, *The Culture of Professionalism: The Middle Class and the Development of Higher Education in America* (New York: Norton, 1976); Ryan, *Cradle of the Middle Class;* Karen Halttunen, *Confidence Men and Painted Women: A Study of Middle-Class Culture in America, 1830–1870* (New Haven: Yale University Press, 1982); John S. Gilkeson, Jr., *Middle-Class Providence, 1820–1940* (Princeton: Princeton University Press, 1986); Cindy Sondik Aron, *Ladies and Gentlemen of the Civil Service: Middle-Class Workers in Victorian America* (New York: Oxford University Press, 1987); and Rose, *Victorian America and the Civil War.*

4. These figures are cited in Brownlee, *Dynamics of Ascent*, 127. The percentages are based on the definition of a city used by the U.S. Census: a place of 2,500 or more inhabitants.

5. *A New England Girlhood*, 182, 183, 184.

6. Ibid., 183.

7. The analysis in this paragraph is based on Halttunen, *Confidence Men and Painted Women*. The figures on etiquette books are found on 92.

8. *Herman Melville: Selected Tales and Poems* (New York: Holt, Rinehart & Winston, 1950), esp. 99 and 101. "Bartleby" was written between 1852 and 1856, when Melville lived on a farm outside Pittsfield, Massachusetts. The story was first published in 1857.

9. Ibid., 105, 103, 111.

10. Margaret Fuller Ossoli, *Summer on the Lakes*, in *At Home and Abroad, or Things*

and Thoughts in America and Europe, ed. Arthur B. Fuller (Boston: Crosby, Nichols & Co., 1856), 5.

11. "Essay on American Scenery," in John W. McCoubrey, ed., *American Art, 1700–1960: Sources and Documents* (Englewood Cliffs, N.J.: Prentice-Hall, 1965), 103, 100, 102; for Durand's views, see the selection from his "Letters on Landscape Painting" (1855), 100–15.

12. "Letter from the Mouth of the Yellowstone River" (1832), in ibid., 94.

13. Ibid., 94.

14. Ibid., 95. For a discussion of the romantic view of nature, see John B. Halsted, ed., *Romanticism* (New York: Harper & Row, 1969), 12–13. For two quite different interpretations of the depiction of nature in antebellum American art, see Barbara Novak, *Nature and Culture: American Landscape Painting, 1825–1875* (New York: Oxford University Press, 1980), and Bryan Jay Wolf, *Romantic Re-Vision: Culture and Consciousness in Nineteenth-Century American Painting and Literature* (Chicago: University of Chicago Press, 1982). For a related discussion of the ideological implications of portrayals of Indians in white antebellum writings, see Lucy Maddox, *Removals: Nineteenth-Century American Literature and the Politics of Indian Affairs* (New York: Oxford University Press, 1991). The history of the frontier, more generally, should be the context in which romanticism is understood. Two excellent studies of the frontier, though concerning different historical periods, are Richard White, *The Middle Ground: Indians, Empires, and Republics in the Great Lakes Region, 1650–1815* (Cambridge: Cambridge University Press, 1991), and Patricia Nelson Limerick, *The Legacy of Conquest: The Unbroken Past of the American West* (New York: Norton, 1987).

15. *The Machine in the Garden: Technology and the Pastoral Ideal in America* (London: Oxford University Press, 1964), 23. Marx's book is the definitive work on American pastoralism. My comments are indebted to his study.

16. Marx focused on pastoralism in the writings of leading intellectuals (among them Herman Melville, Mark Twain, and F. Scott Fitzgerald) and argued that they became painfully aware of the incongruity between the pastoral ideal and urban society. See ibid., esp. 364–65. In contrast, popular culture, perhaps less attentive to this tension, multiplied urban versions of pastoralism.

17. Douglas, *Feminization of American Culture*, 208–12.

18. Quoted in ibid., 213. Downing viewed cottages on the edge of cities as appropriate for working-class families; the well-to-do might afford something larger, such as a country "villa." See his *The Architecture of Country Houses* (1850; rpt., New York: Da Capo Press, 1968), 39–48.

19. On Central Park, see Roy Rosenzweig and Elizabeth Blackmar, *The Park and the People: A History of Central Park* (Ithaca: Cornell University Press, 1992), pts. 1–3, and Laura Wood Roper, *FLO: A Biography of Frederick Law Olmsted* (Baltimore: Johns Hopkins University Press, 1973), chap. 12. Rosenzweig and Blackmar note that even such a comparatively democratic leisure space as Central Park tended to be used more freely and intensively by the well-to-do (see pt. 3).

20. "American Country Life: October Afternoon" (1855); "View of New York: From Brooklyn Heights" (1849), in John Lowell Pratt, ed., *Currier and Ives: Chronicles of America* (Maplewood, N.J.: Hammond Inc., 1968), 232, 116.

21. For some of Strong's more unusual fascinations with fires and drugs, see entries for 16 July 1857 and 1 September 1855, *Diary of Strong*, ed. Nevins and Thomas, 2: 349, 290–91.

22. Perry Miller, *The Raven and the Whale: The War of Words and Wits in Era of Poe and Melville* (New York: Harcourt, Brace, 1956), 82.

23. Characteristic melodramatic stories by Poe such as "The Masque of the Red Death" (1842) may be found in *Selected Writings of Edgar Allan Poe*, ed. Edward H. Davidson (Boston: Houghton Mifflin, 1956), 174–80. Among several of Melville's satiric romances, see *Typee: A Peep at Polynesian Life during a Four Months' Residence in a Valley of the Marquesas* (1846) (New York: New American Library, 1964). For another of his critiques of social change, see "The Paradise of Bachelors and the Tartarus of Maids," in *Herman Melville: Selected Tales*, 206–29.

24. This discussion is based on David S. Reynolds's provocative study of antebellum popular writing, *Beneath the American Renaissance: The Subversive Imagination in the Age of Emerson and Melville* (New York: Knopf, 1988), esp. chap. 2.

25. *Roots of Southern Populism*, 52.

26. On post–Civil War populism, see Lawrence Goodwyn, *The Populist Movement: A Short History of the Agrarian Revolt in America* (New York: Oxford University Press, 1978). For discussion of regionalism in literature during the antebellum period, an approach that celebrated the extent to which country areas escaped mass culture, see Chapter 6.

27. *The Complete Novels and Selected Tales of Nathaniel Hawthorne*, ed. Norman Holmes Pearson (New York: Modern Library, 1965), 1209–23.

28. On these social changes, see Cott, *Bonds of Womanhood*, chap. 1. It is imporant to keep in mind that in homes other than those of the urban middle class, women's labor remained necessary for a family's survival in the market economy. Households, including women workers, became places of production of commodities for sale. See, for example, Clark, *Roots of Rural Capitalism*, esp. chaps. 4 and 8.

29. "Sweethearts and Wives," in Cott, ed., *Root of Bitterness*, 169.

30. Ibid., 169.

31. Ibid., 166.

32. *The Transformation of Virginia, 1740–1790* (Chapel Hill: University of North Carolina Press, 1982), 303.

33. *Bonds of Womanhood*, esp. chaps. 1 and 2.

34. "The Wants of the Age: Part II, Moral Culture," *Godey's Lady's Book* 15 (1837): 24. The title of *Godey's Lady's Book* varied considerably over the years. To simplify references, I have called all volumes by the periodical's final name, *Godey's Lady's Book*.

35. *A Lecture to Young Men, on Chastity: Intended also for the Serious Consideration of Parents and Guardians*, 2d ed. (Boston: Light & Stearns, 1837), 136–39.

36. Ibid., 131–35.

37. For a good discussion of these agencies, see Gilkeson, *Middle-Class Providence*, chap. 2.

38. For an analysis of this advice literature that focuses on nineteenth-century ideas on the relation of sexual self-control to economic success, see G. J. Barker-Benfield, "The Spermatic Economy: A Nineteenth-Century View of Sexuality," in Michael Gordon, ed., *The American Family in Social-Historical Perspective*, 2d ed. (New York: St. Martin's Press, 1978), 374–402.

39. Finley, *Lady of Godey's*, 23.

40. "Editor's Table," *Godey's Lady's Book* 29 (1844): 143.

41. See, for example, "Authoresses—No. I" and "Authoresses—No. II," *Ladies' Magazine* 2 (1829): 30–34, 130–34.

42. "On the Elevation of the Laboring Classes," quoted in Rose, *Transcendentalism as a Social Movement*, 111.

43. *Treatise*, excerpted in Cott, ed., *Root of Bitterness*, 173. For an excellent discussion of Beecher's book, see Sklar, *Catharine Beecher*, chap. 11.

44. Ibid., 173.

45. Quoted in Blumin, *Emergence of the Middle Class*, 108. In addition to Blumin's excellent discussion of the various social changes that contributed to class formation, see Paul Johnson's treatment of these themes in *Shopkeeper's Millennium*, esp. chap. 2.

46. Quoted in Mary Kupiec Cayton, "The Making of an American Prophet: Emerson, His Audiences, and the Rise of the Culture Industry in Nineteenth-Century America," *American Historical Review* 92 (1987): 612.

47. Ibid., 612.

48. *Cradle of the Middle Class*, 168. See also Irvin G. Wyllie, *The Self-Made Man in America: The Myth of Rags to Riches* (New Brunswick, N.J.: Rutgers University Press, 1954).

49. Aron, *Ladies and Gentlemen of the Civil Service*, 28–36.

50. See Max Weber, *The Protestant Ethic and the Spirit of Capitalism*, trans. Talcott Parsons (New York: Scribners, 1958), chap. 5.

51. *The Private City* (1968), quoted in Blumin, *Emergence of the Middle Class*, 157.

52. Oliver W. Larkin, *Art and Life in America*, rev. ed. (New York: Holt, Rinehart & Winston, 1960), 175.

53. Quoted in Karen Lystra, *Searching the Heart: Women, Men, and Romantic Love in Nineteenth-Century America* (New York: Oxford University Press, 1989), 60. Variant spellings that appear in this and subsequent quotations appear in the original texts.

54. I have developed the theme of emotionalism within Victorian families in *Victorian America and the Civil War*, chap. 4.

55. *Emergence of the Middle Class*, 185.

56. On the probate records, see ibid., 159, 162. Blumin discusses the inclination of working-class families to keep wives and children out of the labor force on 188.

57. Quoted in ibid., 123.

58. *Cannibals All!; or, Slaves without Masters*, ed. Woodward.

59. On this image see *Cavalier and Yankee*. See also my discussion in Chapter 2 of the extent to which enterprising northerners, as well as southern gentry, idealized aristocratic traits until the 1850s. For an interpretation of the motives of southern intellectuals, see Drew Gilpin Faust, *A Sacred Circle: The Dilemma of the Intellectual in the Old South, 1840–1860* (Baltimore: Johns Hopkins University Press, 1977).

60. The most persuasive interpretations of southern capitalism have been Oakes, *The Ruling Race*, and Robert William Fogel and Stanley L. Engerman, *Time on the Cross: The Economics of American Negro Slavery* (Boston: Little, Brown, 1974). Eugene D. Genovese has developed the opposing view that slavery deterred the growth of a modern market economy in the South. See, for example, his *The Political Economy of Slavery: Studies in the Economy and Society of the Slave South* (New York: Vintage, 1967).

61. *Uncle Tom's Cabin; or, Life among the Lowly* (Garden City, N.Y.: Doubleday, 1960), 430–31.

62. Rose, *Transcendentalism as a Social Movement*, 117–30.

63. *Woman in the Nineteenth Century, and Kindred Papers*, ed. Arthur B. Fuller (1874; rpt., New York: Greenwood Press, 1968), 38. See Charles Capper's excellent discussion of these years in *Margaret Fuller: An American Romantic*, vol. 1, *The Private Years* (New York: Oxford University Press, 1992), chaps. 7–9.

64. "Hawthorne and His Mosses," included in *Moby-Dick*, ed. Harrison Hayford and Hershel Parker (New York: Norton, 1967), 541. The review appeared anonymously in *The Literary World*, 17 and 24 August 1850.

65. Ibid., 551.

66. *The Intelligence of a People* (Princeton: Princeton University Press, 1973), 256.

67. On Scottish common sense realism, see Bruce Kuklick, *The Rise of American Philosophy: Cambridge, Massachusetts, 1860–1930* (New Haven: Yale University Press, 1977), 11–21, and Theodore Dwight Bozeman, *Protestants in an Age of Science: The Baconian Ideal and Antebellum Religious Thought* (Chapel Hill: University of North Carolina Press, 1977), esp. chap. 1.

68. *The Autobiography of Benjamin Franklin*, ed. Leonard W. Labaree et al. (New Haven: Yale University Press, 1964); *A Treatise Concerning Religious Affections*, excerpted in *Jonathan Edwards*, ed. Clarence H. Faust and Thomas H. Johnson, rev. ed. (New York: Hill & Wang, 1962), 206–54.

69. *Religious History of the American People* (New Haven: Yale University Press, 1972), 414.

70. Ibid., 405.

71. Patricia Cline Cohen, *A Calculating People: The Spread of Numeracy in Early America* (Chicago: University of Chicago Press, 1982), 134–38, 149.

72. *The Cotton Kingdom: A Traveller's Observations on Cotton and Slavery in the American Slave States*, ed. Arthur M. Schlesinger, Sr., intro. by Lawrence N. Powell (New York: Modern Library, 1984), esp. 10–11, 21–22, 480–93.

73. *The Launching of Modern American Science, 1846–1876* (Ithaca: Cornell University Press, 1987), 84.

74. Quoted in ibid., 134. The information contained in this discussion of science may be found in ibid., esp. 83–84, 132–34.

75. *Rise of American Philosophy*, 39.

76. Ibid., 39.

77. Quoted in Bruce, *Launching of Modern American Science*, 193; for more information on the Smithsonian see chap. 14.

78. James D. Hart, *The Popular Book: A History of America's Literary Taste* (New York: Oxford University Press, 1950), 95, 94, 111. On the importance of the Bible in family reading habits, see Gilmore, *Reading Becomes a Necessity of Life*, 257.

79. *Uncle Tom's Cabin*, chaps. 22–26.

80. Ibid., 45.

81. *Intelligence of a People*, 306.

82. Quoted in Hart, *Popular Book*, 93.

83. Anon., "Some Thoughts upon Works of Fiction," *American Monthly Magazine* 2 (1831): 692. Because an unprecedented number of women did write fiction during this period, there has been much scholarly commentary on their work. See esp. Douglas, *Feminization of American Culture*, and Kelley, *Private Woman, Public Stage*.

84. On correspondence between courting couples and between friends, see, respectively, Lystra, *Searching the Heart*, chap. 1, and Carroll Smith-Rosenberg, "The Female World of Love and Ritual: Relations between Women in Nineteenth-Century America," in Smith-Rosenberg, *Disorderly Conduct*, 53–76.

85. For discussion of these aspects of romanticism, see Ahlstrom, *Religious History of the American People*, chap. 36.

4. American Renaissance

1. *Hawthorne*, ed. Tony Tanner (London: Macmillan, 1967), 23. Variant spellings in this and subsequent quotations appear in the original texts.

2. For an informative overview of trends in twentieth-century evaluations of the American Renaissance by literary critics, see Myra Jehlen, "Introduction: Beyond Transcendence," in Sacvan Bercovitch and Myra Jehlen, eds., *Ideology and Classic American Literature* (Cambridge: Cambridge University Press, 1986), 1–18. During the 1980s interest in contextual criticism among literary scholars brought a deeper appreciation of the indebtedness of "classic" texts to popular culture. See, for example, Reynolds, *Beneath the American Renaissance*. Historians have written on the artistic products of the American Renaissance less frequently than have scholars in the fields of literature and the fine arts, but they have probably been more consistently concerned with the social context of thought, as I was, for example, in *Transcendentalism as a Social Movement*.

3. On the obstacles to artistic development in the early republic, see Harris, *Artist in American Society*, chap. 2; Brooks et al., eds., *American Literature*, 1: 118–19; and Jean V. Matthews, *Toward a New Society: American Thought and Culture, 1800–1830* (Boston: Twayne Publishers, 1991), 59–62. Matthews also shows, however, that institutions and means of communication such as literary clubs and periodicals did lay a foundation for the literary and fine arts before 1830 (62–65). Michael Warner makes a brilliant case for the rise of print culture in the eighteenth century, particularly in cities, in *The Letters of the Republic: Publication and the Public Sphere in Eighteenth-Century America* (Cambridge, Mass.: Harvard University Press, 1990). On the period before 1830, see also Brown, *Knowledge Is Power*, and Gilmore, *Reading Becomes a Necessity of Life*. On the expansion of the literary market and the growth of the reading public after about 1830, see Buell, *New England Literary Culture*, chaps. 2 and 3; Kelley, *Private Woman, Public Stage*, chap. 1; and O'Brien, *Rethinking the South*, chap. 1.

4. "The Intellectual History, Condition and Prospects of the Country," in Griswold, ed., *The Prose Writers of America*, 4th ed. (Philadelphia: Parry & McMillan, 1854), 13, 51.

5. Ibid., 14.

6. "Introduction," *The United States Magazine and Democratic Review* 1 (1837): 1, 14. The capitalization that appears in the quotation belonged to the original text.

7. "Marginal Notes—No. 2," *Godey's Lady's Book* 31 (1845): 121. This periodical had different names at different times. To simplify citations, it is designated *Godey's Lady's Book* throughout this chapter.

8. K.K. [*sic*], "The Profession of Authorship," *American Monthly Magazine* 1 (1829): 592, 594. I assume "K.K." was a man because the subject of professionalism was, by convention, a masculine concern. It is possible, however, that the author was a woman.

9. Information on Longfellow is cited in Kelley, *Private Woman, Public Stage*, 4. On the emergence of professional authors, see William Charvat, *The Profession of Authorship in America, 1800–1870: The Papers of William Charvat*, ed. Matthew J. Broccoli (Columbus: Ohio State University Press, 1968), esp. chaps. 3, 10, 14, 15. For a more focused study of the reaction of major authors to writing under market conditions, see Gilmore, *American Romanticism and the Marketplace*.

10. *Artist in American Society*, 41.

11. Ibid., 52.

12. Ibid., 52. For a survey of activity in the fine arts during this period, see Larkin, *Art and Life in America*, bk. 3. For an interpretation of some connections between the fine arts and literature, see Wolf, *Romantic Re-Vision*.

13. P.Q. [*sic*], "National Literature," *American Monthly Magazine* 1 (1829): 380.

14. Ibid., 381, 382.

15. "Twice-Told Tales," reprinted in *Selected Writings of Poe*, ed. Davidson, 441, 442, 450. Poe's review first appeared in *Graham's Magazine* in 1842 and again in *Godey's Lady's Book* in 1847.

16. "Leaves of Grass," in Brooks et al., eds., *American Literature*, 1: 1105.

17. Ibid., 1: 956.

18. "Hawthorne and his Mosses," reprinted in *Moby-Dick*, ed. Hayford and Parker, 536–37.

19. Ibid., 544, 546, 545.

20. Ibid., 549.

21. "The Custom House," in *Complete Novels and Selected Tales of Hawthorne*, ed. Pearson, 110.

22. Ibid., 85.

23. Ibid., 23.

24. On the reputations of Melville and Hawthorne, respectively, see Charvat, *Profession of Authorship*, chap. 13, and Jane Tompkins, *Sensational Designs: The Cultural Work of American Fiction, 1790–1860* (New York: Oxford University Press, 1985), chap. 1.

25. Melville to Hawthorne, 1(?) June 1851, in *Moby-Dick*, ed. Hayford and Parker, 556. Melville described his visit to Hawthorne in a letter to Evert A. Duyckinck, 12 February 1851, in ibid., 553–54. See also selected letters from Melville to Hawthorne in 1851, in ibid., 554–62, 563–64, 566–68.

26. *American Humor: A Study in the National Character* (New York: Harcourt, Brace, 1931), 106.

27. See Robert C. Toll, *Blacking Up: The Minstrel Show in Nineteenth-Century America* (New York: Oxford University Press, 1974), esp. 28–31; despite the origin of antebellum minstrelsy in the creativity of white entertainers, they did borrow from the artistry of black folk culture (see chap. 2).

28. On Longfellow and Lowell, see Brooks et al., eds., *American Literature*, 1: 584–93, 603–12. On the Lowell Institute, see Bruce, *Launching of Modern American Science*, 41–42. On the Town and Country Club and Saturday Club, see Kenneth Cameron, "Emerson, Thoreau, and the Town and Country Club," *Emerson Society Quarterly*, no. 8 (1957): 2–17, and Edward Waldo Emerson, *The Early Years of the Saturday Club, 1855–1870* (Boston: Houghton Mifflin, 1918). The best general discussion of Boston's cultural life is Martin Green, *The Problem of Boston: Some Readings in Cultural History* (London: Longmans, 1966).

29. Emerson, *Early Years of the Saturday Club*, 4, 21.

30. *New England Literary Culture*, 50.

31. Ibid., 51.

32. *Artist in American Society*, 266–67.

33. Quoted in Fred Lewis Pattee, *The Feminine Fifties* (New York: D. Appleton-Century Company, 1940), 303.

34. See Reynolds's pioneering work on popular literature, *Beneath the American Renaissance*, particularly his remarks on the penny press (172–74).

35. *Artist in American Society*, 281. On the intellectual life of New York during this period, see also Thomas Bender's excellent, *New York Intellect: A History of Intellectual Life in New York City, from 1750 to the Beginnings of Our Own Time* (New York: Knopf, 1987), esp. chap. 4.

36. *New England Literary Culture*, 36–37.

37. *The Autobiography of Benjamin Franklin*, ed. Labaree, esp. 70–75.

38. Quoted in Finley, *Lady of Godey's*, 193. On these family magazines, see Baym, *Novels, Readers, and Reviewers*, 14–16.

39. It might be argued that this utilitarian approach to culture was related, more formally, to the philosophical pragmatism developed by William James, John Dewey, and others at the turn of the twentieth century. See Kuklick, *Rise of American Philosophy*, esp. chaps. 14, 16, 17, and Robert B. Westbrook, *John Dewey and American Democracy* (Ithaca: Cornell University Press, 1991).

40. See O'Brien, *Rethinking the South*, 21–22.

41. *Sacred Circle*. For an excellent study of southern thinkers who worked within the traditional vocation of the ministry, see E. Brooks Holifield, *Gentlemen Theologians: American Theology in Southern Culture, 1795–1860* (Durham: Duke University Press, 1978).

42. On Poe's professional life, see Kenneth Silverman, *Edgar A. Poe: A Mournful and Never-Ending Remembrance* (New York: HarperCollins, 1991).

43. Samuel Eliot Morison, *Three Centuries of Harvard, 1636–1936* (1936; rpt., Cambridge, Mass.: Harvard University Press, 1963), 242; on Eliot's innovations, see chap. 14, as well as Kuklick, *Rise of American Philosophy*, chap. 7.

44. On postwar Harvard, see Kuklick, *Rise of American Philosophy*, pt. 3. On post–Civil War university education more generally, see Laurence Veysey, *The Emergence of the American University* (Chicago: University of Chicago Press, 1965).

45. On Felton and Sparks, see Morison, *Three Centuries of Harvard*, 263–64. On Longfellow, see Edward Wagenknect, *Henry Wadsworth Longfellow: Portrait of an American Humanist* (New York: Oxford University Press, 1966), 100–1 and chap. 3.

46. Morison, *Three Centuries of Harvard*, 257. Contemporary Yale, in comparison, remained more homogeneously Congregationalist. See Louise L. Stevenson, *Scholarly Means to Evangelical Ends: The New Haven Scholars and the Transformation of Higher Learning in America, 1830–1890* (Baltimore: Johns Hopkins University Press, 1986), esp. chap. 2.

47. Wagenknect, *Longfellow*, 192–200.

48. Robert Bruce covers these topics in his informative study, *The Launching of Modern American Science*; on Agassiz and Loomis in particular see 233, 46.

49. Kenneth S. Lynn, *William Dean Howells: An American Life* (New York: Harcourt, Brace, Jovanovich, 1970), 98–100.

50. March, Week X [1838], *The Journals of Bronson Alcott*, ed. Odell Shepard (Boston: Little, Brown, 1938), 100. On the formation of the Concord intellectual community, see my *Transcendentalism as a Social Movement*, 94–100. Concord residents also produced many reminiscences at the end of their lives. Among the best are A. Bronson Alcott, *Concord Days* (1872; rpt., Philadelphia: Albert Saifer, 1962), and F. B. Sanborn, *Recollections of Seventy Years* (Boston: Richard G. Badger, 1909), 2: esp. chap. 13.

51. See, for example, Mary Kupiec Cayton's analysis of Emerson's career as a lecturer, "The Making of an American Prophet."

52. Harris, *Artist in American Society*, 284.

53. On these various aspects of Story's life abroad, see *William Wetmore Story and His Friends: From Letters, Diaries, and Recollections* (1903; rpt., New York: Grove Press, n.d.), 1: 98, 114, 116, 126, 132, 172, 249–50, 254.

54. Mount to Charles Lanman, 7 January 1850, quoted in Harris, *Artist in American Society*, 285.

55. *Private Woman, Public Stage*. For an analysis of the careers and writing of southern women, see Elizabeth Moss, *Domestic Novelists in the Old South: Defenders of Southern Culture* (Baton Rouge: Louisiana State University Press, 1992).

56. Jane Tompkins makes the important point that women's fiction should be evaluated by standards appropriate to the genre, in "Sentimental Power: Uncle Tom's Cabin and the Politics of Literary History," in Bercovitch and Jehlen, eds., *Ideology and Classic American Literature*, 267–92.

57. *Woman in the Nineteenth Century, and Kindred Papers*, ed. Arthur Fuller. See also Capper, *Margaret Fuller*, vol. 1, *The Private Years*.

58. One way to measure the strength of connections between antebellum intellectuals and the American public is to contrast their situation with the far more alienated feelings and circumstances of the expatriate writers of the "lost generation" during the 1920s. See Malcolm Cowley's classic account of the later intellectuals, *Exile's Return: A Literary Odyssey of the 1920s* (1934; rpt., New York: Viking, 1963).

59. "Grayling," in *The Wigwam and the Cabin*, rev. ed. (New York: Lovell, Coryell & Co., n.d.), 1.

60. "Grayling," 1. The divergence of rational and imaginative modes of thinking is discussed in this study in Chapter 3. Charles Feidelson, Jr., has argued similarly that the literature of this period aimed to reintegrate sensible perceptions of material objects and abstract thought, in *Symbolism and American Literature* (Chicago: University of Chicago Press, 1953). I propose that this artistic impulse informed a wide range of cultural products because many groups of Americans wondered about, and indeed were troubled by, the relationship between facts and meanings. I use the term "romance" or "romantic" in this chapter to refer this style and frame of mind. This kind of romanticism was related to the romantic love of nature discussed in Chapter 3, because both perspectives valued the search for integrity and envisioned the source of emotional gratification to be a sense of wholeness.

61. For an excellent survey of literature and the fine arts during this period, see Bode, *Anatomy of American Popular Culture*. Bode's lively and informative book covers some themes that I have omitted due to considerations of space, including theater, painting, and music. One additional genre that is particularly important is the travel narrative, including Richard Henry Dana, Jr., *Two Years before the Mast: A Personal Narrative of Life at Sea*, ed. Thomas Philbrick (1840; rpt., Penguin, 1981).

62. Alan Trachtenberg, *Reading American Photographs: Images as History, Mathew Brady to Walker Evans* (New York: Hill & Wang, 1989), 3.

63. "The Daguerreotype," reprinted in Alan Trachtenberg, ed., *Classic Essays in Photography* (New Haven: Leete's Island Books, 1980), 38.

64. "The Stereoscope and the Stereograph" (1859), in ibid., 77, 82. Not all observers of photography praised the medium in these terms. The poet Charles

Baudelaire criticized the mechanistic quality of photographs in 1859 in "The Modern Public and Photography," in ibid., 83–89.

65. Harold Francis Pfister, *Facing the Light: Historic American Portrait Daguerreotypes* (Washington, D.C.: National Portrait Gallery, Smithsonian Institution Press, 1978), 18.

66. Trachtenberg discusses the rituals surrounding sitting for and displaying photographs, in *Reading American Photographs*, 26–27.

67. Cole to William Adams, 26 February 1840, quoted in Pfister, *Facing the Light*, 42.

68. On the galleries where photographs were displayed and on Brady's *Gallery*, see Trachtenberg, *Reading American Photographs*, 39–43, 45–53.

69. Eugene Current-Garcia, *The American Short Story before 1850: A Critical History* (Boston: Twayne Publishers, 1985), 1. Among literary critics, the term "short story" sometimes refers narrowly to short fiction that aims at a description of social life in accord with ordinary experience and common sense. "Tales," in contrast, are thought to be more allegorical, less ambiguous, and more complex from the viewpoint of characterization. Because of the general nature of my discussion, these terms are used more or less interchangeably in the text. But most of the fiction analyzed here would be considered "tales" in the more precise usage. For an interesting argument that tales as a narrative form developed into short stories during the antebellum decades, see Robert F. Marler, "From Tale to Short Story: The Emergence of a New Genre in the 1850s," *American Literature* 46 (1974): 153–69.

70. On Poe and Hawthorne, respectively, see Current-Garcia, *American Short Story*, 59, and Michael J. Colacurcio, *The Province of Piety: Moral History in Hawthorne's Early Tales* (Cambridge, Mass.: Harvard University Press, 1984), 29.

71. This argument is made, for example, by Marler in "From Tale to Short Story," but it is important to acknowledge that this viewpoint is based on the value judgment that "real" life is rational in the sense of capable of being comprehensible by reason, even though also complex in human psychology and social relationships.

72. Marler, "From Tale to Short Story," 155.

73. *The Complete Tales and Poems of Edgar Allan Poe* (New York: Modern Library, 1965), 141–68, 246–57.

74. See, for example, "The Poetic Principle," in ibid., 889–907. "The Colloquoy of Monos and Una" also appears in this edition of Poe's works, 444–51.

75. "Preface to the 1851 Edition of *Twice-Told Tales*," in *Hawthorne: Selected Tales and Sketches*, 3d ed. (New York: Holt, Rinehart & Winston, 1970), 586, 588.

76. This evaluation of public taste in the 1850s is offered by Current-Garcia in *American Short Story*, 119–24.

77. *Hawthorne: Tales and Sketches*, 153, 151.

78. Ibid., 162.

79. Ibid., 149, 150, 151.

80. Colacurcio presents this thesis in *Province of Piety*, 5–36. He discusses "Young Goodman Brown" in chap. 5.

81. "Uncle Lot," in *The May Flower and Miscellaneous Writings*, 26th ed. (Boston: Houghton Mifflin, 1888), 9–42.

82. David D. Van Tassel, *Recording America's Past: An Interpretation of the Development of Historical Studies in America, 1607–1884* (Chicago: University of Chicago Press, 1960), 100.

83. An exemplary local history is Lemuel Shattuck, *A History of the Town of Concord* [Massachusetts] (Boston: Russell, Idiorne, 1835). Characteristic works among the numerous volumes and editions of Bancroft and Parkman, respectively, are *History of the United States from the Discovery of the American Continent*, 10 vols. (Boston: Little, Brown, 1834–75), and *The California and Oregon Trail, Being Sketches of Prairie and Rocky Mountain Life* (New York: George P. Putnam, 1849).

84. *History of the Conquest of Mexico and History of the Conquest of Peru* (New York: Modern Library, n.d.), 3–4.

85. Ibid., 4, 681, 289, 162–63.

86. Ibid., 437, 289, 615, 48–51.

87. Buell thoroughly documents the rise of regional and historical interests in New England literature in *New England Literary Culture*, pts. 3 and 4. See also further discussion of literary regionalism in Chapter 6.

88. *The Yemassee: A Romance of Carolina*, ed. Joseph V. Ridgely (New Haven: College & University Press, 1964). For an analysis of the novel, see Mary Ann Wimsatt, *The Major Fiction of William Gilmore Simms: Cultural Traditions and Literary Form* (Baton Rouge: Louisiana State University Press, 1989), chap. 2.

89. For an excellent discussion of the essay tradition in eighteenth- and early nineteenth-century Britain and America, see Lawrence Buell, *Literary Transcendentalism: Style and Vision in the American Renaissance* (Ithaca: Cornell University Press, 1973), 94–96. In his chapter 3, "From Conversation to Essay," Buell explores the transcendentalists' indebtedness to speech in their writing. I think that his insight pertains more generally to antebellum prose and that this style may have roots in changing social relationships.

90. Thoreau's "Resistance to Civil Government" was first presented as a lecture to his neighbors at the Concord lyceum in 1848. Margaret Fuller hosted several series of conversations around 1840 to which patrons bought tickets. None was devoted specifically to the subject of women, but gender was nonetheless a recurrent theme. One participant, Caroline Wells Healey Dall, later published a purported transcript of conversations held in 1841 as *Margaret and Her Friends, or Conversations with Margaret Fuller upon the Mythology of the Greeks and Its Expression in Art* (1895; rpt., New York: Arno Press, 1972). The first version of Fuller's book, *Woman in the Nineteenth Century*, appeared as a long essay entitled "The Great Lawsuit" in the transcendentalist periodical, *The Dial*, in 1843.

91. Journal, 7 October 1840, in *Selections from Emerson*, ed. Whicher, 144.

92. Journal, 31(?) January 1841, in ibid., 146.

93. "Self-Reliance," in ibid., 147.

94. "Self-Reliance," in ibid., 149, 153.

95. "Self-Reliance," in ibid., 152, 156.

96. Some of the most important proslavery essays were collected as *The Pro-Slavery Argument; as Maintained by the Most Distinguished Writers of the Southern States, Containing the Several Essays, on the Subject, of Chancellor Harper, Governor Hammond, Dr. Simms, and Professor Dew* (1852; rpt., New York: Negro Universities Press, 1968). Drew Gilpin Faust has edited a volume of similar writings, *The Ideology of Slavery: Proslavery Thought in the Antebellum South, 1830–1860*.

97. Faust, ed., *Ideology of Slavery*, 170. Hammond wrote two letters to Clarkson, published first in the Columbia *South Carolinian* and reissued as a pamphlet with the

title *Two Letters on Slavery in the United States, Addressed to Thomas Clarkson, Esq.* (1845). Drew Faust chose to reprint only the first letter. I have used that text.

98. Ibid., 170.

99. Ibid., 172.

100. Ibid., 172–73.

101. Jane Tompkins makes a strong case for the need for a critical reexamination of the standard canon, in *Sensational Designs*, esp. introduction and chap. 7. Tompkins identifies F. O. Matthiessen as a modernist (200), a judgment that may surprise some. To the extent that his classic work, *American Renaissance: Art and Expression in the Age of Whitman and Emerson*, appreciated the philosophical depth of American Renaissance literature as well as honored its democratic impulse, there is much truth in her judgment. For a sense of the various issues raised by more recent critics, see Bercovitch and Jehlen, eds., *Ideology and Classic American Literature*.

102. *Uncle Tom's Cabin* has received a variety of critical judgments. Consider the difference between Jane Tompkins's evaluation of the novel as an exemplary work of domestic fiction in *Sensational Designs*, chap. 5, and Ann Douglas's sharp criticism of Stowe's "infantile heroine [who] anticipates the exaltation of the average which is the trademark of mass culture," in *The Feminization of American Culture*, 4.

103. *Uncle Tom's Cabin; or, Life among the Lowly*, 35.

104. Ibid., 500.

105. Ibid., 510. Although scholars have often noted the voluntary self-restriction of women authors to themes concerning private relationships, it should be noted that Stowe's choice of a public and controversial subject was not unprecedented. On the one hand, Mary Kelley argues in *Private Woman, Public Stage* that women writers were uncomfortable in public roles and, because of their socialization, shied away from political materials. Yet Sarah Hale, for one, although a caretaker of domestic orthodoxy, wrote on sectional issues in what she probably considered a moral and social, as opposed to a political, way. Her first novel, *Northwood* (1827), dealt with sectional character and, indirectly, slavery. After Stowe's success, Hale reissued *Northwood* in 1852 as a conservative voice in growing sectional controversy. In so doing, she, too, tested the limits of women's proper role. See *Northwood; a Tale of New England* (Boston: Bowles & Dearborn, 1827); *Northwood, or Life North and South; Showing the True Character of Both* (New York: H. Long & Brothers, 1852); and Taylor's excellent discussion of the novels in *Cavalier and Yankee*, 115–41.

106. *The Scarlet Letter*, in *Complete Novels and Selected Tales of Hawthorne*, ed. Pearson, 112.

107. The most accessible view of the Hutchinson controversy is the excerpt from Hutchinson's trial in 1637 reprinted as "Examination of Mrs. Ann Hutchinson," in Cott, ed., *Root of Bitterness*, 34–46.

108. The artistry of Hester and the mechanistic qualities of Chillingworth are described in *The Scarlet Letter*, in *Complete Novels and Selected Tales of Hawthorne*, ed. Pearson, 133, 154.

109. Ibid., 209.

110. Ibid., 239.

111. *Moby-Dick*, ed. Hayford and Parker, 2.

112. Ibid., esp. 160, 163.

113. Ibid., 169.

114. Ibid., 12–13.

115. Ibid., 354.

116. Ibid., 324–25.

117. *Walden and Civil Disobedience*, ed. Meyer, 45, 46.

118. Ibid., 160–61, 206–7, 275–79.

119. Ibid., 50.

120. Ibid., 95

121. Ibid., 135.

122. Ibid., 372.

123. Ibid., 372.

124. *Narrative of the Life of Frederick Douglass, an American Slave, Written by Himself* (New York: New American Library, 1968). See also William S. McFeely's biography, *Frederick Douglass* (New York: Norton, 1991).

125. Douglass, *Narrative*, 21, 22–23, 77–83.

126. Douglass became a converted Christian in 1833 and was in close contact with northern Christians, black and white, around 1840. But by 1845, he was critical of most Christians, and particularly of ministers, for their inaction on the slavery issue. See McFeely, *Douglass*, 41, 81–85, 124, 127–28; on Douglass's career as an antislavery lecturer see 86–118.

127. Further discussion of slave narratives as a genre and African-American writing more generally appears in Chapter 5.

5. The Flowering of Minority Cultures

1. *Figures in Black: Words, Signs, and the "Racial" Self* (New York: Oxford University Press, 1987), 129. The text of *Our Nig; or, Sketches from the Life of a Free Black by "Our Nig"* can be found in William L. Andrews, ed., *Three Classic African-American Novels* (New York: Mentor, 1990), 285–366.

2. There seems to be more critical discussion of the work of racial minorities than antebellum ethnic writers. Consider the broad interests represented in two anthologies of criticism, Charles T. Davis and Henry Louis Gates, Jr., eds., *The Slave's Narrative* (Oxford: Oxford University Press, 1985), and Andrew Wiget, ed., *Critical Essays on Native American Literature* (Boston: G. K. Hall, 1985). Scholarly writing on nineteenth-century Catholicism and Judaism tends to focus on religious beliefs and institutions more than on values and literature. One study indicative of emerging interest in Catholic culture is McDannell, *The Christian Home in Victorian America*. Although Lawrence J. McCaffrey does not focus on the antebellum period, see also his *Textures of Irish America* (Syracuse, N.Y.: Syracuse University Press, 1992). Jacob Rader Marcus integrates discussion of religion and customs in his indispensable synthesis on Judaism, *United States Jewry, 1776–1985*, vols. 1 and 2.

3. *Our Nig*, in Andrews, ed., *African-American Novels*; *The Scarlet Letter*, in *Complete Novels and Selected Tales of Hawthorne*, ed. Pearson, 85–240.

4. Introduction, Davis and Gates, eds., *Slave's Narrative*, xxiii. The italics that appear in this and subsequent quotations are found in the original texts.

5. *The Life, History, and Travels of Kah-Ge-Ga-Gah-Bowh (George Copway), a Young Indian Chief of the Ojebwa Nation, a Convert to the Christian Faith, and a Missionary to His People for Twelve Years, . . . Written by Himself*, 2d ed. (Philadelphia: James Harmstead, 1847). "Ojebwa" is the spelling used in this title, although today the more common spelling is "Ojibwa," as it appears in my text.

6. Andrew Wiget, *Native American Literature* (Boston: Twayne Publishers, 1985), 22.

7. *Life, History, and Travels of Kah-Ge-Ga-Gah-Bowh*, 26. Although Copway's language in this passage sounds suspiciously ornate for a man of limited education in English, it is well to keep in mind that one manifestation of nineteenth-century racism was the expectation that blacks were only capable of simple prose, as I discuss below. On the conventionalized elements in autobiographical narratives, see Robert Burns Stepto, "'I Rose and Found My Voice': Narration, Authentication, and Authorial Control in Four Slaves Narratives," in Davis and Gates, eds., *Slave's Narrative*, 225–41. James Olney proposes that these narrators ought not to be considered individual authors because of the restrictive influence of literary conventions, in "'I was Born': Slave Narratives, Their Status as Autobiography and as Literature," in *Slave's Narrative*, 148–75. John W. Blassingame, on the other hand, defends the basic reliability of slave narratives, in "Using the Testimony of Ex-Slaves: Approaches and Problems," in *Slave's Narrative*, esp. 81.

8. On Wise's background and activities, see Sefton D. Temkin, *Isaac Mayer Wise: Shaping American Judaism* (Oxford: Oxford University Press, 1992), esp. pts. 1 and 2, as well as the biographical introduction (by the editors) to *Selected Writings of Isaac M. Wise*, ed. David Philipson and Louis Grossmann (1900; rpt., New York: Arno Press and The New York Times, 1969), 1–44. The subtitle of *Die Deborah* was "A Supplement to the *Israelite*, Devoted to the Daughters of Israel" (Temkin, *Wise*, 124). It seems that part of the reason that Wise published a German-language periodical was to provide women, who did not generally learn English as quickly as men, with Jewish reading material. Wise was reacting to an extent to the situation in his own family. Virtually all of the correspondence to Wise's first wife, Therese (d. 1874), was written in either German or Yiddish. See, for example, Emily Wise (her daughter) to Therese Wise, 27 July [18]63, Family and Miscellaneous Correspondence, Isaac Mayer Wise Papers, American Jewish Archives, Hebrew Union College, Cincinnati.

9. On the conflict over language in the Catholic church, see Dolan, *American Catholic Experience*, chap. 11, and Ahlstrom, *Religious History of the American People*, chap. 49. The rise of Yiddish literature produced less actual controversy than did the language issue among Catholics, perhaps because the Jewish community was less centralized than the Catholic church. But there were subtle tensions between more and less assimilated American Jews over the use of Yiddish in the late nineteenth century. See Marcus, *United States Jewry* (1993), 3: 568–72; he notes that Isaac Wise in particular did not approve of the use of Yiddish (570).

10. *American Catholic Experience*, 243. Other scholars who have commented on the scarcity of Catholic institutions and the importance of reading include Randall M. Miller, "A Church in Cultural Captivity: Some Speculations on Catholic Identity in the Old South," in Miller and Jon L. Wakelyn, eds., *Catholics in the Old South* (Macon, Ga.: Mercer University Press, 1983), 11–52, and Mary Stephana Cavanaugh, "Catholic Book Publishing in the United States, 1784–1850," M.A. thesis, University of Illinois, 1937, 125.

11. Dolan comments on the formation of the Catholic middle class in *American Catholic Experience*, 141. On Jewish learning, see Marcus, *United States Jewry*, 1: 407–15, 2: 249–78.

12. On the difficulty of penetrating images of Hawthorne to understand the man and writer, see Colacurcio, *Province of Piety*, prologue. For a recent attempt to sift facts from myths about Poe, see Silverman, *Poe*.

13. John Bierhorst, quoted in Arnold Krupat, "An Approach to Native American Texts," in Wiget, ed., *Essays in Native American Literature*, 121.

14. On Wise's fiction, see Temkin, *Wise*, 113–14, 161. On Sadlier, see Thomas N. Brown, "Mary Anne Madden Sadlier," in Edward T. James, Janet Wilson James, and Paul S. Boyer, eds., *Notable American Women* (Cambridge, Mass.: Harvard University Press, 1971), 3: 219–20, and *A Round Table of Representative American Catholic Novelists, at Which Is Served a Feast of Excellent Stories by Eleanor C. Donnelly and Ten Others* (New York: Benziger Brothers, 1897), 239–40.

15. *Our Nig*, in Andrews, ed., *African-American Novels*, 287.

16. Ibid., 365.

17. Anon., review of *The Kidnapped and the Ransomed*, in *New Englander*, in Davis and Gates, eds., *Slave's Narrative*, 31; Ephraim Peabody, "Narratives of Fugitive Slaves," in *Christian Examiner*, in *Slave's Narrative*, 19.

18. Introduction (by the editor) to *Letters of Rebecca Gratz*, ed. David Philipson (Philadelphia: Jewish Publication Society of America, 1929), xviii–xix. For a more general view of the Jewish community in Philadelphia, see Maxwell Whiteman, "The Legacy of Isaac Leeser," in Murray Friedman, ed., *Jewish Life in Philadelphia, 1830–1940* (Philadelphia: ISHI Publications, 1983), 26–47.

19. Rebecca Gratz to Maria Gratz, 16 February 1832, [1832], 12 October [1833], *Letters of Gratz*, ed. Philipson, 141, 159, 185. Among the popular authors Gratz named in her letters were Lydia Maria Child, Harriet Martineau, James Paulding, and John Pendelton Kennedy.

20. On Moïse, see Charles Reznikoff, "Penina Moïse," in James, James, and Boyer, eds., *Notable American Women*, 2: 559–60. Her poems have been published as *Secular and Religious Works of Penina Moïse, with Brief Sketch of Her Life*, ed. Charleston Section, Council of Jewish Women (Charleston: Nicholas G. Duffy, 1911).

21. *Works of Moïse*, 299–301.

22. Rebecca Gratz to Maria Gratz, 6 January 1834, *Letters of Gratz*, ed. Philipson, 191.

23. The conclusion that Gratz chose to remain single to avoid intermarriage is reported by Reznikoff in his entry on Penina Moïse in James, James, and Boyer, eds., *Notable American Women*, 2: 559. Dianne Ashton questions the accuracy of this often-repeated explanation of Gratz's celibacy in a penetrating essay, "The Legend of Rebecca Gratz: Jewish Women and Companionate Marriage in America" (1986), typescript, American Jewish Archives. Whether or not loyalty to Judaism was the reason that Gratz never married, she rejected interfaith marriage in principle and stated her view in a number of letters, including Gratz to Maria Fenno Hoffman, 12 July 1819, Rebecca Gratz Papers, American Jewish Archives.

24. Rebecca Gratz to Maria Gratz, 21 September, *Letters of Gratz*, ed. Philipson, 181. She wrote similar letters to Ann Gratz about Jewish naming customs and Yom Kippur on 24 November 1845 and 12 September 1861, *Letters of Gratz*, 319–20, 427.

25. On Moïse's spinsterhood, see *Works of Moïse*, 9; the collection includes these poems (212–13, 269–70, 270–72).

26. Whiteman, "Legacy of Leeser," in Friedman, ed., *Jewish Life in Philadelphia*, 28–29, 32–36. My discussion of the development of Jewish culture after 1830 should not be taken to mean that American Jews did not engage in intellectual pursuits in previous years. In the early national period, however, there was less of a self-conscious attempt to produce a specifically Jewish body of literature. It seems that the leadership

of rabbis was the catalyst of change. For an informative biography of a Jewish intellectual, Mordecai Noah (1785–1851), who made his mark in the early republic and continued to be active after 1830, see Jonathan D. Sarna, *Jacksonian Jew: The Two Worlds of Mordecai Noah* (New York: Holmes & Meier, 1981) esp. chap. 7.

27. On Wise's efforts as a fiction writer, see the biographical introduction to *Selected Writings of Wise*, ed. Philipson and Grossmann, 99–100, and Temkin, *Wise*, 113–14, 161.

28. Brownson to Hecker, 25 June 1845, quoted in Margaret Mary Reher, *Catholic Intellectual Life in America: A Historical Study of Persons and Movements* (New York: Macmillan, 1989), 41.

29. "Women's Novels," quoted in Paul R. Messbarger, *Fiction with a Parochial Purpose: Social Uses of American Catholic Literature, 1884–1900* (Boston: Boston University Press, 1971), 28. Messbarger's discussion (chap. 3) of antebellum Catholic literature focuses on Anglo-Saxon Catholic writing, as does the discussion of Reher in *Catholic Intellectual Life*, chaps. 2 and 3. The best introduction to Irish-Catholic writing in America is Cavanaugh, "Catholic Book Publishing in the United States."

30. Messbarger, *Fiction with a Parochial Purpose*, 20.

31. On Donahoe, see Cavanaugh, "Catholic Book Publishing in the United States," 74–78. Information on other Irish-American publishers may also be found in this source, which is organized according to city or region.

32. Peter Guilday, *John Gilmary Shea: Father of American Catholic History, 1824–1892* (New York: United States Catholic Historical Society, 1926), 14, 19, 18, 52.

33. *Catholic Missions among the Indian Tribes of the United States* (1855; rpt., New York: Arno Press and The New York Times, 1969), 20.

34. Ibid., 438.

35. *The First of the Maccabees: A Historical Novel* (Cincinnati: Bloch Publishing and Printing Co., n.d.). Temkin gives the date of the novel as 1860 in *Wise*, 161.

36. *Catholic Missions*, 19.

37. Ibid., 17.

38. This biographical information is based on Brown, "Sadlier," in James, James, and Boyer, eds., *Notable American Women*, 3: 219–20.

39. *Willy Burke; or, The Irish Orphan in America* (Boston: Patrick Donahoe, [1850]), 163.

40. Ibid., 122, 132–3, 184–91, 204–33.

41. Ibid., 256–80.

42. William Edward Farrison, *William Wells Brown: Author and Reformer* (Chicago: University of Chicago Press, 1969), 314.

43. Blyden Jackson, *A History of Afro-American Literature: The Long Beginning, 1746–1895* (Baton Rouge: Louisiana State University Press, 1989), 122–27.

44. Ibid., 191, 195. The intellectual achievements of African Americans who were born in freedom have received too little attention in comparison with the scholarship on the writings of fugitive slaves. An excellent corrective to this imbalance is Moses, *Alexander Crummell*. See also Moses's edition of Crummell's writings, *Destiny and Race: Selected Writings, 1840–1898* (Amherst: University of Massachusetts Press, 1992).

45. Farrison, *Brown*, 72–73, 116.

46. On segregation in Boston schools, see Farrison, *Brown*, 127; on Brown's years abroad see chap. 12.

47. See Moses, *Crummell*, chaps. 6–10.

48. *The Slave Narrative: Its Place in American History*, 2d ed. (Washington: Howard University Press, 1988), 106.

49. For example, Olney, "'I was Born,'" in Davis and Gates, eds., *Slave's Narrative*, 148–75. Historians are becoming increasingly aware that free African Americans played a crucial role in the abolitionist movement, particularly during its earliest phase in the 1830s. Yet it does not seem that their writing style was as decisive in setting the tone of abolitionist prose as was the language of white reformers such as William Lloyd Garrison. Nor does it appear that black abolitionists were as aggressive about encouraging fugitives to publicize their experiences or perhaps as capable of helping escaped slaves reach white audiences as were white antislavery advocates. I assume in this discussion that fugitive slaves were more strongly influenced in a literary sense by white than black abolitionists. But the relationship between white and black reformers has not been fully explored by historians, and my conclusions must be interpreted as tentative. For an excellent sample of black abolitionist prose, see Ripley, ed., *The Black Abolitionist Papers*, vols. 3–5.

50. Farrison, *Brown*, 62; McFeely, *Douglass*, 80.

51. McFeely, *Douglass*, 89; Farrison, *Brown*, 81.

52. McFeely, *Douglass*, 116–18; Farrison, *Brown*, 112–14.

53. McFeely, *Douglass*, 146–62, 173–75; Farrison, *Brown*, chaps. 12–14.

54. The 1856 edition is *Archy Moore, The White Slave; or, Memoirs of a Fugitive* (1856; rpt., New York: Negro Universities Press, 1969). The 1836 edition consisted of chaps. 1–37 of the 1856 edition.

55. *The Fugitive Blacksmith; or, Events in the History of James W. C. Pennington, Pastor of a Presbyterian Church, New York, Formerly a Slave in the State of Maryland*, in Arna Bontemps, ed. *Great Slave Narratives* (Boston: Beacon Press, 1969), 193–267 and esp. chap. 5.

56. Jackson, *History of Afro-American Literature*, 136.

57. *The Heroic Slave*, in Andrews, ed., *African-American Novels*, 53.

58. "Narrative of the Life and Escape of William Wells Brown," in *Clotel; or The President's Daughter: A Narrative of Slave Life in the United States*, in Andrews, ed., *African-American Novels*, 77–112.

59. *Heroic Slave*, in Andrews, ed., *African-American Novels*, 25.

60. *Clotel*, in Andrews, ed., *African-American Novels*, 258.

61. Ibid., chaps. 8 and 15.

62. Ibid., 248–50.

63. Ibid., 225.

64. Gates, *Figures in Black*, 138–39; see also Gates's critical discussion of *Our Nig* (chap. 5).

65. *Our Nig* in Andrews, ed. *African-American Novels*, 357–58.

66. Ibid., 333.

67. Wiget, *Native American Literature*, chaps. 1 and 2, esp. p. 43. On Native-American writing, see also David Murray, *Forked Tongues: Speech, Writing, and Representation in North American Indian Texts* (Bloomington: Indiana University Press, 1991).

68. *Life, History, and Travels of Kah-Ge-Ga-Gah-Bowh*, esp. chaps. 7–9, 13.

69. James W. Parins, *John Rollin Ridge: His Life and Works* (Lincoln: University of Nebraska Press, 1991), esp. 3, 9–10, 14–18, 36, 53.

70. *Life, History, and Travels of Kah-Ge-Ga-Gah-Bowh*, 20–21, 139. See also Richard White's excellent analysis of changing Indian-white relations in the Great Lakes region during the colonial era and in the early republic, *The Middle Ground.*

71. Parins, *Ridge*, 29–31. For useful background on the *Cherokee Phoenix*, issued in Georgia from 1828 to 1834 and written partly in transliterated Cherokee and partly in English, see Jack Frederick Kilpatrick and Anna Gritts Kilpatrick, eds., *New Echota Letters: Contributions of Samuel A. Worcester to the Cherokee Phoenix* (Dallas: Southern Methodist University Press, 1968). Samuel Worcester was the ABCFM missionary who encouraged the periodical. Elias Boudinot was its first editor.

72. *Life, History, and Travels of Kah-Ge-Ga-Gah-Bowh*, 29. On Apes's *A Son of the Forest* and the autobiographical tradition in Native-American literature, see Wiget, *Native American Literature*, 50–56.

73. *Life, History, and Travels of Kah-Ge-Ga-Gah-Bowh*, 127, 131.

74. Ibid., 107–8

75. Ibid., 43.

76. Parins, *Ridge*, 60–61, 120–39, 184–85.

77. Ridge to Watie, 9 October 1854, quoted in Parins, *Ridge*, 113–14.

78. Ibid., 180–94.

79. The poem appears in Yellow Bird [John Rollin Ridge], *The Life and Adventures of Joaquín Murieta: The Celebrated California Bandit* (1854; rpt., Norman: University of Oklahoma Press, 1955) 23–25.

80. Ibid., 9.

81. Ibid., 10, 12, 13.

82. Ibid., 158.

83. Ibid., 7.

84. Ibid., 158. *Joaquín Murieta* combined a serious message with a sensational narrative and was thus linked to a large body of antebellum popular fiction described by Reynolds in *Beneath the American Renaissance*. Although I do not altogether agree with Reynolds that the stated moralistic purposes of such fiction should be dismissed as simply a device to ease public acceptance of more questionable content, Reynolds has recovered a group of works that should make scholars reassess the literary consciousness of this period.

85. *Joaquín Murieta*, 139, 75.

86. Ibid., 67.

87. Ibid., 50, 64.

88. See Colacurcio, *Province of Piety*, as well as my discussion of *The Scarlet Letter* in Chapter 4.

89. Kelley, *Private Woman, Public Stage*, 18. The most informative general studies of antebellum women's fiction are Kelley's book and Douglas, *Feminization of American Culture*. For a discussion of critical principles appropriate to women's fiction, see Susan K. Harris, *19th-Century American Women's Novels: Interpretative Strategies* (Cambridge: Cambridge University Press, 1990).

90. *The Wide, Wide World* (1850; rpt., New York: Grosset & Dunlap, n. d.), 269–82.

91. Ibid., chaps. 47–52.

92. Ibid., 384.

93. On Lippard's life, see David Reynolds's study, *George Lippard* (Boston: Twayne Publishers, 1982).

94. *The Quaker City; or, The Monks of Monk Hall: A Romance of Philadelphia Life,*

Mystery and Crime, [16th ed.] (Philadelphia: T. B. Peterson and Brothers, [1876]), 112, 113.

95. Ibid., 1.

96. Ibid., 149.

6. America at a Crossroads

1. On the artistic and literary events cited, see Pattee, *The Feminine Fifties*, esp. 148–56, 159–66. On the revival of 1857 and 1858, see Smith, *Revivalism and Social Reform*, chap. 4, and Miller, *Life of the Mind in America*, 88–95. The most synthetic interpretation of the sectional crisis is David M. Potter, *The Impending Crisis, 1848–1861*, ed. Don E. Fehrenbacher (New York: Harper & Row, 1976).

2. "Mr. Douglas' Opening Speech," Ottawa, Illinois, 21 August 1858, in Harold Holzer, ed., *The Lincoln-Douglas Debates* (New York: HarperCollins, 1993), 53. For the text of Lincoln's "House Divided" speech, 16 June 1858, see *Lincoln: Speeches and Writings*, ed. Basler, 372–81.

3. "Speech at Corinth," as paraphrased by the Corinth *True Democrat*, 21 September 1860, in *The Papers of Jefferson Davis, 1856–1860*, ed. Lynda Lasswell Crist (Baton Rouge: Louisiana State University Press, 1989), 6: 365. The italics in this and subsequent quotations appear in the original texts.

4. Ibid., 365.

5. For an example of constitutional argument at the beginning of the antebellum period, see Daniel Webster, "Second Reply to Hayne, Jan. 26–27, 1830," in *Papers of Daniel Webster*, ed. Wiltse, 1: 290–348. For the abolitionists' criticism of the Constitution's compromises on slavery, see Perry, *Radical Abolitionism*, 188–208.

6. "First Inaugural Address, March 4, 1861," in *Lincoln: Speeches and Writings*, ed. Basler, 582.

7. "Opening Speech," in Holzer, ed., *Lincoln-Douglas Debates*, 56.

8. Ibid., 54–55.

9. "Mr. Lincoln's Reply," Ottawa, Illinois, 21 August 1858, in Holzer, ed., *Lincoln-Douglas Debates*, 63.

10. Parker to Francis Jackson, 24 November 1859, in *Theodore Parker: An Anthology*, ed. Henry Steele Commager (Boston: Beacon Press, 1960), 265.

11. On the increasing prominence of racial theories in antebellum thinking, see George M. Fredrickson, *The Black Image in the White Mind: The Debate on Afro-American Character and Destiny, 1817–1914* (New York: Harper & Row, 1971), esp. chaps. 3–5.

12. *Cannibals All!*, ed. Woodward, 256.

13. Ibid., 15.

14. *The Cotton Kingdom*, ed. Arthur Schlesinger, Sr. (with an introduction by Lawrence N. Powell), 8. In *The Cotton Kingdom* Olmsted abridged three of his previous books on slavery, published between 1856 and 1860, and issued them in a single volume. The quotation in the text appeared in a new introduction, "Introductory: The Present Crisis," that he wrote for the 1861 edition.

15. On these developments see Chapter 1.

16. On later Protestant fundamentalism, see Marsden, *Fundamentalism and American Culture*, and Ahlstrom, *Religious History of the American People*, chap. 48.

17. *Entire Devotion to God*, excerpted in *Palmer: Selected Writings*, ed. Oden, 185, 186.

18. Ibid., 196.

19. Ibid., 188.

20. Ibid., 188. For an analysis of Palmer's theology, see Harold E. Raser, *Phoebe Palmer: Her Life and Thought* (Lewiston, N.Y.: Edwin Mellen Press, 1987), esp. chaps. 4 and 5.

21. Clifford E. Clark, Jr., *Henry Ward Beecher: Spokesman for a Middle-Class America* (Urbana: University of Illinois Press, 1978), 133. On Palmer's revival activities between the mid-1850s and her death in 1874, see *Palmer*, ed. Oden, chaps. 8–10.

22. Clark, *Beecher*, 109; for Beecher's critique of revivalism see 135–36.

23. *Star Papers; or, Experiences of Art and Nature* (New York: J. C. Derby, 1855), 27–40, 121–28, 144–51, 293–302.

24. Ibid., 122.

25. Ibid., 297, 299.

26. Quoted in Clark, *Beecher*, 134.

27. On this frame of mind see Chapter 3.

28. *The Autocrat of the Breakfast Table* (London: Dent/Everyman's Library, [1965]), 14, 22–24, 21. Most literary critics assume that Holmes closely identified himself with the "autocrat" and presented the "autocrat" uncritically. I think it is unlikely that in a society well aware of pretension Holmes portrayed the "autocrat" without irony. Even if the "autocrat's" conversation grew out of Holmes's own experience, Holmes probably embellished facts for the sake of satire. Analyses of Holmes's humor include Miriam Rossiter Small, *Oliver Wendell Holmes* (New York: Twayne Publishers, 1962), chap. 3, and Lewis Leary, "Oliver Wendell Holmes," in Louis D. Rubin, ed., *The Comic Imagination in American Literature* (New Brunswick, N.J.: Rutgers University Press, 1973), 113–26. Social satire as a literary genre should be seen in the context of antebellum humor. See esp. Pattee, *Feminine Fifties*, chap. 14; Rubin, *Comic Imagination in American Literature*, esp. Cecil D. Eby, "Yankee Humor," Hennig Cohen, "A Comic Mode of the Romantic Imagination: Poe, Hawthorne, Melville," James M. Cox, "Humor of the Old Southwest," and Brom Weber, "The Misspellers," 77–112, 127–38; and Nancy Pogez and Paul P. Somers, Jr., "Literary Humor," in Lawrence E. Mintz, ed., *Humor in America: A Research Guide to Genres and Topics* (New York: Greenwood Press, 1988), 1–34.

29. *The Potiphar Papers* (New York: G. P. Putnam, 1853), 63. On Curtis, see Gordon Milne, *George William Curtis and the Genteel Tradition* (Bloomington: Indiana University Press, 1956). The satiric writing in the 1850s about snobbery and class distinctions was part of a broader trend in antebellum humor to focus on encounters between gentlemen and provincials. This theme was prominent in the work of southwestern humorists such as Joseph Glover Baldwin, a genre discussed by James M. Cox in "Humor of the Old Southwest," in Rubin, ed., *Comic Imagination in American Literature*, 101–12. The prose of Curtis especially played similarly on the distinction between high and low life but treated the subject in an urban setting and with more political awareness.

30. Ibid., 75.

31. Ibid., 86.

32. Ibid., 87.

33. "Nothing to Wear: An Episode of City Life," *Harper's New Monthly Magazine* 15 (1857): 749.

34. Ibid., 751.

35. Ibid., 752.

36. Ibid., 753.

37. *Maggie: A Girl of the Streets (A Story of New York)* (Lexington: University of Kentucky Press, 1970); *The House of Mirth* (New York: Holt, Rinehart & Winston, 1962). Representative late nineteenth-century nonfiction criticizing social inequality includes Henry George, *Progress and Poverty* (1879), Jacob Riis, *How the Other Half Lives* (1890), and Henry Demarest Lloyd, *Wealth against Commonwealth* (1894). For a good discussion of economic themes in postwar fiction, see Walter Fuller Taylor, *The Economic Novel in America* (Chapel Hill: University of North Carolina Press, 1942).

38. For an overview of the role of regionalism in American culture, see Merrill Jensen, ed., *Regionalism in America* (Madison: University of Wisconsin Press, 1952), esp. Benjamin T. Spencer, "Regionalism in American Literature," 219–60. The "local color" movement usually refers to writers who avowed their commitment around the turn of the twentieth century to a kind of realism highly focused on the manners and mores of out-of-the-way communities. In contrast, literature of a regional orientation was a less self-conscious form of writing produced over a longer period of time. For discussion of local-color prose in relation to women writers, see Josephine Donovan, *New England Local Color Literature: A Women's Tradition* (New York: Frederick Ungar, 1983). For a defense of the value of local-color writing, see Alice Hall Petry, "Universal and Particular: The Local-Color Phenomenon Reconsidered," *American Literary Realism* 12 (1979): 111–26.

39. The best collection of polemical works that defended southern society is Faust, ed., *The Ideology of Slavery*. Perhaps the most comparable northern body of writings consisted of apologies for free-labor capitalism by partisans of the new Republican party. The standard explanation of this ideology is Foner, *Free Soil, Free Labor, Free Men*.

40. See the excellent discussion by Lawrence Buell of the use of literature to create a sense of regional identity in *New England Literary Culture*, esp. pt. 4.

41. "The Courtship of Miles Standish," in *The Courtship of Miles Standish and Other Poems* (Boston: Ticknor & Fields, 1858), 62, 36. For Buell's explanation of works about New England's Puritan history, see *New England Literary Culture*, pt. 3.

42. "Courtship of Miles Standish," in *Miles Standish*, 8, 14, 9.

43. *Georgia Scenes: Characters, Incidents, &c., in the First Half Century of the Republic* (New York: Sagamore Press, 1957); *Sut Lovingood's Yarns*, ed. M. Thomas Inge (New Haven, Conn.: College & University Press, 1966); R. Bruce Bickley, Jr., *Joel Chandler Harris* (Boston: Twayne Publishers, 1978); and, among many editions of the "Uncle Remus" stories, Harris, *Uncle Remus: His Songs and His Sayings* (1880), rev. ed. (New York: D. Appleton-Century Co., 1938).

44. See William Perry Fidler, *Augusta Evans Wilson, 1835–1909: A Biography* (University: University of Alabama Press, 1951), 70, 91, and chap. 9. On southern writing by women, including Augusta Evans, see Moss, *Domestic Novelists in the Old South*.

45. The review is discussed in Fidler, *Augusta Evans Wilson*, 80.

46. *Beulah, a Novel* (New York: Carleton, 1884), 53, 293, 148.

47. For a comprehensive overview of contemporary arts and entertainments, see Bode, *Anatomy of American Popular Culture*.

48. On Howells's critical theory, see *Criticism and Fiction* (1891; rpt., New York: Hill & Wang, 1967). This volume also includes the text of Frank Norris's *The Responsibilities of the Novelist* (1903). Terms such as "idealism" and "realism" are more commonly used in literary studies than intellectual history, but they can be helpful to historians of culture to connote general orientations of values and perceptions. For detailed descriptions of the literary transformation, see Floyd Stovall, "The

Decline of Romantic Idealism, 1855–1870," and Robert P. Falk, "The Rise of Realism, 1871–1891," in Harry Hayden Clark, ed., *Transitions in American Literary History* (Durham, N.C.: Duke University Press, 1954), 317–78, 381–442. Leonard Lutwack reminds scholars that Howells's literary realism remained a contested position in American aesthetics until at least the 1890s, in "William Dean Howells, and the 'Editor's Study,'" *American Literature* 24 (1952): 195–207. In other words, a genteel tradition, descended in part from antebellum idealism coexisted in tension with realism. For a historical account that explains the transition from romanticism to realism as a result of the Civil War, see my *Victorian America and the Civil War*, esp. chap. 6.

49. "My First Visit to New England," *Harper's New Monthly Magazine* 88 (1894): 822, 820. The article was published in four parts between May and August 1894. The first part appeared in *Harper's* volume 88 and the next three in volume 89. The circumstances surrounding the composition of the articles are explained in Lutwack, "Howells," 206–7. For an account of Howells's trip, see Lynn, *Howells*, chap. 5.

50. "First Visit," *Harper's* 89 (1894): 230.

51. Ibid., 444, 445.

52. Ibid., 445.

53. Ibid., 450.

54. Ibid., 449.

55. Ibid., 451.

56. Ibid., 442.

57. On Twain's trip, see Everett Emerson, *The Authentic Mark Twain: A Literary Biography of Samuel L. Clemens* (Philadelphia: University of Pennsylvania Press, 1984), 5–6. The text of "The Dandy Frightening the Squatter" and a representative letter of "Thomas Jefferson Snodgrass" are included in *Selected Shorter Writings of Mark Twain*, ed. Walter Blair (Boston: Houghton Mifflin, 1962), 1–2, 5–7.

58. Emerson, *Twain*, 6.

59. Ibid., 8.

60. Ibid., 20. On Twain's life in the West in the 1850s and 1860s, see Edgar Marquess Branch, *The Literary Apprenticeship of Mark Twain* (Urbana: University of Illinois Press, 1950), chaps. 3 and 4; *Clemens of the "Call": Mark Twain in San Francisco*, ed. Edgar M. Branch (Berkeley: University of California Press, 1969); and Franklin Walker, *San Francisco's Literary Frontier* (Seattle: University of Washington Press, 1939), 89–97.

61. Susan K. Harris reminds readers of Twain, however, that his philosophical skepticism stood in tension with a persistent longing for transcendence. See her provocative *Mark Twain's "Escape from Time": A Study of Patterns and Images* (Columbia: University of Missouri Press, 1982). In addition, it is important to keep in mind that although Twain based much of his fiction on the development of western themes, he chose to reside in the East, primarily in Hartford, Connecticut, and Elmira, New York, after he gained fame as a writer. There was significant ambivalence, in other words, in Twain's movement toward new intellectual solutions.

62. "Maya, the Princess," in *"How Celia Changed Her Mind" and Selected Stories*, ed. Elizabeth Ammons (New Brunswick, N.J.: Rutgers University Press, 1986), 1–13. For biographical information on Cooke, see Ammons's Introduction, ix–xxxv. For a good critical analysis of Cooke's writing, see Donovan, *New England Local Color Literature*, chap. 5.

63. "The Ring Fetter: A New England Tragedy," in *"How Celia Changed Her Mind,"* ed. Ammons, 32–58.

64. Cooke had also published several realistic stories, some about marriage, in *Putnam's Monthly* beginning in 1855, as Donovan notes in *New England Local Color Literature*, 70. Although romantic and realistic approaches were mixed in Cooke's early career, the direction of her writing was toward social themes presented in unadorned prose.

65. For an informative synthesis of the American intellectual experience in the years immediately before 1830, see Matthews, *Toward a New Society*.

66. The study that best underscores the importance of Christianity to Americans, as well as the varied interpretations of Christian doctrine, is Hatch, *Democratization of American Christianity*.

67. For an excellent discussion of this artistic transformation, see Bode, *Anatomy of American Popular Culture*.

68. For an explanation of the extent to which Americans came to terms with public identities that might not match a private sense of self, see Halttunen, *Confidence Men and Painted Women*, chap. 6.

69. George Forgie comments on the retrospective temper of the 1850s in *Patricide in the House Divided*, chap. 5.

Bibliographic Essay

The first modern scholars to study antebellum American culture focused on the period's literature and arts. F. O. Matthiessen made the democratic impulse behind the major writings of the American Renaissance his theme in *American Renaissance: Art and Expression in the Age of Emerson and Whitman* (1941; rpt., New York: Oxford University Press, 1972). Other early commentators were attracted to popular expression, including Constance Rourke, *American Humor: A Study in the National Character* (New York: Harcourt, Brace, 1931), and Fred Lewis Pattee, *The Feminine Fifties* (New York: D. Appleton-Century Co., 1940). The most informative survey of the popular arts, including theater, music, painting, architecture, and literature, remains Carl Bode, *The Anatomy of American Popular Culture, 1840–1861* (Berkeley: University of California Press, 1959). Perry Miller was one scholar who moved beyond an interest in the arts and planned a comprehensive analysis of early nineteenth-century modes of thought. He lived only long enough to produce essays on the religious, legal, and technological frames of mind, published as *The Life of the Mind in America: From the Revolution to the Civil War* (New York: Harcourt, Brace & World, 1965).

More recent works of a general nature include interpretive analyses, informative surveys, and accounts of long-term trends. Studies that attempt to synthesize and explain broad cultural patterns often center on the question of how a society initially open to many possibilities settled into definite patterns of thought and behavior. Among the most compelling interpretations are John Higham, *From Boundlessness to Consolidation: The Transformation of American Culture, 1848–1860* (Ann Arbor, Mich.: William L. Clements Library, 1969); Robert H. Wiebe, *The Opening of American Society: From the Adoption of the Constitution to the Eve of Disunion* (New York: Knopf, 1984); Nathan O. Hatch,

The Democratization of American Christianity (New Haven: Yale University Press, 1989); and Lewis Perry, *Boats against the Current: American Culture between Revolution and Modernity, 1820–1860* (New York: Oxford University Press, 1993). I attempt to amend these views by arguing that a mood of questioning and experimentation persisted through the Civil War era in *Victorian America and the Civil War* (Cambridge: Cambridge University Press, 1992). With less concern for advancing a thesis, David Brion Davis provides the best overview of antebellum culture seen through the lens of primary documents in *Antebellum American Culture: An Interpretive Anthology* (Lexington, Mass.: D. C. Heath, 1979). Lewis O. Saum offers readers a capable survey in *The Popular Mood of Pre–Civil War America* (Westport, Conn.: Greenwood Press, 1980). Three highly original studies that place antebellum intellectual developments in a broad historical perspective are Daniel Calhoun, *The Intelligence of a People* (Princeton: Princeton University Press, 1973); Bruce Kuklick, *Churchmen and Philosophers: From Jonathan Edwards to John Dewey* (New Haven: Yale University Press, 1985); and James Hoopes, *Consciousness in New England: From Puritanism and Ideas to Psychoanalysis and Semiotic* (Baltimore: Johns Hopkins University Press, 1989).

The role of intellectuals in society changed dramatically during the antebellum period. Thinkers became more self-conscious of themselves as people who worked with ideas for a living and who expressed their views most often in writing. The development of a marketplace for publications was a critical part for this transformation. The rise of professionalism in literature has been studied by William Charvat, *The Profession of Authorship in America, 1800–1870: The Papers of William Charvat*, ed. Matthew J. Broccoli (Columbus: Ohio State University Press, 1968); Michael T. Gilmore, *American Romanticism and the Marketplace* (Chicago: University of Chicago Press, 1985); and, with special attention to women, Mary Kelley, *Private Woman, Public Stage: Literary Domesticity in Nineteenth-Century America* (New York: Oxford University Press, 1984). The definitive study of the social role of artists is Neil Harris, *The Artist in American Society: The Formative Years, 1790–1860* (New York: Simon & Schuster, 1966). Southern intellectuals faced unusual moral and social difficulties because of their participation in a slave society. Excellent discussions of writers in the South include Drew Gilpin Faust, *A Sacred Circle: The Dilemma of the Intellectual in the Old South, 1840–1860* (Baltimore: Johns Hopkins University Press, 1977), and Michael O'Brien, *Rethinking the South: Essays in Intellectual History* (Baltimore: Johns Hopkins University Press, 1988). In the North, some intellectuals became social critics and experimented with an activist role for thinkers. That pattern of choices for intellectuals is the theme of my *Transcendentalism as a Social Movement, 1830–1850* (New Haven: Yale University Press, 1981).

The religious history of the antebellum decades includes a wide variety of beliefs and movements. The best general discussion consists of chapters on the period in Sydney E. Ahlstrom, *A Religious History of the American People* (New

Haven: Yale University Press, 1972). Edwin S. Gaustad has compiled an anthology that emphasizes the diversity of religious perspectives, *A Documentary History of Religion in America to the Civil War* (Grand Rapids, Mich.: William B. Eerdmans, 1982). Sydney E. Ahlstrom included selections from leading theologians in *Theology in America: The Major Protestant Voices from Puritanism to Neo-Orthodoxy* (Indianapolis: Bobbs-Merrill Co., 1967). The most revealing studies of antebellum Catholicism are Jay P. Dolan, *The American Catholic Experience: A History from Colonial Times to the Present* (Garden City, N.Y.: Doubleday, 1985); Ann Taves, *The Household of Faith: Roman Catholic Devotions in Mid-Nineteenth-Century America* (Notre Dame, Ind.: University of Notre Dame Press, 1986); and Randall M. Miller and Jon L. Wakelyn, eds., *Catholics in the Old South* (Macon, Ga.: Mercer University Press, 1983). The indispensable introduction to antebellum Judaism are the encyclopedic volumes by Jacob Rader Marcus, *United States Jewry, 1776–1985*, vols. 1–3 (Detroit: Wayne State University Press, 1989–93).

Broad interpretations of American spiritual development that, in effect, debate the much-disputed issue of secularization provide essential background for studying antebellum religion. Among the most sophisticated of these analyses are Jon Butler, *Awash in a Sea of Faith: Christianizing the American People* (Cambridge, Mass.: Harvard University Press, 1990); Richard Rabinowitz, *The Spiritual Self in Everyday Life: The Transformation of Personal Religious Experience in Nineteenth-Century New England* (Boston: Northeastern University Press, 1989); and James Turner, *Without God, without Creed: The Origins of Unbelief in America* (Baltimore: Johns Hopkins University Press, 1985).

Studies of revivalism and reform have long anchored scholarly work on antebellum religion. Among the most provocative analyses of revivals are Timothy L. Smith, *Revivalism and Social Reform: American Protestantism on the Eve of the Civil War* (New York: Harcourt, Brace & World, 1965); Paul E. Johnson, *A Shopkeeper's Millennium: Society and Revivals in Rochester, New York, 1815–1837* (New York: Hill & Wang, 1978); and Jay P. Dolan, *Catholic Revivalism: The American Experience, 1830–1900* (Notre Dame, Ind.: University of Notre Dame Press, 1978). Benevolent activites of women that grew out of revivalism have been the subject of excellent studies by Carroll Smith–Rosenberg, *Religion and the Rise of the American City: The New York City Mission Movement, 1812–1870* (Ithaca: Cornell University Press, 1971), and Lori D. Ginzberg, *Women and the Work of Benevolence: Morality, Politics, and Class in the Nineteenth-Century United States* (New Haven: Yale University Press, 1990). Ronald G. Walters offers a general account of reform movements in *American Reformers, 1815–1860* (New York: Hill & Wang, 1978). How much the emerging middle class aimed to control the behavior of working people through moral reform is a question that has shaped scholarly debate on benevolence. Lawrence Frederick Kohl examines the issue in "The Concept of Social Control and the History of Jacksonian America," *Journal of the Early*

Republic 5 (1985): 21–34. In recent years there has been rising interest in the transformation of revivalism, and the voluntary associations the revivals inspired, into Victorian religious institutions. Stimulating interpretations include Anne M. Boylan, *Sunday School: The Formation of an American Institution, 1790–1880* (New Haven: Yale University Press, 1986); Donald M. Scott, *From Office to Profession: The New England Ministry, 1750–1850* (Philadelphia: University of Pennsylvania Press, 1978); Colleen McDannell, *The Christian Home in Victorian America, 1840–1900* (Bloomington: Indiana University Press, 1986); and Kathryn Kish Sklar, *Catharine Beecher: A Study in American Domesticity* (New Haven: Yale University Press, 1972).

Radical religious movements that restated commonplace beliefs in ways that challenged conventional morals or institutions continue to fascinate scholars and readers. The history of Mormonism has occasioned many fine interpretations, including Jan Shipps, *Mormonism: The Story of a New Religious Tradition* (Urbana: University of Illinois Press, 1985), and Kenneth H. Winn, *Exiles in a Land of Liberty: Mormons in America, 1830–1846* (Chapel Hill: University of North Carolina Press, 1989). The millennial expectations stirred by William Miller have been ably studied by Ruth Alden Doan, *The Miller Heresy, Millennialism, and American Culture* (Philadelphia: Temple University Press, 1987). Fourierism, a reform often driven by a Christian vision though not a religious theory in itself, was the dominant expression of communitarianism during the antebellum period. Carl J. Guarneri offers a masterful analysis in *The Utopian Alternative: Fourierism in Nineteenth-Century America* (Ithaca: Cornell University Press, 1991). Shakerism originated in the early republic but continued to flourish in the pre–Civil War era, as Stephen J. Stein demonstrates in his fascinating book, *The Shaker Experience in America: A History of the United Society of Believers* (New Haven: Yale University Press, 1992). The religious debates initiated by transcendentalism may be understood through the primary documents collected by Perry Miller in *The Transcendentalists: An Anthology* (Cambridge, Mass.: Harvard University Press, 1950).

Abolitionism is the best-known radical reform movement with roots in antebellum revivalism. Works that lucidly introduce the religious and reform issues include Lawrence J. Friedman, *Gregarious Saints: Self and Community in American Abolitionism, 1830–1870* (Cambridge: Cambridge University Press, 1982), and James Brewer Stewart, *William Lloyd Garrison and the Challenge of Emancipation* (Arlington Heights, Ill.: Harlan Davidson, 1992). The scholarship of David Brion Davis is indispensable to an understanding of antislavery. Among Davis's key studies of antebellum antislavery reform are "The Emergence of Immediatism in British and American Antislavery Thought," in his *From Homicide to Slavery: Studies in American Culture* (New York: Oxford University Press, 1986), 238–57, and *Slavery and Human Progress* (New York: Oxford University Press, 1984). Lewis Perry traces the transformation of abolitionist ideas into a religiously inspired form of anarchism in *Radical Abolitionism: Anarchy and the Government of God in Antislavery Thought* (Ithaca:

Cornell University Press, 1973). C. C. Goen documents a less extreme but far more widespread expression of religious antislavery in his thought-provoking book on controversies in Protestant churches over slavery, *Broken Churches, Broken Nation: Denominational Schisms and the Coming of the American Civil War* (Macon, Ga.: Mercer University Press, 1985). There is a growing literature, too, on black abolitionists, including David E. Swift, *Black Prophets of Justice: Activist Clergy before the Civil War* (Baton Rouge: Louisiana State University Press, 1989), and Peter C. Ripley, ed., *The Black Abolitonist Papers*, vols. 3–5 (Chapel Hill: University of North Carolina Press, 1991–92).

African American religion has been the subject of several path-breaking studies. These works have often developed creative approaches in order to recover reliable information from scarce or questionable sources. Albert J. Raboteau combines the techniques of anthropology and more conventional text-based religious history in *Slave Religion: The "Invisible Institution" in the Antebellum South* (Oxford: Oxford University Press, 1978). Eugene D. Genovese argues that black and white religions in the slaveholding South were intimately interconnected and must be interpreted together, in *Roll, Jordan, Roll: The World the Slaves Made* (New York: Vintage, 1974). Donald Mathews pursues that strategy in *Religion in the Old South* (Chicago: University of Chicago Press, 1977). An excellent biography that makes the crucial point that not all black American Christians were born in slavery or were evangelicals is Wilson Jeremiah Moses, *Alexander Crummell: A Study of Civilization and Discontent* (New York: Oxford University Press, 1989).

Topics in antebellum American religion that have received less attention from historians include conservative movements, religious prejudice, and the challenge of science. On Catholic movements among Protestants, see Robert Bruce Mullin, *Episcopal Vision/American Reality: High Church Theology and Social Thought in Evangelical America* (New Haven: Yale University Press, 1986), as well as published primary sources written by transcendentalists who converted to Roman Catholicism, including Joseph Gower and Richard Leliaert, eds., *The Brownson-Hecker Correspondence* (Notre Dame, Ind.: University of Notre Dame Press, 1979), and Isaac T. Hecker, *The Diary: Romantic Religion in Ante-Bellum America*, ed. John Farina (New York: Paulist Press, 1988). A different kind of conservatism that foreshadowed Protestant fundamentalism also emerged during this period. Ernest Sandeen documents the appearance of commitments to biblical literalism and premillennialism in *The Roots of Fundamentalism: British and American Millenarianism, 1800–1930* (Chicago: University of Chicago Press, 1970). Religious bias and conflict accompanied diversity in the antebellum decades. The seminal explanation of intolerance is David Brion Davis, "Some Themes of Counter-Subversion: An Analysis of Anti-Masonic, Anti-Catholic, and Anti-Mormon Literature," in his *From Homicide to Slavery*, 137–54. The changing relationship between Christianity and science has been discussed by Theodore Dwight Bozeman, *Protestants in an Age of Science: The Baconian Ideal and Antebellum Religous Thought* (Chapel

Hill: University of North Carolina Press, 1977), and Bruce Kuklick, *The Rise of American Philosophy: Cambridge, Massachusetts, 1860–1930* (New Haven: Yale University Press, 1977). Essential studies of the rise of a quantitative and scientific outlook include Patricia Cline Cohen, *A Calculating People: The Spread of Numeracy in Early America* (Chicago: University of Chicago Press, 1982), and Robert V. Bruce, *The Launching of Modern American Science, 1846–1876* (Ithaca: Cornell University Press, 1987).

The study of political culture involves attention to the attitudes and ceremonies that shape civic commitments. To cast light on the most general level of political loyalty, historians have analyzed the influence of collective memory and mythmaking on national development. Excellent works include Fred Somkin, *Unquiet Eagle: Memory and Desire in the Idea of American Freedom, 1815–1860* (Ithaca: Cornell University Press, 1967); George B. Forgie, *Patricide in the House Divided: A Psychological Interpretation of Lincoln and His Age* (New York: Norton, 1979); and Michael Kammen, *The Mystic Chords of Memory: The Transformation of Tradition in American Culture* (New York: Knopf, 1991). More specifically, scholars have probed the intellectual commitments associated with partisan politics. Compelling interpretations of party ideologies have been offered by Jean H. Baker, *Affairs of Party: The Political Culture of Northern Democrats in the Mid-Nineteenth-Century* (Ithaca: Cornell University Press, 1983); Daniel Walker Howe, *The Political Culture of the American Whigs* (Chicago: University of Chicago Press, 1979); and Eric Foner, *Free Soil, Free Labor, Free Men: The Ideology of the Republican Party before the Civil War* (London: Oxford University Press, 1970). It is also essential to ask about the assumptions that led Americans to embrace party politics during the Jacksonian era. Among many works that propose answers are Richard Hofstadter, *The Idea of a Party System: The Rise of Legitimate Opposition in the United States, 1780–1840* (Berkeley: University of California Press, 1969); Johanna Nicol Shields, *The Line of Duty: Maverick Congressmen and the Development of American Political Culture, 1836–1860* (Westport, Conn.: Greenwood Press, 1985); and Richard L. McCormick, *The Party Period and Public Policy: American Politics from the Age of Jackson to the Progressive Era* (New York: Oxford University Press, 1986). In an able assessment of minority values, Kenneth S. Greenberg writes about the distinctive political customs of the slaveholding South in *Masters and Statesmen: The Political Culture of American Slavery* (Baltimore: Johns Hopkins University Press, 1985).

This was an era of great statesmen, and historians have produced numerous biographies of public figures that give readers a personal view of politicians and a sense of what their constituents expected. Among the best biographies of political leaders are John William Ward, *Andrew Jackson: Symbol for an Age* (New York: Oxford University Press, 1962); Irving H. Bartlett, *Daniel Webster* (New York: Norton, 1978); Robert W. Johannsen, *Stephen A. Douglas* (New York: Oxford University Press, 1973); and Robert V. Remini, *Henry Clay* (New York: Norton, 1991). The many interpretations of the life of

Abraham Lincoln may be approached through the readable volume by Oscar and Lilian Handlin, *Abraham Lincoln and the Union* (Boston: Little, Brown, 1980). Jean H. Baker presents a different and valuable perspective on the nation's leaders in her study *Mary Todd Lincoln: A Biography* (New York: Norton, 1987).

The transformation of a republican concept of government, with an emphasis on personal responsibility and community consensus, into a liberal or democratic system, based on individual aspiration and competition, has been much discussed by historians. Most agree that the process of change was well advanced by 1830, but opinions differ on how to assess the relative importance of traditional and progressive elements in political culture. In a challenging interpretation, Lawrence Frederick Kohl proposes that Jacksonian Democrats, far from being the champions of egalitarianism of legend, stood for traditional communal values, in *The Politics of Individualism: Parties and the American Character in the Jacksonian Era* (New York: Oxford University Press, 1989). On the other side, James Oakes has underscored the liberalism of the age by insisting on its dominance in the most unlikely part of the nation, the slaveholding South, in *The Ruling Race: A History of American Slaveholders* (New York: Vintage, 1982) and *Slavery and Freedom: An Interpretation of the Old South* (New York: Knopf, 1990). Summaries of the debate on republicanism and liberalism may be found in Daniel T. Rodgers, "Republicanism: The Career of a Concept," *Journal of American History* 79 (1992): 11–38, and Joyce Appleby, ed., "Republicanism in the History and Historiography of the United States," *American Quarterly* (special issue) 37 (1985).

Despite recent interest in partisan culture and ideological transformation, the central issue in studies of antebellum politics remains the reasons for the sectional crisis. Cultural historians contribute to analyses of the coming of the Civil War by identifying the influence of perceptions and values. Ambitious books that trace long-term changes in the concepts of nationalism and constitutional compromise are Paul C. Nagel, *One Nation Indivisible: The Union in American Thought, 1776–1861* (New York: Oxford University Press, 1964), and Peter B. Knupfer, *The Union as It Is: Constitutional Unionism and Sectional Compromise, 1787–1861* (Chapel Hill: University of North Carolina Press, 1991). David Brion Davis points out the divisive effects of conspiracy theories in *The Slave Power Conspiracy and the Paranoid Style* (Baton Rouge: Louisiana State University Press, 1969). A recurring question is whether sectional cultures were so different that conflict was inevitable. The strongest case for the distinctiveness of the South has been made by Bertram Wyatt-Brown, *Southern Honor: Ethics and Behavior in the Old South* (New York: Oxford University Press, 1982). Whatever the depth of sectional differences, northerners and southerners believed that they were unlike one another, as William R. Taylor has shown in *Cavalier and Yankee: The Old South and American National Character* (New York: Harper & Row, 1961). To defend slavery, proslavery advocates transformed the distinguishing characteristics of southern society into a coherent and aggressive ideology. Drew Gilpin Faust has issued an excellent collection of primary documents, *The Ideology of Slavery: Proslavery Thought in the Antebellum South, 1830–1860* (Baton Rouge: Louisiana State University Press, 1981). In a provocative argument once again opening the issue of the relationship of nationalism and sectionalism in the mounting crisis, Larry E. Tise writes that proslavery thought was part of a nationwide conservative ideology, in *Proslavery: A History of the Defense of Slavery in America, 1701–1840* (Athens: University of Georgia Press, 1987).

The cultural effects of market expansion is a challenging subject because it serves to remind historians that sectional divisions were not the only sources of tension in pre–Civil War America. Studies of capitalism emphasize differences between rural and urban life and between the working and middle classes. Analyses of changing mores in the countryside chronicle the advent of self-interested behavior that contested an older ethic of mutual helpfulness. Exemplary interpetations are Steven Hahn, *The Roots of Southern Populism: Yeoman Farmers and the Transformation of the Georgia Upcountry, 1850–1890* (New York: Oxford University Press, 1983); John Mack Faragher, *Sugar Creek: Life on the Illinois Prairie* (New Haven: Yale University Press, 1986); and Christopher Clark, *The Roots of Rural Capitalism: Western Massachusetts, 1780–1860* (Ithaca: Cornell University Press, 1990). The history of the frontier, countryside of a special kind, has been revitalized as a scholarly field by bold new interpretations such as Patricia Nelson Limerick, *The Legacy of Conquest: The Unbroken Past of the American West* (New York: Norton, 1987). Among many works on the culture of cities are William H. Pease and Jane H. Pease, *The Web of Progress: Private Values and Public Style in Boston and Charleston, 1828–1843* (New York: Oxford University Press, 1985), and Thomas Bender, *New York Intellect: A History of Intellectual Life in New York City from 1750 to the Beginnings of Our Own Time* (New York: Knopf, 1987). No primary source provides a better day-to-day view of urban attitudes and customs than *The Diary of George Templeton Strong*, ed. Allan Nevins and Milton Halsey Thomas, 4 vols. (New York: Macmillan, 1952).

Commentaries on urban culture have tended in recent years to focus on class formation. The best books on the lives and values of urban workers are Sean Wilentz, *Chants Democratic: New York City and the Rise of the American Working Class, 1788–1850* (New York: Oxford University Press, 1984), and Christine Stansell, *City of Women: Sex and Class in New York, 1789–1860* (New York: Knopf, 1986). Historians have written extensively on the middle class. A comprehensive introduction is Stuart M. Blumin, *The Emergence of the Middle Class: Social Experience in the American City, 1760–1900* (Cambridge: Cambridge University Press, 1989). Studies that look at key institutions created by the middle class, including voluntary associations and a kind of home intended to assist upward mobility, are John S. Gilkeson, Jr., *Middle-Class Providence, 1840–1940* (Princeton: Princeton University Press, 1986), and Mary P. Ryan, *Cradle of the Middle Class: The Family in Oneida County, New York, 1790–1865*

(Cambridge: Cambridge University Press, 1981). Karen Halttunen interprets changing middle-class ideas of self and society in an original and compelling reading of advice literature, *Confidence Men and Painted Women: A Study of Middle-Class Culture in America, 1830–1870* (New Haven: Yale University Press, 1982). The career goals and concepts of labor of the middle class have been discussed, respectively, by Burton J. Bledstein, *The Culture of Professionalism: The Middle Class and the Development of Higher Education in America* (New York: Norton, 1976), and Jonathan A. Glickstein, *Concepts of Free Labor in Antebellum America* (New Haven: Yale University Press, 1991). The middle class also defined itself by codes of manners. One important set of customs regulated romantic love, as Karen Lystra explains in *Searching the Heart: Women, Men, and Romantic Love in Nineteenth-Century America* (New York: Oxford University Press, 1989).

The development of the antebellum marketplace also facilitated the transmission of ideas and supported the dramatic expansion of literary and artistic expression. In addition to informative older works on the circulation of printed material, such as James D. Hart, *The Popular Book: A History of America's Literary Taste* (New York: Oxford University Press, 1950), and Frank Luther Mott, *A History of American Magazines*, vols. 1–2 (Cambridge, Mass.: Harvard University Press, 1930–38), there are excellent new analyses of the communication and reception of ideas. Books that trace networks of information are Richard D. Brown, *Knowledge Is Power: The Diffusion of Information in Early America, 1700–1865* (New York: Oxford University Press, 1989), and William J. Gilmore, *Reading Becomes a Necessity of Life: Material and Cultural Life in Rural New England, 1780–1835* (Knoxville: University of Tennessee Press, 1989). Nina Baym highlights the importance of reading as part of literary culture in her study of the influence of reviewers on audiences, *Novels, Readers, and Reviewers: Responses to Fiction in Antebellum America* (Ithaca: Cornell University Press, 1984). The existence of a growing reading public depended, in turn, on the availability of education and the spread of literacy, subjects treated by Carl F. Kaestle, *Pillars of the Republic: Common Schools and American Society, 1789–1860* (New York: Hill & Wang, 1983), and David D. Hall, "Introduction: The Uses of Literacy in New England, 1600–1850," in William L. Joyce et al., eds., *Printing and Society in Early America* (Worcester, Mass.: American Antiquarian Society, 1985), 1–47. Donald M. Scott points out that reading was not the only source of knowledge in his excellent article on lyceums, "The Popular Lecture and the Creation of a Public in Mid-Nineteenth-Century America," *Journal of American History* 66 (1980): 791–809.

Literary critics have produced numerous commentaries on the prose and poetry of the American Renaissance, but some studies are more useful to cultural historians than others. Scholars who investigate connections between popular and highbrow expression are able to ground literature in society in ways that are especially helpful. Lawrence Buell offers a brilliant analysis of the role of imaginative literature in the formation of regional identity in *New*

England Literary Culture: From Revolution through Renaissance (Cambridge: Cambridge University Press, 1986). David S. Reynolds places the major texts of the American Renaissance against the hitherto unexplored background of sensational literature in his revealing book, *Beneath the American Renaissance: The Subversive Imagination in the Age of Emerson and Melville* (New York: Knopf, 1988). Sacvan Bercovitch and Myra Jehlen have edited a collection of essays that insist on acknowledging the limiting interests both of historical figures and modern critics, *Ideology and Classic American Literature* (Cambridge: Cambridge University Press, 1986). Efforts to broaden the canon of works considered worthy of study open questions about how to judge intellectual and aesthetic value. This is a central issue of Jane Tompkins, *Sensational Designs: The Cultural Work of American Fiction, 1790–1860* (New York: Oxford University Press, 1985). The significance of fiction by women has been especially disputed. Ann Douglas casts women's literature in a negative light in her influential *The Feminization of American Culture* (New York: Knopf, 1977). Susan K. Harris, on the other hand, presents women's fiction as important instruments of cultural change in *19th-Century American Women's Novels: Interpretive Strategies* (Cambridge: Cambridge University Press, 1990).

Specific intellectual movements and writers have also occasioned essential works of criticism. On the writings of the transcendentalists, the best study is Lawrence Buell, *Literary Transcendentalism: Style and Vision in the American Renaissance* (Ithaca: Cornell University Press, 1973). Excellent biographies of transcendentalists include Mary Kupiec Cayton, *Emerson's Emergence: Self and Society in the Transformation of New England, 1800–1845* (Chapel Hill: University of North Carolina Press, 1989), and Charles Capper, *Margaret Fuller: An American Romantic Life*, vol. 1, *The Private Years* (Oxford: Oxford University Press, 1992). Michael J. Colacurcio offers a compelling view of Hawthorne's appreciation of history in *The Province of Piety: Moral History in Hawthorne's Early Tales* (Cambridge, Mass.: Harvard University Press, 1984). The classic study of literary pastoralism is Leo Marx, *The Machine in the Garden: Technology and the Pastoral Ideal in America* (London: Oxford University Press, 1964).

The cultures of ethnic and racial minorities are the subject of much productive recent scholarship. Even so, special obstacles, including scarce primary sources and scholarly traditions long informed by prejudice, continue to make it difficult to achieve satisfying interpretations in these fields. In addition to the comprehensive works on American Judaism by Jacob Rader Marcus, a sense of Jewish culture may be gained through his anthology, *The American Jewish Woman: A Documentary History* (New York: Ktav Publishing House, 1981). An excellent biography of a leading Jewish American is Eli N. Evans, *Judah P. Benjamin: The Jewish Confederate* (New York: Free Press, 1988). Popular Catholic devotional literature has been ably explained by Ann Taves and Colleen McDannell (cited earlier), but antebellum Catholic philosophy and imaginative literature have been studied less thoroughly. A good introduction to the thought of Anglo-Saxon converts is Margaret Mary Reher, *Catholic Intellectual life in America: A Historical Study of Persons and Movements* (New York: Macmillan, 1989). The best source of information on Irish-American intellectual activity is Mary Stephana Cavanaugh, "Catholic Book Publishing in the United States, 1784–1850," M.A. thesis, University of Illinois, 1937.

An informative introduction to African-American literature is Blyden Jackson, *A History of Afro-American Literature: The Long Beginning, 1746–1895* (Baton Rouge: Louisiana State University Press, 1989). Much critical commentary of antebellum black writing has focused on the narratives of fugitive slaves. One scholarly collection that includes varying opinions on how to evaluate the narratives is Charles T. Davis and Henry Louis Gates, Jr., eds., *The Slave's Narrative* (Oxford: Oxford University Press, 1985). There are a number of anthologies of the slave narratives themselves, such as Arna Bontempts, ed., *Great Slave Narratives* (Boston: Beacon Press, 1969). Basic as slave narratives were to African-American writing, it is important to look more broadly at other forms of black prose. Essential volumes of primary documents include William L. Andrews, ed., *Three Classic African-American Novels* (New York: Mentor, 1990), and Alexander Crummell, *Destiny and Race: Selected Writings, 1840–1898*, ed. Wilson Jeremiah Moses (Amherst: University of Massachusetts Press, 1992). Henry Louis Gates, Jr., offers a theoretical framework for understanding African-American literature in *Figures in Black: Words, Signs, and the "Racial" Self* (New York: Oxford University Press, 1987). William S. McFeely provides an incisive view of the life of a leading black intellectual in *Frederick Douglass* (New York: Norton, 1991).

Microfilm editions are the best source for unabridged texts of antebellum Native-Americans works. Despite the difficulty of acquiring primary sources, however, theoretical discussions of Indian writings are available. The best introduction is Andrew Wiget, *Native American Literature* (Boston: Twayne Publishers, 1985). Other helpful studies are Andrew Wiget, ed., *Critical Essays in Native American Literature* (Boston: G. K. Hall, 1985); David Murray, *Forked Tongues: Speech, Writing, and Representation in North American Indian Texts* (Bloomington: Indiana University Press, 1991), and, focusing on ideas about Indians articulated by whites, Lucy Maddox, *Removals: Nineteenth-Century American Literature and the Politics of Indian Affairs* (New York: Oxford University Press, 1991).

Studies that underscore the atmosphere of racial prejudice in which minority intellectuals worked are Fredrickson, *The Black Image in the White Mind*, and Alexander Saxton, *The Rise and Fall of the White Republic: Class Politics and Mass Culture in Nineteenth-Century America* (London: Verso, 1990).

The antebellum decades were the first era in American history when large numbers of people had contact with the visual and plastic arts. Oliver W. Larkin provides an overview of American artistic development in *Art and Life in America*, rev. ed. (New York: Holt, Rinehart & Winston, 1960). An excellent collection of primary writings by artists is John W. McCoubrey, ed., *American Art, 1700–1960: Sources and Documents* (Englewood Cliffs, N.J.: Prentice-Hall, 1965). Studies of key genres of antebellum painting include Barbara Novak, *Nature and Culture: American Landscape and Painting, 1825–1875* (New York: Oxford University Press, 1980), and Elizabeth Johns, *American Genre Painting: The Politics of Everyday Life* (New Haven: Yale University Press, 1991). Intriguing studies that interpret texts and images in relation to one another are Bryan Jay Wolf, *Romantic Re-Vision: Culture and Consciousness in Nineteenth-Century American Painting and Literature* (Chicago: University of Chicago Press, 1982), and Jean Fagan Yellin, *Women and Sisters: The Antislavery Feminists in American Culture* (New Haven: Yale University Press, 1989). Daguerreotypes and photographs provided Americans with a democratic art form in the sense that these processes allowed affordable, personalized images to be displayed in individual homes. Harold Francis Pfister explains the history of daguerreotypes in *Facing the Light: Historic American Portrait Daguerreotypes* (Washington, D.C.: National Portrait Gallery, Smithsonian Institution, 1978). Alan Trachtenberg has compiled a useful collection of primary sources on photography in *Classic Essays in Photography* (New Haven: Leete's Island Books, 1980). He provides an important analysis of photography as part of American culture in *Reading American Photographs: Images as History, Mathew Brady to Walker Evans* (New York: Hill & Wang, 1989).

Index

Page numbers in italics refer to illustrations.

Abolitionist movement, 1; free
  blacks and former slaves in, 15,
  147; morality of, xvi, 17; and
  religious radicalism, 11, 15–19,
  21, 47; role of clergy in,
  xviii–xix; split in, 21; and
  women's rights, 18–19. *See also*
  Slavery
Adams, Henry, 102
Adventism, 1, 13, 28
African Americans: autobiographies
  by, 132–33, 136–37; literature of,
  146–53; role in United States,
  165–66
African Free School (New York
  City), 146
Agassiz, Louis, 103
Age of Reason, The (Paine), 8
Ahlstrom, Sydney, 84
Albany Regency, xx
Alcott, Bronson, 81–82, 94, 103, 104
Alcott, Louisa May, 103
Alexander's Weekly Magazine, 109
Allston, Washington, 92, 100
American and Foreign Anti-Slavery
  Society, 18
American Anti-Slavery Society, 11,
  15, 17, 18

American Board of Commissioners
  of Foreign Missions (ABCFM),
  154
American Female Guardian Society,
  6
American Humor (Rourke), 97
American Indians. *See* Native
  Americans
American Jewish Publication
  Society, 139
American Monthly Magazine, 87, 93
American (Know-Nothing) party, 38
American Renaissance, xv, xvii, 91,
  164, 177, 184
American Renaissance (Matthiessen),
  119, 215n101
American Revolution: anniversary
  of, 32–33; ideology of, 41
American Society to Promote the
  Principles of the Protestant
  Reformation, 9
American Victorian culture: emer-
  gence of, 7; and politics, 40–41;
  and religion, 22
Anarchism, 18, 41, 46–47, 48, 49, 51
Anglican church. *See* Episcopal
  (Anglican) church
Anti-Catholicism, 9–10, 23–24, 161

Anti-Semitism, 161
Antislavery movement, 55–56, 147, 194n38. *See also* Abolitionist movement
Apes, William, 155
Apologia Pro Vita Sua (Newman), 24
Appleton, Nathan, 76
Architecture: "cottage" style of, 67; domestic, 78; and national culture, 93; neoclassical, 32
Art, promotion of, 93–94
"Artemus Ward" (pseud.), 178
Arthur, T. S., 71, 73
Artistic freedom, 94
Atheism, 1
Atlantic Monthly, 109, 178, 179–80
Authors of the United States (engraving), *121*
Autobiographies, by minorities, 132–33, 154–55
Autocrat of the Breakfast Table, The (Holmes), 170
Awful Disclosures of the Hotel Dieu Nunnery of Montreal (Monk), 9

Baldwin, Joseph Glover, 223n29
Ballou, Adin, 18
Baltimore *Daily Exchange*, 176
Bancroft, George, 114
Baptist church, xix, 1, 17
Barnum, P. T., xxii, 14
"Bartleby the Scrivener" (Melville), 64, 69, 70, 71
Beecher, Catharine, xix, 6, 76, 179
Beecher, Henry Ward, 168–69
Beecher, Lyman, 5, 8, 40, 168
Behemoth: A Legend of the Moundbuilders (Mathews), 70
Benevolent associations. *See* Social reform
Bennett, James Gordon, 99
Beulah (Evans), 176
Biblical literalism, 13
Birney, James G., 15, 55
Blacks. *See* African Americans
Blakes and Flanagans: A Tale Illustrative of Irish Life in the United States, The (M. Sadlier), 143

Blumin, Stuart, 79
Bonner, Robert, xxii
Book of Mormon, The, 11, 12
Boston, intellectual culture of, 97–98
Boston *Christian Examiner*, 137
Boston *Investigator*, 8
Boston Pilot (journal), 141
Boudinot, Elias, 154
Bowen, Francis, 85–86
Brady, Mathew, 111
Broadway Journal, 101
Brontë, Charlotte, 176
Brook Farm community, 20–21
Brotherhood of the Union, 160
Brown, John, 50, 164
Brown, William Wells, 130, 146–53, 158
Browne, William R., 34
Browning, Elizabeth Barrett, 104
Browning, Robert, 104
Brownson, Orestes, 8, 25, 140
Brownson's Quarterly Review, 140
Bruce, Robert, 85
Buell, Lawrence, 98
Buntline, Ned, 160
"Burned-over district" (New York), 12, 21
Burns, Anthony, 202n66
Burton's Gentleman's Magazine, 101
Bushnell, Horace, 5, 6, 7, 98, 169
Butler, William Allen, 171–74, *172, 173*

Cable, George Washington, 175
Calhoun, Daniel, 83, 87
Calhoun, John C., 42–44, 46, 51, 57, 100
Calvin, John, 23
Cane Ridge, Kentucky, revival meeting (1801), 2
Cannibals All! (Fitzhugh), 80–81, 166–67
Capitalism: as a central concept, xv, xvi–xvii; development of, 60–62; and science, 86
Carey, Mathew, 140
Carpet-Bag, The (magazine), 179
Catholicism. *See* Roman Catholicism

Catholic Missions among the Indian Tribes of the United States (Shea), 141, 142
Catlin, George, 65, 66
Cemeteries, design of, 67
Central Park (New York City), 67
Channing, William Ellery, 7, 75–76
Charleston (South Carolina), intellectual culture of, 100
Cherokee (tribe), 154, 156
Cherokee Phoenix, 154
Chesnut, Mary, xxi–xxii
Christian humanism, 28–29
Christianity: as a central concept, xv–xvi; conservatism in, 22–28; radicalism in, 10–22, 28; revivalism in, 1, 2–5, 7, 8, 12, 21, 22, 162, 168–69; and slavery, xvi; and social reforms, 2–3, 5; women's role in, xix, 6
Christian Nurture (Bushnell), 5
Church and state, separation of, xix
Circuses, xxii
Civic virtue, 31, 32, 36, 41
"Civil Disobedience" (Thoreau), 45
Civil rights movement, 45
Clarke, Lewis, 149
Clarkson, Thomas, 118
Class, social. *See* Class conflict; Class consciousness; Gentry; Middle class; Working-class values
Class conflict, 164, 169–74
Class consciousness: and capitalism, 76–83; and politics, 52–53; and religion, 7–8
Clergy: Catholic, 10; opposition to politics, 40; professionalization of, xviii
Clotel; or, The President's Daughter (Brown), 130, 149–52, 158
Cognition. *See* Knowledge
Colacurio, Michael, 114
Cole, Thomas, 65, 111
Colleges, intellectual communities at, 101–3
"Colloquoy of Monos and Una, The" (Poe), 112
Colonization, of blacks, 15

Commerford, John, 53
Common schools movement, 24, 84
Communitarianism, 1, 11, 19–21, 28, 81
Communities: decline of, 61; intellectual, 97–108
Complex marriage, 20
Compromise of 1850, 122, 164
Concord (Massachusetts): historical preservation of, 33; Howells in, 178; intellectual community in, 103–4, 116, 117
"Concord Hymn" (Emerson), 33
Confederate States of America, 50
Confidence Men and Painted Women (Halttunen), 63
Congregationalism, xviii, xix, 7, 8, 19, 98
Congregation B'nai Yeshurun (Cincinnati), 26, 139
Congregation Mikveh Israel (Philadelphia), 138, 139
Constitution, United States, xviii, 18, 31, 36, 47, 164–65
Consumerism, 80, 126
Conversation Club (Charleston, S.C.), 100
Conversion narratives, 155
Cooke, Rose Terry, 177, 179–80, 183
Cooper, James Fenimore, 86, 92
Copway, Elizabeth Howell, 154, 155
Copway, George (Kah-Ge-Ga-Gah-Bowh), 133, 153, 154–56, 158
Copyright laws, 93
Corinth *True Democrat*, 165
Cornish, Samuel, 15
Cortés, Hernando, 115
Cott, Nancy, 73
Cottage architecture, 67
Cotton, Rev. John, 123
Cotton, trade in, xxi
Cotton Kingdom, The (Olmsted), 85, 167
Country party, British, 41
"Courtship of Miles Standish, The" (Longfellow), 175, 176
Crane, Stephen, 174
Crummell, Alexander, 146, 147

Culture, definition of, 91
Cummins, Maria, 86
Currier, Nathaniel, 68, *68, 69*
Curtis, George William, 99, 170–71
Cushman, Charlotte, 104

Daguerre, Louis, 109
Daguerreotypes and photographs, 108, 109–11, 181
Dall, Caroline Wells Healey, 214n90
"Dandy Frightening the Squatter, The" (Twain), 178
Dante Alighieri, 102
Darwin, Charles, 85
Davis, David Brion, 10
Davis, Jefferson, 165
Deborah, Die (German-language newspaper), 134
De Bow's Review, 100
Declaration of Independence, 32
DeForest, John William, 98
Democracy: as a central concept, xv–xvi; definition of, 31; and national literature, 92–93; and party loyalty, xx; and political instability, 41–52; Tocqueville's view of, 30–31, 32, 40, 41, 42, 46
Democracy in America (Tocqueville), 30, 42
Democratic party, xx, 32, 33, 36, 37, 38, 56
Democratic-Republican party, 38
Democratic Review, 92–93
Dewey, John, 211n39
Dickens, Charles, 93
Dickinson, Emily, 9, 98
Disquisition on Government, A (Calhoun), 43
Dolan, Jay, 135
Domestic fiction, 121–22, 123, 127
Domesticity, cult of, xvii, 6, 73–74, 75–76, 79
Donahoe, Patrick, 140, 141
Dorsey, Anna, 141
Douglas, Stephen, 37, 39, 50, 164–66
Douglass, Frederick, *16*, 26, 120, 127–28, 147–53, *150*
Downing, Andrew Jackson, 67

Durand, Asher B., 65
Düsseldorf, intellectual community in, 104

Eclogues (Virgil), 67
Edwards, Jonathan, 5, 84
Elections, turnout for, xxi. *See also* Voting rights
Eliot, Charles William, 101–2
Emerson, Everett, 179
Emerson, Ralph Waldo: as an essayist, 116, 117–18; critical judgment of, 119; as friend of Margaret Fuller, 65, 82; Howells's visit to, 178; lectures by, xxii; as part of Concord intellectual community, 103, 104, 117; and self-reliance, 77; and state power, 45; and transcendentalism, 13, 14
English language, 132–37, 138, 153
Entertainment, popular, xxii–xxiii
Entire Devotion to God (Palmer), 4, 168
Episcopal (Anglican) church, 1, 8, 22, 23–24, 28
Erie Canal, 8, 12, 65
Essays, 108, 116–19, 126
Essays: First Series (Emerson), 117
Ethnic groups. *See* Minorities
Ethno-cultural and ethno-religious perspectives, 200n27
Etiquette: among strangers, 63; and middle-class propriety, 79
Eugenics, 20
Evangelicalism, xvi, 2–8, 21, 24, 54, 61
Evangeline (Longfellow), 102
Evans (Wilson), Augusta Jane, 176
Everett, Edward, 33
Exposition and Protest (Calhoun), 43

Faith and Its Effects (Palmer), 4
Family: and middle-class development, 77; as a religious institution, 6; and slavery as a familial institution, 23, 27
Fancy's Sketch Book (Moïse), 138

Faust, Drew, 100
Federalist Papers, The, 31, 116
Felton, Cornelius, 102
Fields, Annie, xxii
Fields, James T., xxii, 178
Fine arts, promotion of, 93–94
Finney, Charles Grandison, xviii, 4, 16
Finney, Lydia, xix
First International Exposition (New York), 162
First of the Maccabees, The (Wise), 140, 142
Fitzgerald, F. Scott, 205n16
Fitzhugh, George, 48, 80–81, 118, 166–67
Florence, intellectual community in, 103, 104
Foner, Eric, 58
Forgie, George, 32
Foster, Charlotte, 49
Foster, Stephen S., 18
Fourier, Charles, 21, 28
Fourth of July orations and celebrations, 32, 38, 181
Fox, Katherine, 14
Fox, Margaret, 14
Franklin, Benjamin, 74, 84, 99
Frederick Douglass' Paper, 148
Free blacks: in abolitionist movement, 15; voting rights of, xx
Freedom's Journal, 15, 146
Free labor ideology, 37, 48, 58, 85, 167
Freemasonry, 10
Free-Soil party, 44, 55
Free Will Baptist church, 8
Frémont, John C., 56
Fruitlands community, 81–82
Fugitive Blacksmith, The (Pennington), 149
Fuller, Margaret, 65, 82, 104, 108, 117, 214n90

Gallery of Illustrious Americans, The (Brady), 111
Garland, Hamlin, 175
Garnet, Henry Highland, 146

Garrison, William Lloyd, 15, 17, 18, 85, 220n49
Gates, Henry Louis, Jr., 131, 132–33
Gender relations. *See* Domesticity, cult of; Separate spheres
Genovese, Eugene, 27
Genre painting, 107
Gentry, 80–81
Geography, divisions based on, 174–76
Georgia Scenes (Longstreet), 175
German immigrants, 23, 26, 135, 138
German Reformed church, 23
Gettysburg Address, xx
Godey, Louis, 75
Godey's Lady's Book, 73, 74, 75, 99, 100, 138
Graham, Sylvester, 74
Graham's Lady's and Gentleman's Magazine, 100, 101
Gratz, Ann, 139
Gratz, Benjamin, 139
Gratz, Maria, 138, 139
Gratz, Rebecca, 25, 26, 138–39
"Grayling" (Simms), 108
"Great Lawsuit, The" (Fuller), 117, 214n90
Greenough, Horatio, 104
Grimké, Angelina, 11, 16, 17, 18–19, 54
Grimké, Sarah, 11, 15, 18–19
Griswold, Rufus Wilmot, 92
Guiney, Louise, 141

Hahn, Steven, 71
Hale, Sarah, xxii, 75, 100, 215n105
Halttunen, Karen, 63
Hammond, James Henry, 48, 116, 118
Harper's New Monthly Magazine, 99, 171–74, 177
Harris, George Washington, 175
Harris, Joel Chandler, 175
Harris, Neil, 94, 99
Harrison, William Henry, 37
Harte, Bret, 175
Harvard Divinity School, 101–2

Harvard University, intellectual community at, 101–2

Hawthorne, Nathaniel: critical judgment of, 119; depiction of urban experience by, 72; and gap between literature and popular culture, 94–95; historical fiction by, 113–14, 115, 123–24, 142; Howells's visit to, 178; H. James's critical study of, 90; and knowledge, 83; myths about, 136; opinion of American society, 125; opinion of "scribbling women," 87; as part of Concord intellectual community, 103, 104; popularity of, 87, 94–97; and realism, 113–14; and regional literature, 175; romanticism of, 100; and short story genre, 112, 113–14, 115; and victimization of women, 132

Hayne, Robert, 49

Hazard of New Fortunes, A (Howells), 177

Hebrew Sunday School Society, 138

Hecker, Isaac, 140

Henry, Joseph, 86

Heroic Slave, The (Douglass), 148, 149–52

Hicks, Thomas, *121*

Higham, John, 189n1

Hildreth, Richard, 148–49

Historical fiction, 115–16, 123–24

Historical societies, development of, 33, 114

Histories: by minorities, 131, 142–45; popular, 108, 114–16, 119

History of the Conquest of Mexico (Prescott), 115

Holmes, Oliver Wendell, Sr., 109, 111, 170, 178

Holt, Michael, 56

Home, as center of consumption, xxiii, 77–78

Hooper, Johnson ("Captain Simon Suggs"), 40

Hopedale Community (Massachusetts), 18

House of Mirth, The (Wharton), 174

Howe, Daniel, 36

Howells, William Dean, 103, 177–78, 180, 183

Hudson River School (of painting), 65

Hunter, Robert, 44

Hutchinson, Ann, 123

Imagination, and knowledge, 83–84, 86–89, 108

Immigrants: and immigrant narratives, 143–45; voting rights of, xx. *See also* German immigrants; Irish immigrants; Jewish immigrants

Indians. *See* Native Americans

Individualism, 46, 61

Intelligence. *See* Knowledge

International trade, xxi

Intuition: and knowledge, 83; and transcendentalism, 13

Irish immigrants: and Catholicism, 1, 9; literature of, 130, 135, 136, 140–45

Irving, Washington, 92

Isaac, Rhys, 73

Israelite, The (journal), 130, 133, 140

Ives, James, 68

Jackson, Andrew, xv, xix, *34*, 36–39, 42, 154

James, Henry, 90, 91, 92, 104

James, William, 102, 211n39

Jane Eyre (Brontë), 176

Jefferson, Thomas, 38, 48, 57, 151, 152

Jesuit; or, Catholic Sentinel, 141

Jesuit order, 9

Jesus Christ, 11, 13, 23

Jewett, Sarah Orne, 175

Jewish Heroine, The (Wise), 140

Jewish immigrants, 26, 135, 138. *See also* Judaism

"John Phoenix" (pseud.), 178

Judaism: literature of, 130, 133–35, 136, 138–40, 142–45; relationship to Protestant culture, 1, 2, 23, 25–26
Julian, George, 44

Kansas, statehood for, 49–50
Kelley, Mary, 107
Kenedy, John, 140
Kennedy, John Pendleton, 100
Kidnapped and the Ransomed, The (Pickard), 137
King, Martin Luther, Jr., 45
Kneeland, Abner, 8
Knights of the Golden Circle, 156
Knowledge, fragmentation of, 83–89
Know-Nothing party, 38
Kuklick, Bruce, 85

Ladies' Industrial Association (New York City), 53
Ladies' Magazine, 75
Ladies' Repository, xviii
Lafayette, Marquis de, 33
Laissez-faire economics, 36
Lamplighter, The (Cummins), 86
Landscape design, 61, 62–72
Larcom, Lucy, 8, 63
Lawrence, Abbott, 103
Leaves of Grass (Whitman), 95
Lecture circuit, xxii
Lectures on Revivals of Religion (Finney), 4
Lecture to Young Men, on Chastity, A (Graham), 74
Leeser, Rabbi Isaac, 138, 139
Legaré, Hugh, 38, 100
Leslie, Frank, 141
Letters on the Equality of the Sexes and the Condition of Women (S. Grimké), 19
Letter to an English Abolitionist (Hammond), 48, 118
Liberalism, religious, 168
Liberator, 15, 17
Liberty party, 38, 55
Lieber, Francis, 100
Life, History, and Travels of Kah-Ge-Ga-

Gah-Bowh, The (Copway), 133, 154–56, 158
Life and Adventures of Joaquín Murieta: The Celebrated California Bandit, The (Ridge), 130, 154, 156–57, 158, 179
Life of George Washington (Sparks), 102
Life of Washington (Weems), 32
"Ligeia" (Poe), 113
Lincoln, Abraham: distrust of unregulated freedoms, 49–50; elected to presidency, xix, 56, 164; on equality of blacks, 166; home of, 33; opinion of slavery, 44, 49–50, 55; and political instability, 47; as a public speaker, xx, 39; respect for law, 47, 51; and secession, 49, 50, 165
Lincoln-Douglas debates, 39, 164
Lind, Jenny, xxii, 162
Lippard, George, 159, 160–61
Literacy, xix, 54, 133, 135
Literary professionalism, xxii, 93
Literary societies, xxi
Literature: changing taste in, 86; masterpieces of, 119–29; and national culture, 94–97; popularity of, 87–88; professionalization of, 93; of reform, 70–71; regional, 174–76; by women, 87, 107–8
Local color movement, 174–75, 224n38
Local history, 33, 114
Logic, and science, 83, 84, 85, 88, 89
Longacre, James Barton, 35
Longfellow, Henry Wadsworth, xxii, 93, 97, 102, 119, 175, 176, 179
Longstreet, A. B., 175
Loomis, Elias, 103
Lovejoy, Elijah, 17
Lowell, James Russell, xxii, 97, 119, 178
Lowell Institute (Boston), 98

Macaria (Evans), 176
Macdonald, A. J., 19
McGee, Thomas D'Arcy, 141
Madison, James, 31–32

Magazines, xxi
Maggie: A Girl of the Streets (Crane), 174
Mail service, 60, 63
Man, The (New York newspaper), 53
Manufacturing, xxi
Market economy, xvi, xxi, 60, 83
Marx, Leo, 67
Massachusetts Anti-Slavery Society, 50, 148
Mathematics, 84
Mathews, Cornelius, 70
Matthiessen, F. O., 119, 215n101
"Maya, the Princess" (Cooke), 179–80
May Flower, The (Stowe), 114
May, Samuel J., 16
Melville, Herman: critical judgment of, 119; depiction of nature by, 70; and knowledge, 83; opinion of American society, 124–25, 126; and pastoralism, 205n16; popularity of, 95–97; portrayal of cities by, 64, 69; romanticism of, 100; skepticism of, 136
Mercersburg movement, 22–23, 28
Mesmerism, 14
Methodist church, xviii, 1, 4, 8, 17
Mexican War, 44, 45
Middle class: development of, 60–61, 62, 77–78, 83, 88, 204n3; dominance of values of, 167, 181
Miller, Perry, 2
Miller, William, 12–13
Millerism, xix, 11, 12–13, 21, 28, 81
Minorities: definition of, 131; in politics, 42–44; relationship to popular culture, 91, 127, 129, 130–61; values of, xxiii; voting rights for, xx
Missionaries, 7, 141, 142, 154
Missouri Compromise (1820), 50, 55
Mobile *Daily Advertiser*, 176
Moby-Dick (Melville), 112, 120, 124–25
Modern Instance, A (Howells), 177
Moïse, Penina, 138, 139
Monk, Maria, 9

Monroe, James, 33
Montezuma, 115
Morality: and men, 74–75; and moral improvement, xxiii, 11; and Scottish common sense philosophy, 4; of slavery, xvi, 17, 26, 27, 44, 55–56; and women, xix, 54, 75
Mormon church, xix, 1, 10, 11, 12, 21, 81
Morse, Samuel F. B., 9
Mosses from the Old Manse (Hawthorne), 95
Mott, James, 16
Mott, Lucretia, 16, 54
Mount, William Sidney, *106*, 107
Mount Auburn Cemetery (near Boston), 67
Mount Vernon, restoration of, 33, 183
Munich, intellectual community in, 104
Municipal parks, 67
"Murders of the Rue Morgue, The" (Poe), 112
"My Kinsman, Major Molineux" (Hawthorne), 72
Mystical Presence, The (Nevin), 23

Narrative of the Life of Frederick Douglass (Douglass), 26, 120, 127–28, 148
Narrative of the Sufferings of Lewis Clarke (Clarke), 149
Narrative of William W. Brown (Brown), 146, 148
National Era (journal), xxii
Nationalism, 167
National Republican party, 32
National Trades' Union, 53
National unity, xviii, 32, 49
Native Americans: autobiographies by, 132, 133, 154–55; literature of, 153–57; romantic depictions of, 65, 70, 116; and tribal identity over individualism, 136
Native culture, development of, 90, 92–97, 107, 119

Nativism, 9, 24, 156
Natural selection, 85
Nature (Emerson), 14
Nebraska, statehood for, 50
Nevin, John Williamson, 23
"New Divinity" ministers, 84
New England Anti-Slavery Society, 15
New Englander, 137
New England Girlhood, A (Larcom), 8, 63
New England Non-Resistance Society, 18
New Haven Perfectionism, 20
New Lights; or, Life in Galway (M. Sadlier), 143
Newman, John Henry Cardinal, 24
New Views of Christianity, Society, and the Church (Brownson), 25
New York City, intellectual culture of, 98–99
New York Crystal Palace, 85, 162, *163*
New York Female Moral Reform Society, xix, 6
New York *Herald*, 99
New-York Historical Society, 141
New York *Literary World*, 95
Niagara Falls, 65
Noah, Mordecai, 218–19n26
Nonresistant anarchism, 18
Northwood (Hale), 75, 215n105
"Nothing to Wear" (Butler), 171–74, *172, 173*
"Notorious Jumping Frog of Calaveras County, The" (Twain), 179
Noyes, John Humphrey, 20, 21
Nullification Crisis, 42–43, 165
Numeracy, 84

Occident, and American Jewish Advocate, The, 138, 139
Ojibwa (tribe), 133, 155, 158
Olmsted, Frederick Law, 67, 85, 166, 167
Oneida community, 20
Oral traditions, 181

Order of the Star-Spangled Banner, 38
O'Reilly, John Boyce, 141
Origin of Species, The (Darwin), 85
Orr, J. W., *163*
Otis, Harrison Gray, 47
Our Nig (Wilson), 131, 132, 137, 152–53, 158
Owen, Robert, 19
Owen, Robert Dale, 1, 53
Oxford movement, 24

Paine, Thomas, 8
Painting, 93, 104–7, 111
Palmer, Phoebe, 4, 168–69
Paris, intellectual community in, 104
Parker, Theodore, 166
Parkman, Francis, 114
Parks, municipal, 67
Pastoralism, 61, 64–65, 66–68, 69, 72
Paul, Nathaniel, 15
Pennington, James W. C., 149
Perfectionism, 4, 15, 20, 21, 168
Peterson's Magazine, 99–100
"Petroleum Nasby" (pseud.), 178
Philadelphia, intellectual culture of, 99–100
Philadelphia *Mechanic's Free Press*, 80
Philadelphia Orphan Society, 138
Photographs and daguerreotypes, 108, 109–11, 119, 181
Pickard, Kate, 137
"Pit and the Pendulum, The" (Poe), 112
Pluralism, 158, 161, 164, 183
Poe, Edgar Allan: and Beulah Benton, 176; and copyright laws, 93; depiction of nature by, 70; and gap between literature and popular culture, 94–95; migration to northern cities by, 100, 101; myths about, 136; and photography, 109, *110*, 111; and realism, 112–13; and short story genre, 112–14
Poetry, 112–13

Political parties: as expressions of political identity, 33; and increasing participation in politics, xxi, 40; and partisanship, xix–xx, xxiii, 32, 36–40; rise of, 32; and sectionalism, 56–57; urban working class in, xix, 52–53

Politics: increasing participation in, xx–xxi, 54–55; professionalization of, xx; and sectionalism, xx; and self-expression, xix

Popular culture: development of, 90, 97, 119; relationship of intellectuals to, 91, 108; relationship of minorities to, 91, 127, 129, 130–61

Popular Monthly, 141

Popular sovereignty, 37, 50

Populism, rise of, 71

Potiphar Papers, The (Curtis), 170–71

Powers, Hiram, 104, *105*

Pragmatism, 211n39

Presbyterian church, 1, 3, 17

Prescott, William, 115, 116, 142

Professionalization: of authors, xxii; of clergy, xviii; of literature, 93; of politicians, xx; rise of, xviii; of social reform, 6

Progressive reform, 174

Prose Writers of America, The (Griswold), 92

Proslavery: Calhoun's defense of slavery, 43–44; essays for, 118. *See also* Slavery

Protestantism: changes in participation in, 1–2; dominance of, 2, 3; goals of, xvi; new divisions within, 167–69; values of, 10; and work ethic, xvii, 78. *See also* Evangelicalism

Public speaking, rise of, xx

Puritanism, 4, 98, 113–14, 123, 168

Putnam's Monthly Magazine, 170, 226n64

Quaker City; or, the Monks of Monks Hall, The (Lippard), 159, 160–61

Quakerism, 11

Raboteau, Albert, 3, 27

Racial minorities. *See* Minorities

Railroads, development of, xxi, 60, 63, 71

Rationalism, 9, 80

Realism: of essays, 117; in ethnic literature, 142; literary, 108, 112–14, 127, 177; photographic, 109–11; and Scottish common sense philosophy, 85

Reason: and knowledge, 83–89, 108; and theological reasoning, 84

Regionalism, 174–76. *See also* Sectionalism

Religion: gradualism of conversion in, 2, 5–6, 15, 22, 28, 41, 51, 167, 181; and literacy, xix; secularization of, 29, 169; separation of church and state, xix. *See also* Atheism; Christianity; Clergy; Morality; Second Great Awakening; specific denominations

Representative government, xvi

Republicanism, 31, 33, 47–48, 61, 80

Republican party, xx, xxi, 32, 37, 38, 56, 58, 164

"Resistance to Civil Government" (Thoreau), 45, 117, 214n90

Rice, Thomas D., 97

Ridge, John, 154

Ridge, John Rollin (Yellow Bird), 130, 153–54, 156–57, 158, 179

"Ring Fetter, The" (Cooke), 180

Ripley, George, 20–21

Ripley, Sophia, 20

Risso, Charles, 34

Ritchie, Alexander Hay, *121*

Roman Catholicism: literature of, 135, 140–42; relationship to Protestant culture, xix, 1, 2, 8–10, 22–25, 28, 102

Romanticism: development of, 64–65, 69, 72; and history, 114–15; in literature, 88, 112

Romantic love, 78–79

Rome, intellectual community in, 103, 104

Rourke, Constance, 97
Royce, Josiah, 102
Ryan, Mary, 77

Sabbath observance, 13
Sadlier, Denis, 140
Sadlier, James, 140, 143
Sadlier, Mary Anne Madden, 130, 136, 143–45, *144*, 157, 158
Santayana, George, 102
Saturday Club (Boston), 98
Scarlet Letter, The (Hawthorne), 96, 112, 120, 122–24, 132, 159
Science, rising interest in, 85–86, 102–3
Scott, Dred, 164
Scott, Sir Walter, 86, 181
Scottish common sense philosophy, 4, 84, 85–86
Sculpture, 93, 104, *105*
Second Great Awakening, xv, 2, 3, 5, 10, 20, 22, 84
Sectionalism: and abolitionist movement, 17; of intellectual culture, 99; and political parties, 56–57; and regionalism, 174–76; rise of, xvi, xx, 57–59, 163
Self-made man, 77
"Self-Reliance" (Emerson), 117
Seneca Falls Convention (1848), 18, 53–54
Sentimentalism, 5, 6, 29
Sentimentality, of fiction, 86–87
Separate spheres, xvii, 61, 72–76
Shea, John Gilmary, 141, 142, 143
Short stories, 108, 112–14, 119, 213n69
Sigourney, Lydia, 98
Simms, William Gilmore, 27, 100, 108, 115–16, 118, 175
Skidmore, Thomas, 53
Slave, or Memoirs of Archy Moore, The (Hildreth), 148–49
Slave narratives, 136–37, 146, 147–52, 155
Slave rebellions, 48, 116
Slavery: and Christianity, 3, 22, 26–28; as a familial institution, 23, 27; laws governing, 48, 122, 147; morality of, xvi, 17, 26, 27, 44, 55–56; opposing views of, xvi; reasoning against, 85; and westward expansion, 44, 45, 55. *See also* Abolitionist movement; Proslavery
Smith, Joseph, 11, 12
Smith, Seba ("Major Jack Downing"), 39–40
Smith, Timothy, 7
Smithsonian Institution, 86
Social Gospel, 174
Socialism, 174
Social mobility, upward, xxiii, 8, 76–80, 181
Social reform: development of, 2, 5, 81–83; and literature of dissent, 159–61; and pragmatic reasoning, 84–85; professionalization of, 6
Society for Christian Union and Progress, 25
Somkin, Fred, 33
Son of the Forest, A (Apes), 155
Southern Literary Messenger, 100, 101
Sparks, Jared, 102, 141
Spiritualism, 11, 13, 14–15
Stanton, Elizabeth Cady, 54, 203n75
Starling, Marion, 147
Star Papers; or, Experiences of Art and Nature (H. W. Beecher), 169
States' rights, 43, 165
Steamboats, 63
Stirpiculture, 20
Stowe, Harriet Beecher: castigated by Mary Chesnut, xxi–xxii; depiction of southern gentry by, 81; and domestic fiction, 121–22; in Hartford's intellectual community, 98; popularity of, 86, 87, 107, 120, 182; and short story genre, 114; and slave narratives, 149
Strong, George Templeton, 14, 22, 24, 70
Suffrage. *See* Voting rights
Sumner, Charles, 162

"Sut Lovingood" (G. W. Harris), 175
Swedenborg, Emanuel, 14
Swedenborgianism, 14
"Sweethearts and Wives" (Arthur), 73

Tappan, Arthur, 16
Tappan, Lewis, 16
Tariffs. *See* Nullification Crisis
Taylor, William R., 57
Taylor, Zachary, 38
Telegraph, 60, 63, 162
"Tell-Tale Heart, The" (Poe), 113
Temperance, 3, 146
Ten Nights in a Bar-room (Arthur), 71
"Thomas Jefferson Snodgrass" (Twain), 178
Thompson, George, 160
Thoreau, Henry David: as an essayist, 117, 125–27; communitarianism of, 11; and conscientious political action, 45–46; as part of Concord intellectual community, 103, 117; pastoralism of, 125–27
Thorn, Margaretta, 137
Thought, analytic versus personal, 83, 84
Time, changing conceptions of, 11–12, 13, 14–15
Tocqueville, Alexis de, 30–31, 32, 40, 41, 42, 46
Tolstoy, Leo, 18
Tom Thumb, xxii
Town and Country Club (Boston), 98
Tracts for the Times, 24
Transcendentalism, 1, 11, 13–14, 21, 25, 45, 81–82
Transcendentalist Club (Boston), 98
Treatise concerning Religious Affections, A (Edwards), 84
Treatise on Domestic Economy (C. Beecher), 6, 76
Turner, Nat, 48
Twain, Mark, 85, 177, 178–79, 180, 183, 205n16

Twice-Told Tales (Hawthorne), 94, 113
Tyler, John, 47
Tyranny (of the majority), 41, 42–43, 51

"Uncle Lot" (Stowe), 114
"Uncle Remus" stories (J. C. Harris), 175
Uncle Tom's Cabin (Stowe), xxii, 81, 86, 87, 112, 120–22, 149, 182
Unionism, 49, 50
Unitarian church, 1, 4, 6, 7, 13, 14, 102

Universalist church, 8
Universities, intellectual communities at, 101–3
Urbanization: impact on popular culture, 97; rise of, 61, 63–72; and urban vs. rural population, 180, 182
Utopian communities. *See* Communitarianism

Van Buren, Martin, xx
Vance, Zebulon, 56
Vaux, Calvert, 67
Vegetarianism, 13
Vesey, Denmark, 48, 116
Victorianism. *See* American Victorian Culture
Virgil, 67
Virtue. *See* Civic virtue
Voluntary associations. *See* Social reform
Voting rights: denied to women, 40, 54; for immigrants, xx; for minorities, xx; for white males (only), xxi, 52; universal suffrage, xxi

Walden (Thoreau), 11, 120, 125–27, 183
Wallace, Lew, 56
Walsh, Mike, 160
Warner, Sam Bass, Jr., 78
Warner, Susan, 86, 159–60

Washington, George, 32, 33, 121, 152, 183
Watie, Stand, 156
Webster, Daniel, xx, *35*, 36, 49, 58
Weems, Mason, 32
Weld, Theodore, 16, 19
Wesleyan University, xviii
Western New York Anti-Slavery Society, 148
Westward expansion, 44, 55
Wharton, Edith, 174
Whig party, xx, 32, 33, 36, 37–38, 56, 181
Whiskey Rebellion, 46
Whitman, Walt, xxii, 95, 119
Wide, Wide World, The (Warner), 86, 159–60
Wide Awakes, xxi, 162
Williams, Peter, Jr., 15
William Wetmore Story and His Friends (H. James), 104
Willy Burke; or, The Irish Orphan in America (M. Sadlier), 130, 143–45, 157, 158
Wilson, George, 152

Wilson, Harriet E. Adams, 131, 132, 137, 152–53, 158
Wilson, Thomas, 152
Winthrop, John, 202n63
Wise, Rabbi Isaac Mayer, 26, 130, 133–35, *134*, 136, 139–40, 142, 143
Wise, Therese, 217n8
Woman in the Nineteenth Century (Fuller), 82, 108
Women: barred from voting, 40, 54; and morality, xix, 54, 75; role in Christianity, xix, 6, 54; and women's rights movement, 18–19, 53–54, 82–83; as writers, 87, 107–8
Working-class values, 80
Wright, Fanny, 1
Wright, Henry Clarke, 11, 16

Yamassee (tribe), 116
Yemassee, The (Simms), 116
"Young Goodman Brown" (Hawthorne), 96, 113, 114, 115, 124